Emma Mason is senior lecturer in medieval history at Birkbeck College, University of London. She has published extensively in the fields of medieval religious and social history, and her recent works include *The Beauchamp Cartulary: Charters 1100–1268* (1980) and *Westminster Abbey Charters 1066–c.1214* (1988).

St Wulfstan of Worcester

To the Memory of
REGINALD RALPH DARLINGTON
who first introduced me to St Wulfstan and his neighbours

St Wulfstan of Worcester
*c.*1008–1095

Emma Mason

Basil Blackwell

Copyright © Emma Mason 1990

First published 1990

Basil Blackwell Ltd
108 Cowley Road, Oxford, OX4 1JF, UK

Basil Blackwell, Inc.
3 Cambridge Center
Cambridge, Massachusetts 02142, USA

British Library Cataloguing in Publication Data
A CIP catalogue record for this book is available from the British Library.

Library of Congress Cataloging in Publication Data

Mason, Emma.
Saint Wulfstan of Worcester, C. 1008–1095 / Emma Mason.
p. cm.
Includes bibliographical references.
ISBN 0–631–15041–2
1. Wulfstan, Saint, 1012?–1095. 2 Christian saints—England–
–Worcestershire—Biography. I. Title.
BR754.W84M37 1990
282'.092—dc203
[B]   89–18595
CIP

Typeset in 10 on 12pt Sabon
by TecSet Ltd, Wallington, Surrey
Printed in Great Britain by TJ Press Ltd., Padstow

Contents

Acknowledgements

My warmest thanks are due to all those who read one or more chapters of this work in a draft version: Frank Barlow, Brenda Bolton, James Campbell, Marjorie Chibnall, Diana Greenway, Henry Loyn, Patrick McGurk and Ann Williams. Their comments and suggestions, together with those of Blackwell's anonymous reader, have contributed to the completed book in many ways, and any remaining errors or omissions are my own responsibility.

The Battle Conference on Anglo-Norman Studies was the setting in which the idea for this biography was first conceived, with the strong encouragement of Marjorie Chibnall. Subsequent meetings of the Conference provided the opportunity for stimulating discussions with specialists on many aspects of life in eleventh-century England. There and elsewhere, expertise and insights of various kinds have been contributed in particular by Janet Barnes, David Bates, the late Jennifer Bray, Roger Fearnside, Margaret Gibson, John Hayward, John Moore, Kevan Pearson, Amanda Martin, David Pelteret and Ian Short.

In Birkbeck College, my seminars on Hagiography and Propaganda, and Church, Religion and Society, each provided a forum in which I began to formulate ideas which have been developed in this work, and my thanks are due to all participants.

At Worcester Cathedral Library, Canon Librarian Jeffery Fenwick and, in particular, Ronald Stratton, the Assistant Librarian, did much to forward my investigations. Jane Dobson expertly and energetically turned successive draft chapters into immaculate typescript. Among those at Basil Blackwell whose expertise contributed to the production of this book are Jan Chamier, Margaret Hardwidge, Sarah McNamee, Virginia Murphy, Ginny Stroud-Lewis and especially John Davey, to all of whom my thanks are offered.

Plates

1 *The Portiforium of Saint Wulfstan:* a prayer-book which probably belonged to him. It includes this full page portrait of King David playing upon the harp. (MS 391 f. 24 is reproduced by kind permission of The Master and Fellows of Corpus Christi College, Cambridge)

2 *Charter B.1680: The Alveston Charter.* This is the original version of a grant which St Wulfstan made and witnessed. Reproduced by kind permission of the Dean and Chapter of Worcester Cathedral (Photograph: J. R. Thoumine)

3 *'Hemming's Cartulary'.* This is a composite manuscript, the second part of which was composed under the direction of St Wulfstan and is an important illustration of his activities. There are three folios reproduced here: MS Cotton Tiberius A.XIII, folios 119, 131v and 144. (Reproduced by kind permission of the British Library)

4 *Dialogues:* Clare College MS 30 Gregory the Great (produced at Worcester in the late 11th century). Five splendid historiated initials. (Reproduced by kind permission of Cambridge University Library)

5 *MS Cotton Claudius A.V.* folios 160v–199v comprise a late 12th-century text of the *Life* of St Wulfstan. Illustrated here is the first page, 160 verso. (Reproduced by kind permission of the British Library)

6 *MS Latin Theol. d, 33 folio lr Augustine, Enchiridion* (Reproduced by kind permission of the Bodleian Library, Oxford)

1
The Inheritance of Bishop Wulfstan

Wulfstan was born in the reign of Ethelred II (Unraed), and died in that of William II (Rufus). Eleventh-century people are in the main shadowy figures, but Wulfstan's long career, and more especially his subsequent canonization, ensured that his activities were recorded in a variety of writings. Each was composed for some specific purpose, and recorded only those facts relating to Wulfstan which contributed towards the function of the text. Some matters are recorded more than once, from different angles; others are mentioned only in passing, or entirely omitted. The most important source, the near-contemporary English *Life*, which survives only in an amended Latin translation, is a work of hagiography consciously designed to depict Wulfstan in the traditional mould of the holy man. This text leaves important questions unanswered, and raises others by its episodic and selective presentation. The sources are discussed in the Appendix. Taken together, they build up a convincing and consistent portrait of Wulfstan, even though important details are now lost beyond recall.

Wulfstan's life was largely spent in the west Midlands of England. Contemporaries would have referred to his home region as south-west Mercia, a fragment of the great earldom which, in the middle decades of the eleventh century, stretched south from the Pennines to within a few miles of Gloucester, and eastwards from the Welsh borders for some distance beyond Coventry.[1] Within these wider boundaries, the core of Wulfstan's home territory encompassed the more fertile valleys of the rivers Severn and Avon, flowing south-west towards the Bristol Channel, and hence to the Irish Sea and the Atlantic. This was a lowland region, with uplands on parts of its borders. In an era when road transport left much to be desired, the waterways of this region were often a surer

[1]F. Barlow, *Edward the Confessor* (1970), pp. 358–9.

means of communication. Much of the lowlands was already cleared for arable farming, although the bordering uplands were still thickly wooded.[2]

Wulfstan's diocese was probably based on a tribal territory of the late Iron Age, that of the Dobunni. Traditional medieval sub-divisions of the region perhaps originated in pre-existing Celtic units.[3] The commanding heights of the region were naturally occupied by hill forts during the Iron Age. The British Camp, which still survives, dominated a southern ridge of the Malvern Hills; a major fort on Bredon Hill loomed over the junction of the rivers Severn and Avon,[4] while an important crossing of the River Severn was defended on the site later occupied by medieval Worcester.[5] In Wulfstan's lifetime these three sites had a continuing significance. Elmley castle was built on the north-easterly slopes of Bredon Hill, from where its occupant could control the rich agricultural land of the river valleys. During Wulfstan's episcopate, Elmley was taken from the cathedral priory by a royal officer, Robert Dispenser, "by the power of the king."[6] When he died, shortly after Wulfstan, Elmley came into the hands of Robert's brother, Urse de Abetot, the formidable sheriff of Worcester, who looms large in the events of Wulfstan's episcopate.[7] Urse shared with Wulfstan responsibility for safeguarding the Severn crossing. He constructed a castle at Worcester, next to the cathedral, but also virtually on the site of the old Iron Age defences. Bishop and sheriff alike had interests in the priory established in the later eleventh century at Great Malvern. These interests were overtly spiritual in nature, although the sheriff at least perhaps also bore territorial considerations in mind.[8]

During the Roman occupation of Britain, the region was extensively settled, and various sites were fortified. As its southern limits lay the most important one, Cirencester. Others included Gloucester (*Glevium*) on the lower Severn, and Worcester (*Vertis*) itself.[9] The Roman settlement at

[2]D. Hooke, *The Anglo-Saxon Landscape: the Kingdom of the Hwicce* (1985), pp. 1–2.
[3]Ibid., p. 6, fig. 1; p. 17.
[4]Ibid., p. 180; D. Hooke, *Anglo-Saxon Landscapes of the West Midlands: the Charter Evidence* (1981), p. 281.
[5]M. O. H. Carver (ed.), *Medieval Worcestershire: An Archaeological Framework* (1980), pp. 1, 19, 25.
[6]*Hemingi Chartularium ecclesiae Wigorniensis*, ed. T. Hearne, 2 vols (1723), I, p. 268.
[7]An early twelfth-century list of the lands of Oswaldslow records Elmley as held by Walter de Beauchamp (son-in-law of Urse de Abetot): ibid., I, p. 315. Walter's descendants were habitually styled Beauchamp "of Elmley."
[8]*The Vita Wulfstani of William of Malmesbury*, ed. R. R. Darlington (1928), pp. xli–xlii; *The Beauchamp Cartulary: charters 1100–1268*, ed. Emma Mason (1980), p. xvi.
[9]Hooke, *The Anglo-Saxon Landscape*, p. 3; Hooke, *Anglo-Saxon Landscapes of the West Midlands*, pp. 288–9. The Roman place-name, *Vertis*, is possibly to be identified with Worcester, but is not the basis of the latter name: A. L. F. Rivet and C. Smith, *The Place-Names of Roman Britain* (1979), p. 496.

Worcester, like the British one before it, partly occupied the high ridge overlooking the Severn, above the line of its notorious floods, although three distinct nuclei have now been identified.[10] The Roman town was small, but archaeological excavations have revealed that it was an important centre for iron-working on a large scale. Iron ores were probably brought down the Severn from outcrops in Shropshire and Staffordshire. The quality of the iron-slag closely resembles that of the Forest of Dean, downriver, but it is unclear why ore from that area should have been transported upstream. At Worcester the ores were processed and transformed into wrought iron. The end product would then be transported, via the Severn and the Bristol Channel, to other provinces of the Roman Empire.[11] Urban occupation was intensive in the area to the south of the site later occupied by the cathedral. Archaeological finds indicate that the Roman occupation of Worcester lasted at least from the mid-first century to the late third.[12]

Christianity was perhaps introduced to Worcester during this time. Its existence can tentatively be surmised in the Romano-Celtic society which survived there after the withdrawal of the legions. Two burials, carbon-dated to between the late fifth century and the late seventh, have been discovered beneath the refectory of the cathedral.[13] It may be that a pre-existing Christian site was deliberately chosen for the location of the first cathedral church, when it was built in Anglo-Saxon times. More diffuse evidence for the existence of Christianity among the Romano-Celtic population of the region is found in two places in Warwickshire, both named Exhall, which contains the element *ecles*, a survival of the Roman word *ecclesia*, or church.[14]

The native population was not destroyed by the Anglo-Saxon invasions. The Severn and other rivers retained their Celtic names, as did hills and woods throughout the region. This indicates that the British inhabitants survived in considerable numbers, even though they were now subject to a Germanic ruling class. Place-name evidence also suggests that the native population was later reinforced by an influx of

[10]Carver (ed.), *Medieval Worcestershire*, pp. 25–6.

[11]Ibid., pp. 26, 88; G. Webster, "Prehistoric settlement and land use in the West Midlands and the impact of Rome," in T. R. Slater and P. J. Jarvis (ed.), *Field and Forest: an historical geography of Warwickshire and Worcestershire* (1982), pp. 31–58, esp. pp. 46, 50–1.

[12]Carver (ed.), *Medieval Worcestershire*, p. 2.

[13]P. A. Barker, A. L. Cubberley, Elisabeth Crowfoot and C. A. Ralegh Radford, "Two Burials under the refectory of Worcester Cathedral," *Medieval Archaeology*, 18 (1974), pp. 146–51. See also Carver (ed.), *Medieval Worcestershire*, p. 3.

[14]Hooke, *The Anglo-Saxon Landscape*, p. 93. But see Barker et al., p. 151.

Welsh-speakers from beyond the Severn.[15] The native British of the region were defeated in 577 by a West Saxon army, led by Cuthwine and Ceawlin, and Cirencester, Bath and Gloucester were captured.[16] The men of Wessex fought at Cirencester in 628 against an army led by Penda, ruler of the Anglian kingdom of Mercia, but were forced to make terms.

The resulting settlement established Mercian rule in the region, with control over the Severn waterway, important Roman roads, and the extensive sheep-pastures of the Cotswolds.[17] Penda's campaign was probably supported by a strong Northumbrian war-band, led, it is believed, by the exiled Bernician princes Oslaf and Oswudu. The conquered territory in the lower Severn valley was now used by Penda to create a buffer-stage against the Welsh, and probably also against the Saxons. The distinctive identity of this area within the kingdom of Mercia was probably due to the survival of Celtic elements within its society, despite the introduction of a Germanic upper class. The government of the region was assigned to Penda's princely allies from Northumbria, and the name of Oslaf was commemorated in a landmark, *Oslafeshlaw*, "the mound of Oslaf." The name of this mound was later changed in honour of the tenth-century Bishop Oswald, when the site became the meeting-place of the court of a new unit of episcopal and local government, the triple hundred of Oswaldslow.[18] The ruling dynasty of this "Kingdom of the Hwicce" can be traced from the later seventh century to the end of the eighth. Its members had personal names in common with the Northumbrian dynasties, indicating ties of kinship.[19] Links established during the seventh century between the territory of the Hwicce and Northumbria were to be maintained, in one form or another, down to the end of the eleventh century.

The Roman capital of the region, Cirencester, was unsuitable as the administrative centre of the Hwiccian lands, since it was too remote from the centre of Mercian power, and dangerously close to the borders of the kingdom of Wessex. Winchcombe was the chief centre of the rulers of the Hwicce, chosen perhaps for its location at the junction of the valley of the

---

[15]Hooke, *The Anglo-Saxon Landscape*, p. 9. For Celtic forms of the river name Severn, see E. Ekwall, *English River Names* (1928), pp. 358–9.

[16]*The Anglo-Saxon Chronicle*, transl. and ed. Dorothy Whitelock, with D. C. Douglas and Susie I. Tucker (1961), p. 14.

[17]*Anglo-Saxon Chronicle*, p. 17; H. P. R. Finberg, *The Early Charters of the West Midlands* (1981), p. 167.

[18]Finberg, *Early Charters of the West Midlands*, pp. 168–9; Hooke, *The Anglo-Saxon Landscape*, pp. 8–9. On Oswaldslow Hundred, see O. S. Anderson, *The English Hundred-Names*, I (Lund, 1934), pp. 140–2; A. Mawer and F. M. Stenton, with F. T. S. Houghton, *The Place-Names of Worcestershire* (1927), pp. 87–8.

[19]Finberg, *Early Charters of the West Midlands*, p. 168.

Avon with the northern approaches to the Cotswold hills. The surrounding district formed the basis of the early medieval Winchcombshire, which was incorporated into Gloucestershire only in the eleventh century. A royal mausoleum was established at Winchcombe, and became the focus of the cult of a member of the Mercian royal house, Saint Cynhelm, who died early in the ninth century.[20] The subordinate condition of the kingdom of the Hwicce is indicated by the titles ascribed to its rulers in Mercian documents: *subreguli*; *comites*; *ministri*. The kings of Mercia ensured that these Hwiccian sub-kings were progressively relegated to the position of regional governors, or ealdormen. The change was effected by about 800, but the territorial unit retained its distinct identity until the period after the Danish wars.[21]

The name of Worcester is first documented in 691, and possibly reflects an earlier tribal name.[22] Despite its ancient origins, it remained a small site until Archbishop Theodore (668–90) divided the large diocese of Lichfield, coterminous with the Mercian realm, into several smaller bishoprics. Worcester lay at the centre of one such new unit of episcopal administration, and in the mid-eighth century it was described as "the metropolis or capital of the Hwicce." This concept of Worcester as the centre of a distinctive region survived into the twelfth century, when a writer described it as "the metropolis of all the Hwicca or Magesitonia," reviving the ancient tribal names for the inhabitants of this diocese and its westerly neighbour.[23] The writer evidently perceived them as branches of the same people, a notion revived in the late twentieth-century government re-organization which designated this grouping as Hereford and Worcester. The Magonsaetan occupied the area between the Wrekin and the River Wye, the most remote buffer-state of the Mercian kingdom.[24] They, like the Hwicce, were given their own bishop, and

[20]S. R. Bassett, "A Probable Mercian Royal Mausoleum at Winchcombe, Gloucestershire," *The Antiquaries Journal*, LXV (1985), pp. 82–94; Finberg, ibid., pp. 229–25. For more detailed discussion, see J. Whybra, *A Lost English County: Winchcombeshire in the Tenth and Eleventh Centuries* (The Boydell Press, Studies in Anglo-Saxon History I, Woodbridge, 1990).

[21]James Campbell, "Bede's *Reges* and *Principes*," Jarrow Lecture, 1979, reprinted in his *Essays in Anglo-Saxon History* (1986), pp. 87–92; Finberg, ibid., pp. 172–7, 180.

[22]Mawer and Stenton, *ThePlace-Names of Worcestershire*, pp. 19–20; Carver (ed.), *Medieval Worcestershire*, p. 2.

[23]Hooke, *The Anglo-Saxon Landscape*, pp. 12–13, 18.

[24]The inhabitants of this region were first described as the Western Hecani: Finberg, *Early Charters of the West Midlands*, p. 217. See also Wendy Davies and H. Vierck, "The Contexts of Tribal Hidage: Social Aggregates and Settlement Patterns," *Frühmittelalterliche Studien*, 8 (1974), pp. 223–93, esp. pp. 231, 290.

Putta of Hereford was in office in 676, four years earlier than his colleague east of the Severn.[25]

The diocese of Worcester was largely identical with the territory of the Hwicce. The jurisdiction of the bishop extended over almost the whole of the later Worcestershire, Gloucestershire, apart from the Forest of Dean and certain other land west of the rivers Severn and Leadon, and also the south-western part of the later county of Warwickshire, the home territory of Bishop Wulfstan. This virtual identity of diocese and tribal kingdom was quite deliberate, and reflects the usual policy of Archbishop Theodore.[26] The rulers of the Hwicce also had a part to play. The foundation of the see of Worcester is described in differing accounts concerning King Osric (c.675–85) and King Oshere (c.679–93). Oshere is likely to have been the founder of Worcester, and King Osric was claimed as founder of two minster churches, founded on other former Roman sites, at Bath (c.675) and Gloucester (c.679). While Oshere was lineal ancestor of all later kings of the Hwicce, the practice of co-rulership, which can be glimpsed in this era, revived at intervals over the ensuing centuries in the form of overlapping and at times competing jurisdictions.[27] In the tenth century, the rival powers were those of the bishop of Worcester and the ealdorman of Mercia, whereas, following the Norman Conquest, Bishop Wulfstan was to contend with the jurisdiction of the sheriff of Worcester.

The conversion of central England was, in its earlier phases, under-taken by Northumbrian priests who were imbued with Celtic traditions of Christianity. This early link between the diocese of Worcester and the Northumbrian church was to manifest itself again during the episcopate of Bishop Wulfstan. The first three men designated as bishops of the Hwicce came from the Northumbrian monastery of Whitby, thus reinforcing the indications that the royal house of the Hwicce was itself Northumbrian in origin. Tatfrith, the first choice as bishop, died before he could take up office. His immediate successors were Bosel (680–91), and Oftfor (691 to 693 or later).[28] The first local man to be elected bishop was Egwuin (693 or later to 717), a kinsman of King Ethelred of

---

[25]E. B. Fryde, D. E. Greenway, S. Porter and I. Roy (eds), *Handbook of British Chronology* (1986), pp. 217, 223.

[26]Davies and Vierck, "The Contexts of Tribal Hidage," p. 281; James Campbell, "The Church in Anglo-Saxon Towns," in *The Church in Town and Countryside*, ed. D. Baker (1979), pp. 119–35, reprinted in his *Essays in Anglo-Saxon History* (1986), pp. 139–54, esp. pp. 139–40; Hooke, *The Anglo-Saxon Landscape*, p. 13.

[27]Finberg, *Early Charters of the West Midlands*, pp. 172, 174–5.

[28]Fryde et al., *Handbook of British Chronology*, p. 223; *Bede's Ecclesiastical History of the English People*, ed. B. Colgrave and R. A. B. Mynors (1969), p. 410.

Mercia. Egwuin eventually moved from Worcester to live in his monastic foundation at Evesham.[29] In later generations he was locally regarded as a holy man. His relics were prized by the monks of Evesham, who subsequently claimed a large degree of independence from the bishops of Worcester. Evesham's assertion of its jurisdictional claims, reinforced by confidence in the relics of Saint Egwuin, was one of the many pressing issues which later confronted Bishop Wulfstan.[30]

The Northumbrian church had elected to adopt Roman practices at the Synod of Whitby in 664.[31] Subsequent Northumbrian influence on the diocese of Worcester probably explains why Saint Peter was dedicatee both of the first cathedral church of Worcester and of the minster churches of Bath and Gloucester.[32] Gloucester was initially a mixed community of both men and women, presided over by an abbess, as in the Northumbrian abbey of Whitby. Both Bath and Winchcombe were also established as houses of this type.[33] The cathedral minster at Worcester was staffed only by men. Some indication of the respective numbers of priests, deacons and clerks appears from their attestations to surviving charters of the early bishops.[34] Local landed families probably supplied recruits for the service of the cathedral. This employment carried with it a certain social status, as well as an income secured by direct control over part of the cathedral's landed estate. Individuals could, and did, support a wife and children in some comfort, and were likely to treat their benefices as hereditary tenures.[35] Conversely the cathedral would have a ready supply of educated young recruits, already familiar with the traditions and requirements of the Church. Clergy enlisted from such a background were likely to prove at least as well

[29]Fryde et al., *Handbook of British Chronology*, p. 223; William of Malmesbury, *De Gestis Pontificum Anglorum*, ed. N. E. S. A. Hamilton (1870), pp. 296–7; *Chronicon Abbatiae de Evesham ad annum 1418*, ed. W. D. Macray (1863), pp. 8–14.

[30]*Placita Anglo-Normannica: Law Cases from William I to Richard I preserved in historical records*, ed. M. M. Bigelow (1879), pp. 16–22, 288–90; Jane Sayers, "'Original', Cartulary and Chronicle: the Case of the Abbey of Evesham," *Falschungen im Mittelalter*, *Monumenta Germaniae Historica*, ed. H. Fuhrmann, 6 vols, Teil IV, *Diplomatische Falschungen* II (1988), pp. 371–95, see esp. p. 385.

[31]*Bede's Ecclesiastical History*, pp. 298–308.

[32]G. Hickes, *Linguarum vett. septentrionalium thesaurus grammaticocriticus et archaeologicus* (1703–1705), I, p. 169; I. Atkins, "The Church of Worcester from the Eighth to the Twelfth Centuries, " Part I, *The Antiquaries Journal*, 17 (1937), pp. 371–91, esp. p. 378; Finberg, *The Early Charters of the West Midlands*, p. 172.

[33]D. Knowles and R. N. Hadcock, *Medieval Religious Houses England and Wales* (1971), pp. 59, 66, 80. On the early minsters of the region, see Hooke, *The Anglo-Saxon Landscape*, pp. 90–3.

[34]G. W. O. Addleshaw, *The Beginnings of the Parochial System* (1959), p. 12.

[35]Eric John, *Orbis Britanniae and Other Studies* (1966), pp. 163–4, 170.

fitted for their employment as those recruited by other means, a point to be borne in mind when considering Bishop Wulfstan's family origins.

The countryside was largely evangelized from similar minster churches. In the territory encompassed by the later Worcestershire, besides the cathedral minster itself, there were minsters at Hanbury, Kempsey and Kidderminster in the district between the rivers Severn and Avon, while further east there were others at Bredon, Fladbury and Pershore, together with the monastic minster at Evesham. The early minsters each had a sphere of influence probably equivalent to an early tribal sub-division of the diocese, but there is little evidence to connect these Anglo-Saxon minster sites with earlier British ones, which were denoted by the *ecles* element in their place-names.[36] The clergy of a minster were employed in saying Mass, and celebrating the Divine Office. Neighbouring laity would attend the church on Sundays and great festivals. The minster might have attached to it a school, in which boys in minor orders were trained for the priesthood.[37] The school at Evesham was to be the first educational establishment attended by the young Wulfstan.[38] The clergy of any one of these early minsters might have pastoral responsibility for an area covering several villages. Each minster was the base of what would be termed, in the late twentieth century, a team-ministry. From the minster, its clergy would travel out to officiate in the surrounding villages, baptizing, preaching and teaching.[39]

Over the centuries, there were changes in the organization of the diocese for pastoral purposes. Archbishop Boniface and his episcopal colleagues complained in 746–7 that landed families were encroaching on the lands of religious houses.[40] During the eighth and ninth centuries, pressure from such critics resulted in the gradual absorption by the cathedral church of the estates of other Hwiccian minsters. Only those which had powerful patrons were able to retain their separate identity.[41]

---

[36]Addleshaw, *Beginnings of the Parochial System*, pp. 13–14; Hooke, *The Anglo-Saxon Landscape*, pp. 90–3.

[37]Addleshaw, *Beginnings of the Parochial System*, p. 12.

[38]*Vita Wulfstani*, p. 4.

[39]Addleshaw, *Beginnings of the Parochial System*, p. 12; Jane Sayers, "The Proprietary Church in England: a note on *Ex ore sedentis* (X 5.33.17)," *Zeitschrift der Savigny-Stiftung für Rechtsgeschichte*, Kanonistische Abteilung LXXIV, ed. Th. Mayer-Maly et al. (1988), pp. 231–45, esp. pp. 236–7.

[40]*Councils and Ecclesiastical Documents*, ed. A. W. Haddan and W. Stubbs, III (1871), pp. 350–6, translated in *English Historical Documents* I, *c.500–1042*, ed. Dorothy Whitelock (1979), p. 820.

[41]C. Dyer, *Lords and Peasants in a Changing Society: the estates of the bishopric of Worcester, 680–1540* (1980), pp. 12, 14–15, 30.

Between the late ninth century and the mid-eleventh, the gradual emergence of a broader thegnly class resulted in the fragmentation of the extensive estates of the early Anglo-Saxon period into many smaller ones. Each thegn, for reasons which included status, patronage and finance, wanted to build a church on his own estate, an aspiration which was facilitated by King Edgar's law of 959–63 ordering the diversion of one-third of a thegn's tithes to any church which he had built on his bookland.[42] The social devolution which indirectly led to the proliferation of parish churches also provided them with ready-made congregations, for there was a corresponding move by the new thegnly class to organize their tenants into nucleated, planned villages. These changes were worked out over several generations. Some minsters survived, even prospered, well after the Norman Conquest, especially in the west of England and the Midlands.[43]

The pastoral ministry based on this network of minsters resembled in some respects the method earlier used to evangelize the laity in Northumbria and elsewhere in England, during the time of the Heptarchy. The concept of the itinerant missionary cleric was perhaps transmitted from Northumbria to Mercia through the *Lives* of holy men such as Aidan, bishop of Lindisfarne, or Chad, bishop of Lichfield.[44] Their simple lifestyle and evangelizing priorities would be known to Wulfstan through lections prescribed on their feastdays. His zealous pursuit of his pastoral responsibilities was perhaps inspired by their example. Yet such narratives were also available to Wulfstan's biographers and their informants. Whether consciously or not, they selected and emphasized aspects of his work in the light of these older models. Kalendars of both Worcester and Evesham reveal that cults of numerous Northumbrian saints continued to be observed in the diocese throughout the eleventh century.[45]

The pastoral achievement which resulted from the work of the minster clergy was gravely threatened during the ninth century when England was devastated by successive waves of Danish raids. The hope of plunder drew the invaders towards monasteries and churches, with their ornate

---

[42]*English Historical Documents, I, c.500–1042*, no. 40.2, p. 431.

[43]J. Blair, "From Minster to Parish Church," in *Minsters and Parish Churches: the Local Church in Transition 950–1200*, ed. John Blair (1988), pp. 1–19, esp. pp. 7–8; Sayers, "The Proprietary Church in England," p. 236. On the development of minsters, see also John Blair, "Minister Churches in the Landscape," in *Anglo-Saxon Settlements*, ed. Della Hooke (1988), pp. 35–58.

[44]*Bede's Ecclesiastical History*, pp. 226, 316.

[45]*English Kalendars before A.D.1100*, ed. Francis Wormald, I: Texts (1934), Kalendars 16–18.

furnishings. Worcester was not saved by its inland setting, since raiders would sail up the Severn to loot the town and the cathedral church. One Viking raider reputedly became separated from his war-band while he was stealing the sanctuary bell from the cathedral. He was seized by angry citizens and monks, who flayed him alive, and his skin was nailed on the inner side of one of the great west doors.[46] More successful looters stole considerable quantities of church ornaments in gold and silver, including chalices, crosses, book-covers and clasps, which were melted down for bullion.[47]

The fortifications of Worcester can be traced in the late Iron Age and Roman periods, but there is no firm evidence of early Anglo-Saxon defences.[48] At the end of the ninth century, new defences were built by the ealdorman of Mercia, Ethelred, and his wife Ethelfled, who "ordered the *burh* at Worcester to be built for the protection of all the people."[49] A nationwide defensive and administrative reorganization followed in the wake of the Danish invasions and the unification of England. The territory of the Hwicce was divided into shires, each containing about 1,200 hides of land and a defensible, urbanized centre. These shire's were based on Gloucester, Warwick, Worcester and Winchcombe, the last merging with Gloucestershire during the reign of Ethelred II.[50]

A major jurisdictional reorganization of Worcestershire arose from the nationwide monastic reform movement of the mid-tenth century. Two of the three leaders of this movement had direct associations with Worcester. Dunstan, abbot of Glastonbury from 940, was also bishop of Worcester between 957 and 959, after which he became successively bishop of London (959) and archbishop of Canterbury (959–88). Oswald, nephew of the Danish Archbishop Osketel of York, succeeded Dunstan at Worcester in 961. He was translated to York in 971, but continued to hold the see of Worcester in plurality until his death in 992. The third leader of the reform was Ethelwold, bishop of Winchester (963–84). All were influenced by monastic reforms on the European mainland, in particular those achieved at Fleury (now St Benoît-sur-

[46]The story of the flayed Viking recurs in accounts of the raids during the reign of Ethelred. In the 1840s the gruesome relic at Worcester was subjected to microscopic examination, which indicated that it was indeed human skin: A. Way, "Some Notes on the Tradition of Flaying, inflicted in punishment of sacrilege, the skin of the offender being affixed to the church doors," *The Archaeological Journal*, V (1848), pp. 185–92.

[47]*Hemingi Chartularium*, I, p. 256.

[48]Carver (ed.), *Medieval Worcestershire*, pp. 1–5.

[49]*English Historical Documents*, I, no. 99, pp. 540–1. See also Hooke, *The Anglo-Saxon Landscape*, pp. 118–19; P. A. Rahtz, "The Archaeology of West Mercian Towns," in A. Dornier (ed.) *Mercian Studies* (1977), pp. 107–30, see esp. p. 115.

[50]Hooke, *The Anglo-Saxon Landscape*, pp. 94–5, 104–6, 119–20; Finberg, *Early Charters of the West Midlands*, pp. 234–5.

Loire) in France, and at Ghent in Lower Lotharingia (in the present-day Belgium). A third reform movement was centred on Gorze, in Upper Lotharingia.[51] The English reformers were strongly supported by Edgar, king of the Mercians and Northumbrians from 957, and king of all England from 959. Under his auspices, a synod was convened at Easter 964, in the royal capital of Winchester, where a debate was held on the best means of restoring monasticism in England.[52] It was decided to reinforce the monastic Rule of Saint Benedict by making certain adaptations based on the customs of leading reformed monasteries on the Continent. A distillation of these customs, the *Regularis Concordia* (*The Monastic Agreement*) was drawn up by Bishop Ethelwold, in order to adapt the Rule, which was first devised in sixth-century Italy, to conditions in mid-tenth-century England.[53]

The disciplinary reform was accompanied by a major extension of monastic lands and jurisdiction, effected by King Edgar. This had a revolutionary impact upon national and regional politics, but was justified by the reforming party as a move to restore an earlier state of "right order" in English monastic life, and hence in the overall effectiveness of the Church hierarchy.[54] The argument put forward by the reformers was somewhat tenuous. They maintained that, over the centuries since monasticism was first introduced into England, the inmates of religious houses had relaxed the monastic discipline prescribed in the Rule of Saint Benedict. This argument stemmed from an ambiguity in the term *monasterium*, which when used by early writers such as Bede, could denote either a monastery, in the modern sense of the word, or a minster. The reformers of the mid-tenth century assumed that every *monasterium* was a monastery, hence it was almost invariably in a decadent state, and consequently in need of a drastic purge.[55] The zeal of the reformers in attempting to implement this programme has been attributed to a determination to effect a spiritual revival which would in

---

[51]Fryde et al., *Handbook of British Chronology*, pp. 214, 223–4; J. Armitage Robinson, *The Times of Saint Dunstan* (1923), pp. 82–8.

[52]*Regularis Concordia*, ed. T. Symons (1953), pp. xxiii–xxv, 1–2.

[53]Ibid., pp. xlv–lii, 3–4. For the original Rule, see *The Rule of Saint Benedict*, ed. and transl. J. McCann (1951). See also M. Lapidge, "Ethelwold as Scholar and Teacher," in *Bishop Aethelwold: His Career and Influence*, ed. Barbara Yorke (1988), pp. 89–117, esp. pp. 98–9, 101–2; Mechthild Gretsch, "Ethelwold's translation of the *Regula Sancti Benedicti* and its Latin exemplar," *Anglo-Saxon England*, 3, ed. P. Clemoes (1974), pp. 125–51.

[54]John, *Orbis Britanniae*, pp. 56–60, 175–9.

[55]*Regularis Concordia*, pp. 1–2; P. Wormald, "Aethelwold and his Continental Counterparts: contact, comparison, contrast," in *Bishop Aethelwold: His Career and Influence*, ed. Barbara Yorke (1988), pp. 13–42, esp. pp. 40–1.

turn ensure the physical safety of the nation. Bishop Ethelwold, like King Alfred in an earlier generation, believed that only decisive moral re-generation could avert the overwhelming disaster which was due to befall a sinful nation.[56]

King Edgar perhaps accepted this viewpoint, yet there were more immediate political grounds for his support of the reformers. In effect he created a powerful group of clerical magnates, whose support for the monarchy was virtually automatic. In addition to confirming and enlarging monastic estates, he granted to the bishops and abbots wide jurisdictional powers, in order to guarantee the title to their lands, and secure control over their tenants, in the face of anticipated resistance from lay magnates. In particular, the prelates were given their own local courts, in which pleas concerning the land law might be heard, to the exclusion of the authority of the ealdorman, who was usually the most powerful lay magnate of a region.[57] The clerical reformers would remain loyal to the king, if only out of self-interest, while their celibacy prevented them from founding powerful dynasties on their wide estates. Insistence on the staffing of religious houses by monks, rather than secular clerks, was designed to prevent the continued existence of a sub-stratum of clerical families with entrenched tenants' rights in church lands. King Edgar, by acting as patron of the reform movement, had created a new political force designed to counterbalance any separatist tendencies on the part of the lay magnates.[58] The monastic reformers had good reason to be grateful to the king, and to wish him a long and stable reign, the better to ensure their renewed prosperity.

A pronounced feature of the *Regularis Concordia* was its introduction into the monastic liturgy of extensive prayers for the King, the Queen (the patroness of the reformed nunneries), and for the royal house. This feature was not paralleled in the customs of the Continental reform movements, originating as they did in areas where the assertion of royal government was minimal or non-existent.[59] The English monks were well aware that the achievements of the reform would be threatened by a backlash if Edgar's rule was endangered, whether by foreign invaders or by native opposition, or if he was succeeded by a weaker ruler. The perceived community of interest between monarchy and monasticism imbued ensuing generations of monastic leaders. Political events in the

---

[56]Wormald, "Aethelwold and his Continental Counterparts," p. 41.

[57]John, *Orbis Britanniae*, pp. 172–6, 179.

[58]Ibid., pp. 174–9.

[59]*Regularis Concordia*, xxxii, xlvi, 5, 13–14, 16, 21–2. See also B. Tierney, *The Crisis of Church and State, 1050–1300* (1964); H. R. Loyn, "The King and the Structure of Society in late Anglo-Saxon England," *History*, 42 (1957), pp. 87–100, esp. pp. 92–3, 100.

reigns of Edgar's successors ensured that this royalist bias continued to affect the activities of monastic leaders down to the time of Bishop Wulfstan and his contemporaries. This was in marked contrast to the situation on the Continent in the mid-eleventh century, where a further reform movement centred on the papal *Curia*, or court, led to the assertion of the claim to superiority of the *sacerdotium*, or clerical power, over that of the *regnum*, or royal power.[60]

Yet there were decided limits to the extent to which the English reformers succeeded in revitalizing monasticism. Bishop Ethelwold was able to ensure that secular clerks were removed from the Old Minster and other houses in and around Winchester, the royal capital. Elsewhere, however, the vested interests of magnates, and of their kinsmen who were clerks in the minsters, ensured that the reform was patchily enforced.[61] The reformers had little success overall in regions of old and intensive settlement. They came to see the advantages of concentrating their efforts in comparatively unpopulated areas, and notably in the Fenlands of East Anglia. The religious houses, converted to pure Benedictine monasticism, or newly established in remote island fastnesses were comparatively safe, both from marauders offering physical violence, and from the secularizing attitudes of lay magnates and their clerical kinsmen.[62] Those educated in these new, purer monasteries would be averse to the old minsters with their secular, and often married, priests, a point to be borne in mind when considering the formulation of Bishop Wulfstan's attitudes.

Bishop Oswald's attempt to reform his *familia*, or his resident community of clerks, at Worcester was far from successful, and the well-entrenched secular clerks firmly resisted efforts to convert them to the monastic life. The evidence for this resistance lies in the attestations of members of the *familia* to seventy-one of seventy-nine leases of land known to have been granted by Oswald. Since most of these leases are dated, their chronological sequence can be established, hence it is possible to chart any changes in the composition of the community. The

[60]Tierney, *Crisis of Church and State*, pp. 35, 41–2, 49–50.

[61]*Regularis Concordia*, xxi–xxii; Wormald, "Aethelwold and his Continental Counterparts," p. 41; Barbara Yorke, "Aethelwold and the Politics of the Tenth Century," in *Bishop Aethelwold: His Career and Influence*, ed. Barbara Yorke (1988), pp. 65–88, esp. p. 86. For the extent of the reform movement, its ethos, and its influence on subsequent generations of English monks, see Antonia Gransden, "Traditionalism and Continuity during the last Century of Anglo-Saxon Monasticism," *Journal of Ecclesiastical History*, 40 (1989), pp. 159–207.

[62]Major Fenland abbeys founded, or refounded, in this period, include Crowland, Ely, Peterborough, Ramsey and Thorney: Knowles and Hadcock, *Medieval Religious Houses*, pp. 63–4, 73, 78.

majority of witnesses at any date attested as priests, deacons or clerks, but rarely as monks. At two periods, 964–5 and 969–77, there is marked evidence of recruiting, but losses occurred through natural wastage rather than from any dramatic expulsions such as Bishop Ethelwold was able to effect at Winchester.[63] Throughout Oswald's long episcopate at Worcester, there was marked continuity in the composition of the *familia*, and only two men regularly attested as monks. Some men perhaps preferred the style of priest or deacon, if they were entitled to it, but there is no obvious reason why any monk should prefer the style of clerk, so frequently used by witnesses. The presumption is that numbers of monks remained comparatively small.[64] Moreover, several of the *familia* were granted leases of land by Oswald.[65] The Rule of St Benedict forbade monks to hold private property, and the inference is that the recipients did not regard themselves as bound by its provisions.[66] Perhaps the majority were, and remained, secular clerks, but one lease was certainly granted to a monk.[67] The resistance of the Worcester *familia* to the thoroughgoing introduction of monasticism probably accounts for Oswald's founding genuine monastic communities some distance away. The first of these was a small house established at Westbury-on-Trym, in Gloucestershire. Its first head was Germanus, an associate of Oswald, who had followed him to Fleury and trained in monasticism there.[68] From Westbury, Oswald colonized (*c*.969) another monastic foundation at Ramsey, in the Fenlands, and, subsequently, Winchcombe.[69]

In 971 Oswald was promoted archbishop of York, while retaining the bishopric of Worcester.[70] At this time the community at Worcester was headed by Wulfric, one of the unreformed clerks. Another senior clerk, Wynsige, became drawn to the monastic life during the 970s. It perhaps occurred to him that monasticism was a road to promotion. He was sent to Ramsey to undertake his noviciate, and was back at Worcester, as

[63]P. Sawyer, "Charters of the Reform Movement: the Worcester archive," in *Tenth Century Studies: essays in Commemoration of the Millennium of the Council of Winchester and Regularis Concordia*, ed. D. Parsons (1975), pp. 84–93, esp. pp. 87–93.

[64]Sawyer, "Charters of the Reform Movement," pp. 92–3.

[65]Ibid., p. 92.

[66]*Rule of Saint Benedict*, pp. 84, 122, 126, 132, 134.

[67]Sawyer, "Charters of the Reform Movement," pp. 92–3.

[68]Knowles and Hadcock, *Medieval Religious Houses*, p. 79; "Vita Oswaldi," in *The Historians of the Church of York*, ed. J. Raine (1879, 1886, 1894), I, p. 435; J. A. Robinson, "St. Oswald and the Church of Worcester" (1919), pp. 15–16.

[69]Knowles and Hadcock, ibid., pp. 73, 80. "Vita Oswaldi," in *Historians of the Church of York*, I, pp. 427–35; *Chronicon Abbatiae Ramesiensis*, ed. W. D. Macray (1886), pp. 29, 42.

[70]Fryde et al., *Handbook of British Chronology*, p. 224.

prior, in 977, whereupon Wulfric dropped to second place in the hierarchy. By training at Ramsey, Wynsige was able to assume his post as head of the community at Worcester without risk of his authority, or his newly established monastic status, being undermined by communal recollections of any shortcomings he had displayed as a novice. The questionable nature of his conversion, and indeed, the extent to which monastic rule was observed at Worcester, even among professed monks, is shown by his receiving a lease of land from Bishop Oswald in 977.[71]

Wynsige was later said to have been the best-born of the Worcester chapter. As such, he probably had influential kindred, most likely in the districts where his chief benefices lay. His eventual willingness to accept the new dispensation, and to assume a place of authority within the monastic hierarchy, rendered it likely that he could allay the disquiet of his own kindred, and those of his fellow converts to monasticism, over the disruption to long-standing tenurial arrangements.[72] The *Regularis Concordia* provided safeguards against any part of the monastic patrimony being diverted to the use of individual monks,[73] yet in 977 Bishop Oswald granted three hides of land to his "brother monk Wynsige." Some pressing reason must underlie Oswald's circumvention of the very rule he had helped introduce into England. Most likely it was represented to him in no uncertain terms that, in order to ensure the stability of the new monastic dispensation, he must enlist the support of Wynsige's powerful connections by recognizing his hereditary claim to the land in question.[74] The peaceful administration of the monastic estates was the more easily assured if the prior could rely on the goodwill of influential lay kinsfolk. Similarly his authority over his fellow monks was the better assured if he had better social connections than they. There was an innate assumption that the higher the breeding, the more potential for virtue an individual possessed. Genuine virtue would not pass unnoticed, but in a hierarchical society a man could more easily exercise authority if he had been bred to the assumption that he would do so.[75] While Wynsige had perhaps little in common, temperamentally, with a subsequent prior, Wulfstan, there were perhaps certain common considerations underlying their respective appointments to that office.

[71]Sawyer, "Charters of the Reform Movement," pp. 91–3; I. Atkins, "The Church of Worcester from the Eighth to the Twelfth Centuries," Part II, *The Antiquaries Journal*, 20 (1940), pp. 1–38 and 203–28, see esp. p. 11; *Anglo-Saxon Charters: an annotated list and Bibliography*, compiled by P. H. Sawyer (1968), no. 1336.

[72]*Chronicon Abbatiae Ramesiensis*, p. 41; John, *Orbis Britanniae*, p. 170.

[73]*Regularis Concordia*, p. 69; *Rule of Saint Benedict*, ch. 34.

[74]John, *Orbis Britanniae*, pp. 167, 170, 245. John's suggestion that the grant was intended to support dependents (p. 245) is discounted by Sawyer, "Charters of the Reform Movement," p. 92.

[75]A. Murray, *Reason and Society in the Middle Ages* (1978), pp. 336–67.

In the wake of the monastic reform, the church of Worcester was secured in its large estates, reorganized into the triple hundred of Oswaldslow. An alleged charter of King Edgar, styled *Altitonantis* from its opening word, and purportedly dating from 964, was later used to "prove" Worcester's right to exercise extensive franchisal rights, or "liberties", over this triple hundred.[76] In the generations prior to the Norman Conquest, franchisal rights were exercised over their respective estates by the religious houses of Evesham, Pershore and Worcester, but any delegated royal power would be vested in the head of each house, which, in the case of Worcester, was the bishop.[77] The estates of the monks of Worcester were administered separately from those of the bishop, and monastic claims to exercise franchisal rights over the monastic estates developed as a result of the prolonged absences of several bishops in the late tenth and earlier eleventh centuries. The three hundred hides of the church of Worcester were held by bishop and monks in a ratio of approximtely 2:1 at the time of the Domesday Survey.[78] By 1086 the dean, or prior, and monks genuinely possessed certain jurisdictional rights over their own estates, guaranteed by grants of King Edward and King William, during Wulfstan's episcopate.[79] Yet the monks claimed that their rights originated in the charter *Altitonantis*, which is now generally acknowledged to be an ambitious forgery, composed in support of the monks' interests, after the Norman Conquest. Until modern textual criticism proved this document to be a forgery, the charter was accepted as proof of the establishment of monasticism at Worcester in 964. The discrediting of this charter, and detailed analysis of the attestations of Bishop Oswald's leases, have combined to suggest a more gradual alteration in the nature of his *familia* from that year onwards.[80]

The religious community at Worcester in permanent local residence was able to administer the hundred hides directly, if it chose. This did not apply to Bishop Oswald, who was in addition archbishop of York from 971, and also had oversight of other religious houses. He provided for the practical needs of his bishopric, besides meeting his military obliga-

[76]The earliest surviving text of *Altitonantis* is a twelfth-century copy, and the charter is generally believed to be a post-Conquest forgery: *Anglo-Saxon Charters*, no. 731; Sawyer, "Charters of the Reform Movement," pp. 85–7. For an alternative view, see E. John, *Land Tenure in Early England* (1960), pp. 80–139 (the text follows as Appendix I, pp. 162–7).

[77]*Domesday Book 16: Worcestershire*, ed. F. and C. Thorn (1982), 2: Land of the Church of Worcester; Appendix V, Worcester F.

[78]Ibid., 2: Land of the Church of Worcester.

[79]*Anglo-Saxon Charters*, no. 1157; *Regesta Regum Anglo-Normannorum 1066–1154: I Regesta Willelmi Conquestoris et Willelmi Rufi*, ed. H. W. C. Davis (1913), no. 252.

[80]Sawyer, "Charters of the Reform Movement," pp. 84–93.

tions to the crown, by leasing out 190 of his 200 hides. The remaining ten were presumably retained as home farms. The texts of many of Oswald's leases survive, showing that these were usually made "for three lives", that of the recipient and two successors. On the termination of the third tenancy, it was for the bishop to decide whether to hold the estate directly, himself, or to renew the tenancy in favour of someone else. Any failure to render the prescribed service was to result in the land reverting to the bishop.

Oswald's *Libellus*, or general statement of the terms upon which the leases were granted, was drawn up in triplicate. One copy was to be retained at Worcester; one deposited with Archbishop Dunstan at Canterbury; and the third sent to Bishop Ethelwold at Winchester for safekeeping.[81] As a short term arrangement, this could not be faulted, for these three men were among King Edgar's chief advisers, but there was no guarantee that the terms of the leases would continue to be observed after the deaths of the king and bishops. The king's goodwill was essential in order to implement the mechanism by which land reverted to the bishop on the termination of the third life. This goodwill was not automatically forthcoming after the death of King Edgar in 975.

Bishop Oswald granted several such leasehold tenures to his kinsfolk. Nepotism was a fact of life in medieval society, and was practised by even the most ardent clerical reformers. Its continued occurrence during the episcopates of his successors, combined with the natural reluctance of lay families to surrender lands on the extinction of the "third life", ensured that by Bishop's Wulfstan's day, the problem of alienated tenancies loomed large.[82] Each leasehold was required to contribute to one or more of the specific needs of the bishopric, and the services which Oswald required of his tenants varied widely. Ready cash accrued from the tolls exacted on buying and selling, but the tenant's contribution might equally be in kind. Duties included pottery-making; brewing; minting new coins (the Worcester mint is thought to date from the reign of Ethelred II); providing fish or hunting-spears; maintaining a deer-hedge; defending the walls of the city; building bridges; repairing fortifications; riding as messenger or escort; and military service in time of emergency.[83]

---

[81]*Hemingi Chartularium*, I, pp. 292–6, printed in translation, R. Allen Brown, *Origins of English Feudalism* (1973), no. 42, pp. 133–5; *Anglo-Saxon Charters*, no. 1368. Oswald's charters are calendared in *Anglo-Saxon Charters*, nos 1297–1375.

[82]Oswald made written grants to the following kinsfolk: Athelstan his brother: *Anglo-Saxon Charters*, nos 1308, 1340; Osulf his brother: nos 1315, 1370; Osulf his kinsman: no. 1326; Eadwig his kinsman: no. 1348; Gardulf his kinsman: nos 1345, 1361; Alfwin his nephew: no. 1355; Edric, his *compater*: no. 1310.

[83]Brown, *Origins of English Feudalism*, no. 42, pp. 133–5.

The tenurial reorganization accompanying the monastic reform resulted in the designation of the bishop, in place of the ealdorman, as military commander of the tenants of the see. Oswaldslow formed a shipsoke, an administrative unit required to build a warship, which was presumably based on the Severn, and to provide its crew. Oswaldslow was also required to provide a guaranteed number of men to serve with the *fyrd*, the national defence force. The tenants of the bishop presumably underwent some form of commendation to him, and in time of war they followed his banner.[84] The bishop himself would not normally take a direct part in hostilities. Successive individuals are documented as steersmen of his warship, and, by analogy, a designated layman would lead the bishop's men into battle when the need arose.[85] Yet the bishop retained overall responsibiity for the military preparedness of his lands. In due course Bishop Wulfstan assumed responsibility for the defence of the bishopric and fulfilled his duty with devastating effect.[86]

Tenancy agreements were designed to contribute towards the military capacity of the bishopric. A tenant unable to perform military service in person was bound to provide an adequate substitute.[87] In order to ensure that services were properly rendered, the bishop kept control over women's marriages, and could therefore bar any unsuitable potential tenant from settling on episcopal lands.[88] In important respects, the conditions binding the tenants of the bishopric anticipated classic feudal

[84]C. Warren Hollister, *Anglo-Saxon Military Obligations on the eve of the Norman Conquest* (1962), pp. 54–5, 66, 96–7. Some of the assumptions in this work concerning the pre-Conquest military obligations of Worcester, and ship service, are criticized and corrected by R. P. Abels, *Lordship and Military Obligation in Anglo-Saxon England* (British Museum Publications, London, 1988), pp. 113, 122–3, 152–7. See also R. P. Abels, "Bookland and Fyrd Service in late Anglo-Saxon England," *Anglo-Norman Studies VII*, ed. R. Allen Brown (1985), pp. 1–25, esp. pp. 7–12, 14. Among Oswald's leases listed in *Anglo-Saxon Charters*, three were granted to recipients styled *cniht*, nos 1326, 1332, 1373; three to men styled *miles*, nos 1341, 1343, 1346; one to a *cliens*, no. 1367; three to "his man", nos 1354, 1362, 1364; and seven to tenants styled *fidelis*, nos 1318–19, 1321, 1325, 1330–31, 1335.

[85]In the years before the Norman Conquest, Edric was both steersman of the ship of the bishop of Worcester, and also leader of the bishop's army in the king's service: *Domesday Book 16: Worcestershire*, Appendix V, Worcester H. King Edward's steersman, Thorkell, held land in Pershore before 1086: ibid., 8:1. Other steersmen recorded are Wulfheah (Beds) and Stephen (Warwicks). Note C2, 52.

[86]*Florentii Wigorniensis monachi Chronicon ex Chronicis*, ed B. Thorpe (1848–9), II, 11, under 1074 AD. The true date of the revolt of 1075, but no mention of the attack on Worcester, is given in the *Anglo-Saxon Chronicle*, p. 157. For the attack of 1088, see ibid., pp. 166–7; *Florentii Wigorniensis Chronicon*, II, p. 35.

[87]*Domesday Book 16: Worcestershire*, [c].5.

[88]The Domesday Survey records that the bishop, probably Wulfstan, granted a female tenant at Croome, with her land, to one of his men at arms: ibid., 2.33.

tenures.[89] From the bishop's point of view, there were both advantages and disadvantages in these leasehold, or *laen*, tenancies. They still existed during Wulfstan's episcopate when they were gradually replaced by "classic" feudal tenures.[90] By granting leasehold tenancies, the bishop also delegated most of the routine agricultural management of his land. Food rents could be consumed as he and his household travelled around the diocese on administrative business. These rents appear low in proportion to the size of the estates, perhaps due to low yields, but there would be little point in requiring a large surplus in a region where there were currently few guaranteed market outlets.[91]

King Edgar's death in 975 occasioned a lay reaction against the newly-privileged monasteries. In the Mercian region the chief instigator of this backlash was Ealdorman Alfhere. Worcester, under Bishop Oswald, was powerful enough to withstand the worst effects of his activity, but other religious houses in the region, including Evesham, Deerhurst, Winchcombe and, possibly, Pershore, suffered major depredations. Alfhere's hostility was not directed against the Christian religion, nor even against monasticism as such, for he was, and remained, a patron of Glastonbury abbey in Somerset, where Archbishop Dunstan had formerly been abbot. Alfhere's grievance was against the recent extension of monastic jurisdiction, which encroached on his authority throughout Mercia.[92] During the episcopate of Bishop Wulfstan, a comparable, but more localized, tension resulted when the Norman sheriff, Urse de Abetot, found that the extensive monastic liberties of Worcestershire limited his capacity to administer the revenues of the shire.[93]

Pastoral activity at Worcester flourished in Bishop Oswald's lifetime. His preaching attracted a growing lay population, too large for the old church of St Peter's. For a time, Oswald was obliged to preach in the open air, while a new, larger church was built. This was dedicated to the Blessed Virgin, whose cult was becoming increasingly popular in England. St Peter's church remained standing for some time after the completion of its successor, which now accommodated the clergy of the

---

[89]The military implications of the bishop's tenancy agreements are discussed by Hollister, *Anglo-Saxon Military Obligations*, pp. 54–5, 67, 97–8. See also Abels, *Lordship and Military Obligation*, pp. 113, 122–3, 152–7.

[90]Emma Mason, "Change and Continuity in Eleventh-Century Mercia: the experience of St. Wulfstan of Worcester," *Anglo-Norman Studies VIII*, ed. R. Allen Brown (1986), pp. 154–76, esp. pp. 163–6.

[91]Dyer, *Lords and Peasants in a Changing Society*, pp. 28–31.

[92]Ann Williams, "*Princeps Merciorum gentis*: the family, career and connections of Aelfhere, ealdorman of Mercia, 956–83," *Anglo-Saxon England*, 10 (1982), pp. 143–72.

[93]*Domesday Book 16: Worcestershire*, [c].3.

cathedral. St Mary's, built on the impressive scale of the great churches which Oswald had seen on the Continent, was completed in 983.[94] Cumulative evidence from the attestations to episcopal charters from Oswald's time onwards suggests that, despite two waves of recruitment to the *familia*, the community at Worcester decreased in size from c.977.[95] Wulfstan's well-known saying, that at the outset of his ministry he found barely a dozen monks in the cathedral priory,[96] could equally have been said by his immediate predecessors. Because of the contracting numbers, the first church of St. Mary remained adequate for the needs of the community for almost a century, until the renewed expansion of the community under Wulfstan caused him to replace Oswald's church with an even larger one.[97]

Contrasting reasons might be offered for this fluctuation in the size of the community. Bishops who were perceived as holy men would perhaps be more likely to attract recruits than would some of those who presided at Worcester between the episcopates of Oswald and Wulfstan. But, since the decline in numbers began in Oswald's lifetime, it appears that political and social changes in Mercia largely determined the numbers of recruits. The two waves of recruitment observed between 964 and 977 were probably the result of tenurial restructuring caused by the monastic reform movement. The royal guarantee of monastic endowments curtailed former modes of land distribution, and Oswald's leasehold policy further limited the chance for younger sons to acquire a competence. Inadvertently, therefore, the reformation which guaranteed the prosperity of the reformed religious houses also ensured them a supply of novices. The falling off in recruitment after 977 can be attributed to the lay reaction, headed by Ealdorman Alfhere, which swept the region after the death of King Edgar. Ironically, numbers began to tail off just as Oswald appointed his first monastic deputy, Wynsige. The peculiar circumstances surrounding the latter's appointment may reflect an awareness that secular pressures now militated against the continuing expansion of monastic interests in the diocese. The subsequent relaxation of the episcopal grip upon the leaseholds, combined with the destabilizing effect of the renewed Danish incursions, would maintain the brake on recruitment. The size of the community at Worcester in Oswald's day can be estimated, to some extent, by the numbers of witnesses to his leases.

[94]Robinson, *The Times of Saint Dunstan*, pp. 123–4, 126, 130.

[95]Sawyer, "Charters of the Reform Movement: the Worcester archive," p. 89; Atkins, "The Church of Worcester," Part II, p. 10.

[96]*The Cartulary of Worcester Cathedral Priory (Register I)*, ed. R. R. Darlington (1968), no. 3.

[97]*Vita Wulfstani*, p. 52.

Since they attested in order of precedence it is possible to chart the progress of individuals in the hierarchy of the *familia*. Probably only the more senior would be required to witness leases. Not all the *seniores* would be available to attest on any given occasion, as is shown by comparing the witness lists of two or more leases issued in any given year, while some may have been too old or infirm to witness these transactions. The size of the community can therefore be estimated, but only cautiously.[98]

Oswald was esteemed at Worcester on account of his character, but also because of his work in furthering the interests of the community there. Although he was archbishop of York, he was buried at Worcester in 992, and quickly venerated as a saint. On 17 May 1002, his body was solemnly "translated" to a place of honour, in recognition of his sanctity.[99]

Danish raids which began in the last years of the tenth century brought a new threat to the lands of the church of Worcester. These incursions rose to the crescendo of a full-scale invasion during the early years of the eleventh century, culminating in the triumph of Cnut in 1016, and the establishment of a Danish line of kings.[100] Scandinavian settlers arrived in Mercia in considerable numbers. There was even a Danish earl (*jarl*) of Worcester between 1019 and 1026. This man, Hakon Ericson, was the son of the earl of Northumbria, Eric of Hladir. Once again Worcester's links with the North were reinforced.[101] Danes were admitted as tenants on episcopal estates by Bishop Wulfstan I (1002–16) and later by Bishop Brihtheah (1033–8). Danes such as Sigmund of Crowle, and Ocea ("the Toad") of Astley, were admitted to manors of the church of Worcester[102] but the bishops did not necessarily have much say in the choice of their new tenants. The laws of Cnut directed that if taxes were not rendered promptly from a manor or a village, any Dane could deposit the sum due with the sheriff, the royal officer whose duties included the collection of money due to the king. The Dane could then take immediate possession, and hold the manor for life, displacing the former tenant.[103] Not only

[98]Sawyer, "Charters of the Reform Movement," pp. 87–93; Atkins, "The Church of Worcester," Part II, pp. 6–12.

[99]*Historians of the Church of York*, I, pp. 472–3; II, p. 39.

[100]*Anglo-Saxon Chronicle*, pp. 83–97.

[101]Ann Williams,"'Cockles among the Wheat:' Danes and English in the Western Midlands in the first half of the Eleventh Century," *Midland History*, 11 (1987), pp. 1–22, esp. p. 2.

[102]Williams, "Cockles among the Wheat," pp. 13–14.

[103]Cnut II: Secular Code: 79; *English Historical Documents, I, c.500–1042*, no. 49, pp. 466–7 and n. 1. Hemming stated that at a time of unbearable taxation, land could be acquired by paying the outstanding geld which the former occupants could not raise; *Hemingi Chartularium I*, p. 278.

Danes took advantage of this legislation. Edwin, the brother of Earl Leofric, acquired in this way lands in Shropshire which belonged to the church of Worcester. The bishop was obliged to accept such tenants, provided they acknowledged his overlordship and rendered a money payment in recognition.[104]

This process of infiltration was recorded by the Worcester writer Hemming (itself a Danish name), who claimed that other lands were seized outright. Some of these, he reveals, were recovered in the time of Bishop Wulfstan. Hemming is generally critical of the activities of the Danish settlers, with the notable exception of Earl Eilaf, uncle of Harold Godwinson. It might be questioned whether Hemming was trying to discount his own racial origins, but in fact he was equally scathing about everyone whom he perceived as an enemy of the church of Worcester. His recurring theme was the spoilation of the lands of his church by the laity – virtually all of them, with a few notable exceptions who were regarded as patrons and friends of the church.[105] So as far as the Danes were concerned it may be conjectured that, by Wulfstan's episcopate, recruits to the monastery would include the younger sons of Danish settlers, as well as native English. One instance of such recruitment is that Northman, sheriff of Northamptonshire, gave the manor of Pendock to the church of Worcester when his son became a monk there.[106]

The integrity of Worcester's endowment was threatened in another way by successive appointments of bishops of Worcester to the archbishopric of York. Bishop Oswald himself was also archbishop of York from 971 until his death in 992. His successor, Ealdwulf (992–1002) retained the bishopric of Worcester when he was appointed to York in 995. Subsequently, Wulfstan, bishop of London, was translated simultaneously to Worcester (1002–16) and York (1002–23).[107] The formal excuse for the occupancy of these sees in plurality was that the wealthy bishopric of Worcester provided economic support for the man who governed the devastated archdiocese of York. The underlying reason for this pluralism was that, by permitting successive archbishops of York to retain Worcester, King Edgar, and his son Ethelred II, were encouraging them to remain loyal to the king of England, rather than throw in their lot with potential separatists in the Danelaw or (in Ethelred's reign)

---

[104]Ibid., I, pp. 277–8, 280; Williams, "Cockles among the Wheat," p. 13.

[105]Williams, "Cockles among the Wheat," p. 15. There were some marked exceptions to this general condemnation of lay magnates. Chief among them were the Godwinsons (Sweyn was censured only because he claimed to be a son of Cnut), Ralph of Hereford and Odda of Deerhurst.

[106]Hemingi Chartularium, pp. 249–50.

[107]Fryde et al., Handbook of British Chronology, p. 224.

actual Danish invaders, as an earlier Archbishop Wulfstan I of York (931–56) had done.[108] The northern province of Deira was governed from York by a series of Danish kings, between 855/6 and 954. While the sanction for their rule was force of arms, pagan warlords might also have a use for the services of a defecting archbishop. Following the conversion of the Danish King Harold Bluetooth in c.965, and the renewal of highly organized Danish raids on England in the late tenth century, there was an increasing possibility that a successful invader might seek to legitimize his conquest of the North, and that an opportunist archbishop of York might be willing to consecrate him.[109]

A third possible reason for the English king permitting the joint tenure of York and Worcester was to provide adequate financial recompense for an able administrator who would defend the North in his name, much as the bishops of Durham were to defend the border with Scotland, in the centuries after the Norman Conquest. A bishop, by virtue of his presumed celibacy, was unable to found an entrenched territorial dynasty which might undermine royal authority in the very region he was supposedly guarding. Political considerations such as these almost certainly motivated the king of all England in permitting the joint occupancy of Worcester and York, so long as northern separatism was a live issue. It ceased, for the time being, in 1016, when Cnut succeeded to the English throne. He intended to rule England as a civilized, Christian king, and to demonstrate this to other European rulers, including the pope, in furtherance of his wider European ambitions.[110] A good Christian ruler should not permit blatant pluralism, nor did Cnut do so, in this instance. Archbishop Wulfstan accordingly relinquished the bishopric of Worcester, and the Danish Earl, Hakon Ericson, was shortly afterwards installed in the region. Yet the archbishop succeeded in retaining much of the revenues of the bishopric, by transferring certain of the episcopal estates into his archiepiscopal administration. The archbishop's

---

[108]Archbishop Wulfstan I of York threw in his lot with Danish rulers of York: A. P. Smyth, *Scandinavian York and Dublin*, 2 vols (1975–9), I, p. 46; II, pp. 43, 92–4, 99, 102, 107, 114, 135, 155–7, 160–2, 164–5, 172–4. He himself was partly responsible for the impoverishment of his see: pp. 170–1.

[109]Guthfrith was consecrated King of the Danes in Northumbria by Bishop Eardwulf of Lindisfarne c.895, Smyth, *Scandinavian York and Dublin*, I, p. 43; II, pp. 267, 293.

[110]Cnut's depiction of his rule as that of a Christian king is illustrated in his Ecclesiastical and Secular Codes: *English Historical Documents*, I, c.500–1042, no. 49, pp. 454–67. See also Dorothy Whitelock, "Wulfstan and the Laws of Cnut," *English Historical Review*, 63 (1948), pp. 433–52; Dorothy Whitelock, "Wulfstan's authorship of Cnut's laws," ibid., 70 (1955), pp. 72–85.

successors at York contrived to retain control of these lands, which were recovered by Bishop Wulfstan only after the Norman Conquest.[111]

Archbishop Wulfstan was a noted preacher. His homilies, or sermons designed for a lay congregation, were much admired by his contemporaries. Present-day readers might find them repetitive and stodgy, but the younger Wulfstan is said to have admired them, and to have drawn on them. Eleventh-century churchmen were thoroughly grounded in the Old Testament, and hence imbued its reiterated message concerning the calamities which befall a nation of wrongdoers.[112] Modern scholarship has demonstrated that the reign of King Ethelred was not as uniformly disastrous as propagandists once claimed; nevertheless there was an ominous and growing threat from the Danes, and consequently the king's last years were punctuated by invasion and military defeat.[113] It was the contention of Archbishop Wulfstan II, notably in his most famous homily *Sermo Lupi ad Anglos* (The Sermon of the Wolf to the English) that the nation was being punished for its sins.[114] This theme of national sin and retribution was one which appealed strongly to the archbishop's younger namesake.[115] Despite the pessimistic note of his famous sermon, Archbishop Wulfstan did not brood over the Danish conquest of England. Having supported the rule of Ethelred, he was willing to do the same for Cnut, presenting him as a lawgiver and peacemaker in the tradition of his English royal predecessors. Cynicism and opportunism perhaps played a part, but are less relevant than the archbishop's grounding in the values of the Old Testament. Since God had permitted the change of dynasty, it was clearly His will, to which mere mortals must submit. Moreover, the peace and stability of the nation could best be served by co-operation with the new ruler.[116] Men reared in the

---

[111]The monks of Worcester remembered Archbishop Wulfstan as a reprobate (*reprobus*), who despoiled them of their lands: *Cartulary of Worcester Cathedral Priory*, p. 1. Archbishop Ealdred retained these lands on his translation from Worcester to York, William of Malmesbury, *De Gestis Pontificum Anglorum*, ed. N. E. S. A. Hamilton (1870), p. 280; *Vita Wulfstani*, pp. 19–20; Hugh the Chantor, *The History of the Church of York 1066–1127*, transl. and introd. C. Johnson (1961), p. 1.

[112]*The Anglo-Saxons*, ed. J. Campbell (1982), p. 202; Dorothy Bethurum, *The Homilies of Wulfstan* (1957), esp. pp. 87–98.

[113]S. D. Keynes, "The Declining Reputation of King Aethelred the Unready," in *Ethelred the Unready: papers from the Millenary Conference*, ed. D. Hill (1978), pp. 227–53; S.D. Keynes, *The Diplomas of King Aethelred "the Unready", 978–1016* (1980), pp. 209–28.

[114]The Sermon of the Wolf to the English, *English Historical Documents c.500–1042*, no. 240, pp. 928–34; Keynes, "The Declining Reputation of King Aethelred the Unready," p. 235.

[115]*Vita Wulfstani*, p. 23.

[116]Whitelock, "Wulfstan and the Laws of Cnut," pp. 433–52; Whitelock, "Wulfstan's authorship of Cnut's laws," pp. 72–85; Bethurum, *The Homilies of Wulfstan*, p. 64.

traditions of the tenth-century reform venerated the king as the *Christus Domini*, the anointed one of God, whose consecration with chrism raised him to a higher plane than his subjects. Whatever the circumstances preceding Cnut's accession, obedience was due to him once he was consecrated.[117] Some fifty years later, similar considerations guided the archbishop's namesake after the Norman Conquest.

Archbishop Wulfstan was a major statesman and law-maker, but at Worcester his contribution to the public welfare counted for little compared with the monks' allegations that he pilfered Worcester's lands, and had practised extortion and nepotism. Like most bishops or abbots, he was chiefly remembered on his home territory for what he had done, or had neglected to do, to maintain the property of his house.[118] This monastic attitude stemmed from the conviction that it was the duty of a prelate to safeguard the estates of the patron saint of his church, for whom he was merely trustee. Bishops or abbots might come and go, but the monastic community, continually regenerated by new recruits, was the living embodiment of the traditions of the house, and zealous in the interests of its patron saint. If the bishop proved to be an unjust or incompetent steward, he had failed in his prime duty, beside which his merits counted for little. The evidence of surviving Worcester charters demonstrates that Archbishop Wulfstan did indeed take some of the possessions formerly assigned to the monks. He is shown to have furthered the interests of his kindred, and granted a lease for three lives to the matron Wulfgiva.[119]

Archbishop Wulfstan took seriously his episcopal role, but placed particular emphasis upon its administrative responsibilities. In his book *The Institutes of Polity*, he writes that a bishop must instruct his flock, and protect it from the wolves. The bishop upholds righteousness and justice; he is a judge, and must join the temporal judges in judging justly. Eminent statesman, intellectual, and homilist though he was, Archbishop Wulfstan was little admired in monastic circles. The tenth-century reformation had generated a revival of the tradition of ecclesiastical biography, and the lives of exemplary clerics were written up sooner or later. But so far as is known, no monastic writer composed a *Life* of Archbishop Wulfstan. This suggests that those who had dealings with

[117]Elfric, abbot of Eynsham, Palm Sunday Homily, *English Historical Documents*, I, c.500–1042, no. 239, pp. 925–6.
[118]William of Malmesbury, *De Gestis Pontificum Anglorum*, p. 250. See, however, Bethurum, *The Homilies of Wulfstan*, pp. 65–6, 68.
[119]*Anglo-Saxon Charters*, Sawyer, nos 1384–5; Finberg, *Early Charters of the West Midlands*, no. 336, p. 126; on the lavish marriage-settlement which he negotiated for his sister, see *Anglo-Saxon Charters*, ed. and transl. A. J. Robertson (1956), no. LXXVI, pp. 148–9, 395–7.

him saw little reason to preserve his memory. Whatever his merits when acting in a public capacity, none of those communities with which he was associated believed that he had acted in their best interests. He promoted the interests of the secular clergy, and this may also help to explain why no monastic house was prompted to commission a biography of him.[120]

When Archbishop Wulfstan resigned Worcester, in 1016, his successor was Leofsige, who left no remarkable impression upon the monastic community there. The Worcester chronicler, writing a century after this bishop's death, described him as "a man of great religion and modesty," in itself an indirect comment upon his predecessor.[121] The devout and unassuming Leofsige, formerly abbot of Thorney, was perhaps introduced to Worcester as a "front" so that Archbishop Wulfstan, while formally surrending the bishopric, could retain effective control of much of the lands of the diocese. A comparable ploy certainly occurred to Archbishop Ealdred in 1062, when he engineered the choice of Prior Wulfstan as bishop. In 1033, Leofsige was succeeded in turn by Archbishop Wulfstan's nephew Brihtheah, but this bishop is best considered in his proper sequence in the life of the future Bishop Wulfstan. Since Bishop Wulfstan II spent many of his earlier years as an obedientiary or monastic officer, he presumably shared the views of his fellow monks on any bishop who proved to be an inadequate steward of the lands of the church of Worcester.

When Wulfstan himself eventually became bishop, none of his recent predecessors offered an ideal model of conduct or character to be emulated, whereas the successive bishops of the reform era, Dunstan and Oswald, had been acclaimed as saints. Wulfstan turned to these two as his intercessors in times of crisis, and it was they, presumably, who represented for him proper models of episcopal conduct. The lives of Dunstan and Oswald are known from biographies which in most respects follow the standard format of hagiography. At Worcester, local tradition also played a part in formulating the received view of its episcopal saints, whose merits loomed the larger in contrast to the activities of their successors.

Dunstan, in his prime, was a major public figure, but in his later years he gave less attention to political activity, and instead devoted himself to the spiritual needs of his archdiocese. Despite the relatively short time he had earlier spent as bishop of Worcester, he was revered there. He had been indirectly responsible for bringing the monastic community into

---

[120]F. Barlow, *The English Church 1000–1066* (1979), pp. 25, 65; H. R. Loyn, "Church and State in England in the Tenth and Eleventh Centuries," *Tenth Century Studies* (1975), pp. 94–102, esp. pp. 100–1; D. Dales, *Dunstan: Saint and Statesman* (1988), pp. 122–7.
    [121]*Florentii Wigorniensis monachi Chronicon*, I, p. 189.

existence, by pioneering the reform of English monasticism, even though he had only presided over a secular chapter during his time as bishop. Moreover, his eventual status, and spiritual merits, were guarantors of the priory's endowment and privileges. Dunstan's achievement as bishop survived largely in verbal tradition at Worcester. His term of office, while uncertain, was at any rate short, and is unlikely to have generated much documentation, especially in the pre-reformation state of the cathedral's endowment. There is no surviving charter of his relating to Worcester, and no contemporary evidence of his work there.[122] Stern when the occasion demanded, Dunstan was also gentle and kind to the poor, and took time to instil in the young *oblates*, child-recruits to the cloister, the traditions of the past. On his death, Dunstan was immediately acclaimed as a saint, because of his unworldliness, humbleness of heart, and love of God.[123]

Oswald governed Worcester for about thirty years. Notwithstanding his translation to York, and his concern for his monastery of Ramsey, he continued to spend much of his time at Worcester, where he died and was buried. Local recognition of his saintly character probably helped to ease the tensions caused by the tenurial and jurisdictional revolution which accompanied the monastic reform.[124] Even discounting the conventions of hagiography, Oswald can be recognized as a man who retained his humility and devotion to the end of his life, which came when he collapsed in the cloister after washing the feet of the poor.[125] By the time of his death, in 992, there had been great changes both in monastic practice and in the public role of a bishop, since the heroic days of the Northumbrian church. Yet the priority given by its early missionary bishops to pastoral activity, and something of their unassuming, outgoing humility, can be discerned in the tenth-century saints, Dunstan and Oswald. It was these virtues, transmitted in biography and tradition, which inspired the future Saint Wulfstan.

---

[122]Dunstan's various biographers have little to say about his time as bishop of Worcester: *Memorials of Saint Dunstan*, ed. W. Stubbs (1874), pp. 36–7, 60, 103–4, 195, 292, 337; although one of these writers, Eadmer, received some information from a monk of Worcester, pp. 163–4; Armitage Robinson, *The Times of Saint Dunstan*, pp. 83–91; Antonia Gransden, *Historical Writing in England c.550 to c.1307* (1974), pp. 82–7, 127–8, 130–1, 184.

[123]*Memorials of Saint Dunstan*, pp. 49–52, 62–8, 217–22, 314–21; Armitage Robinson, *The Times of Saint Dunstan*, pp. 89–90.

[124]Dales, *Dunstan: Saint and Statesman*, p. 76.

[125]*Historians of the Church of York*, I, pp. 471–2. Armitage Robinson, *The Times of Saint Dunstan*, p. 133.

2
Early Years

Wulfstan was born in or about 1008. The date of his birth can be calculated from that of his death, in January 1095, when he was "in about the eighty-seventh year of his age."[1] His birthplace, and early home, was the vill of Itchington, in Warwickshire.[2] There are now two places of this name, both of which are recorded in the Domesday Survey. Long Itchington lies in the valley of the River Itchen, about eight miles east of the town of Warwick. In 1086, Long Itchington was held by Christina, a kinswoman of King Edward. Her estates there was reckoned at twenty-four hides, and containing land for twenty-one ploughs. The demesne, or home farm, employed five of these ploughs and ten slaves. The estate was tenanted by two priests, eighty-three *villani* (peasants who were legally bound to remain on the manor) and four smallholders. Virtually all would have families, making a total population of several hundred. These tenants employed seventeen ploughs. There were also two mills, which rendered 6s 8d; sixteen acres of meadow, and some pastureland. When King William granted this big estate to Christina it was worth £36; it had formerly been worth £12 and in 1086 was valued at £20.[3] Circumstantial evidence suggests that her estate was formerly held by Alfgar, earl of Mercia, and his successor Edwin, and that their ancestors had taken it from the church of Worcester.[4]

Bishop's Itchington lies higher up the Itchen valley, and slightly to the west of the river, about nine miles south-east of Warwick. In 1086 Bishop's Itchington was held by Coventry abbey, which had an estate there valued at five hides, and which contained land for sixteen ploughs.

---

[1]*The Vita Wulfstani of William of Malmesbury*, ed. R. R. Darlington (1928), p. 61.
[2]Ibid., p. 4.
[3]*Domesday Book 23: Warwickshire*, ed. J. Morris (1976), 42:3. It is stated in "The Laws of Edward the Confessor" that King Edward gave Christina her land. *Die Gesetze der Angelsachsen*, ed. F. Liebermann, 3 vols (1903–1916), Erster band, p. 665.
[4]*Vita Wulfstani*, pp. xxii–xxiii, note 3; *Victoria County History of Warwickshire*, ed. H. A. Doubleday and W. Page (London, 1904), I, p. 281, note 1.

The demesne farm employed two ploughs and six slaves. There were thirty *villani* tenants and seven smallholders (who, with their families, would have comprised a total population of over one hundred) and these employed thirteen ploughs. There were fifty acres of meadowland. In 1066 the estate was valued at £10; susequently at £3, and in 1086 at £12.[5] (The political unrest and ensuing devastation of the late 1060s caused the slump in the value of both Itchingtons, and the return to stability contributed to their subsequent recovery.) This estate was granted to Coventry abbey by its founder, Leofric earl of Mercia, probably in 1043, in which year his donation was confirmed by King Edward.[6] In time it came to be known as Bishop's Itchington because it was later held by the bishop of Coventry.[7] On circumstantial grounds, it seems that this estate had been taken from the church of Worcester by Earl Leofric's father, Leofwin.[8] In the Domesday Survey, both places are named simply as Itchington (*Icetone, Icentone*) indicating that they represent the two fragments of one older settlement. This was perhaps the property of the church of Worcester in the tenth century, before being seized by Leofwin, and held subsequently by the earls of Mercia in the earlier eleventh century.[9] Since Wulfstan was already an adult before the southerly part of the original estate was alienated to Coventry abbey, he would naturally speak of having been born and bred in "Itchington," without qualifying the place-name in any way.

Wulfstan's family had lived in Itchington since the time of his great-grandparents. This suggests the possibility that Wulfstan's great-grandfather had been granted a lease for three lives, but evidence for this is lacking.[10] Wulfstan's father, Athelstan, and mother, Wulfgiva, were said to be well-born and comfortably off. If Athelstan was the tenant of the church of Worcester in the original, undivided estate, his yearly

---

[5] *Domesday Book 23: Warwickshire*, 6:12.

[6] *Anglo-Saxon Charters: an annotated list and bibliography*, compiled by P. H. Sawyer (1968), nos 1000, 1226.

[7] J. E. B. Gover, A. Mawer and F. M. Stenton, with F. T. S. Houghton, *The Place-Names of Warwickshire* (1936), p. 171.

[8] *Vita Wulfstani*, p. xxii, note 3.

[9] Ibid., pp. xxii–xxiii.

[10] Ibid., p. 4. Clofti, who received land at (Long) Itchington and Arley, Warwickshire, from King Ethelred in 1001 (*Anglo-Saxon Charters*, compiled Sawyer, no. 898), is not known to have been an ancestor of Wulfstan. Three of Bishop Oswald's leases for three lives concern land in Itchington, but this is another place of that name, in Tytherington, Gloucestershire: *Hemingi Chartularium ecclesiae Wigorniensis*, ed. T. Hearne, 2 vols (1723), I, pp. 126–9; *Anglo-Saxon Charters*, compiled Sawyer, nos 1312, 1316, 1364. See H. P. R. Finberg, *The Early Charters of the West Midlands* (1981), nos 114–15, 137 and notes.

income was perhaps £22, a considerable sum, although of course the 1066 values may have been more than those of the early eleventh century. Their affluence is borne out by the nature of their son's education, and the ease with which he attained the first steps of his ecclesiastical career. Athelstan and Wulfgiva were reputedly energetic, generous and virtuous. They are said to have given their son the first element of his mother's name and the last of his father's, "as if to transfer to him the holiness of both."[11] In fact Wulfstan was probably named after the current bishop of Worcester (and archbishop of York). In view of Athelstan's connection with the church of Worcester, and the circumstantial evidence implying that Wulfgiva was the Archbishop's sister (both points are discussed below), the elder Wulfstan perhaps stood godfather to the younger, but the *Life* of the younger Wulfstan would not mention such possibilities in view of the senior Wulfstan's poor reputation at Worcester.[12] In naming their son after the bishop, both parents by a happy coincidence would be commemorated in their offspring.

Following the usual conventions of hagiography, the *Vita Wulfstani* omits everything irrelevant to its overriding spiritual message. Works of this type usually record heavenly signs to the mother-to-be that she would give birth to a child of outstanding spiritual merit, but there is nothing of this sort in Wulfstan's *Life*. Either Wulfgiva received no such intimations, or they were not transmitted to posterity by her practical son, who firmly suppressed efforts by contemporaries to regard him as a wonder-worker.[13] Wulfstan himself is cited as the sole source of information on his early years. Evidently he saw no reason to hand on stories concerning his infancy or early childhood which could be interpreted as precocious signs of wonder-working sanctity. In a formal *Vita*, any discussion of the family background of the subject was omitted as an irrelevance. It could even detract from the message of the work, if the activities of its hero's kinsfolk were liable to attract the censure of a clerical readership. At the end of the eleventh century, when Wulfstan's life came to be recorded, there might still be people, both in his native south-east Warwickshire and in the city of Worcester, who could recall his well-born family, but certain recollections would be embarrassing in a work of this nature.

First and foremost, Wulfstan was the son of a priest. This is clear from the *obit* list which includes "Athelstan the priest, father of Bishop

---

[11] *Vita Wulfstani*, p. 4. See also Olaf von Feilitzen, *The Pre-Conquest Personal Names of Domesday Book* (1937), pp. 13, 31–2.

[12] *The Cartulary of Worcester Cathedral Priory* (Register I), ed. R. R. Darlington (1968), p. 1.

[13] *Vita Wulfstani*, pp. 30–1.

Wulfstan." Athelstan's relationship to the bishop is recorded in a cipher, which substitutes for each vowel its ensuing consonant. [14] The *obit* list occurs in a homiliary, or sermon collection, believed to have been used by Bishop Wulfstan. This list was therefore perhaps composed for his personal use.[15] The monastic community as a whole might not have access to the homiliary, but the use of the cipher suggests that Wulfstan was concerned to prevent a casual reader from discovering grounds for spreading unseemly gossip.[16] In the earlier eleventh century there were still many married priests, despite the censure of clerical reformers. Wulfstan and his siblings would not have experienced social embarrassment in their early years, on account of their father's profession. On the contrary, the apparent ease with which Wulfstan attained the early stages of his career suggests that his path was smoothed by a network of clerical connections arising from a Barchester-like environment. The major disciplinary reform of the Church throughout western Europe, which occurred in the middle decades of the eleventh century, was accompanied by renewed insistence upon clerical celibacy.[17] Just as Wulfstan attained his bishopric, it became necessary to deflect attention from his family origins.

Athelstan can probably be identified with one of the men of that name who were in the *familia* of Bishop Oswald. There were five of these, and the most likely candidate is the Athelstan who frequently witnessed the bishops' charters between 984 and 996, almost always as priest, and on one occasion as *Secundus* (second-in-command).[18] Since charters of Bishop Oswald's successors are comparatively scarce, it need not be assumed that the career of this Athelstan terminated in 996. Wulfstan's father probably married about the year 1000. It was a contemporary observation that, as priests became better off, in the course of their careers, so they were more apt to contract a marriage.[19] A benefice must

[14]I. Atkins, "The Church of Worcester from the Eighth to the Twelfth Centuries," Part II, *The Antiquaries Journal*, 20 (1940), pp. 1–38 and 203–28, see esp. p. 30.

[15]Atkins, "The Church of Worcester," Part II, p. 28.

[16]The Worcester monk Edric appears to have copied this Kalendar from an earlier exemplar: Atkins, "The Church of Worcester," Part II, p. 29.

[17]*The Epistolae Vagantes of Pope Gregory VII*, ed. and transl. H. E. J. Cowdrey (1972), no. 9. See also R. I. Moore, "Family, Community and Cult on the Eve of the Gregorian Reform," *Transactions of the Royal Historical Society*, fifth series, 30 (1980), pp. 49–69, esp. pp. 61–2, 66–8; J. A. Brundage, *Law, Sex and Christian Society in Medieval Europe* (1987), p. 183.

[18]P. H. Sawyer, "Charters of the Reform Movement: the Worcester archive," in *Tenth Century Studies: essays in commemoration of the Millennium of the Council of Winchester and Regularis Concordia*, ed. D. Parsons (1975), p. 90.

[19]Atto of Vercelli, *Epistola* IX, addressed to the priests of the diocese of Vercelli, *Patrologia Latina*, 134, cols 116–17.

first be secured to enable the priest to negotiate a marriage settlement
which would satisfy the family of his prospective wife.[20] Wulfgiva,
Wulfstan's mother, can almost certainly be identified with the married
woman of that name who received from Archbishop Wulfstan a grant of
half a hide of land (approximately fifty acres) at Perry Wood in St
Martins without Worcester, to hold for her life and those of two heirs.
The recipient of this land can be shown on tenurial grounds to have been
the unnamed sister of Archbishop Wulfstan who, between 1014 and
1016, married a certain Wulfric, who gave her a substantial dowry. This
sister of the archbishop is also believed to have been the mother of Bishop
Brihtheah of Worcester. The identification of the archbishop's sister with
Wulfstan's mother would assume that she married at least twice, and
more likely three times, since Brihtheah was evidently older than
Wulfstan.[21] On this hypothesis, Wulfstan would have been reared by a
stepfather. Athelstan is mentioned by name only once in Wulfstan's Life.
Subsequent references are to Wulfstan's parents, or to his "father and
mother." The writer would see no reason to relate the remarriage of his
subject's mother, especially since Wulfstan left home to begin his
education about the same time the archbishop's sister married Wulfric. It
is stated in the Vita Wulfstani that the memory of Wulfstan's parents
would have vanished entirely, had they not produced so eminent a son.[22]

Wulfstan's siblings may have had a father other than Athelstan.
Wulfstan's brother Byrcstan was a source of embarrassment, even a
cause of positive annoyance, in later years. His relationship to Wulfstan,
like that of Athelstan, was recorded in cipher in the bishop's obit list[23]
probably for the reason discussed below. Byrcstan was a layman,
whereas Wulfstan's other brother, Alfstan, became a monk at Worcester
in due course. From documentary references indicating their relative

[20]Moore, "Family, Community and Cult," p. 62.

[21]A Handbook to the Land-Charters, and other Saxonic Documents, ed. J. Earle (1888),
pp. 234–5; calendared Finberg, Early Charters of the West Midlands, no. 336, p. 126;
Anglo-Saxon Charters, compiled Sawyer, no. 1385, p. 392. In 1086 a whole hide of land at
"Perry" was held of the bishop by Herlebald. Its previous tenant, Godric, held it at the will
of Bishop Wulfstan. (Domesday Book 16: Worcestershire, ed. F. and C. Thorn (1982),
2:61.) I am grateful to Dr Ann Williams for help on the question of Wulfstan's parentage. In
a personal communication she stated that the Wulfgiva at Perry can be shown, on the
descent of the relevant estates, to be the unnamed sister of Archbishop Wulfstan who, on
the occasion of her wedding to Wulfric (between 1014 and 1016), was granted a substantial
dowry by her husband (Anglo-Saxon Charters, compiled Sawyer, no. 1459).

[22]Vita Wulfstani, p. 4

[23]Atkins, "The Church of Worcester," Part II, p. 30.

seniority, it seems that Alfstan was younger than Wulfstan.[24] Byrcstan, as the one who remained a layman in later years, was probably the eldest brother. Conventionally, at least from the later eleventh century, only younger sons were normally educated for a career in the Church, but on the other hand, since boys born into a clerical family could expect to receive advancement in the Church hierarchy, it is also possible that the clerically educated Wulfstan was the eldest. Wulfstan also had one sister, who died shortly before him, apparently towards the end of 1094.[25] She is not identified in any source, but is probably among several women recorded in the Worcester *obit* lists. A likely candidate is the nun Ragnhild, the only woman besides Wulfgiva and Earl Leofric's wife ("Lady Godiva") to occur in the list in Wulfstan's Homiliary.[26] A second *obit* list includes four women: a second Godiva; Lifgiva; Seburga and Segitha.[27]

Wulfstan's earliest years were overshadowed by a series of Danish invasions which destabilized the rule of King Ethelred Unraed (the ill-counselled) and culminated in the struggle between the king's son, Edmund Ironside, and the Danish Cnut.[28] The triumph of Cnut in 1016 led to renewed stability at national level, and royal government resumed on traditional lines, thanks in large measure to the activities of Archbishop Wulfstan.[29] The Earl of Mercia, Edric Streona, played a double game during the political upheavals, and was executed in 1017.[30] Danish

[24]Alfstan was still in deacon's orders when Wulfstan was already a priest (Atkins, "The Church of Worcester," p. 19). He served as prior of Worcester during the earlier part of Wulfstan's episcopate (*Cartulary of Worcester Cathedral Priory*, no. 2; *Diplomatarium Anglicum Aevi Saxonici*, ed. and transl. B. Thorpe (1865), p. 615).

[25]William of Malmesbury, *De Gestis Pontificum Anglorum*, ed. N. E. S. A. Hamilton (1870), p. 287.

[26]Atkins, "The Church of Worcester," p. 31. Ragnhild's ancestry was perhaps partly Danish, although people of English race occasionally bore fashionable Scandinavian names in the earlier eleventh century; Ann Williams, "'Cockles among the Wheat:' Danes and English in the Western Midlands in the first half of the eleventh century," *Midland History*, 11 (1987), pp. 1–22, esp. p. 11.

[27]Atkins, "The Church of Worcester," Part II, p. 32. A list of Worcester monks compiled *c*.1104 contains several later additions, including the women Agnes Mahald (presumably a "Frenchwoman"), Berchtild, Lefhild and Theodgivu: Atkins, "The Church of Worcester," Part II, pp. 218–19.

[28]*The Anglo-Saxon Chronicle*, transl. and ed. Dorothy Whitelock with D. C. Douglas and Susie I. Tucker (1961), 1009–1016, C (D, E); S. D. Keynes, *The Diplomas of King Aethelred "the Unready"*, 978–1016 (1980), pp. 213–28.

[29]Dorothy Bethurum, *The Homilies of Wulfstan* (1957), pp. 62–4; Dorothy Whitelock, "Wulfstan and the Laws of Cnut," *English Historical Review*, 63 (1948), pp. 433–52; Dorothy Whitelock, "Wulfstan's authorship of Cnut's Laws," ibid., 70 (1955), pp. 72–85.

[30]*Anglo-Saxon Chronicle*, 1015–17, C (D, E); Keynes, *The Diplomas of King Aethelred "the Unready"*, pp. 211–15, 220, 227–8; Williams "Cockles among the Wheat," pp. 3–6.

settlers arrived in Mercia, displacing some English landholders,[31] but there is no evidence to suggest that Wulfstan's family suffered deprivation at this time. The very fact that Wulfstan was able to embark on a lengthy education indicates that the family was far from impoverished.

Wulfstan was sent for elementary schooling to Evesham abbey,[32] which had suffered from Ealdorman Alfhere's anti-monastic campaign, but had quickly recovered.[33] Evesham lies about twenty-eight miles south-west of Long Itchington, and in the eleventh century was more than a day's journey from either of the Itchingtons. Wulfstan would necessarily be a boarding-pupil, an unnerving experience for a small child. He was probably about five years old when he began his education.[34] Residence at Evesham would provide his first experience of a monastic environment, even though the discipline might be somewhat relaxed for infant pupils, particularly those who were not *oblates*.[35] Since the *Vita Wulfstani* has very little to say about Wulfstan's time at Evesham, it seems that either his stay there was short, or he did not regard it as providing any major formative experience. In this monastic environment, he was possibly taught, for the first time, the undesirability of clerical marriage, yet his family evidently believed that he would be acceptable there. Wulfstan's education at Evesham was largely confined to acquiring the rudiments of his letters,[36] that is, learning to read and write, probably both in English and in Latin. The memorizing of psalms and hymns was probably also included in the curriculum.[37] This basic education may have been painfully acquired. Medieval writers and sculptors depicted Grammar as a stern disciplinarian, who beat the elements of language into small boys.[38] Since Wulfstan was still a child when he embarked on the next stage of his education, he perhaps remained at Evesham for two or three years at most.

The second phase of Wulfstan's education took place at Peterborough

---

[31]Williams, "Cockles among the Wheat," pp. 1–22.

[32]*Vita Wulfstani*, p. 4

[33]Ann Williams, "Princeps Merciorum gentis: the family, career and connections of Aelfhere, ealdorman of Mercia, 956–83," *Anglo-Saxon England*, 10 (1982), pp. 143–72.

[34]This is the age at which the chronicler Orderic Vitalis began his education in 1080: *The Ecclesiastical History of Orderic Vitalis*, ed. and transl. Marjorie Chibnall, 6 vols (1969–80), VI, pp. 550–2.

[35]*The Rule of Saint Benedict*, ed. and transl. J. McCann (1951), ch. 37, pp. 92–3; *Regularis Concordia*, ed. T. Symons (1953), p. xxxvi. Mayke de Jong, "Growing up in a Carolingian Monastery: Magister Hildemar and his Oblates," *Journal of Medieval History*, 9 (1983), pp. 99–128, esp. pp. 103–19.

[36]*Vita Wulfstani*, p. 4.

[37]*Ecclesiastical History of Orderic Vitalis*, VI, p. 552.

[38]Emile Mâle, *The Gothic Image: Religious Art in France of the Thirteenth Century*, transl. from the third edn by Dora Nussey (1961), pp. 79–80, 87.

abbey, on the edge of the Fenlands.[39] In the early eleventh century, this was a remote spot, far removed in travelling time from the family home. Holiday visits, if any, to Itchington would be few and far between, possible at all only if a group of people was travelling in each direction. Peterborough was originally founded in 655–6, under the name of Medehamstede, but was destroyed by the Danes in 870, and remained derelict for almost a century. About 966, Ethelwold, bishop of Winchester, refounded the monastery as the Benedictine abbey of Saint Peter (hence its later name) with the help of King Edgar and Archbishop Dunstan. The church and other buildings were completed in 972.[40] Ethelwold's influence would ensure that this house was a genuine monastery, rather than a still-secularized house such as Worcester. The reputation which Peterborough enjoyed at Worcester perhaps dated from the time of Ealdwulf, bishop of Worcester from 992, and simultaneously archbishop of York from 995 until his death in 1002. Previously, he had been abbot of Peterborough from the time of the monastery's refoundation.[41] Ealdwulf's successor at Peterborough, Coenwulf, was an energetic man who, by his learning, attracted monks and clerks from far and wide.[42] Yet the choice of Peterborough for Wulfstan's schooling was perhaps made on the recommendation of Archbishop Wulfstan. Peterborough was the nearest Benedictine monastery to York, and the archbishop maintained close links with this house.[43] The practical difficulties involved in conveying a young child across the Midlands suggests that Wulfstan travelled in the retinue of someone able to ensure safe passage. Such a journey would be potentially dangerous if it was made in the turbulent period before Cnut was established as king of England.

The hagiographer does not discuss the composition of the school at Peterborough. We do not know how many boys were being educated simultaneously, what proportion of them had influential parents or patrons, or how many of the boys were *oblates*. The latter were strictly disciplined, but firm precautions were enjoined to ensure that the boys were never placed in circumstances where they might be prey to

---

[39] *Vita Wulfstani*, p. 4

[40] D. Knowles and R. N. Hadcock, *Medieval Religious Houses England and Wales* (1971), p. 73; F. M. Stenton, "Medeshamstede and its Colonies," in J. G. Edwards, V. H. Galbraith, E. F. Jacob (eds), *Historical Essays in Honour of James Tait* (1933), pp. 313–26, reprinted in *Preparatory to Anglo-Saxon England: being the collected papers of Frank Merry Stenton*, ed. Doris Mary Stenton (1970), pp. 179–92.

[41] D. Knowles, C. N. L. Brooke and Vera C. M. London, *The Heads of Religious Houses England and Wales 940–1216* (1972), p. 59.

[42] Ibid., p. 59; *The Chronicle of Hugh Candidus, a monk of Peterborough*, ed. W. T. Mellows, with *La Geste de Burch*, ed. A. Bell (1949), pp. 48–9.

[43] *Chronicle of Hugh Candidus*, p. 73

homosexual advances from their seniors.[44] Presumably schoolboys were similarly protected.

On arrival, Wulfstan was "barely across the threshold of infancy,"[45] perhaps seven or eight years old, at an age when there is often a strong predisposition towards conformity with a generally accepted line of conduct. The hagiographer would naturally stress Wulfstan's precocious manifestation of spiritual merit, but the following account has a factual base. Isolated as Wulfstan was from his family circle, he could expect to receive acceptance and approval only by conforming to the standards established by adult mentors. He soon adapted to the new regime. He prayed and fasted; checked frivolous chatter, first in himself and then in others, and organized both the boys of his own age and those rather older into a group mutually bound to observe self-discipline.[46] This implies exceptional force of character, yet we should like to know something of the relative social standing, and future expectations, of Wulfstan and his schoolfellows. Any natural authority which he possessed at this age would be enhanced if he had arrived as a protégé of Archbishop Wulfstan. The young Wulfstan was determined upon self-improval. If he did wrong, he instructed his associates to censure him, and he gladly submitted to correction. He took as his example any conduct which seemed worth imitating. Such behaviour, says his hagiographer, demonstrated that he was a wise boy, and the he would be a wise man, a living illustration of the Scriptural saying "Rebuke a wise man and he will love you" (Proverbs 19:25). He also assimilated a philosophical precept, "ever set before the eyes of the mind some good man, recollection of whom may order your thoughts and actions. The man will not easily depart from righteousness who is always pondering on some God or man, fear of whom will restrain him from wrong-doing."[47]

This account of the young Wulfstan's programme of self-discipline has didactic overtones which he introduced himself. He used this glimpse of his early years to instruct successive groups of *oblates* at Worcester, encouraging them to conform to standards of behaviour appropriate to their years.[48] As bishop, Wulfstan was entrusted with the education of the sons of local notables,[49] and his account of his self-imposed programme of personal betterment was perhaps also used to encourage these arrogant young boys to learn some humility. The hagiographer

---

[44]*Rule of Saint Benedict*, ch. 30, p. 80; ch. 45, p. 106; ch. 63, p. 144; ch. 70, p. 156. *Regularis Concordia*, pp. xli, 7–8.

[45]*Vita Wulfstani*, p. 4.

[46]Ibid., pp. 4–5.

[47]Ibid., p. 5.

[48]Ibid., p. 7.

[49]Ibid., p. 50.

incorporated this account of Wulfstan's early spiritual development to demonstrate that he had a natural inclination towards the monastic life. It was a convention of hagiography that its subject displayed precocious spiritual merit, yet this depiction of the young Wulfstan is perhaps no exaggeration. Whereas children reared to the life of the cloister were apt to think themselves perfect,[50] Wulfstan was a secular pupil, perhaps conscious of a gap to be bridged.

The *oblates* had a defined part to play in the monastic liturgy,[51] and the other schoolboys presumably joined them in some, at least, of the monastic offices. Regular participation would ensure that they acquired considerable fluency in the Psalms, and absorbed a good deal of the Scriptures. Since it was no part of the hagiographer's brief to introduce mundane facts for their own sake, the wider intellectual content of Wulfstan's education is not known. Bishop Ethelwold had donated numerous books to Peterborough, including scriptural and patristic commentaries, saints' lives and miracle-collections, and works on both medicine and natural history. These, with any additions introduced by Abbots Ealdwulf and Coenwulf, would have formed the basis of those academic subjects which were taught to Wulfstan and his school-fellows.[52]

The only information about Wulfstan's formal training is that he was instructed by Ernwin, an expert in writing and painting pictures of all manner of subjects. Ernwin illuminated with gold the capital letters of a sacramentary and a psalter, which he then gave to Wulfstan to look after. The boy was fascinated by the rich decorations, eagerly assimilating their beauty while at the same time taking in the meaning of the words. At this period, the Psalms were often used to teach children to read, and Wulfstan was probably allowed custody or the books for this purpose. They did not remain with him for long. Ernwin, hoping for worldly advantage and profit, presented the sacramentary to King Cnut and the psalter to Queen Emma. Wulfstan was heartbroken at the loss, but was consoled by a dream, in which a man with an angelic countenance promised that the books would be returned, which they were, at a much

---

[50]*Ecclesiastical History of Orderic Vitalis*, II, pp. 84–6, 128; C. Harper-Bill, "The Piety of the Anglo-Norman Knightly Class," in *Proceedings of the Battle Conference on Anglo-Norman Studies II. 1979*, ed. R. Allen Brown (1980), pp. 63–77, esp. pp. 68–9.

[51]*Regularis Concordia*, pp. 13, 16, 23, 28, 35–6, 51, 61.

[52]M. Lapidge, "Surviving Booklists from Anglo-Saxon England," in *Learning and Literature in Anglo-Saxon England*, ed. M. Lapidge and H. Gneuss (1985), pp. 33–89, esp. pp. 52–5, 76–82. See also N. R. Ker, *Medieval Libraries of Great Britain: a list of surviving books*, second edn (1964), pp. 150–1. N. R. Ker, *Catalogue of Manuscripts containing Anglo-Saxon* (1957), no. 304.

later date.[53] This story, too, has survived in the form in which Wulfstan related it to the boys of Worcester.[54]

The leaders of the tenth century reform movement had demonstrated by their own artistic output that the practice of the arts in the service of the Church was fully justified. Ethelwold had been a skilful metal-worker,[55] while Dunstan was a scribe, an illuminator and also a musician.[56] Monastic patrons ensured that great care was taken over the production of a whole range of beautiful artefacts which were intended to enhance the setting of the liturgy.[57] In the generations following the monastic reformation, English scribes produced liturgical manuscripts of great beauty, ornamented with expensive paints, gilding and even jewelled book-covers.[58] Scribes would begin their training at an early age, achieving their best work before their fingers were stiffened by rheumatism, and their eyes strained by long years of intensive close work. Wulfstan's experience with the Peterborough manuscripts apparently occurred before he was adolescent.[59] The story was transmitted to posterity to demonstrate that he already received divine guidance at a tender age. It also suggests that his family intended him to be trained as a clerk and illuminator, like Ernwin. Presumably not every boy then being educated at Peterborough was given custody of valuable manuscripts, but most were not protégés of Archbishop Wulfstan.

The young Wulfstan is said to have been firmly committed to a life of chastity by the time he was an adolescent.[60] Years of schooling in an all-male climate, imbued with the spirituality of the reformed Benedictines, would condition many pupils in this way. In such circles, there was total censure of clerical marriage. Even sexual relations between married laity were becoming increasingly hedged with theoretical restrictions, and were regarded as permissible only when the conception of children

[53]*Vita Wulfstani*, pp. 5, 16.

[54]Ibid., p. 7.

[55]*Chronicon Monasterii de Abingdon*, ed. J. Stevenson, 2 vols (1858), I, pp. 344–5; II, p. 278.

[56]*Memorials of Saint Dunstan, Archbishop of Canterbury*, ed. W. Stubbs (1874), pp. 20–1, 49, 78–80, 169–70, 257.

[57]Janet Backhouse, D. H. Turner and Leslie Webster (eds), *The Golden Age of Anglo-Saxon Art 966–1066* (1984), pp. 46–169. See also Theophilus, *The Various Arts: De Diversis Artibus*, ed. and transl. C. R. Dodwell (1986). This work was apparently produced in north-west Germany by a monastic craftsman during the earlier decades of the twelfth century (ibid., pp. xxxiii, xxxix–xlii).

[58]Backhouse, Turner and Webster (eds), *The Golden Age of Anglo-Saxon Art*, pp. 46–87; plates IV–XVI.

[59]*Vita Wulfstani*, p. 5.

[60]Ibid., p. 6.

was intended.[61] Wulfstan's upbringing, isolated from a demonstrative family circle, would reinforce his instruction in the virtue of celibacy, lead him to regard it as a normal condition, and prompt him to encourage others in the same view. His hagiographer relates that, thanks to his being imbued with divine grace, Wulfstan never faltered in preserving his chastity, "but carried the palm of modesty unimpaired to Heaven."[62] Wulfstan's decisive commitment to a life of celibacy resulted from a traumatic experience which occurred when he eventually returned to his native village. The arrival in the neighbourhood of the good-looking young man was seen as a challenge by an amorous girl. She took to squeezing his hand, giving him come-hither looks, and flaunting provocative body-language, the meaning of which was quite unmistakable. For a time, Wulfstan's instinctive chastity frustrated her sexual designs on him, until the day when a large crowd of young people gathered for a sports meeting in a field. Wulfstan was probably always robust, since he lived to a ripe old age. After his years in the cloister, outdoor activities on the family estate would enable him to work off youthful energies. This village sports-day was one such occasion. The atmosphere was excitable, heightened by the crowd shouting and cheering for the contestants. Wulfstan did particularly well in the competition, and the villagers shouted his praises again and again. Most young men would have been encouraged by this, and become a little vain but Wulfstan neither acknowledged the adulation nor grew exultant.[63] This cool reaction probably resulted in part from his disciplined monastic education. Besides, as a member of Itchington's foremost family, he perhaps took part in the village sports only from a sense of *noblesse oblige*.

When the temptation of vainglory failed, another presented itself, in the shape of the immodest young girl. She began to dance in front of Wulfstan, to the accompaniment of a harp, using uninhibited gestures and gyrations intended to excite a lover. Whereas her previous approaches, whether in words or hand-holding, had failed, Wulfstan was now completely overwhelmed by her alluring dance. The discreet account in the *Life* does not make clear just what happened next, but before matters had gone too far, Wulfstan realized the error of his ways, burst into tears, and fled away into the rough and prickly undergrowth.[64]

[61]E. John, "The World of Abbot Aelfric," in *Ideal and Reality in Frankish and Anglo-Saxon Society: studies presented to J. M. Wallace-Hadrill*, ed. P. Wormald with D. Bullough and R. Collins (1983), p. 308; Brundage, *Law, Sex and Christian Society*, pp. 150–228.

[62]*Vita Wulfstani*, p. 6.
[63]Ibid., p. 6.
[64]Ibid., p. 6.

His monastic upbringing had perhaps rendered him frigid and impotent, quite possibly homosexual in inclination and certainly very confused. His education would not have brought him into close contact with young girls, and probably he had not experienced such strong feelings before.

Mercifully, the other young people were too absorbed in their own activities (unspecified, but imaginable) to notice that Wulfstan had disappeared. He lurked in hiding, a prey to self-recrimination and agonizing, until he fell asleep. A bright and gleaming mist then began settling over a wide tract of land. This glistening and spectacular phenomenon stopped the young people's fun, and sobered them up. They rushed to the mist-covered bushes, and finding Wulfstan, asked him what the occurrence meant.[65] So writes the hagiographer. This was probably not their only, or even their chief, reaction. Country-dwellers must often have seen patches of mist before. In view of the likely reaction of the frustrated girl, the young people were more likely trying to flush Wulfstan out of hiding, to taunt him for not making the most of his chances with the village flirt. As the hagiographer tells the story, Wulfstan replied to them authoritatively (the consequence of his superior and prolonged education, coupled with the social standing of his family). He interpreted the glistening and drenching mist as a divine manifestation, the flame of heavenly love, sent to bring him spiritual illumination. Eager to enlighten his associates, he explained events as he had experienced them: "Just then," he said, "I was overwhelmed with physical urges, but now, watered with the divine dew, both my guts and all my vital parts are cool. I hope that from now on, by God's mercy I shall be free from sexual arousal, and no longer troubled by such turmoil." The hagiographer reported that Wulfstan's prophetic utterance was fulfilled by the course of events. Never, from that day onwards, was he distracted, in fact or in fantasy, by any seductive figure, nor was the peace of his sleep disturbed by wet dreams.[66] Whether Wulfstan could really exercise such self-control over his unconscious mind is questionable, although he might be able to train himself to forget the details of dreams on waking, the more easily because he now realized that he could never fulfil their fantasies in his waking life. Monastic discipline required that wet dreams were to be followed by purification and penance,[67] and the hagiographer is indicating that Wulfstan had no need of these.

This episode, and its interpretation, were probably glossed by Wulfstan for didactic purposes. In later years, he related the story to the monk Hemming, who in turn told it to Coleman, the bishop's bio-

[65]Ibid., pp. 6–7.
[66]Ibid., p. 7.
[67]De Jong, "Growing up in a Carolingian Monestery," p. 112.

grapher. Wulfstan generally adapted his conversation to the age and understanding of his hearers. He sometimes introduced things he himself had done, so that his listeners would not despair of being able to accomplish what they heard that he had been able to achieve by the grace of God. Just as the boys being trained at Worcester were told of episodes from Wulfstan's schooldays, so this story was related to the novices "with joking cheerfulness."[68] Wulfstan's shattering experience, and his interpretation of it, were transformed into an *exemplum* to instil into the adolescents the need to accept the celibacy imposed upon them for the duration of their lives.

The telling and re-telling of the tale pruned it of some of its original features. The earthy reactions of the villagers to Wulfstan's rejection of the girl, and her own frustrated recriminations, would be shed as he later rationalized the incident. Editing of the story would excise embarrassing recollections, before Wulfstan repeated the basic tale in a light-hearted way to later generations of adolescents. The surviving version probably also owes something to a sense of decorum on the part of those through whom it was later transmitted. Wulfstan's education would have trained him to view his experiences – even the drenching in the mist – as having a spiritual dimension. Long years of ascetic training would leave him completely distanced from the outlook and experiences of young people reared in the secular world, and he could the more easily see the mortification of his sexual misadventure as embodying a spiritual lesson. By accepting the interpretation of events which he later expounded to the novices, he could come to terms with limitations which, even if he fully understood their origins and implications, he could not express in any other language.[69] These rare stories of Wulfstan's childhood and youth have survived only because he could put them to good use in training the younger members of his community. The three episodes perhaps represented for him major landmarks which directed his course towards the religious life. This is the more likely in that Wulfstan's eventual acceptance of the monastic habit was not a course imposed upon him by family pressure, but a free choice which he made as an adult.

Some time before his own monastic conversion occurred, both his parents entered religious houses in the city of Worcester. We are told that their decision was prompted by an increasing vocation for the religious

---

[68] *Vita Wulfstani*, p. 7.

[69] Wulfstan's interpretation of the episode has parallels with the reactions of those who experienced visions, often at times of stress, and which guided their subsequent actions and attitudes: see C. J. Holdsworth, "Visions and Visionaries in the Middle Ages," *History*, 48 (1963), pp. 141–53; *The Life of Christina of Markyate: a twelfth century recluse*, ed. and transl. C. H. Talbot (1987), p. 31; C.J. Holdsworth, "Christina of Markate," in *Medieval Women*, ed. D. Baker (1978), pp. 185–204.

life, coupled with advancing age and the prospect of poverty. They adapted to their new lifestyle, increasing in virtue until they died.[70] This statement reflects the normal monastic assumption that life within the cloister was invariably more virtuous than that of the secular world.[71] Elderly people sometimes did enter monasteries as their health declined, rendering them unequal to the continued management of a household and landed property. Wulfstan's parents were still living at home when he completed his schooling, perhaps about 1024, while he remained in the secular world for some time after their conversion, before entering the *familia* of Bishop Brihtheah (1033–8).[72]

The reason for the couple's approaching poverty is less obvious. Confiscation of land following non-payment of taxes was a potential cause of impoverishment,[73] but it is more likely that the territorial aggression of Earl Leofric and his kindred caused problems. All land owed secular service, possibly including military duties. Failure to render the service due might lead to forfeiture.[74] The obligation to render service was confused by the question of who might lawfully exact it. While Itchington was legally an estate of the church of Worcester, it fell under the control of the earl of Mercia. Efforts to placate one lord with a claim on this service would antagonize the other. The ealdorman of the Hwicce from c.993 was Leofwin, whose precedence at court was diminished by the rise of the notorious Edric Streona.[75] Following the execution of Earl Edric in 1017, and the consequent appointment of Hakon Ericson as earl of Worcester, Leofwin was promoted to the earldom of Mercia, an office which he held until his death, probably in 1023, when he was succeeded by his son Leofric.[76] Earl Leofric earned a bad reputation in the eyes of

[70]*Vita Wulfstani*, p. 7. The years in which Athelstan and Wulfgiva died are not known, but the dates of their deaths are recorded in Wulfstan's *obit* list as 5 July and 31 December, respectively; Atkins, "The Church of Worcester," Part II, pp. 30–1.

[71]See, for instance, Eadmer, *The Life of St. Anselm*, ed. and transl. R. W. Southern (1962), pp. 35–6, 94–7; R. W. Southern, *Saint Anselm and his Biographer: a study of monastic life and thought 1059–c.1130* (1966), p. 109.

[72]*Vita Wulfstani*, p. 7.

[73]Cnut II: Secular Code: 79: *English Historical Documents, I, c.500–1042*, ed. Dorothy Whitelock, second edn (1979), no. 49, pp. 466–7 and n. 1; *Hemingi Chartularium*, I, p. 278.

[74]*Domesday Book 16: Worcestershire*, 2:1, sets out the terms on which land was held of the estates of the church of Worcester. See also C. Warren Hollister, *Anglo-Saxon Military Obligations on the Eve of the Norman Conquest* (1962), p. 96.

[75]Keynes, *The Diplomas of King Aethelred "the Unready"*, pp. 197, 213–14 and table 6.

[76]D. J. V. Fisher, *The Anglo-Saxon Age c.400–1042* (1973), p. 330; Williams, "Cockles among the Wheat," pp. 6–7.

the monks of Worcester as a predator upon their estates.[77] He played a major role in the political struggle of 1035–6, supporting the succession to the throne of Harold Harefoot.[78] In a crisis of this kind, Earl Leofric would demand the loyalty of those whom he regarded as his tenants. It was perhaps during this crisis that Byrcstan commended himself to Earl Leofric, that is, entered into a dependent relationship towards him. Most likely it was by such means that Itchington came to be controlled by the earl. The reversal in the family fortunes would be grounds enough to prompt Byrcstan to seek the earl's patronage. This explanation for Byrcstan's later reputation at Worcester depends upon his identification with the Bricstuin who, in the reign of King Edward (1042–66), held an estate of the bishop of Worcester's Warwickshire manor of Alveston. This Bricstuin "served Earl Leofric," and consequently it became uncertain whether overlordship of Alveston pertained to the bishop or the earl. In the reign of William I, Bishop Wulfstan encountered much trouble in establishing his title to this estate.[79]

Wulfstan remained for a time in the outside world after his parents embarked on the religious life.[80] His occupation is not recorded, but secular activities would not seem worthy of notice by his hagiographer. This silence prompts a wider question. What in fact was Wulfstan's occupation over the decade or so between completing his schooling and beginning his ecclesiastical career? The scanty chronology of his early life indicates that he was still a child when he went to Peterborough, perhaps in about 1016, or 1018 at the latest. His formal education is unlikely to have continued beyond the age of fifteen or sixteen at most, and probably ceased about 1024. Yet Wulfstan embarked upon his ecclesiastical career only during the episcopate of Bishop Brihtheah (1033–8).[81] In view of his careful education, which was evidently designed to train him as a clerk, his apparent lack of employment is surprising.

When Wulfstan eventually embarked on his clerical career, his family connections were a strong recommendation,[82] and the only wonder is that this influence was not deployed earlier. It may be that he was employed as a clerk at an earlier date, but that his prospects were curtailed by the loss of a patron. Even if the young Wulfstan was briefly

---

[77]*Hemingi Chartularium*, I, p. 261; Williams, "Cockles among the Wheat," pp. 13–14.
[78]F. Barlow, *Edward the Confessor* (1970), p. 43; Fisher, *The Anglo-Saxon Age*, p. 339.
[79]*Domesday Book 23: Warwickshire*, 2.4.
[80]*Vita Wulfstani*, p. 7.
[81]Ibid., p. 7. Wulfstan's earliest surviving attestation as a member of the episcopal *familia* is to a charter of Brihtheah's successor, Bishop Lyfing (1038/9–1040 and 1041–6); Atkins, "The Church of Worcester," Part II, p. 19. Surviving episcopal charters from this period are rare, so that undue emphasis cannot be placed on the date of this attestation.
[82]*Vita Wulfstani*, p. 7.

recruited into the service of Archbishop Wulfstan, the latter's death in 1023 occurred far too early to account for the lost years. Conversely, the long abbacy at Peterborough of Alfsige (1006/7–42)[83] makes it unlikely that Wulfstan incurred loss of employment as a secular clerk there. Well-born, well-educated clerks might be recruited into the royal household. Abbot Alfsige supported Queen Emma during her exile towards the end of Ethelred's reign,[84] and was later well placed to recommend promising scribes to the royal service. Wulfstan's teacher, Ernwin, was perhaps hoping for an offer of such employment when he presented the manuscripts to the royal couple, although his sights were probably set even higher.[85] King Cnut's death in November 1035, followed by Queen Emma's isolation from political influence,[86] might account for the end of a clerical career in the royal service. Yet Wulfstan was remarkably unsophisticated for a former habitué of court circles.

It is probably safest to assume that, as the hagiographer implies, Wulfstan returned directly to Warwickshire when his schooling ended. Yet his expensive education was not put to good use in the service of Bishop Leofsige (1016–33). Earl Leofric was another potential employer of young clerks; he was also a predator upon the estates of the church of Worcester, so that if the young Wulfstan was in his service, Worcester writers would be inclined to suppress the fact. Yet the earl's wife Godiva was included in the *obit* list preserved in Wulfstan's homiliary, and Earl Alfgar, the son of Leofric, played an important part in ensuring Wulfstan's election to the bishopric, so that some personal connection may perhaps be deduced.

An intensive education such as Wulfstan received was normally given only to those who were in minor clerical orders from an early age. By the time that Wulfstan's parents retired, he himself was probably at least a subdeacon, and perhaps already in deacon's orders. The pastoral sphere of the two priests employed on the big estate of Long Itchington in 1086[87] extended over several square miles of the upper Itchen valley. Fifty or sixty years earlier Wulfstan perhaps served in some parochial capacity, but any such occupation would be only a stopgap. His prolonged education was most likely designed to fit him for a career in the *familia*, or household staff, of the bishop of Worcester, and he could

[83]Knowles, Brooke and London, *The Heads of Religious Houses*, pp. 59–60.
[84]Ibid., pp. 59–60; *The Anglo-Saxon Chronicle*, 1013, C (D, E).
[85]Ernwin can probably be identified with Earnwig, abbot of Peterborough 1041–52; *Heads of Religious Houses*, p. 60; *Vita Wulfstani*, p. 5 and note 2.
[86]*Anglo-Saxon Chronicle*, 1035, C (D), E (F); Barlow, *Edward the Confessor*, pp. 42, 44.
[87]*Domesday Book 23: Warwickshire*, p. 42.

simply have been waiting either for a vacancy to be offered to him, or else for the canonical age for priesting.

In view of his formative experiences, it is doubtful whether Wulfstan fitted contentedly into the secular life. The resumption of close ties with his family might present difficulties, after the long years of his monastic education. At this period, almost all priests were themselves the sons of priests, even if they were conceived while their fathers were still in minor orders, so that the clerical profession was virtually a hereditary caste. Yet there were always some tender consciences, most probably found among those influenced by the monastic reformers. Wulfstan's later drive against married priests in his diocese[88] implies that his monastic education had led him to question the values of his family background. The hagiographer says nothing of his relationship with any of his family. In terms of education, and eventual profession, he had most in common with his brother Alfstan, whom he later appointed as his prior, or dean.[89]

Relationships outside the family were perhaps even more difficult to establish. Wulfstan's monastic education would have distanced him from contemporaries in the secular world, and while he was willing to join in the village sports, he derived less pleasure from them than did the other young men of the neighbourhood. A clerk in minor orders was still free to wed, and it is possible that his family considered arranging a marriage for him.[90] But the latter's traumatic experience with the village temptress demonstrated that he was unsuited to marriage and founding a family of his own, even if his kindred was willing to provide a marriage settlement and his own career prospects were considered to be good. The episode on the sports field was evidently the last conflict between his sexual urges and his monastic conditioning. His reaction on that occasion would have consequences for his reputation among local girls which would reinforce his inculcated disposition towards celibacy. If his education convinced him that his parents had done wrong to marry, he would be yet further resistant to emotional entanglements on his own account.

The silence on Wulfstan's wilderness years implies that the bishop did not choose to discuss them later in life, perhaps considering them unsuited to didactic adaptation. Equally, there is no record of the reasoning, or of a dawning sense of vocation, which led Wulfstan by stages to the monastic life. Since he was so frank about several of his formative experiences, the absence of any anecdotes on this important

---

[88] *Vita Wulfstani*, p. 53.

[89] John Le Neve, *Fasti Ecclesiae Anglicanae 1066–1300: II. Monastic Cathedrals*, compiled by Diana E. Greenway (1971), p. 102.

[90] On the lifestyle of clerks in minor orders at this period see Frank Barlow, *The English Church 1000–1066*, second edition (1979), p. 333.

subject is conspicuous. It may be that he was self-revealing only about matters on which he believed his own example might prompt unformed or immature minds to accept a vocation which they had not chosen of their own volition. His own monastic vocation was recognized fully only when he was a mature adult. Other adult converts to monasticism would come to recognize their vocation through their individual experiences,[91] and would not need the additional encouragement of his example. Wulfstan's reticence was also due, perhaps, to a wish to maintain discretion about his father and brother, if not for their sakes, then to preserve his own authority. Discipline in the diocese would not be enhanced by the knowledge that the bishop was the son of a priest, nor that his brother had been instrumental in conveying estates of the church of Worcester to the predatory Earl Leofric. For these, or other reasons, Wulfstan's wilderness years remain a mystery, until he embarked on the career for which he had been equipped, and joined the *familia* of Bishop Brihtheah.[92]

---

[91]Harper-Bill, "The Piety of the Anglo-Norman Knightly Class," pp. 71–2.
[92]*Vita Wulfstani*, p. 7.

3

Priest and Monk of Worcester

Brihtheah was the first of four bishops whom Wulfstan served before his own consecration. As a nephew of Archbishop Wulfstan,[1] Brihtheah enjoyed a successful monastic career in the diocese of Worcester. He had been a monk of Worcester, or perhaps of Evesham, then abbot of Pershore, before his appointment to Worcester in 1033.[2] Like his uncle before him, he granted lands of the church of Worcester to friends and associates, and to his brother Ethelric, not always with the consent of the monastic chapter.[3] The monks of Worcester deplored his nepotism when it affected their landed interests, but responded more favourably when it was exercised in a good cause. We learn that the bishop gladly received Wulfstan into his *familia*, "both on the recommendation of Wulfstan's kinsfolk and because of his own open-heartedness."[4] As indicated above, it is likely that he was actually receiving a younger halfbrother at the petition of their mutual kindred.

According to Wulfstan's *Life*, Brihtheah was doing himself a favour in appointing the well-connected young clerk, whose character earned approval even from wicked and hard-hearted men. Wulfstan, we learn, was entirely lacking in arrogance or insolence; he did not indulge in loose conduct or disorderly behaviour, and was neither bumptious nor cheeky. In particular, he "most carefully guarded his modesty."[5] By inference, he was something of an exception among the staff of the *familia*. The men

---

[1] *Florentii Wigorniensis monachi Chronicon ex Chronicis*, ed. B. Thorpe, 2 vols (1848–9), I, p. 189.

[2] I. Atkins, "The Church of Worcester from the Eighth to the Twelfth Centuries," Part II, *The Antiquaries Journal*, 20 (1940), pp. 1–38 and 203–28, see esp. p. 17; *The Heads of Religious Houses England and Wales 940–1216*, ed. D. Knowles, C. N. L. Brooke and Vera C. M. London (1972), p. 58.

[3] *Hemingi Chartularium ecclesiae Wigorniensis*, ed. T. Hearne, 2 vols (1723), I, pp. 255, 266–9.

[4] *The Vita Wulfstani of William of Malmesbury*, ed. R. R. Darlington (1928), p. 7.

[5] Ibid., pp. 7–8.

who became episcopal clerks were frequently sophisticated careerists, not necessarily given to plain living and high thinking. Provided they remained in minor orders, they were not obliged to remain unmarried, and in fact, there were still married priests in Worcestershire later in the century.[6]

At the time of his entry into the episcopal *familia*, Wulfstan was a handsome young man. The hagiographer conceded that this was not a cardinal virtue, but believed that his appearance reflected and set off his spiritual merits.[7] Contemporaries would generally have agreed with this correlation. Bishop Brihtheah was impressed by his new recruit, and promoted Wulfstan to the priesthood, despite some difficulty in persuading him to agree to this.[8] It was a commonplace of hagiography for the subject's humility to be emphasized by such hesitation, although it is clear from other episodes that he was in fact over-conscientious. Brihtheah had reasons to urge Wulfstan to ordination quite apart from his personal merits. The expectations of Wulfstan's importunate and seemingly influential kinsfolk had perhaps to be fulfilled. As suggested in the previous chapter, these kinsfolk were probably related to the former Archbishop Wulfstan, and hence they were also the kindred of Brihtheah. Most likely the bishop was being urged to ordain his own brother. Wulfstan's relations would know that he must be in priest's orders if he were to take full advantage of any patronage, in the form of rich livings, which the bishop might choose to dispense. Since the *familia* at Worcester was not large at this period,[9] it would be helpful to the bishop himself to have as many of his clerks as possible in priest's orders, to maintain the liturgical round. Brihtheah was a public figure, with other calls on his time. One such task was to escort King Cnut's daughter Gunnhild to her wedding in Germany with the son of the Emperor.[10]

Wulfstan is said at this stage of his career to have become a model priest, embarking on a programme of fasting and abstinence, in order to subdue his flesh and grow in spiritual strength.[11] This determination arose from his drastic reaction to a seemingly minor incident. Bishop Brihtheah committed the church of Hawkesbury, in Gloucestershire, to his new priest. At that time Wulfstan still ate meat occasionally, and one day he ordered a goose to be roasted. The bird was spitted, and put to roast. A scullion tended it carefully, and as the hot coals were heaped up

---

[6]Ibid., p. 53.

[7]Ibid., p. 8.

[8]Ibid., p. 8.

[9]Atkins, "The Church of Worcester," Part II, p. 20.

[10]*Hemingi Chartularium* I, p. 267; W. Dugdale, *Monasticon Anglicanum*, rev. edn by J. Caley, H. Ellis and B. Bandinel, 6 vols in 8 (1817–30), I, p. 596a.

[11]*Vita Wulfstani*, p. 8.

underneath, the heat of the fire caused the dripping to run. As the sauce was being prepared, the aroma was mouth-watering. Even Wulfstan was looking forward to the roast goose with delighted anticipation, but just as the table was being laid, he and his steward were called out on urgent business. This was very inconvenient, but could not be delayed. William of Malmesbury, in his *De Gestis Pontificum Anglorum (Deeds of the English Bishops)*, added a further circumstance which was discreetly omitted from Wulfstan's *Life*: it was then the time to celebrate Mass, and as Wulstan reached the most solemn point in the liturgy the smell of roasting goose wafted into the chancel from his house nearby. The aroma completely distracted his thoughts for a while, before he recovered himself and became aware of his lapse. Angered at his own weakness, he instantly took an oath on the Blessed Sacrament never again to eat that sort of food. From then on, his meals comprised fish and sauces, with dishes prepared from dairy products, but he was often quite content to eat only vegetables. By persisting in this vow, he found that in the course of time he had no inclination to eat meat, and this was several years before he took monastic vows.[12] This story was probably told by Wulfstan himself when training the novices to accept the monastic discipline concerning food, and also to exercise self-control over their thoughts when in church.

At this stage of his career, Wulfstan was soberly inclined; serious in his speech; reverential in bearing and cheerful in disposition, traits which his disciplined academic education would encourage.[13] The episode of the roast goose suggests that Wulfstan's schooling had also conditioned him to be both strong-minded and over-conscientious. Yet he was sensitive to the reactions of those around him. If it was necessary for him to rebuke anyone, he worded his criticism in such a way that, at the same time, he could also find something to praise in the conduct of the culprit.[14]

Bishop Brihtheah, perhaps in recognition of Wulfstan's merits, or else responding to the expectations of Wulfstan's kinsfolk, offered him a church on the outskirts of the city, one with a good income which would more than meet his daily needs. Wulfstan repeatedly evaded the offer, and when he was pressed to explain his refusal, declared that this transitory world was losing its value for him. He wanted to become a monk, longing to offer God not only fragments of his life, but the whole of it.[15]

---

[12] William of Malmesbury, *De Gestis Pontificum Anglorum*, ed. N. E. S. A. Hamilton (1870), p. 279; *Vita Wulfstani*, pp. 47 (in part), 94–5.

[13] *Vita Wulfstani*, p. 8; on Wulfstan's education, see also William of Malmesbury, *De Gestis Pontificum Anglorum*, p. 278.

[14] *Vita Wulfstani*, p. 8.

[15] Ibid., p. 8.

Wulfstan's vocation seems to have developed gradually over a long period of time. His eventual resolution is understandable, given that his formative years had been passed in an environment where even those pupils being educated for the career of a secular clerk were continually taught that the monastic life was the ideal one. Yet the mystery of Wulfstan's "wilderness years" suggests that his vocation appeared by no means as inevitable to him, in his early manhood, as the hagiographer implies. Wulfstan perhaps joined the episcopal *familia* only after a series of personal disappointments curtailed other options, and steered him towards the one career in which the influence of his family would ensure success. Once he was established in the routine of the cathedral's liturgical round, emotive aspects of his early conditioning would re-surface, and help formulate his resolve to take the further step of becoming a monk. There was also the example set by Wulfstan's father (or his stepfather?), who had earlier become a monk of the cathedral priory, while Wulfstan's mother had strongly urged her son to take monastic vows – it is not clear whether this was after her own entry into a nunnery.[16] Those who entered religious houses might well believe that they had chosen the best manner of life, and the only one guaranteed to earn eternal salvation. Naturally they would try to influence others to follow their example. But Wulfgiva perhaps also considered that Wulfstan would have better opportunities for further advancement if he became a monk like Brihtheah, who would then be able to ensure his promotion in the hierarchy of the cathedral priory.

The hagiographer naturally says that Brihtheah joyfully responded to Wulfstan's request to become a monk, warmly encouraging and advising him, as though with a call to arms:

> It is a happy man who tires of the attractions of the world. Its pleasures vanish in a moment, while the pangs of conscience remain active for the whole of man's life. Happy the man who wants to become a monk. For someone in that position, so long as he doesn't dishonour his way of life by abandoning his calling, the more he is despised and crucified in the world, the more blessedly close he is to God.[17]

This speech is a literary set-piece, probably composed by the hagio-grapher, Coleman, some sixty years after the death of Bishop Brihtheah. If it is actually the work of the translator, William of Malmesbury, then it is thirty years later again. It occurs in a text written by a monk, for monks, and is a panegyric on the monastic life, designed to indicate the significance of the first major act of the hero of the work. Yet Brihtheah's

---

[16]*Florentii Wigorniensis monachi Chronicon*, I, p. 219.
[17]*Vita Wulfstani*, p. 8.

actual response was perhaps as enthusiastic in its own way. The bishop's long monastic career had presumably convinced him of the merits of the cloistered life. We are told that he encouraged Wulfstan's dawning vocation, and gave him both his blessing, and the monastic habit.[18] Monks perceived themselves, and were generally perceived by others, to be on a higher spiritual plane than were secular clergy. The disciplined liturgical round observed by the monks led to their depiction as Soldiers of Christ, fighting spiritual battles both for their own salvation and on behalf of those less worthy to offer up prayers to God. The only truly religious life – religious in the sense of following a *religio*, or rule of spiritual conduct – was that of the monks. Their disciplined lifestyle was held to bring them far closer to God than were the secular priests, let alone the unregenerate and aggressive laity.[19]

The slow conversion to the monastic life of the *familia* at Worcester observed during the episcopate of Bishop Oswald perhaps continued in the time of his immediate successors, Archbishop Wulfstan and Leofsige, although developments cannot easily be discerned from the attestations to their few surviving charters. Its seems that at most their *familia* numbered sixteen, taking together monks, priests, deacons and clerks. Few charters have survived for the period between 1017 and 1038, even from the episcopate of Brihtheah.[20] Any further changes in the composition of the *familia* are obscured by its members continuing to subscribe to charters as "priest" or "deacon," after they are known to have become monks. While Wulfstan became a monk in the time of Bishop Brihtheah, he styled himself priest in his earliest surviving attestation, to a charter of Bishop Lyfing. Alfstan (brother of Wulfstan) attested this charter as deacon.[21]

The monastic observance at Worcester in the earlier eleventh century probably followed the routine prescribed in the *Regularis Concordia*. This laid down a regular round of offices, largely comprising Psalms and readings from the Scriptures, with certain additional Masses, and prayers for the royal family. The remainder of the day would be given to intellectual activities, including the writing and illuminating of manuscripts. It was ordained that no-one should be excused work in the kitchen or the bakehouse, but it is likely that lay servants were employed in various capacities.[22]

---

[18]Ibid., p. 8.

[19]Barbara H. Rosenwein, "Feudal War and Monastic Peace: Cluniac Liturgy as Ritual Aggression," *Viator*, 2 (1971), pp. 129–57, esp. pp. 145–6, 152–3.

[20]Atkins, "The Church of Worcester," pp. 14–15, 17–18; *Anglo-Saxon Charters: an annotated list and bibliography*, compiled P. H. Sawyer (1968), no. 1399.

[21]Atkins, "The Church of Worcester," Part II, p. 19; *Anglo-Saxon Charters*, compiled Sawyer, no. 1392.

[22]*Regularis Concordia*, transl. and ed. T. Symons (1953), pp. xxxii–xxxv.

The monastic diet varied with the liturgical seasons of the year. Between Easter and 14 September, but excluding certain fast days, there were two daily meals, one at midday and the other in the early evening, between Vespers and Compline. Two meals were also permitted on all Sundays and on major festivals at other times of the year, including Lent. From 14 September to the beginning of Lent one daily meal was prescribed, to be eaten between the early evening offices of None and Vespers, while in Lent itself, this one meal was postponed until after Vespers.[23] The tenth-century reformers did not lay down rules about the monastic diet, beyond a general reminder that the instructions of the Rule of St Benedict were to be followed, both as regards the amount and quality of food to be eaten, and the directions concerning abstinence and fasting.[24] The Rule itself forbade the eating of meat, except by the sick, and prescribed further austerities in Lent. These points are not specifically discussed in the *Regularis Concordia*. The fact that St Ethelwold was praised for his abstinence suggests that in general the Rule was not strictly observed on questions of diet.[25] In addition to the prescribed meals, drinks were permitted at certain times of the day.[26] The monastic life was also intended to be largely silent;[27] the *Regularis Concordia* encouraged this, while permitting quiet conversations about urgent matters.[28] How well this silence was maintained at Worcester Cathedral priory is conjectural. The anecdotal content of much of Wulfstan's official *Life* suggests that the monks indulged in a good deal of talking, not always on matters of urgency.

Wulfstan's *Life* implies that he earned rapid promotion in the monastic hierarchy due to the purity and perfection of his conduct. His family connections probably also contributed towards his advancement. He was apparently made novice-master soon after entering the monastic community,[29] since his first office is described as *custos puerorum*, indicating that he directed the education of *oblates*. He perhaps also had charge of any lay schoolboys being educated with them, as Wulfstan himself had been educated at Evesham and Peterborough. Children offered by their families for the monastic life were not necessarily enthusiastic about their enforced vocation, let alone temperamentally suited to it. The stories of

---

[23]Ibid., pp. xxxv–xxxvi; *The Rule of Saint Benedict*, ed. and transl. J. McCann (1951), chs 39–41.

[24]*Regularis Concordia*, pp. xxxv, 8.

[25]*Rule of Saint Benedict*, chs 36, 39, 49; *Regularis Concordia*, pp. xxxv–xxxvi.

[26]*Regularis Concordia*, p. xxxvi.

[27]*Rule of Saint Benedict*, chs 6–7.

[28]*Regularis Concordia*, pp. xxxviii–xxxix; 19–20, 25, 54–5.

[29]*Vita Wulfstani*, p. 91; *Florentii Wigorniensis monachi Chronicon* I, p. 219.

Wulfstan's own schooldays at Peterborough[30] were perhaps first told to the *oblates* of Worcester while he had charge of them, as *exempla* of how they might grow in faith and self-discipline. The Rule of St Benedict prescribed for the boys a strict, but not excessive discipline.[31] The *Regularis Concordia* defined the duties of a novice-master with particular emphasis on the need to avoid demonstrative conduct, which might give occasion for scandal.[32] The *oblates* received both a formal education and also training in their particular role in the liturgy. There was emphasis on decorous conduct, and, perhaps, instruction in projecting the voice when reading in church.[33] Wulfstan's next promotion was to the office of cantor, or precentor,[34] the monastic officer who played the leading role in the conduct of the liturgy, with particular responsibilities on major feasts such as Christmas, Palm Sunday and Easter.[35] He was transferred again to the office of sacrist "so that he might have more free time for prayer."[36] It is not obvious why this was so, because the sacrist was the officer who had the charge of the church and of the church services. Among his other duties was that of controlling the timing of the liturgy,[37] a responsibility which perhaps conditioned Wulfstan to appreciate the need for punctuality in attending the offices, a trait which is observed at a later stage of his monastic career.[38]

At this time of his life, Wulfstan was driving himself hard, fasting, and passing whole nights in a continuous vigil. During the liturgy he would genuflect at each verse of the seven (penitential) psalms, and the same at night during the lengthy Psalm 119. In the western porch of the church, there was an altar to All Saints, with a banner depicting Christ. Wulfstan would shut himself into this porch, and invoke Christ, "assaulting heaven with his tears and making noisy lamentations." No explanation is given for this distress, clearly the outcome of some personal or spiritual crisis. He had no feather bed (which implies that others did), and at this time of crisis he used no bed at all, snatching at sleep, instead of indulging

---

[30]*Vita Wulfstani*, pp. 4–5.

[31]*Rule of Saint Benedict*, chs 30, 45, 63, 70.

[32]*Regularis Concordia*, pp. xli, 7–8; see also Mayke De Jong, "Growing up in a Carolingian monastery: Magister Hildemar and his oblates," *Journal of Medieval History*, 9 (1983), pp. 99–128.

[33]*Rule of Saint Benedict*, chs 38, 45; *Regularis Concordia*, e.g. pp. 28, 35, 48.

[34]*Vita Wulfstani*, p. 9.

[35]*Regularis Concordia*, pp. xxxi, 21, 28, 35, 48n, 49, 51.

[36]*Vita Wulfstani*, p. 9. Another account records that he was appointed simultaneously cantor and sacrist on the order of the senior monks, *Florentii Wigorniensis monachi Chronicon*, I, p. 219.

[37]*Regularis Concordia*, pp. xxxi, 16 and note, 24, 26, 39, 49.

[38]*Vita Wulfstani*, p. 51; William of Malmesbury, *De Gestis Pontificum Anglorum*, p. 282.

in it. He would stretch out on the ground with his head on the step in front of the altar. Occasionally he would put a book under his head, and sleep on bare boards.[39] Since books at this period were produced individually and laboriously, they were rare and expensive objects. Wulfstan's treatment of them is astonishing, in view of his early training at Peterborough, and no doubt resulted from the intensity of the crisis through which he was passing. He was known to deprive himself of sleep for four days and nights at a stretch, and was in danger of a complete mental breakdown, if nature had not taken charge, so that he eventually fell asleep in the chapel where he was praying.[40]

Seven times each day he prostrated himself before every one of the eighteen altars in the Old Church of St Peter's, considering this no hardship. On the contrary, what others thought a hardship, he would copy. Although he exceeded everyone else in virtue, he humbly deferred to each of them, instantly performing any menial task from which the others turned in disgust.[41] His conduct was ascetic to the point of being excessive, yet the *Life* gives no indication of what had induced it. The literary presentation of Wulfstan's austerities echoes those of the early Northumbrian saints. There are comparable episodes in Bede's *Life* of Saint Cuthbert, and it may be that Coleman, Wulfstan's biographer, exaggerated his activities to match such examples. On the other hand, Wulfstan himself was perhaps influenced by Saint Cuthbert's example when his spiritual crisis led him to embark on his own intensive cycle of prayer.[42] The austerities of the Celtic monks were sometimes designed to overcome physical urges, and it may be that Wulfstan also felt tempted towards some forbidden relationship with one of the other inmates of the cathedral priory. Another, and perhaps more likely, explanation is that he was agonizing over his capacity to live up to the standards of a self-imposed ideal. His initial advancement as a secular clerk and later as a priest, and then as a monk, perhaps owed more to family influence than to his perception of his monastic vocation. His awareness of this might grow as he assumed increasing responsibility for exacting proper conduct from his subordinates.

Wulfstan's devotional practices perhaps orginated in a penance imposed by a confessor – the *Regularis Concordia* prescribed weekly confession for monks, and it was available as often as individual consciences might require it.[43] Yet the extremes to which Wulfstan went

[39]Ibid., p. 9.
[40]*Florentii Wigorniensis monachi Chronicon*, I, p. 219.
[41]*Vita Wulfstani*, p. 9.
[42]*Two Lives of Saint Cuthbert*, ed. B. Colgrave (1985), pp. 188, 210–12.
[43]*Regularis Concordia*, pp. xxxix, 18.

were evidently not prompted by a spiritual director, but rather by his own sense of unworthiness. His deliberately depriving himself of sleep, and more especially his absence from the dormitory,[44] were surely breaches of monastic discipline, yet there is no recorded objection by his seniors to his conduct. It was the business of the hagiographer to be economical with the truth, when the remainder could be displayed to the advantage of his subject, and this selective presentation was exercised even in recounting an episode in which an intruder disturbed Wulfstan's solitary vigils.

Wulfstan began visiting other churches in the neighbourhood at night, in order to recite the Psalms, and pray, in each one of them.[45] The hagiographer records this practice without comment, as though it was quite in order for Wulfstan to go about in this way, regardless of the monastic vow of stability, and setting an unfortunate precedent for junior members of the community, who might have less commendable reasons for being out of bounds late at night. It is odd that Wulfstan did not use the cathedral church for his devotions, unless his fervent prayers were the outcome of some tension between himself and others in the community. To achieve privacy for these private prayers, Wulfstan needed to walk through the cemetery. Despite the late hour, he did this without hesitation or fear – presumably of ghosts, rather than of muggers. Neither the darkness nor the isolation concerned him, and soon he was going every night to St Peter's, formerly the cathedral before the move to St Mary's, built in Bishop Oswald's time.[46]

Wulfstan was standing before the altar one night when his prayers were rudely interrupted. He was not the only one to take advantage of the quiet and seclusion of the Old Church. A peasant was also on the premises – perhaps sleeping off too much beer, or using the deserted building as a shelter, or even a hide-out. He told Wulfstan in no uncertain terms that he had arrived at a bad time, and that he was unwelcome there. In snarling tones, and grinning ferociously, he challenged Wulfstan to a fight. Wulfstan saw this apparition as a temptation of the Devil. As the hagiographer presents the story, the occurrence was due to malign supernatural intervention. Wulfstan continued reciting the Psalms, and had just reached Psalm 118:6, "The Lord is my helper; I will not fear what man can do to me," when the peasant rushed forward and seized him in a wrestler's lock. Wulfstan's body was weak from fasting, but he managed to push back his assailant and then go on to the attack. As he

---

[44] *Rule of Saint Benedict*, ch. 22.
[45] *Vita Wulfstani*, p. 9. For the churches in Worcester at this period, see M. O. H. Carver (ed.), *Medieval Worcestershire: An Archaeological Framework* (1980), pp. 31–7, 115–24.
[46] *Vita Wulfstani*, p. 9.

recalled afterwards, the fight lasted much of the night. He fought confidently, armed with faith, in a struggle which he believed was intended to test his spiritual resolution. At last the peasant gave way, vanishing in a blast of foul stench. But as a parting shot, he stamped heavily on Wulfstan's foot, piercing it as though with a scorching branding iron. Godric, one of the monks of Worcester, told Coleman he had often seen this scar or sore – the wound penetrated right to the bones. Coleman knew the peasant, a man of savage strength, monstrous wickedness and a hideously deformed face, altogether an appropriate guise in which, he believed, the Devil appeared.[47] More precisely, Wulfstan, while recognizing the peasant as a human being, apparently believed that his presence in that place, at that time, had been prompted by the Devil, in order to disrupt his prayers.

The occurrence is explicable enough in natural terms, although Wulfstan viewed it as a spiritual temptation. Episodes of this kind often occur in saints' lives, while the emphasis given to Wulfstan's stamina as a wrestler may owe something to a story of the boyhood of St Cuthbert, an influence which perhaps derived from the Northumbrian associations of the Church of Worcester.[48] Wulfstan's age at the time of this episode is uncertain, but evidently he was still quite young, and retained something of his earlier physical prowess, despite his recent austerities. This is virtually the only episode recorded from the first fifteen years or more during which Wulfstan was a monk of Worcester. We are told that he continued to grow in the virtues, especially those of obedience and submission to his superiors, and that he was always willing to take on the hardest task, even if he lacked the power to accomplish it.[49] With hindsight, we know that he was destined for higher things, but probably this was not obvious either to Wulfstan or to his fellow monks. On the other hand, his spiritual crisis resulted in a determination on his part to observe the monastic Rule zealously, and to ensure that his subordinates did likewise.

The works which focus on Wulfstan's career, his *Life*, and the long section devoted to him in William of Malmesbury's *De Gestis Pontificum Anglorum (Deeds of the English Bishops)* were written by clerics for the edification of their fellows, and consequently indicated the wider world of ecclesiastical and secular politics only to provide the background for

---

[47]Ibid., pp. 10–11. Coleman's informant was probably Godric Wirl, the monastic chamberlain in 1092: *The Cartulary of Worcester Cathedral Priory* (Register I), ed. R. R. Darlington (1968), no. 52. Godric, without a title, is among the monks of Worcester listed in 1104; *Durham Liber Vitae*, ed. A. H. Thompson (1923), folio 22 recto; Atkins, "The Church of Worcester," Part II, pp. 218–20.

[48]*Two Lives of Saint Cuthbert*, ed. Colgrave, p. 156.

[49]*Vita Wulfstani*, p. 11.

some telling anecdote. Yet life outside the cathedral precincts, and sometimes within them, was periodically disrupted by the ambitions of clerics and lay magnates alike. In order to understand the constraints upon Wulfstan, it is necessary to know something of what was happen ing in the wider world beyond the cloister. During these years, too, he was first brought into contact with several men who would play important roles in his later career.

Following the death of Bishop Brihtheah in December 1038, his successor was an outsider, Lyfing, who had been bishop of both Cornwall and Crediton since 1027. He retained both these sees down to his death, but his tenure of Worcester was at first more precarious.[50] Lyfing's reputation among his fellow churchmen was low. He was said to be ambitious, arrogant and uncontrollable, a man who trampled on the laws of the Church, and who was chiefly concerned to get his own way.[51] When Harthacnut succeeded to the throne in 1040, one of his priorities was to arraign those accused of the betrayal and death of his uterine brother Alfred, who had been summoned from exile in Normandy by his mother in 1036, only to face ambush, arrest, and a miserable end.[52] The chief culprits were identified by Harthacnut as Earl Godwin and Bishop Lyfing. The earl bribed his way out of trouble; he presented a fitting *wergild*, or blood-price, for the deceased aetheling, a gilded warship manned by eighty chosen warriors. Either Bishop Lyfing could not match this, or else he was not allowed the opportunity to do so, and accordingly suffered deprivation of his see of Worcester. The prosecutor in the case was Archbishop Elfric of York, who was rewarded for services rendered by the grant of the see of Worcester, to hold in plurality[53] as several previous archbishops had done. Yet Elfric's triumph was short-lived. The *familia* of Worcester raised strong objections to him, and in practice the archbishop never occupied the see.[54] Wulfstan would have had strong views on these events, but the format of his *Life* ensured that they are lost.

More traumatic events were to follow, when King Harthacnut greatly increased the taxation levied to pay off the royal war-fleet.[55] In May

[50]*Handbook of British Chronology*, ed. E. B. Fryde, D. E. Greenway, S. Porter and I. Roy (1986), pp. 215, 224. See also Knowles et al., *The Heads of Religious Houses*, p. 72.

[51]William of Malmesbury, *De Gestis Pontificum Anglorum*, p. 200. See also F. Barlow, *The English Church 1000–1066* (1979), pp. 73–4.

[52]*The Anglo-Saxon Chronicle*, transl. and ed. Dorothy Whitelock, with D. C. Douglas and Susie I. Tucker (1961), 1036, C (D); *Encomium Emmae Reginae*, ed. A. Campbell (1949), pp. lxiv–lxvii; F. Barlow, *Edward the Confessor* (1970), pp. 45–6.

[53]*Florentii Wigorniensis monachi Chronicon*, ed. B. Thorpe (1848–9), I, pp. 194–5.

[54]Ibid., p. 195; Fryde et al., *Handbook of British Chronology*, p. 224.

[55]*The Anglo-Saxon Chronicle*, 1040 C (D); 1039, 1040, E (F).

1041 two royal housecarls, Feader and Thurstan, arrived in Worcester to collect the tax owed from the city, but their demands provoked unrest. The housecarls fled to the tower of the cathedral priory, but were pursued and killed by the outraged citizens. Archbishop Elfric, with reasons of his own for wanting to teach a lesson to the people of Worcester, urged the king not to tolerate this act of defiance to his authority. There was an ominous lull, then in November the king sent an expedition with orders to kill all the citizens and to lay waste the city and the surrounding countryside. Almost all the royal housecarls took part in this punitive raid, together with five earls, including Leofric of Mercia and Godwin of the West Saxons. Thanks to advance warning, very few of the citizens were killed. Many were able to flee to the safety of Beaver Island in the River Severn, which they fortified and used as a base for resistance. The royal forces plundered the city for four days, and burned it on the fifth, before leaving with the booty, whereupon King Harthacnut's wrath was calmed.[56] The retribution meted out to Worcester was standard procedure in such a case. Several of the king's predecessors, and later, his brother Edward, also ordered the ravaging of rebellious towns.[57]

The reputation at Worcester of Archbishop Elfric was not enhanced by this episode, and in 1041, Bishop Lyfing was permitted to make his peace with the king, who restored him to his see.[58] Whatever Wulfstan thought of Bishop Lyfing, his own responsibilities as an increasingly senior member of the community threw them together. Consequently several of the bishops's surviving charters are attested by Wulfstan as priest.[59] At the bishop's death, in March 1046, a great clap of thunder was heard, and many people believed the Day of Judgement had arrived. Lyfing was buried at Tavistock abbey, which he had repaired and re-founded, and where, for many years, the fifteen Psalms of Degrees were chanted for the repose of his soul.[60]

Ealdred, his successor at Worcester (1046–62), was a smoother and more successful operator. He succeeded Lyfing as abbot of Tavistock

---

[56]*Florentii Wigorniensis monachi Chronicon*, I, pp. 195–6; *Anglo-Saxon Chronicle*, 1041, C (D); J. Campbell, "Some Agents and Agencies of the late Anglo-Saxon State," in *Domesday Studies*, ed. J. C. Holt (1987), pp. 201–4.

[57]S.D. Keynes, "A Tale of Two Kings: Alfred the Great and Aethelred the Unready," *Transactions of the Royal Historical Society*, fifth series, 36 (1986), pp. 195–217, esp. p. 211.

[58]*Florentii Wigorniensis monachi Chronicon*, I, p. 195.

[59]Atkins, "The Church of Worcester," Part II, pp. 19–21; *Anglo-Saxon Charters*, compiled Sawyer, nos 1058, 1392–8, 1849, 1850–6.

[60]*Florentii Wigorniensis monachi Chronicon*, I, p. 199; William of Malmesbury, *De Gestis Pontificum Anglorum*, pp. 200–1.

c.1027, and probably acted as his coadjutator at Worcester from c.1043.[61] Ealdred held the see of Hereford 1056–60, held the abbey of Winchcombe in 1053–4, and administered the diocese of Ramsbury during the absence of Bishop Herman, c.1055–8.[62] Given all these responsibilities, and quite apart from his participation in political life on the national level, Ealdred would have travelled a good deal, but he regarded Worcester cathedral and its property as very much under his control. His appointment as bishop of Worcester would have required at least the tacit assent of Earl Godwin,[63] and he subsequently fostered the interests of the earl's family, one of the few lay dynasties not to earn unfavourable notice in the writings of the monks of Worcester. The support of the earl and his sons was valued at Worcester as a counterbalance both to the encroaching Earl Leofric and also to the Normans and other "Frenchmen" introduced into the region by King Edward, after his accession in 1042.[64] Godwin himself was earl of Wessex, while in 1043 another earldom, comprising Herefordshire, Gloucestershire, Somerset, Oxfordshire and Berkshire, was created for his eldest son, Sweyn.[65] This new earl was too turbulent a character to be a reliable protector to the monks of Worcester. In 1047 he fled the country after being refused permission to marry the abbess of Leominster (Hereford), whom he had abducted.[66] His disgrace was materially advantageous to his brother Harold, and to their maternal cousin Beorn, who were therefore opposed to his reinstatement in 1049. Sweyn resolved the dispute by murdering Beorn, whereupon he was again outlawed,[67] but Bishop Ealdred arranged a pardon for him.[68] So committed were the monks of Worcester

---

[61]Knowles et al., *The Heads of Religious Houses*, p. 72.

[62]Fryde et al., *Handbook of British Chronology*, p. 217; Knowles et al., *Heads of Religious Houses*, p. 79. On Ealdred's career, see *The Life of King Edward who rests at Westminster*, ed. and transl. F. Barlow (1962), pp. xlvii–xlviii, p. 34, note 4; Barlow, *The English Church 1000–1066*, pp. 86–7, 220–1.

[63]Eric John, in *The Anglo-Saxons*, ed. J. Campbell (1982), p. 230.

[64]On the settlement of Normans as a deliberate counterweight to the house of Godwin, see M. W. Campbell, "A pre-Conquest Norman occupation of England?" *Speculum*, 46 (1971), pp. 21–31, esp. pp. 27–8; Ann Williams, "The King's nephew: the family and career of Ralph, earl of Hereford," *Studies in Medieval History presented to R. Allen Brown*, ed. C. Harper-Bill, C. J. Holdsworth and J. L. Nelson (1989), pp. 327–43, esp. pp. 330–1.

[65]*Florentii Wigorniensis monachi Chronicon*, I, p. 205; Williams, "The King's nephew," pp. 327, 329.

[66]*Anglo-Saxon Chronicle*, 1046 (C); *Florentii Wigorniensis monachi Chronicon*, I, pp. 201–2; *Hemingi Chartularium* I, pp. 275–6; Knowles et al., *The Heads of Religious Houses*, p. 214.

[67]*Anglo-Saxon Chronicle*, 1049 (C); 1050 (D); 1046 (E); Williams, "The King's nephew," p. 329.

[68]*Florentii Wigorniensis monachi Chronicon*, I, pp. 202–3.

to the house of Godwin that the only one of Sweyn's misdeeds to earn their censure was his allegation that he was actually the son, not of Godwin, but of Cnut – a claim which, if true, would have rendered him throne-worthy.[69]

King Edward's "French" adherents were meanwhile moving into territory which Sweyn had controlled, and there were complaints about the *welesce men* (foreigners) who had built a castle at Hereford.[70] The power struggle in 1051 between Godwin and his sons, and the "French" party resulted in the former being driven from England, although only Sweyn was formally outlawed. Bishop Ealdred was deputed to arrest Harold, but conspicuously failed to do so.[71] The king's nephew Ralph, who had already succeeded to Beorn's earldom of East Mercia, was now also created earl of Hereford. Sweyn died on pilgrimage in Constantinople in 1052, and when Godwin and his other sons returned in triumph to England in that year, Ralph retained his new earldom.[72] His duty was to defend the borders against the Welsh, but in 1055 his forces were defeated by Gruffyd ap Llewelyn, king of North Wales, and his ally, the exiled Earl Alfgar of Mercia. This engagement earned Ralph his nickname of "the Timid": "Before any spear had been thrown, the English host fled, because they were on horseback. And many were killed there – about four or five hundred men – and they killed none in return."[73]

Harold Godwinson, formerly earl of East Anglia, succeeded his father as earl of Wessex in 1053, and he probably took over command of Herefordshire after Ralph's defeat.[74] Leofgar, a former chaplain of Harold's, was appointed to the bishopric of Hereford in March 1056. Until his consecration as bishop, "he wore his moustaches" (in the manner of a warrior). He campaigned against the Welsh but was killed in action in June of that year.[75] Bishop Ealdred of Worcester was now appointed to the bishopric of Hereford, and held this office in plurality down to 1060, assuming some responsibility for the defence of the frontier.[76]

---

[69] *Hemingi Chartularium*, I, p. 275.

[70] *Anglo-Saxon Chronicle*, 1051 (E); Williams, "The King's nephew," pp. 330–1.

[71] *Anglo-Saxon Chronicle*, 1051 (C, D, E).

[72] *Anglo-Saxon Chronicle*, 1052 (C); Williams, "The King's nephew," p. 338.

[73] *Anglo-Saxon Chronicle*, 1055 (C, D, E); Williams, "The King's nephew," p. 329.

[74] *Anglo-Saxon Chronicle*, 1055 (C); Williams, "The King's nephew," p. 329.

[75] *Anglo-Saxon Chronicle*, 1056 (C).

[76] *Anglo-Saxon Chronicle*, 1056 (C, D); Fryde et al., *Handbook of British Chronology*, p. 217. On the politics of the Welsh frontier in this period, see Kari L. Maund, "The Welsh Alliances of Earl Aelfgar of Mercia and his family in the mid-eleventh century," *Anglo-Norman Studies XI: Proceedings of the Battle Conference 1988*, ed. R. Allen Brown (1989), pp. 181–90.

Ealdred was also a leading minister of King Edward. In 1054 he travelled to the Emperor and to Hermann, archbishop of Cologne, to negotiate the return of Edward the Exile, a kinsman and potential successor of the king. This embassy lasted for nearly a year.[77] In 1058 Ealdred journeyed in near-regal state to Jerusalem, via Hungary,[78] a round trip which would take him several months. Given all this activity in public life, Ealdred needed a reliable prior to maintain stability at Worcester. When he first became bishop, the prior was Agelwin, who continued in office until some uncertain date in the mid-1050s.[79] When a successor was required, Ealdred is said to have considered how diligently Wulfstan had carried out his responsibilities in previous posts, and appointed him provost, or prior, evidently not later than 1055.[80] This promotion was most likely due to Wulfstan's real merits, as much as to his seniority within the community, rather than to any residual family influence.

Wulfstan set about his new responsibilities energetically, reforming matters both inside the priory and outside. Externally, his chief task was to retrieve the assets of the cathedral priory which his predecessors had wasted.[81] The official *Life* gives no further details, since these would be inappropriate in a work of hagiography, designed to record Wulfstan's spiritual achievement. The discreet wording of the *Life* suggests that previous priors had injudiciously granted leases in such a way that the monks did not receive the service due, and estates were in real danger of permanent alienation. His experiences while attempting their recovery would lead him to appreciate the need for careful documentation, and would shape the advice which, as bishop, he was later to give to the monk Hemming.[82] Dubious transactions of the kind which Wulfstan was

[77]*Anglo-Saxon Chronicle*, 1054 (C, D); *Florentii Wigorniensis monachi Chronicon*, I, p. 212; Barlow, *Edward the Confessor*, pp. 215–17.

[78]*Anglo-Saxon Chronicle*, 1058 (D); *Florentii Wigorniensis monachi Chronicon*, I, p. 217; Barlow, *Edward the Confessor*, p. 218.

[79]Knowles et al., *Heads of Religious Houses*, p. 83.

[80]*Vita Wulfstani*, p. 11; *Florentii Wigorniensis monachi Chronicon* I, p. 219. At Worcester this office was usually termed provost, rather than prior, down to the late eleventh century. The appointment is dated pre-1057 by Knowles et al., *Heads of Religious Houses*, p. 83, who argue that "too much weight should perhaps not be laid on" the dating of the episode of Ealdred's gift to Wulfstan upon his return from Cologne (*Vita Wulfstani*, pp. 15–16). The *Vita* is explicit on the circumstances under which the gift was made, presumably in 1055, and places it in the narrative some time after Wulfstan's appointment as prior. Against this it might be argued that the psalter and sacramentary were appropriate gifts to entrust to the sacrist, and that the episode is perhaps recorded out of sequence in the *Vita Wulfstani*.

[81]*Vita Wulfstani*, p. 11.

[82]*Hemingi Chartularium*, I, pp. 282–6; II, p. 391.

determined to remedy are illustrated in an account which Hemming later recorded concerning land at Condicote (Gloucs). This was bought, with the convent's money, by Prior Agelwin and his brother Orderic, but was later returned to the priory when they dedicated Orderic's son to the monastic life. Orderic himself became a monk soon afterwards. In order to ratify the priory's title, a declaration of the history of this estate was made before King Edward, about January 1053, and witnessed by the prior, or dean, together with the monks Wilstan and Wulfstan.[83] This story illustrates what was perhaps a fairly common occurrence: priors acting in association with their well-placed kinsmen in the secular world, to the enrichment of their lay kinsfolk at the expense of monastic property. Such transactions may never have been discussed in chapter, so that objectors could be ignored. During the later years of Prior Agelwin, Wulfstan and Wilstan, as the monks next in seniority, assumed increasing responsibiity for defending the property rights of the cathedral priory. In two instances land was seized by brothers of Earl Leofric, but in one case Wulfstan and Wilstan were able to put pressure on the culprit, Godwin, who restored the property when on the point of death.[84] Attestations to the surviving episcopal and monastic charters of the mid-eleventh century suggest that the monastic community was still small,[85] making it easier for one high-handed individual such as Prior Agelwin to mismanage the community's lands. Conversely, one or two right-thinking and assertive monks might be able to carry the others with them when acting to defend the interests of the community as a whole.

Within the priory, Wulfstan insisted strongly on the observance of the Benedictine Rule. In order to ensure this, he presented in his own life a religious example to the other monks, since he would have disdained to preach what he was unwilling to practice. His instruction was neither of his own devising nor particularly eloquent, but was based on the teachings of the Fathers of the Church. He was well versed in all the books of Holy Scripture, paying particular attention to all those which commended chastity, a virtue which he himself earnestly maintained, and the lack of which he sharply rebuked in others.[86] He would recognize the

---

[83]Ibid., II, p. 335; *Anglo-Saxon Charters*, compiled Sawyer, no. 1475.

[84]*Hemingi Chartularium*, I, pp. 259, 277–80. The chronology of the episodes concerning Earl Leofric's brothers is uncertain. In the account of the second case, Wulfstan is styled prior and Wilstan *prepositus*; Atkins, "The Church of Worcester," Part II, p. 27. Prior Agelwin's term of office cannot easily be defined: Knowles et al., *Heads of Religious Houses*, p. 83. On the question of his incapacity in later years, see Atkins, "The Church of Worcester," Part II, p. 26.

[85]Atkins, "The Church of Worcester," Part II, pp. 26–7.

[86]*Vita Wulfstani*, p. 11. Wulfstan's continuing austerities at this time were intended to set a good example to others: *Florentii Wigorniensis monachi Chronicon*, I, p. 220.

potential for disruption in any monastic community in which homosexual relationships were condoned, but the real targets of his censure
were probably the secular priests and clerks of the episcopal *familia*.
These were not bound by the same rigorous vows as the monastic
community, although by the mid-eleventh century there were constraints
against clerical marriage. Some of these secular clerics were probably
married, and Wulfstan's censures were most likely directed against
members of this group, even though they were formally subject to the
bishop, not the prior. His *Life*, written for a monastic audience, would
naturally stress the virtue of chastity, but given Wulfstan's early psychological conditioning, we need not doubt either his own chastity or his
failure to understand why others were unable to remain chaste. When
temptation came, he emerged unscathed.

In the city of Worcester there lived a wealthy woman, whose attractive
figure fascinated those who gazed at her. She often came to church, but
more to give people something to look at than to pay attention to the
word of God. She had designs on Prior Wulfstan, and tried flattering
him, but met with no response – he was utterly impervious to her charms.
For a long time she nursed her hurt in secret, and was afraid to show her
feelings, but at last her desire overcame her sense of shame. When the
prior happened to be standing near her in church she ventured to pull at
his monastic habit in a shameless manner. He stopped her with a stern
glance, but she begged him in the name of Almighty God not to despise
what she had to say. Wulfstan innocently supposed that she wanted to
make her confession, and took her on one side. But the woman began to
proposition him. She said that for some time she had considered talking
over with him an idea which might be to their mutual advantage. She had
a house full of material possessions, but these needed some fit person to
look after them, since both her parents were dead, and her husband was
no longer there. She argued that Wulfstan was the proper person to take
charge, a man with the wisdom to decide both how to manage the
household and how to spend the money. Wulfstan advised that she
should give the money to the poor, and that she herself should become a
nun. The women retorted that this was not her idea at all. Wulfstan
should relax his priestly strictness a little, and agree to share her bed,
since it was only a small fault, if it was a fault at all, to enjoy the
embraces of a woman. Yet even if it was a serious fault, Wulfstan could
redeem the guilt by almsgiving from her wealth.[87] She had enough and

---

[87]*Vita Wulfstani*, pp. 11–12. The lady seriously underestimated the gravity with which
the church hierarchy would have regarded her own adultery, let alone any sexual
transgression by a man who was both priest and monk; see J. A. Brundage, *Law, Sex and
Christian Society in Medieval Europe* (1987), pp. 207–9, 214–23. On the woman's
suggestion that penance could be commuted for a money payment, see Barlow, *The English
Church 1000–1066*, p. 268 and notes 4, 6.

some to spare, and would not begrudge it. Wulfstan could stand no more. He made the sign of the cross on his forehead, to ward off temptation, and shouted at her "Clear off, with the hatred you deserve, you provoker of lust; you daughter of death; you agent of Satan." He boxed her ears, giving her such a blow on the side of her head that the sound of the smack was heard outside the door of the church. The news of this incident naturally spread around the town, and was discussed in social gatherings. The hagiographer likened Wulfstan to a second Joseph (who had rejected the amorous wife of Potiphar) (Genesis 39).[88]

While this story is presented in Wulfstan's *Life* as an example of how he upheld the virtue of chastity,[89] it also illustrates the lifestyle of prosperous townspeople in late Anglo-Saxon England. The unnamed woman in the story was evidently separated from her husband, since it was suggested that she might become a nun, yet she enjoyed complete control over her property and her social relationships. From her own point of view, her proposition was not as outrageous as it was perceived by the monks of Worcester. It was not so long since the *familia* had comprised secular priests, whose wives would be women of good social standing, like herself.[90] It is questionable whether she perceived the distinction between secular clerks and Benedictine monks, since the latter were in such close daily contact with the townspeople. If the woman felt the need of a good business head to manage her property, then the competent provost immediately came to mind, since his successful recovery of the alienated lands of the church of Worcester would be well known in the circle in which she moved. The woman's social position was such that propositioning an attractive and competent acquaintance was an obvious course open to her, since she had no vocation for the religious life. A woman separated from her husband could not remarry without certain news of his death.[91] Even then, her choice wold be limited to competing for such unmarried men of appropriate social status as there were in the neighbourhood. Given these uncertainties, a relationship of concubinage was one to which many women willingly resorted at this time.[92]

Wulfstan's vulnerability to such approaches arose from his dedication to his pastoral duties. The provost, or prior, was officially concerned with the administration of the cathedral priory, but Bishop Ealdred's public activities necessitated his frequent absence from Worcester, and

---

[88]*Vita Wulfstani*, p. 12.
[89]Ibid., p. 11.
[90]Cf. Brundage, *Law, Sex and Christian Society*, pp. 216–17.
[91]Ibid., p. 201.
[92]Ibid., p. 183.

many of his pastoral responsibilities would have remained unfulfilled if Wulfstan had not taken these tasks upon himself.[93] His compassion reached out beyond his monastic duties to the common people. When the morning's services were concluded, he could often be seen standing in front of the church door, readily available to those who wanted to speak to him. He was so conscientious in investigating people's troubles that he often continued at his post until midday, or even to the time of the late-afternoon office of Vespers, in order to help those who had suffered from violence of any kind, or to baptize the children of the poor.[94]

While the *Regularis Concordia* prescribed the formal duty of feeding the poor of the neighbourhood, and poor vagrants,[95] Wulfstan's care for the poor extended to remedying the spiritual consequences of their lack of money. Many priests in the surrounding district were refusing to baptize infants without payment. It was believed that a child who died unbaptized would not go to Heaven, and in an age of high infant mortality, the greed of these priests would cause much anxiety to the poor. Wulfstan, while secretly pitying the greed of the rapacious priests, undermined their activities by voluntarily baptizing poor children himself. Parents flocked to him from town and countryside, especially those who were unable to give any money for the baptism of their children.[96] The demands of the priests for payment in return for bestowing the sacrament of baptism might be perceived as simony. Wulfstan was ahead of Continental reforming clerics in his own attitude.[97] Soon, not only poor parents but also rich ones were flocking to Wulfstan to have their children baptized. His holiness, recognized in his ministry to the poor, became an attraction in itself. Throughout the district people quickly came to think that a child was properly baptized only if Wulfstan officiated.[98]

Eminent people also became attracted by Wulfstan's reputation, and sought out his friendship, which they found a spiritual support in times of both prosperity and adversity. Among the nobles drawn to Wulfstan was Harold Godwinson, already, we are told, "feeling himself capable of

---

[93]It was later claimed at Evesham that Abbot Ethelwig (1058–77) was entrusted by Ealdred with responsibility for the external affairs of the diocese, before he became abbot: *Chronicon Abbatiae de Evesham ad annum 1418*, ed. W. D. Macray (1863), p. 87 and note 2.

[94]*Vita Wulfstani*, pp. 12–13.

[95]*Regularis Concordia*, pp. 61–2.

[96]*Vita Wulfstani*, p. 13.

[97]The second Lateran Council of 1139, cap. 2, cap. 24, condemned clerics who accepted money for administering sacraments: *Conciliorum Oecumenicorum Decreta*, ed. J. Alberigo et al., 3rd edn (1973), pp. 197, 202.

[98]*Vita Wulfstani*, p. 13.

greater power and of laying claim to the kingdom by his noble qualities."
When the earl was on a journey, we are told that he would not hestitate
to go thirty miles out of his way, in order to receive Wulfstan's spiritual
guidance. The esteem was mutual, and Wulfstan acted as Harold's
confessor, faithfully mediating his prayers to God.[99] Superficially they
appear ill-assorted friends, but Harold was an intelligent man, quite
capable of recognizing Wulfstan's spiritual qualities. In that era, there
was effectively a demarcation of activity between "those who pray" and
"those who fight," yet the latter would want to enlist the goodwill of
some holy man, whose prayers on their behalf would ensure salvation.
Harold, astute politician and man of action though he was, did not
necessarily lack any religious sense. The trouble which Harold took to
ensure his meetings with Wulfstan shows that he appreciated the
opportunity to get things into perspective. Wulfstan's later determined
rearguard action in defence of English cultural values suggests that he
would sympathize with Earl Harold against King Edward's alien
protégés. It was no doubt gratifying to the English writer, Coleman, to
record this close relationship between the last surviving English spiritual
hero and his secular counterpart.

Earl Harold's acquaintance with Wulfstan perhaps dated from 1055,
when he assumed military control in Herefordshire. His authority there
was formalized after the death of Earl Ralph in 1057, when Harold
succeeded him as earl of Hereford.[100] He acquired considerable lands in
the region, probably with the direct support of King Edward, so that his
territory would form a defensive "marcher lordship" against the Welsh,
who raided intermittently between 1049 and 1066. Much of Harold's
land lay in the valley of the River Wye, but other profitable estates lay
east of Offa's Dyke. The most extensive lands of both Harold and his
men were in Herefordshire, although they had smaller but still considerable holdings in both Gloucestershire and Oxfordshire. In Worcestershire itself Harold held only one estate, and he had none at all in
Warwickshire.[101] He would certainly need to go out of his way in order
to have any conversation with Prior Wulfstan. Ealdred's control of the
bishopric of Hereford in 1056–60[102] and his consequent military respon-

---

[99]Ibid., p. 13.

[100]*Anglo-Saxon Chronicle*, 1055 (C); 1057 (D); Williams, "The King's nephew," pp.
338–40.

[101]Ann Williams, "Land and Power in the eleventh century: the estates of Harold
Godwineson," *Proceedings of the Battle Conference on Anglo-Norman Studies III, 1980*,
ed. R. Allen Brown (1981), pp. 171–87; Robin Fleming, "Domesday Estates of the King
and the Godwines: a study in late Saxon politics," *Speculum*, 58 (1983), pp. 987–1007,
esp. pp. 1004, 1006.

[102]Fryde et al., *Handbook of British Chronology*, p. 217.

sibilities in the area probably accounts for the initial meeting between Harold and Wulfstan. Harold would be well-disposed towards the trustworthy prior of his ally, and perhaps appreciated Wulfstan's earnest spirituality all the more in contrast to Bishop Ealdred's sophistication. While personal confession did not become obligatory for the laity until the Fourth Lateran Council of 1215,[103] eminent individuals had spiritual advisers at a much earlier date. Both Harold's father, Earl Godwin, and Leofric earl of Mercia and the Lady Godiva are said to have had as their confessor and spiritual adviser the hermit Wulsy.[104] The spiritual reliance which Earl Harold placed in Wulfstan was the foundation for the political trust which he placed in him during later and more dangerous times.[105]

Bishop Ealdred also deferred to Wulfstan's sanctity and spiritual guidance. It was said that while the bishop was astute in worldly matters, he was not lacking in religion.[106] The hagiographer was clearly impressed by the spiritual deference shown by the eminent Ealdred, whom he named as successor to Bishop Brihtheah. The *Life* persistently disregards the two unsatisfactory intervening bishops, Lyfing and Elfric Puttoc. Perhaps neither appreciated Wulfstan's merits but in any case he was a comparatively junior monk during their time at Worcester.

Ealdred's absences on matters of national importance presumably prompted Wulfstan's increasing pastoral activities. He noticed a decline in the moral conduct of the laity, which he put down to lack of proper instruction through preaching. Accordingly he began preaching regularly in the cathedral on Sundays and major festivals. Wulfstan's preaching style was said to be very effective, thundering against sinners, while encouraging the others, yet he approached this task in all humility, modestly not seeking any recognition for his achievements.[107] The pragmatic Englishman saw a job which needed to be done, and did it, even though in the eyes of purists he might be said to be usurping the teaching role of the absent bishop. At this period there was at Worcester a Continental monk named Winrich, who was much given to scholarly reading, and was a vigorous and ready speaker. In several respects he would have impressed superficial observers as being more prepossessing than Wulfstan: shrewd and discreet in worldly matters, sophisticated in his conduct, admirably composed and agreeable to everyone. On the other hand, he was very hot-tempered. He enviously attacked whatever

[103]Fourth Lateran Council, ch. 21, *Conciliorum Oecumenicorum Decreta*, p. 245.
[104]*Chronicon Abbatiae de Evesham*, p. 83.
[105]*Vita Wulfstani*, p. 23.
[106]Ibid., p. 13.
[107]Ibid., pp. 13–14.

displeased him – in particular Wulfstan's frequent preaching. Winrich argued that this was quite out of order, since Wulfstan was usurping the episcopal office. Only the bishop should preach to the people, and only the bishop could absolve them from their sins. A monk should be content with the silence of the cloister, and should not insult the people's ears by rhetorical preaching. To Winrich, this preaching seemed more like crafty striving after preferment than an act of piety. He generally spoke in this way behind the prior's back, but one day, in a fit of rage, he said it to Wulfstan's face.[108]

Wulfstan's reported reply seems remarkably low-key, even given his well-known humility. He was perhaps in a difficult position regarding Winrich who, given his Continental origins, was perhaps a protégé of King Edward or of one of his alien courtiers. The sophisticated and cosmopolitan Winrich probably believed himself to be on the road to promotion. He could prove his worth, in his own eyes at least, by asserting the strict interpretation of the canon law against a man whom he could regard as a presumptuous provincial. Winrich's open challenge to the authority of Wulfstan, the head of the priory, indicates that the foreigner enjoyed powerful patronage. Wulfstan met the challenge on pastoral grounds, arguing that nothing pleased God more than when people called sinners to the path of truth. Preaching along these lines must not be neglected. If Winrich could show him anything that was more pleasing to Christ, he would do it instantly.

This argument took place just as the monks were retiring for the night. The force of Wulfstan's words made a deeper impact on Winrich than he was prepared to admit, and as he slept, he was afficted by a violent dream. He seemed to be carried before the judgement seat of an unknown Judge, who demanded to know why Winrich had just censured his servant for the good deed of preaching. Winrich's excuses fell on deaf ears. He was thrown to the ground and was ordered to be beaten. The officers of the Judge thrashed him severely, while Winrich cried out "Have mercy, Lord. Oh Lord, have mercy." At last his torment ceased, and he was asked whether he would continue to silence the messenger of the Lord, and by doing so, cause fewer men to be summoned to his court. By now the desperate Winrich was willing to promise anything. He swore by all that was holy that he would no longer forbid Wulfstan to preach. On the contrary, he would actually encourage him and others to do so. At last the Judge granted him mercy and spared his life. Winrich gave his word not to break his promise, and was then dismissed. On waking, Winrich was still in the same penitent frame of mind. As soon as it was daylight, he threw himself at the feet of Prior Wulfstan, clasped his knees,

---

[108]Ibid., p. 14.

acknowledged his fault, and begged for pardon. When asked what had caused this sudden change of mind, he told the story of his vision, swearing that it was true. His earnest pleas and streaming tears were taken as evidence of this, but the conclusive point was this his shoulders were covered with swollen bruises, and it was accepted that he had undergone severe punishment. Wulfstan quickly pardoned him. On receiving the prior's blessing Winrich was healed, and his pain vanished.

The writer of Wulfstan's *Life* pointed out that St Jerome, one of the Fathers of the Church, had a similar experience to Winrich, although in his case the punishment was inflicted for reading heathen books. The writer considered that in moral terms there was little difference between neglecting the Holy Scriptures in order to read the frivolous works of the heathen, and acting so as to prevent the Scriptures themselves from being preached.[109] This episode is presented in Wulfstan's *Life* to point a moral. The dream demonstrated to Winrich that God valued Wulfstan's concern for the spiritual welfare of his flock above the strict observance of the canon law. Medieval readers and listeners would perceive the story of Winrich's dream as a supernatural vision which vindicated Wulfstan's simple and single-minded goodness. Modern readers would say that Winrich's unconscious mind contradicted his waking verdict on Wulfstan's preaching, recognizing the validity of the prior's moral stance, and that the mental conflict was worked out in a violent dream, in which he was condemned for his wrongful actions and "punished" by psychosomatically induced physical symptoms.[110] At Worcester the story was accepted as denoting heavenly approval of Prior Wulfstan.

At about the same time as Winrich's discomfiture, a second episode occurred which was deemed to illustrate Wulfstan's saintliness. The prior was designing a belfry (or a small bell-cage – William of Malmesbury, when translating the *Life*, said he did not know the proper word). This structure was to be erected above the roof of the cathedral church. The workmen had access by step-ladders, on which they stood while securing further ladders suspended in the air – presumably raised by pulleys from the roof, or the tower, but no technical explanation is given. Eventually a whole series of ladders was in place, fastened to one another by cords. The workmen were instructed to use this hazardous contrivance as their means of access to the site, but they viewed it very warily. At last one of them ventured to climb to the top, bu fell headlong. Wulfstan was standing by, and "placed the Cross between him and destruction." It is not clear whether this was a cross he was wearing, or, more likely, that he

[109]Ibid., pp. 14–15.
[110]C. J. Holdsworth, "Visions and Visionaries in the Middle Ages," *History*, 48 (1963), pp. 141–53, esp. pp. 145–6.

made the sign of the cross. The workman fell at least forty feet, but suffered neither from fractures nor from concussion. He got up, blaming the fall on his own rashness, and blessing Wulfstan's holiness that he had escaped unharmed. It was widely believed that if Wulfstan had not been there, the man would have lost not one life, but, in the words of a popular contemporary saying, "a hundred lives would have gone down the drain" (probably the equivalent in human terms, of saying that a cat had lost all its nine lives at once). The biographer claimed that he could have described this episode in more circumstantial detail, but that this would have been an impertinence when the bare facts evoked so much wonder and admiration.[111] It is not unknown for people to escape a fall from this height with little more than bruising, although such escapes are rare. The fortuitous presence of Wulfstan at the scene of the accident was enough to ascribe the man's survival to miraculous intervention.

Wulfstan's activities were the more "visible" in that the bishop was so much away. At about the same time as these episodes, King Edward sent Ealdred on a mission to the Emperor Henry at Cologne, probably concerning the return to England of the king's kinsman, Edward the Exile.[112] Ealdred's embassy was well received, and having completed his task, he stayed on in Cologne for a few days, for a holiday. Many gifts were showered on him, whether on his own account or because he was the ambassador of King Edward. As a parting gift, the bishop received the psalter and sacramentary which had been produced at Peterborough so many years earlier, and which Ernwin had given to King Cnut and Queen Emma. Cnut had sent the books to Cologne as one goodwill gesture, and now they were returned, as another. Ealdred had never heard of Wulfstan's prophetic saying that the books would one day come back. When he returned to England, he gave them to the prior, as the person most worthy to receive them. Wulfstan joyfully accepted the books as a gift from Heaven, thanking God for the fulfilment of his wish.[113]

The bishop certainly owed a generous present to the loyal Wulfstan, who both governed the cathedral priory and also ministered to the pastoral needs of the diocese. He was so dependable as to be indispensable, which was gratifying up to a point, but a barrier to further promotion. Wulfstan had the satisfaction of knowing that he was doing a

---

[111]*Vita Wulfstani*, p. 15.

[112]Ibid., pp. 15–16; *Anglo-Saxon Chronicle*, 1054 (D); Barlow, *Edward the Confessor*, pp. 215–16.

[113]*Vita Wulfstani*, p. 16, see also p. 5; the books had perhaps been sent to Cologne during negotiations for the marriage of Cnut's daughter Gunnhild to the future Emperor Henry III: cf. *Hemingi Chartularium*, I, p. 267.

worthwhile job, but as he approached his mid-fifties[114] it must have seemed as though, despite his long experience, he was not destined for higher things. Even his influential kinsfolk had not been able to accelerate his previous promotion, since the former prior had survived for so long. When Bishop Ealdred promoted a monk of Worcester to the abbacy of St Peter's, Gloucester, in 1058, this was not Wulfstan but his fellow monk Wilstan,[115] next below Wulfstan in the Worcester hierarchy.[116] Wilstan was now promoted over his head to the superior status of abbot, perhaps because of his kinship to Ealdred,[117] but the bishop was soon compelled to secure an even greater dignity for Wulfstan.

[114]*Florentii Wigorniensis monachi Chronicon*, I, p. 221. Wulfstan was "upwards of fifty years old" at his consecration as bishop.

[115]Wilstan is given this form of his name throughout the present work, to avoid confusion with the future bishop, although he himself was sometimes known as Wulstan (Wulfstan): Knowles et al., *Heads of Religious Houses*, p. 52 and note 2; *Historia et Cartularium Monasterii Sancti Petri Gloucestriae*, ed. W. H. Hart, 3 vols (1863–7), I, pp. 8–9.

[116]Wilstan, abbot of Gloucester, survived to 1072 (Knowles et al., *Heads of Religious Houses*, p. 52). It is therefore unlikely that he is identical with the deacon Wilstan who attested a charter of Bishop Leofsige in 1016. Wilstan, priest and monk, often attested charters in company with Wulfstan from the time of Bishop Lyfing onwards. He was sub-prior, when Wulfstan was prior. The attestations of Wilstan are discussed by Atkins, "The Church of Worcester," Part II, pp. 15, 19–22, 24, 26, 27, although his belief that the witness of 1016 was identical with Wulfstan's contemporary affects his discussion of their relative seniority (p. 26).

[117]*Historia et Cartularium Monasterii Sancti Petri Gloucestriae*, I, p. 9; II, p. 119.

4

Election to the Bishopric

The death of Archbishop Cynesige of York, on 22 December 1060, triggered a chain of events which culminated some twenty months later in Wulfstan's election as bishop of Worcester. King Edward quickly nominated Bishop Ealdred to York,[1] a promotion which the latter had probably anticipated, as a natural and proper reward for the services he had rendered to the crown. Ealdred then set off for Rome to obtain papal approval of his election. On a long and dangerous journey of that kind, safety lay in numbers, and so he travelled in company with Tostig Godwinson, earl of Northumbria; his wife, the Countess Judith; Tostig's young brother Gyrth, and, probably Wulfwig, bishop of Dorchester, besides Gospatric, a young kinsman of King Edward.[2] Such an aristocratic party would of course be accompanied by a retinue of servants and a bodyguard. Their meandering route, "through Saxony and the upper reaches of the Rhine," was probably dictated by some diplomatic mission in which Earl Tostig was concerned.[3] Ealdred himself had been entrusted with business at the papal court by King Edward, and it is possible that the party were also delivering a consignment of Peter's Pence to Rome.[4] Two more bishops-elect, Giso of Wells and Walter of Hereford, both Continental clerks in the royal service, were also travelling to the papal

---

[1]*The Vita Wulfstani of William of Malmesbury*, ed. R. R. Darlington (1928), p. 16; E. B. Fryde, D. E. Greenway, S. Porter and I. Roy (eds), *Handbook of British Chronology*, third edn (1986), p. 224. The appointment was said to have been made on Christmas Day: *Florentii Wigorniensis monachi Chronicon ex Chronicis*, ed. B. Thorpe, 2 vols (1848–9), I, p. 218.

[2]*The Life of King Edward who rests at Westminster*, attributed to a monk of St Bertin, ed. and transl. Frank Barlow (1962), pp. 34–6; for the identity of Gospatric, see p. 36, note 1, and for the probable presence of Bishop Wulfwig, see p. 34, note 2; p. 35, note 2.

[3]Frank Barlow, *The English Church 1000–1066*, second edn (1979), p. 292 and note 6.

[4]*Life of King Edward*, p. 34, note 5.

Curia to obtain confirmation of their recent appointments, but perhaps set out later and used a shorter route.[5]

The main party arrived in Rome just before Easter (15 April) 1061, on which day a papal synod convened. Earl Tostig was graciously received by Pope Nicholas, who invited him to attend the synod and even to sit next to him.[6] The earl, as a brother-in-law of King Edward, would naturally see in this signal honour the recognition due to his exalted status while the pope, as an ardent reformer, could take advantage of his presence to ensure publicity in England for his attacks on abuses in the church, committed at the instigation, or with the connivance, of influential laymen. This supposition is the more likely in that the earl was detained in Rome for some time – whatever business broguht him there was not expedited as quickly as he had hoped.[7]

Bishops Giso and Walter were consecrated on Easter Day.[8] In the normal course of events, they would not have been required to visit the papal court, since their consecration would be the responsibility of their archbishop, but the incumbent at Canterbury at this time was Stigand, a man who was regarded in papal circles as a usurper. Moreover, in 1058, he had accepted the pallium, the vestment which was the insignia of his office, from an anti-pope, Benedict X. This caused a problem for all clerics elected to bishoprics in the province of Canterbury during Stigand's tenure of office.[9] Wulfstan himself later stated that whereas some went to Rome, as Giso and Walter had done, others went either to France for their consecration, or else to neighbouring bishops.[10]

Ealdred's visit to the papal court initially proved disastrous. This was perhaps inevitable, given the pope's zeal to abolish abuses such as simony (the offering of money in return for spiritual benefits) and the holding of benefices in plurality. Ealdred "was examined on how he had come to sacred orders." This phrase refers to his free admission that he had transferred from the bishopric to which he was first ordained, to another, something which was forbidden in canon law. Earlier papal decretals on

[5]*Life of King Edward*, p. 35 and note 3. See, however, William of Malmesbury, *De Gestis Pontificum Anglorum*, ed. N. E. S. A. Hamilton (1870), p. 251, where it is implied that these two bishops-elect travelled with the main party.

[6]*Life of King Edward*, p. 34.

[7]Ibid., p. 36. For the impact of the papal reform upon England in this period, see Barlow, *The English Church 1000–1066*, pp. 294–302.

[8]Fryde et al., *Handbook of British Chronology*, pp. 227, 250.

[9]Barlow, *The English Church 1000–1066*, pp. 300–5.

[10]*Vita Wulfstani*, p. 190; *Canterbury Professions*, ed.M. Richter (1973), p. lxi; no. 31, p. 26.

this point were considered, and the whole synod gave its verdict against him.[11]

In fact, custom was already beginning to permit translations from one see to another and the synod might have stretched a point, if only to oblige the worthy King Edward. But Ealdred further scandalized the assembly by his proposal that he should continue to hold the diocese of Worcester jointly with the archdiocese of York. It was claimed in England that Ealdred "had taken advantage of the simplicity of King Edward" to obtain royal approval for his proposal to unite the sees, as his predecessors at York had done.[12] A Worcester writer later believed that Ealdred "was so bound by ties of love to Worcester that it was dearer to him than the dignity of the archbishopric."[13] More likely Ealdred wanted to combine the prestige of metropolitan status with the revenues of the rich agricultural lands of his Mercian diocese, besides retaining the option of residing in the south-west when he tired of the harsher climate, and, perhaps, the political restiveness, of the north. There was a long argument, which ended in Ealdred not only being refused the pallium for York, but even being deposed from his episcopal rank.[14] Earl Tostig regarded the outcome as an affront to national dignity and threatened that from then onwards Peter's Pence would not be rendered from England.[15]

The clerics and noblemen all left Rome together, but were ambushed that same day, barely fifteen miles from the city.[16] A combined group of prelates and nobles would present a tempting challenge to robbers on the lookout for booty. The value of the haul in this raid was about £1,000 in Pavian currency, but the attack had also a political dimension, since the gang was led by the Tuscan Count Gerard of Galeria, one of those local nobles who were trying to prevent the papacy escaping from their

---

[11]*Life of King Edward*, pp. 34–5 and note 1; William of Malmesbury, *De Gestis Pontificum Anglorum*, p. 251.

[12]William of Malmesbury, *De Gestis Pontificum Anglorum*, p. 251.

[13]*Vita Wulfstani*, p. 16. Ealdred had held the see of Hereford between 1056 and 1060 but surrendered this on acquiring York: The *Anglo-Saxon Chronicle*, trannsl. and ed. Dorothy Whitelock with D. C. Douglas and Susie I. Tucker (1961), 1056 (C, D); 1060 (D, E).

[14]*Life of King Edward*, p. 35; William of Malmesbury, *De Gestis Pontificum Anglorum*, p. 251. On the pallium, see Barlow, *The English Church 1000–1066*, pp. 298–300.

[15]*Vita Wulfstani*, p. 16; William of Malmesbury, *De Gestis Pontificum Anglorum*, pp. 251–2. On the levying of Peter's Pence, and the purpose to which it was put, see Barlow, *The English Church 1000–1066*, pp. 290–1, 295–7.

[16]*Life of King Edward*, p. 35; *Vita Wulfstani*, pp. 16–17. The latter text places the attack at Sutri, but see *Life of King Edward*, p. 35, note 4; William of Malmesbury, *De Gestis Pontificum Anglorum*, p. 251.

control.[17] Well-publicized attacks on prominent personalities might discourage potential visitors to the *Curia* of the reforming popes. Count Gerard evidently had a good intelligence service which notified him of prominent travellers who were about to leave Rome, for as soon as the ambush was sprung, he demanded to know which of the party was Earl Tostig. Fortuitously, the leading rider of the English party at that moment was the young Gospatric, whose distinguished appearance and splendid clothes indicated his high rank. Heroically, he identified himself as the earl, and signalled to Tostig to ride away. The gang led off Gospatric with the rest of the booty, evidently with a view to holding him for ransom. When he thought the others had reached safety, he admitted his real identity under interrogation and at once his life was threatened. Happily others of the gang acknowledged his courage, and insisted that he be set free. His personal possessions were restored to him and he was escorted to safety.[18] This misadventure to the English party resulted from their delay in Rome. Tostig had earlier decided to send his wife homewards, perhaps to avoid the onset of the unaccustomed summer heat. He assigned most of his own armed escort to protect her, in addition to her personal bodyguard, hence the vulnerability of his party. Judith continued on her way, ignorant of the disaster which befell the others.[19]

Wulfstan's promotion to the see of Worcester resulted from this ambush. The English delegation had not the wherewithal to continue their homeward journey, and were obliged to make their way back to Rome. Pope Nicholas could now make Ealdred come to terms.[20] Further blunt representations by Tostig were considered and accepted. The pope also bore in mind that Ealdred had freely confessed his position, and that, when he was degraded, he had accepted his sentence humbly. The *Curia*, moreover, advised the pope that it would be uwise to permit such an important[21] delegation to leave Rome both pillaged and mortified.[21] Ealdred was accordingly restored to his episcopal rank, and now promised that he would resign the bishopric of Worcester, provided that he could find a better priest in the diocese to fill the vacancy. Once he had made this promise, the pope granted him the pallium for York. It was believed that this concession "would cause them to persevere in their realm in greater fidelity and veneration of St Peter." In other words, had

---

[17]*Life of King Edward*, p. 35, note 4.
[18]ibid., pp. 35–6.
[19]Ibid., p. 36.
[20]*Vita Wulfstani*, p. 17.
[21]*Life of King Edward*, p. 37; William of Malmesbury, *De Gestis Pontificum Anglorum*, pp. 251–2.

the pope continued implacable towards Ealdred, not only might Peter's Pence be withheld, but the resentment of the king and his nobles might also lead England into schism. In consideration of the earlier losses of the English party, they were now generously equipped for their return journey, and this time they all reached home unharmed.[22]

Pope Nicholas was too astute to rely solely on Ealdred's own word, and dispatched legates, both to witness to the fulfilment of his promise, and to deal with other ecclesiastical business in England.[23] The new archbishop's disregard of canon law rulings on translation and pluralism perhaps prompted suspicions that a general tour of inspection might be opportune. Archbishop Ealdred presented the legates to King Edward, "who habitually conformed entirely to the customs of the Roman church."[24] He would be glad to earn such a reputation, in view of the privileges which he had been requesting for Westminster Abbey.[25] In recent years, he had assumed the patronage of this monastery, contributed generously to its endowment and instigated a rebuilding programme, so that the abbey church could serve as his mausoleum.[26] The king entertained the papal legates with all due honour and respect before sending them off on their tour throughout the realm. They were to travel under the protection of Archbishop Ealdred, who would bring them back to the royal court at Easter 1062. The official reason given for this arrangement was that they would feel at ease with Ealdred, since he had already accompanied them on their long journey from Rome. They could talk freely with him, and be at ease as though with a familiar friend.[27] The urbane and cosmopolitan Ealdred could certainly smooth their path, and ensure that all necessary introductions were made. At the same time,

---

[22]*Life of King Edward*, p. 37; William of Malmesbury, *De Gestis Pontificum Anglorum*, p. 252; *Vita Wulfstani*, pp. 16–17.

[23]*Vita Wulfstani*, p. 17. The papal envoys are described as cardinals in this text, but not in the Worcester Chronicle. Nicholas II died in Rome, perhaps on 22 July 1061, and Alexander II was elected there on 29 or 30 Sepember, so that either pope might have sent these legates to England. On this mission, see H. E. J. Cowdrey, "Bishop Ermenfrid of Sion and the Penitential Ordinance following the Battle of Hastings," *Journal of Ecclesiastical History*, 20 (1969), pp. 225–42; esp. pp. 229–30.

[24]*Vita Wulfstani*, p. 17.

[25]*Westminster Abbey Charters, 1066–c.1214*, ed. Emma Mason assisted by the late Jennifer Bray, continuing the work of the late Desmond J. Murphy (1988), no. 153; see also *Anglo-Saxon Writs*, ed. F. E. Harmer (1952), pp. 288–95.

[26]*Life of King Edward*, pp. 44–6, 71–4, 80–1; Barbara Harvey, *Westminster Abbey and its Estates in the Middle Ages* (1977), pp. 24–5; R. Gem, "The Romanesque Rebuilding of Westminster Abbey," *Proceedings of the Battle Conference on Anglo-Norman Studies III. 1980*, ed. R. Allen Brown (1981), pp. 33–60; *Westminster Abbey Charters*, pp. 1–2.

[27]*Vita Wulfstani*, p. 17.

the arrangement allowed discreet surveillance to be maintained by both parties. The legates had no doubt been briefed to keep an eye on Ealdred, while he in turn would want to keep an eye on them, both for his own sake and, perhaps, in accordance with secret instructions by King Edward and his advisers. Given the aggressive stance of the reforming papacy towards lay domination of the Church, these legates might uncover various abuses, or long-standing preferential arrangements, depending on the viewpoint of the beholder. In such eventualities, Ealdred could explain the circumstances in as favourable a light as possible, and then negotiate a compromise on the best terms available. Such a task would call for constant vigilance, but was not insuperable. The English Church had perhaps not retained the zeal of the tenth-century reform movement, but the general standard of conduct did not compare unfavourably with that elsewhere in Western Europe at this time.[28] The legates duly carried out their instructions, travelling over much of England in company with Ealdred, during the last months of 1061 and the first weeks of 1062. Eventually, a little before Lent, the party reached Worcester, where the cardinals rested. But Ealdred quickly set off to visit his estates.[29]

The lands of the diocese of Worcester, rather than those of his new archdiocese, were Ealdred's preoccupation at this time. He was bound to renounce his diocese and nominate his successor at the Easter court, where his choice would determine whether or not he would finally lose control of his desirable Mercian property. Within his diocese there were two outstanding candidates: Prior Wulfstan, famed for his spirituality and his pastoral activities, and Abbot Ethelwig of Evesham, an outstanding adminstrator. It was later claimed at Evesham that Ealdred had designated Ethelwig as his deputy in the bishopric during his own absence. This had apparently occurred some years before Ethelwig became abbot in 1058, and perhaps coincided with Ealdred's embassy of 1054. While there were precedents for the appointment of an episcopal coadjutator, Ethelwig cannot have exercised this role, since he was not in episcopal orders, but he perhaps carried out the bishop's administrative and legal fuctions, within certain limits.[30] Ethelwig, if nominated, would be an extremely competent bishop, and even Wulfstan's supporters admitted that he was not lacking in religious qualities. From Ealdred's

---

[28]R. R. Darlington, "Ecclesiastical Reform in the late Old English period," *English Historical Review*, 51 (1936), pp. 385–428; Barlow, *The English Church 1000–1066*, pp. 9–10, 27–9.

[29]*Vita Wulfstani*, p. 17.

[30]*Chronicon Abbatiae de Evesham ad annum 1418*, ed. W. D. Macray (1863), p. 87; R. R. Darlington, "Aethelwig, abbot of Evesham," *English Historical Review*, 48 (1933), pp. 1–22, 177–98, esp. pp. 3–4.

point of view, the big disadvantage of this appointment would be that Ethelwig, with his first-rate managerial skills, would see to it that he took possession of all the lands of the diocese. Yet Ealdred's own worldly outlook would enable him to recognize the abbot's positive qualifications, and Ethelwig himself lobbied strongly for this promotion. We are told that Ealdred hesitated for a long time, weighing up the merits of the two candidates, before allowing worldly prudence to give way to Divine Providence.[31]

In fact, Wulfstan's nomination was probably decided while Ealdred was touring with the papal envoys. This is borne out by his depositing them at Worcester, where they would have a good opportunity of observing the prior in action for six weeks or so at a stretch. The legates were lodged with Wulfstan, and were glad of a rest, after their exhausting travels during the autumn and winter.[32] Pope Nicholas had died in July 1061, and the legates were regarded at Worcester as the envoys of his successor, Pope Alexander II. One of them has remained anonymous, but the name of the other was recalled, perhaps because he was the dominant partner, Ermenfrid, bishop of Sion (in the Valais region of what is now Switzerland).[33] The visitors would naturally observe a Lenten discipline, although secular priests would not have to undergo the rigours imposed upon monks at this season of the Church's year. Wulfstan kindly took all possible care that his guests would experience the generous, liberal hospitality of the English.[34]

Wulfstan's conduct during their visit is described in terms strongly reminiscent of hagiography. Exaggeration may have crept in, but the zealous Wulfstan is likely to have observed Lent solemnly. He is said to have observed his usual discipline of prayer and fasting. He regularly kept vigil during the night, doing entirely without sleep, reciting psalms and punctuating the verses with frequent genuflexions, a movement which would help him not to doze off. Three days a week he abstained completely from food, and continued his fast throughout the night until dawn. On the other three weekdays, he ate only leeks and cabbage, with a crust of bread. Since Sundays were always feast days in the monastic calendar, Wulfstan's meal then comprised fish and wine, but more for basic nourishment than to indulge his appetite. He kept total silence on the three days he fasted, so as not to give offence by any chance word.[35]

---

[31] *Vita Wulfstani*, p. 18.

[32] Ibid., p. 17.

[33] *Florentii Wigorniensis monachi Chronicon*, I, p. 220. On Ermenfrid, see Cowdrey, "Bishop Ermenfrid of Sion," pp. 225–42, esp. pp. 229–30. Neither envoy is named in Wulfstan's *Life*.

[34] *Vita Wulfstani*, p. 17.

[35] Ibid., p. 17.

This verbal abstinence would not greatly inhibit his control of the monastic community, since there was a commonly recognized sign-language in which basic needs could be communicated, while more complex instructions could be given in writing.[36] Every day Wulfstan lovingly entertained three poor men. Following the command of Our Lord (John 13:15) he gave them their daily bread, and washed their feet.[37] The daily washing of the feet of guests was prescribed in the Rule of Saint Benedict,[38] while the *Regularis Concordia* instructed that this service was to be rendered specifically to poor strangers. The duty was required of the head of the house "whenever he can," no less than of the rank and file monks.[39]

Wulfstan's other austerities derived from his conscientious observance of the Lenten discipline prescribed in the Rule of St Benedict. During Lent, monks were required to stint themselves of food, drink, sleep, talk and jesting. Individual monks were allowed some degree of discretion in determining the extent of their self-denial, but were obliged to report their intended programme to the abbot, who forbade those excesses which tended to encourage presumption and vainglory.[40] No check was imposed on the self-denial of the head of the house. While no monk consumed fats during Lent,[41] Wulfstan's dietary restraint was remarkable. Its regular observance throughout the year would surely have impaired his health, especially in conjunction with loss of sleep. Since he lived to a ripe and active old age, the austerities reported at this juncture of his career were surely the result of Lenten self-discipline, rather than his normal routine. Wulfstan no doubt realized Ealdred's intention in bringing the legates to Worcester, and perhaps imposed this severe regime upon himself as a penance designed to crush any vainglory arising from the conjecture that he was next in line for the bishopric. Given his genuine resistance to the appointment when it was eventually made, it is highly improbable that the programme of austerities was designed to impress the legates. Whatever his own intentions, his self-discipline aroused the admiration of the legates. They also praised his teaching, particularly because he himself practised what he preached.[42]

---

[36]*The Rule of Saint Benedict*, ed. and transl. J. McCann (1951), ch. 38. This sign-language was primarily intended for use in the refectory, so as not to render the reader inaudible. See also p. 186, note 60.

[37]*Vita Wulfstani*, p. 17.

[38]*Rule of Saint Benedict*, ch. 53.

[39]*Regularis Concordia*, ed. T. Symons (1953), pp. xxxvii, 62.

[40]*Rule of Saint Benedict*, ch. 49.

[41]*Regularis Concordia*, p. xxxvi.

[42]*Vita Wulfstani*, pp. 17–18.

At Easter the papal envoys joined the royal court, perhaps held at Gloucester, to hear the king's response to their legation.[43] They naturally also took part in the discussions on the appointment to the vacant bishopric of Worcester. The sequence of events leading to Wulfstan's consecration as bishop can be pieced together from his *Life*, with its hagiographical bias, and from the Worcester Chronicle, which is more dramatic in its presentation at times, and emphasizes different aspects of the proceedings. In Wulfstan's *Life* we are told that he was proposed by the legates as a worthy candidate, who added more to the priestly office than he received from it. His character was on a par with his diligence, and his manner of life was guided by wisdom, since he lived well, and his deeds excelled his words. This line of argument, we are told, aroused the goodwill of King Edward, "a man who never supported those covetous people who trafficked in benefices."[44]

So runs the formal account. Wulfstan's genuine goodness and exemplary observance of the monastic rule would impress even sophisticated habitués of the papal *Curia*. His humility and unworldliness would make him a model subject of the reforming papacy, while his pastoral concern for the laity of the diocese had already been amply demonstrated. His administrative talents were apparent in his recovery of alienated lands of the cathedral priory, although no detached observer would have rated his managerial acumen on a par with that of Abbot Ethelwig. It is conjectural whether Ealdred contrived to prevent the ambitious abbot from pressing his claims directly upon the legates. If they did meet him, they perhaps concluded that, once admitted to episcopal office, Ethelwig would be likely to prove just the type of prelate which the papacy was attempting to curb.

Both Archbishop Stigand and Archbishop Ealdred supported the choice of the cardinals. It was said that Stigand did this from goodwill, and Ealdred "from his experience."[45] There is no reason to doubt Stigand's goodwill — many years later, Wulfstan was to write of him in respectful terms to Anselm, a later archbishop of Canterbury.[46] The presence of the papal legates in England was doubtless an embarrassment to Stigand, given the dubious circumstances under which he had obtained

---

[43]*Florentii Wigorniensis monachi Chronicon*, I, p.220. On the location of this Easter court, see Martin Biddle, "Seasonal Festivals and Residence: Winchester, Westminster and Gloucester in the tenth to twelfth centuries," *Anglo-Norman Studies VIII*, ed. R. Allen Brown (1986), pp. 51–72, esp. pp. 69, 71, note 24.

[44]*Vita Wulfstani*, p 18.

[45]Ibid., p. 18.

[46]Eadmer, *Historia Novorum in Anglia*, ed. M. Rule (1884), pp. 46–7. See also Barlow, *The English Church 1000–1066*, p. 305.

his position, but his authority was not under threat at this time, nor indeed for years to come.[47] Even so, it would be as well for him to be seen to side with the legates. Ealdred was well acquainted with Wulfstan's spiritual merits, but his later actions were to show that he supported and, almost certainly, initiated Wulfstan's candidature in the belief that he would prove pliable when faced with continuing archiepiscopal claims on the lands of the diocese.

The chief lay supporters of Wulfstan's appointment were Harold Godwinson, earl of Wessex, and Earl Alfgar of Mercia, "equals in conspicuous courage, if not quite equals in piety," as it was tactfully expressed. They were influential in securing Wulfstan's nomination, sending mounted messengers to sway the discussion in his favour, dispatch riders who covered many miles at great speed, in order to hasten the progress of the negotiations.[48] There had perhaps been some counter-lobbying in support of Ethelwig or yet another candidate, so that influential bishops or abbots remained to be convinced of Wulfstan's superior claims. The concerted support of Earls Alfgar and Harold would be decisive in ensuring the success of Wulfstan's cause in the West Midlands and the border region. Alfgar's earlier career was turbulent. He had twice been exiled. On one occasion he joined a Welsh invasion force, while Earl Harold was a leader of the English defence.[49] Yet there was seemingly no personal animosity between Alfgar and Harold, who married his daughter after Alfgar's death.[50] Alfgar succeeded his father, Earl Leofric, only in October 1057,[51] and his support of Wulfstan in 1062 was one of his last recorded acts, since he apparently died later that year.[52] Harold Godwinson's support of Wulfstan is readily understandable, given that the prior was his confessor,[53] and the earl was an ally of Ealdred. In view of the archbishop's imminent departure from Mercia, Harold might welcome the prospect of having another trustworthy ally in Worcestershire, where his own landholdings were comparatively small.[54]

This account of the concerted action which resulted in the promotion of a new bishop is quite credible – although the proceedings were

[47]Barlow, *The English Church 1000–1066*, pp. 302–8.

[48]*Vita Wulfstani*, p. 18.

[49]*Anglo-Saxon Chronicle*, 1055 (C, D); 1058 (D).

[50]F. Barlow, *Edward the Confessor* (1970), p. 243.

[51]*Anglo-Saxon Chronicle*, 1057 (D, E).

[52]*Life of King Edward*, p. 51, note; Barlow, *Edward the Confessor*, p. 210 and note 3.

[53]*Vita Wulfstani*, p. 13.

[54]Emma Mason, "Change and Continuity in Eleventh-Century Mercia: the experience of Saint Wulfstan of Worcester," *Anglo-Norman Studies VIII*, ed. R. Allen Brown (1986), pp. 168–9.

scarcely in line with those prescribed by the reforming popes. Wulfstan's *Life* probably records the actual course of events in compressed form. There is some discrepancy with the account in the Worcester Chronicle, composed several decades later. In the latter it was claimed that the legates instigated the clergy and people of Worcester to call for Wulfstan's election, which they, by virtue of their authority, then confirmed. This sequence of events was more in line with canonical theory, but it lacks credibility in mid-eleventh century England.[55]

The two accounts agree that Wulfstan experienced great distress when his nomination became inevitable. It was a contention that a candidate for a bishopric should express his unworthiness: *noli episcopari*: "I don't want to be made a bishop," but Wulfstan's reluctance seems genuine. This may seem surprising in one who was a member of an influential clerical family, and who was probably a near kinsman of two former bishops of Worcester. In his earlier years he may well have been encouraged to expect eventual elevation to the bishopric. Yet under the hagiographical gloss of Wulfstan's *Life*, and of the Worcester Chronicle, to a lesser extent, can be glimpsed Wulfstan's agonized self-doubts about his capacity to undertake the major public responsibilities which fell upon bishops in his day. The account in Wulfstan's *Life* states that he was presented at court, and ordered to accept the office of bishop. He earnestly resisted, crying out that he was unworthy of such a great honour, while everyone else shouted that he certainly was up to it.[56] This noisy, emotional and undignified scene carries conviction as an unvarnished glimpse of high society in eleventh-century England. Those urging Wulfstan to accept the bishopric pointed out that obedience was the chief of all the virtues. A man who would not obey could not be reckoned either a faithful monk to his monastery, or a faithful bishop to his flock. He must bear his promotion humbly, thanking God who had raised him to an office which ought to be a blessing to those over whom he was to rule.[57] This appeal to the monastic virtues of obedience[58] and humility[59] was an astute move in persuading Wulfstan to submit – eventually.

The Worcester Chronicle makes a similar point in more dramatic terms. It is said that when deadlock had been reached, he was censured for his disobedience and obstinacy by the anchorite Wulsy, a holy man who had lived an enclosed life for some forty years. Frightened by this oracle, Wulfstan was compelled to give way, although sorrowfully, and

---

[55]*Florentii Wigorniensis monachi Chronicon*, I, p. 220.
[56]*Vita Wulfstani*, p. 18.
[57]Ibid., p. 19.
[58]*Rule of Saint Benedict*, chs 5, 58, 68, 71.
[59]*Rule of Saint Benedict*, ch. 7.

with a heavy heart.[60] Wulsy, one of three anchorites attached to the abbey of Evesham, had been confessor to Earl Leofric and the Lady Godiva,[61] and his support for Wulfstan's candidature was perhaps enlisted by their son Alfgar, dispatching his couriers to Evesham, notwithstanding the rival claims of its abbot. Wulsy was debarred by his profession of enclosure from leaving Evesham to harangue Wulfstan. Either the anchorite summoned the prior to him – or else his dire warnings were conveyed to Wulfstan by messengers such as the earl's men.

Subjected to a barrage of admonitions from all quarters, Wulfstan experienced a great conflict between love and fear: fear in case he should fail in his unaccustomed responsibilities, and love, which forbade him to resist the commanding authority of so many eminent men, and the earnest devotion of the people. The more unworthy he thought himself, the more eagerly his supporters pressed the office upon him. They were said to be the more convinced that he would discharge the duties of his office wisely because he came to it with such anxious heart-searching. Only a fool would plunge thoughtlessly into a position of responsibility without knowing how much effort would be needed to fulfil it.[62] Wulfstan was so reluctant to accept the office of bishop that he declared to those around him that he would rather have had his head cut off than have this office imposed upon him.[63] He planned to escape to some remote part of the country, but his supporters guessed his intentions, and prevented his flight. They then tried to get him into a more positive frame of mind. Some coaxed him, urging him to accept his new role, and reverently prostrating themselves at his knees and his feet, which they kissed repeatedly. Others bullied him, warning him not to spoil the free gift of Heaven by his impatience, but instead to enhance it by meekly bearing his new responsibilities.[64] The court was virtually unanimous in support of Wulfstan's candidature. When he still resisted, the legates and archbishops introduced the clinching argument that it was Wulfstan's duty to obey the pope. He was bound to give way on this, and so he at last agreed under compulsion, submitting to the will of God, and of the people. It was said that God's will was manifested in Wulfstan's promotion, because he never intentionally did anything contrary to the will of God, and always did penance for any accidental transgression.[65]

---

[60]*Florentii Wigorniensis monachi Chronicon*, I, p. 220.
[61]*Chronicon Abbatiae de Evesham*, pp. 83, 219, 266, 308, 322, 394.
[62]*Vita Wulfstani*, p. 19.
[63]Ibid., p. 19; *Florentii Wigorniensis monachi Chronicon*, I, p. 220.
[64]*Vita Wulfstani*, p. 19.
[65]Ibid., p. 18.

Since Wulfstan was so determined to refuse the bishopric, while Abbot Ethelwig was only too eager to obtain it, some of the exasperated courtiers would no doubt have been glad if the prior's candidature had been dropped. But this would be tactically undesirable, given the presence of the legates, who were witnesses to Wulfstan's merits. From the viewpoint of the English court, the recent scandal in Rome caused by the ambitious Ealdred made it essential to redress the balance by securing the election of a man who was truly religious, in both senses of the word. The papal legates, and even Wulfstan's committed supporters, perhaps had doubts about his ability to fulfil the public side of his role – a bishop was expected to take part in secular administration, and to serve as a royal adviser. Yet at this distance in time it is all too easy to overlook the appeal of Wulfstan's genuine holiness, which in turn was a potent force both in his own locality and among those elsewhere who knew him as a mediator with the unseen but all-powerful spiritual world.[66]

This battle to compel Wulfstan to accept the bishopric took place over some months. The royal court convened at Easter, which in 1062 was on 31 March,[67] yet it was only on 29 August that his election was canonically confirmed,[68] presumably by the papal legates. King Edward then invested Wulfstan with the bishopric.[69] In this solemn ceremony, the king presented the new incumbent with his episcopal staff and ring, in token that he conveyed to him the lands and temporal authority of the bishopric. In 1099 Pope Urban II prohibited the ceremony, partly on the grounds that the staff and ring were emblems of the bishop's spiritual office,[70] but in Wulfstan's day they were the most readily identifiable symbols of the dignity which the king was conferring. In years to come, Wulfstan's acceptance of the staff and ring from the hands of King Edward were to acquire new meanings, first for the monks of Westminster, eager to promote the canonization of their patron, and later for King John, defending against the papacy his right to control episcopal appointments.[71]

King Edward's writ formally notifying the thegns of Worcestershire, Gloucestershire and Warwickshire of Wulfstan's appointment was prim-

[66]Barlow, *The English Church 1000–1066*, pp. 7–8.
[67]C. R. Cheney (ed.), *Handbook of Dates for Students of English History* (1948), table 10, pp. 102–3.
[68]*Florentii Wigorniensis monachi Chronicon*, I, p. 220.
[69]*Vita Wulfstani*, p. 19.
[70]Eadmer, *Historia Novorum*, p. 114.
[71]Emma Mason, "St. Wulfstan's staff: a legend and its uses," *Medium Aevum*, 53 (1984), pp. 157–79.

arily addressed to the bishop's lay patrons, Earls Harold and Alfgar.[72] In normal circumstances, Wulfstan would have been consecrated by his own metropolitan, the archbishop of Canterbury, but Stigand's dubious position made this inadvisable.[73] The ceremony was therefore conducted on 8 September by Archbishop Ealdred, who swore in the presence of the king and nobles of the realm that he would not claim any ecclesiastical or secular right over Wulfstan, either by virtue of this ceremony, or because Wulfstan had been one of his monks before his consecration.[74] When Wulfstan came to make his profession of obedience to Archbishop Lanfranc, Stigand's successor, he explained the circumstances which had constrained him to accept consecration from Ealdred, but said that he had not sworn canonical obedience to him.[75] Clearly it was believed at court that Ealdred would try to assert authority over Bishop Wulfstan. Subsequent events imply that the archbishop always regarded him as a subordinate.

At the consecration of a bishop, the Scriptures were opened at random. The verse on which the reader's eye alighted, the prognosticon, was believed to foretell the nature of his episcopate. At Wulfstan's consecration the prognosticon comprised the words of Our Lord on meeting the plain-spoken Nathaniel: "Behold an Israelite indeed – in whom there is no guile" (John 1:47). It was considered that this might be applied to Wulfstan by anyone who saw or heard him, or by those who read of his life.[76] The events which immediately followed the consecration bore out this verdict in an unhappy way. Ealdred left Wulfstan at York for a while, claiming this was intended to do him honour. His enforced stay was extended for some time, to the distress of the community of Worcester.[77] Naturally they would miss the rule of their former prior, and be left wondering what was now in store for them. Their immediate

---

[72] British Library Additional Charter 19802, reproduced in *Facsimiles of English Royal Writs to A.D.1100 presented to Vivian Hunter Galbraith* (1957), plate XXVI, with text printed on the facing page (no foliation); *Anglo-Saxon Writs*, no. 115; *Anglo-Saxon Charters: an annotated list and bibliography*, ed. P. H. Sawyer (1968), no.1156. See also *Councils and Synods with other documents relating to the English Church, I, A.D. 871–1204*, ed. D. Whitelock, M. Brett and C. N. L. Brooke, 2 vols (1981), I, pp. 560–1.

[73] *Vita Wulfstani*, p. 19; William of Malmesbury, *De Gestis Pontificum Anglorum*, pp. 35–6; Barlow, *The English Church 1000–1066*, pp. 302–8; *Canterbury Professions*, pp. lxi; no. 31, p. 26.

[74] *Florentii Wigorniensis monachi Chronicon*, I, pp. 220–1; *Vita Wulfstani*, p. 19. Another account states that the legates ordained Wulfstan, with the consent of Ealdred: William of Malmesbury, *De Gestis Pontificum Anglorum*, p. 252.

[75] *Vita Wulfstani*, p. 190; *Canterbury Professions*, pp. lxi, no. 31, p. 26.

[76] *Vita Wulfstani*, p. 19; William of Malmesbury, *De Gestis Pontificum Anglorum*, p. 280.

[77] *Vita Wulfstani*, p. 19.

cause for alarm was Ealdred's expropriation of almost all the episcopal estates. From the two separate references to this in Wulfstan's *Life*, it seems that Ealdred set this process in motion while the see was still vacant.[78] Wulfstan was distressed but at first did not argue with him, judging it best to yield to circumstances.[79] It was considered that Wulfstan's "simplicity" and holiness were deliberately exploited by Ealdred,[80] who resumed his expropriations during Wulfstan's enforced stay at York, securing control of almost all the revenues of the episcopal estates. When Wulfstan was eventually allowed to return to Worcester, Ealdred restored to him scarcely seven villages.[81] Even the archbishop had not the effrontery to keep the lot, yet by detailing Wulfstan in York during the autumn, Ealdred could appropriate the harvest from those Worcester estates which were then returned.

Ealdred's depredations were difficult for Wulfstan to withstand in view of his long conditioning in monastic obedience. By the time of his consecration, Wulfstan was in his fifties.[82] He had spent well over two decades in a position of subjection to a series of overbearing bishops, and, in his earlier years, perhaps also to domineering monastic obedientiaries. His position as prior, which he had held for six or eight years at most, but perhaps less, allowed him some initiative, but always subject to Ealdred's veto. Any feeling of release prompted by the bishop's frequent absences would be modified by the supervisory role exercised in the diocese by Abbot Ethelwig. People who have undergone long years of strict discipline can often assert it successfully over others, if they suddenly find themselves in positions of authority, because of their innate assumptions about hierarchical role-playing. But even then, this new-found authority is effective only over those whom they unhesitatingly regard as their subordinates, and who share with them common values. When dealing with those who do not, psychological inhibitions are likely to remain. While Prior Wulfstan could assert his authority over his own monks and deferential laity, his limited social contact with the opposite sex had caused his initial failure to grasp the intentions of his importunate woman parishioner. Similarly the intellectual, articulate and cosmopolitan monk Winrich could challenge the prior's pastoral activity.

[78]Ibid., pp. 19–20.

[79]Ibid., p. 19.

[80]*Hemingi Chartularium ecclesiae Wigorniensis*, ed. T. Hearne, 2 vols (1723), II, p. 406; William of Malmesbury, *De Gestis Pontificum Anglorum*, p. 280.

[81]*Vita Wulfstani*, p. 20. Similarly, after consecrating his kinsman Wilstan abbot of Gloucester, Ealdred appropriated certain of its manors on account of the expenses he had incurred in rebuilding the abbey: *Historia et Cartularium Monasterii Sancti Petri Gloucestriae*, ed. W. H. Hart, 3 vols (1863, 1865, 1867), I, p. 9; II, p. 119.

[82]*Florentii Wigorniensis monachi Chronicon*, I, p. 221.

Whether or not Ealdred knew of these telling episodes, he would shrewdly realize that Wulfstan would be inhibited from speaking out publicly against his encroachments on the lands of the church of Worcester, following sixteen years of subjugation to him. During that time Wulfstan probably had to swallow many other criticisms of Ealdred's conduct. The latter had no doubt plenty of smooth-sounding arguments ready if complaints by Wulfstan did reach the king's ears. Besides, Edward was more likely to support his trusted minister than a new and untried bishop who had publicly proclaimed his own unfitness to govern the church of Worcester.

Wulfstan's anger and resentment at these encroachments should not be underestimated. As prior, he had been in practice the custodian of the monks' estates, and now, as the bishop-abbot, his responsibility was all the greater, since he was now custodian of the patrimony of St Mary. If Wulfstan had successfully withstood the efforts to make him bishop, then the lands would have been saved from Ealdred, since the other candidate, Ethelwig, would never have tolerated such encroachments. This thought had perhaps occurred to Wulfstan, even though it was not his chief reason for resisting election. Ealdred stubbornly retained all but the seven villages he had previously restored. Wulfstan knew there was no way of forcing his hand, so he resorted instead to persistent pleading. This gradually wore Ealdred down, and eventually he returned more of the lands. Yet he still retained twelve villages, which were relinquished only by a later archbishop,[83] after Wulfstan had undergone yet more traumatic experiences.

---

[83] *Vita Wulfstani*, p. 20.

5

Wulfstan's Episcopate to Christmas 1066

Wulfstan's new role as a diocesan bishop entailed many public obligations, yet we are told that he kept the balance between the episcopal life
and the monastic one, without losing his grip on either. As a bishop, he
continued to observe the monastic rule, while as a monk he now
displayed the authority of a bishop. The hagiographer tartly observed
that Wulfstan's whole lifestyle was quite unlike that of certain persons at
the time of writing.[1] Probably he had in mind Wulfstan's successor,
Bishop Samson.[2] Wulfstan, despite his new responsibilities, was not one
of those people who claim to be "too busy to be bothered." If people
came to consult him, he had plenty of sound advice to give them. If
petitioners came, he willingly heard their requests, handling them
impartially, and reaching a quick decision.[3] In this respect, too, the
hagiographer is indirectly censoring later bureaucrats of church and
state, who made big play of their self-importance and restricted availability, and who procrastinated as a ploy in the power game. Without
seeking to detract from Wulfstan's manifest abilities, it may be thought
that this passage, like many others in his *Life*, projects onto him the
virtues of a lost Old English golden age, contrasting them with the slick
practices of the secular clerks who increasingly filled the ranks of the
bishops after the Norman Conquest.[4] William of Malmesbury, translator
of the *Life* into Latin, is well known for his views on the demoralizing

---

[1]*The Vita Wulfstani of William of Malmesbury*, ed. R. R. Darlington (1928), p. 20.
[2]For the career of Wulfstan's successor, see V. H. Galbraith, "Notes on the career of
Samson, bishop of Worcester (1096–1112)," *English Historical Review*, 82 (1967), pp.
86–101, reprinted in his *Kings and Chroniclers, essays in English medieval history* (1982),
pp. 86–101.
[3]*Vita Wulfstani*, p. 20.
[4]Frank Barlow, *The English Church 1066–1154* (1979), pp. 58, 318.

consequences for Englishmen of the Norman Conquest.[5] He would have agreed with this depiction of Wulfstan. Yet this presentation of the bishop's career as an extended *exemplum* is all-pervasive, and was most likely the concept of the original English biographer, Coleman, who directly experienced the contrast between Wulfstan and Samson.

This introductory section to Wulfstan's episcopal career in his *Life* continues in the same vein, in the manner of a classical eulogy,[6] on which it was perhaps modelled. The passage may represent a homily preached at the time of his funeral, but in any event it would readily lend itself to adaptation as a *lection*, the prescribed lesson to be read on a saint's feast day, in the event of his cult gaining official recognition. We are told that:

> When he was required to act as a judge, he was ready to make a judgement. He did not favour a rich man for his money, nor did he reject a poor man for his poverty. He never yielded to flattery, nor was he sympathetic towards flatterers. He never deviated from justice for fear of great men, nor rendered any honour unless they had deserved it. When he was praised for doing a good deed, he gave thanks to the Grace of God instead of becoming proud. When he was reviled, he forgave those who reviled him, secure in his good conscience. But that did not often happen because, since he lovingly cherished every man as his offspring, they in return all loved him as a kinsman. With his merry heart and a cheerful countenance he already tasted in hope the celestial joy from the fountain of heavenly gladness, which he now drinks and imbibes unceasingly. His soul was always intent upon inward things, but men did not find him negligent or lazy about outward matters.[7]

Wulfstan could readily be depicted as the perfect bishop after his death, but throughout his episcopate he provoked mixed reactions at Worcester. Tensions chiefly arose from the conflicting assumptions of bishop and chapter about their respective jurisdictions. A series of absentee bishops, preoccupied with affairs of state, had left the monks, headed by their provost, free to manage their own property. During Ealdred's absences, Wulfstan himself had been just such an active provost, but a new situation arose after his consecration. His determination to live as a Benedictine monk, at once bishop and abbot, represented on his part a return to ancient ideals, but for the monks it was a reversion

---

[5]William of Malmesbury, *De Gestis Regum Anglorum*, ed. W. Stubbs, 2 vols (1887, 1889), I, 278.

[6]On the transmission of the classical eulogy to medieval historical writing, see Beryl Smalley, *Historians in the Middle Ages* (1974), p. 21.

[7]*Vita Wulfstani*, pp. 20–1.

so drastic as to be revolutionary. Since the *Life* of Wulfstan was designed to depict him as a saint, it is naturally reticent about this conflict, although it contains evidence of his frequent intervention in the daily routine of the cathedral, and his constant assertion of a strong discipline. His determination to exercise abbatial rule is reflected in his appointment of his brother Alfstan as prior. Wulfstan could thereby hope to contain the monastic reaction, even though his episcopal duties prevented him from exercising a continuous presence in the cathedral priory.[8] Alfstan's appointment dated from soon after that of Wulfstan to the bishopric. The evidence for this lies in an English writ, or sealed mandate, issued by King Edward. In this, he notified Bishop Wulfstan, Earl Alfgar of Mercia, Richard "my housecarl," and all his (Edward's) thegns in Worcestershire, of his grant to the monk Alfstan of certain jurisdictional and financial rights – sake and soke, toll and team, over his land and his men, both within town and without.[9] Alfstan's exercise of jurisdiction was guaranteed by his possession of this document, which he could produce before the most influential men of the region. His brother, the new bishop, was addressed as a matter of course. So was the principal layman, Earl Alfgar who, it will be recalled, apparently died before the end of 1062.[10] Richard, whom the king (or rather the clerk who drew up the writ) called his housecarl, one of his trusted troubleshooters,[11] is better known to historians as Richard Fitz Scrob, one of the French-speaking newcomers who were established by King Edward in the west Midlands.[12] In obtaining the document the bishop inadvertently added a vital link to the evidence which the monks were to produce against him when the conflict over their respective jurisdictions came to a head some thirty years later.[13] The writ was most likely obtained by Wulfstan while he was still at court following his election to the bishopric, when he also

---

[8]Frank Barlow, *The English Church 1000–1066* (1979), pp. 92, 241.

[9]*Anglo-Saxon Writs*, ed. F. E. Harmer (1952), no. 116. For the rights granted to Alfstan, see H. R. Loyn, *The Governance of Anglo-Saxon England 500–1087* (1984), p. 162.

[10]The Life of King Edward who rests at Westminster, attributed to a monk of St Bertin, ed. and transl. Frank Barlow (1962), p. 51, note; Frank Barlow, *Edward the Confessor* (1970), p. 210 and note 3.

[11]J. Campbell, "Some Agents and Agencies of the late Anglo-Saxon State," in *Domesday Studies* (1986) ed. J. C. Holt (1987), pp. 203–4.

[12]*The Cartulary of Worcester Cathedral Priory (Register I)*, ed. R. R. Darlington (1968), p. xxxiii; I. J. Sanders, *English Baronies: a study of their origin and descent 1086–1327* (1960), p. 75.

[13]Barlow, *The English Church 1000–1066*, p. 241; Eric John, *Orbis Britanniae and other Studies* (1966), pp. 241–2, note 1.

obtained a writ notifying the great men of the region of his accession to the see.[14]

It was probably also at this time that he obtained a second royal writ on his own behalf, also addressed to Earl Alfgar, Richard (Fitz Scrob) and the thegns of Worcestershire, notifying them that the Bishop was entitled to a third of the *seamtoll* (toll levied on each horse-load of goods) and the *ceaptoll* (toll levied on market trading) for the "minster of St. Mary's," that is, the cathedral church.[15] This royal grant of a substantial share in the profits derived from Worcester's commercial activities would compensate to some extent for the financial loss caused by Archbishop Ealdred's retention of some of the episcopal estates. Royal grants were seldom issued in a spirit of spontaneous goodwill. Recompense was often expected, although this might not be mentioned in the document issued in the king's name. Evidence of such payments is more often found in the records of the beneficiary. We know from a Worcester source that after the Norman Conquest when Bishop Wulfstan petitioned for help in enforcing the reversion of one of the cathedral's leasehold estates, it was necessary to give King William I a most valuable gold chalice.[16]

Property rights in the diocese of Worcester were manipulated by King Edward in order to increase the endowment of his designated mausoleum, Westminster Abbey. In 972 King Edgar had confirmed to Pershore abbey extensive lands in Worcestershire, with other estates in Gloucestershire and Warwickshire, and added a grant of franchisal and other privileges.[17] During the anti-monastic reaction which followed Edgar's death, Pershore was among those monasteries whose lands were encroached upon by Ealdorman Alfhere and his associates.[18] In the eleventh century, the fortunes of the house recovered, but the abbey faced new and permanent losses when King Edward reassigned some of its most valuable properties to Westminster. The substantial manors of Pershore (Worcs), and Deerhurst (Gloucs), and their dependent vills were alienated, together with franchisal rights in the double hundred of

---

[14]*Anglo-Saxon Writs*, no. 115. See also Loyn, *Governance of Anglo-Saxon England*, pp. 114–15.

[15]*Anglo-Saxon Writs*, no. 117, and pp. 409–10 for a discussion of these tolls.

[16]*Hemingi Chartularium ecclesiae Wigorniensis*, ed. T. Hearne, 2 vols (1723), I, pp. 268–9.

[17]This writ was addressed to "all my headmen, thegns, sheriffs and loyal friends." For reference see *Anglo-Saxon Charters: an annotated list and bibliography, compiled P. H. Sawyer (1968), no. 786.*

[18]Ann Williams, "*Princeps Merciorum gentis*: the family, career and connections of Aelfhere, ealdorman of Mercia, 956–83," *Anglo-Saxon England*, 10 (1982), pp. 143–72, esp. pp. 167–8.

Pershore.[19] Several documents in King Edward's name relate to this appropriation, but since these are of varying degrees of authenticity, the exact date of the transfer is uncertain.[20] Final arrangements were concluded towards the end of his reign, and perhaps during the last few days of his life, when a writ was addressed to Archbishop Ealdred, Bishop Wulfstan and Bishop Wulfwig (of Dorchester), and the officials in Worcestershire, Gloucestershire and Oxfordshire, notifying them of the transfer of certain estates.[21]

As this writ indicates, Wulfstan was now required to play a part in secular administration. His monastic training in the values of the *Regularis Concordia* would have imbued him with its ideal of loyal support for the monarchy.[22] Unhesitating obedience to the anointed king was also proclaimed in the more recent homiletic tradition of the earlier eleventh century.[23] Diocesan bishops were more specifically obliged to render service to the crown by acting jointly with the leading lay officials of the diocese as resident executives of the king's orders. One regular task was to preside as judges in the shire court.[24] While Wulfstan's *Life* focuses on his spiritual qualities, it does occasionally depict him fulfilling the secular obligations of his episcopal office. A story from this period of his career suggests that his fulfilment of these took second place to his observance of his spiritual obligations. No matter how urgent the business upon which Wulfstan was travelling, he insisted upon entering every church or chapel on his route, invariably weeping while praying. One day when he had been summoned to the shire court, his journey took him through Evesham. His companions, probably businesslike clerks, tried to dissuade him from going into the abbey church, but he would not listen. On entering, he prostrated himself before the shrine of Saint Egwuin, an early bishop of Worcester, and prayed earnestly both

[19]Barbara Harvey, *Westminster Abbey and its Estates in the Middle Ages* (1977), pp. 27, 344–5, 360–4; *Anglo-Saxon Charters*, compiled Sawyer, no. 1143. Two-thirds of the lands of Pershore abbey were allocated by King Edward to Westminster Abbey, and were contained in the double hundred of Pershore. The lands remaining to Pershore abbey were contained in the single hundred of Pershore. Neither of these hundreds is named in the Domesday Survey: *Domesday Book 16: Worcestershire*, ed. Frank and Caroline Thorn (1982), Appendix I.

[20]*Anglo-Saxon Charters*, compiled Sawyer, nos 1040, 1043, 1143–45.

[21]*Anglo-Saxon Writs*, no. 102; *Anglo-Saxon Charters*, compiled Sawyer, no. 1146.

[22]*Regularis Concordia*, ed. T. Symons (1953), pp. 5, 7, 12–14, 16, 21–3.

[23]H. R. Loyn, "The King and the Structure of Society in late Anglo-Saxon England," *History*, 42 (1957), pp. 87–100, esp. pp. 92–3, 100; H. R. Loyn, "Anglo-Saxon England: Reflections and Insights," *History*, 64 (1979), pp. 171–81, esp. p. 178.

[24]Loyn, "Anglo-Saxon England: Reflections and Insights," p. 179; Loyn, *Governance of Anglo-Saxon England*, p. 157.

for himself and for the people of his diocese.[25] The monks of Evesham flocked to greet their distinguished visitor. Wulfstan greeted them all with the kiss of peace, and addressed them with a suitable homily.[26] The subject is not recorded, but he perhaps took the opportunity to remind them that it was their bishop, and not the assertive Abbot Ethelwig, who was truly the successor of Saint Egwuin.

One of the monks of Evesham had been ill with a fever for a long time, and was now believed to be dying. He heard that Wulfstan was in the abbey, and sent a messenger to tell the bishop of his distress, and of how he deserved a visit from him before he died. Wulfstan was not the kind of person to make an excuse on the grounds of pressing business elsewhere. When his companions argued that this sick-visit would delay their journey, and the day was well advanced, he answered, "I am commanded by my Creator to visit the sick. If you hinder me, and this man dies, I shall be guilty of evading the order." He went in to visit the sick monk, and eased his distress with the saving promises tht he would survive long enough to be cleansed by the last rites.[27] Since the monk was desperately ill, it seems odd that no resident confessor was at hand. Perhaps the abbot normally acted as confessor, since this community was still small enough for him to do so,[28] as prescribed in the Rule of Saint Benedict and apparently assumed in the *Regularis Concordia*.[29] Abbot Ethelwig had perhaps already set out to attend the shire court towards which Wulfstan was travelling. The sick monk was desperate to receive absolution before he died, and implored Wulfstan in his mercy to obtain for him a prolongation of life. The bishop was greatly moved by the man's spiritual agony. He lifted his heart to God, and raised his hands in prayer, saying, "Almighty and most merciful God, through whose gift confession washes away sins, in Whose sight he who accuses himself is absolved, I humbly beg You to prolong the life of this sick man until You may receive his soul cleansed and better prepared by his penitence."[30]

---

[25]*Vita Wulfstani*, p. 21. On Saint Egwuin, see William of Malmesbury, *De Gestis Pontificum Anglorum*, ed. N. E. S. A. Hamilton (1879), pp. 296–7; *Chronicon Abbatiae de Evesham ad annum 1418*, ed. W. D. Macray (1863), pp. 8–14.

[26]*Vita Wulfstani*, p. 21.

[27]Ibid., p. 21.

[28]When Ethelwig became abbot, there were only twelve monks at Evesham. Their numbers had trebled by 1077, but perhaps this was largely due to the tenurial revolution after 1066: *Chronicon Abbatiae de Evesham*, pp. 95–6.

[29]*The Rule of Saint Benedict*, ed. and transl. J. McCann (1951), ch. 7, lection on the fifth degree of humility; *Regularis Concordia*, p. xxxix; p. 18, note 6.

[30]*Vita Wulfstani*, pp. 21–2

Wulfstan followed his intercession by blessing the sick man. His prayer met with an immediate and spectacular answer. At the very moment the bishop went out, the sick monk was healed. Health and strength returned and his symptoms vanished. He immediately abandoned the bed on which he had lain for so long, struggled to his feet and called for his clothes and shoes. The onlookers thought his mind was wandering; that his brain and powers of reasoning were affected, and that he was delirious. But the monk, Ethelric, continued to bless God and Bishop Wulfstan for his restoration to health and urged others also to give thanks.[31] The hagiographer was doubtless conscious of the scriptural parallel to this episode; Our Lord's healing of the paralytic after first forgiving his sins (Matthew 9: 1–9; Mark 2: 1–12; Luke 5: 17–25) offers an analogy which would at once occur to those who read or heard Wulfstan's *Life*. The spiritual and psychological release from his burden of guilt would in themselves boost Ethelric's morale and aid the healing process.[32] Renewed medical emphasis in recent years on treating the whole personality, rather than prescribing for physical symptoms alone, enlarges our understanding of this incident. Intercession by the caring bishop raised Ethelric's spirits sufficiently to effect a remission, and he was still living in 1077.[33]

Elevation to the episcopate, with its concomitant new duties, in no way lessened Wulfstan's zeal for his pastoral responsibilities. On the very day after he was ordained bishop, he consecrated a church to the Venerable Bede, "the foremost writer among the English."[34] The literary tribute to the author of *The Ecclesiastical History of the English People* probably reflects interest in his work at Worcester, but it may stem from the translator of Wulfstan's *Life*, William of Malmesbury.[35] At the dedication ceremony, Wulfstan preached most fluently, "as though inspired by the Holy Spirit with the same eloquence that had once inspired Bede." Wulfstan was renowned for his preaching, and great crowds gathered on

[31]Ibid., p. 22.

[32]The patient's absolution from sin was believed to be a prerequisite of complete healing: J. Sumption, *Pilgrimage: an image of medieval religion* (1974), pp. 78, 80, 144.

[33]Ethelric was listed among Evesham monks subscribing to a confraternity bond in 1077 (*Historia et Cartularium Monasterii Sancti Petri Gloucestriae*, ed. W. H. Hart, 3 vols (1863, 1865, 1867), III, p. xix). He was also included in a longer list of Evesham monks recorded c.1104 in the *Durham Liber Vitae*, ed. A. H. Thompson (1923, in facsimile), f. 21 verso, but had perhaps died before that date.

[34]*Vita Wulfstani*, pp. 19–20. Since Wulfstan was evidently consecrated in York, where Ealdred then left him, St Bede's church was either in the city or well within a day's travel.

[35]R. H. C. Davis, "Bede after Bede," *Studies in Medieval History presented to R. Allen Brown*, ed. C. Harper-Bill, C. J. Holdsworth and Janet L. Nelson (1989), pp. 103–16, esp. pp. 106–7, 114–16.

subsequent occasions when he dedicated churches.[36] The laity would normally have little opportunity to hear anything more stirring than a homily by their parish priest, so that Wulfstan's sermons on major occasions would be a great rarity. The *Life* naturally emphasizes their spiritual appeal, and this should not be undervalued – even today a famous evangelist can attract huge crowds. Yet in an age when there was little alternative public entertainment, people might be prepared to walk miles to see and hear the celebrated bishop who was such a rousing speaker. We are told that Wulfstan took every opportunity of preaching:

> He continually spoke of Christ, and continually set Christ before his congregation. He would, so to speak, drag Christ to his side against His will. So obstinately did Wulfstan persevere in vigils and fasts; so violently did he assault Heaven with his prayers, that of him, and men like him, Our Lord said: "The Kingdom of Heaven suffers violence, and the violent take it by force". (Matthew 11:12)[37]

In his enthusiasm to describe the power of Wulfstan's preaching, the writer of his *Life* was prepared to twist the meaning of this scriptural quotation. The urgent note of Wulfstan's preaching derived from his conviction that the nation was in a state of moral decline, which in turn would have the most dire consequences.[38] This theme is earlier found in the preaching of his namesake, Archbishop Wulfstan, at the time of the Danish invasions, and the younger Wulfstan drew on the sermons of the elder.[39] Events proved them both right.

Wulfstan also zealously performed other pastoral duties. He was particularly diligent in making visitations in his diocese.[40] After the prolonged absences of his predecessors these tours of inspection would come as something of a novelty. Slackly run religious houses or negligent parish priests might not welcome them, but Wulfstan's travels were necessary if he was to enforce his ideal of moral reform. On these tours, he exhorted the laity to persevere in faith and good works, and administered the sacrament to any unbaptized infants.[41]

Yet public duties limited the time which Wulfstan could now give to pastoral work. Besides presiding regularly at the shire court, he would be expected to attend the formal gatherings of the itinerant royal court

[36]*Vita Wulfstani*, p. 20.

[37]Ibid., p. 20.

[38]Ibid., p. 23.

[39]Dorothy Bethurum, *The Homilies of Wulfstan* (1957), pp. 4–5, 8, 15, 99. The Sermon of the Wolf to the English, *English Historical Documents*, I, *c.500–1042*, ed. Dorothy Whitelock, second edn (1979), no. 240, pp. 928–34.

[40]*Vita Wulfstani*, p. 21.

[41]Ibid., p. 21. The relevant phrase may imply confirmation, rather than baptism.

which convened at the major religious festivals of the year. During King Edward's reign, the three great feasts of Easter, Pentecost and Christmas were increasingly celebrated at one particular group of places, although the evidence for these locations remains fragmentary, even for the 1060s. In 1062, the Easter court at which Wulfstan's appointment was discussed perhaps met at Gloucester. The following Christmas court certainly convened there. No relevant evidence survives for the next eighteen months, but the Christmas court of 1064 perhaps met at Winchester, the city which was in effect the national capital. In 1065, the court met at Windsor for Pentecost, while the drama of King Edward's last days was enacted at the Christmas court held at Westminster. His successor's only Easter court met there in 1066, but the whereabouts of his Pentecost court, if he held one, is unknown.[42] Such festive courts comprised large gatherings of lay nobles and office-holders, together with the archbishops and bishops, and the more prominent abbots and abbesses. The major participants in certain courts are known from their attestations to charters issued in the king's name.[43] Important business of various kinds was transacted, and there are indications that King Edward perhaps wore his crown in solemn ceremony, as his Norman successors did.[44] Wulfstan's presence at court would require him to travel considerable distances. Given the bad state of the roads during the winter months, riding to court at Christmas, or even at Easter, would be an unpleasant experience. In such unfavourable conditions, journeys to Winchester, Windsor or Westminster perhaps took Wulfstan and his entourage a week or more. Gloucester was a relatively easy destination, since a journey by boat down the Severn was the obvious means of travel.

Life at court probably came as a major culture shock to Wulfstan. He had been raised and passed his earlier career in a monastic environment, surrounded by Englishmen. These English monastic values had scarcely ever been challenged. King Edward, in contrast, had spent his youth and early manhood in Normandy and other French-speaking territories.[45] Following his accession to the throne, he introduced various French-speaking clerics and laymen into England. The laymen were mainly

---

[42]M. Biddle, "Seasonal Festivals and Residence: Winchester, Westminster and Gloucester in the tenth to twelfth centuries," *Anglo-Norman Studies VIII*, ed. R. Allen Brown (1986), pp. 56, 69, 71–2. It is possible that the Pentecost court was not summoned in 1066, since King Harold and his forces were on the alert, awaiting the anticipated Norman invasion: cf. *Florentii Wigorniensis monachi Chronicon ex Chronicis*, ed. B. Thorpe, 2 vols (1848–9), I, p. 225.

[43]Loyn, *Governance of Anglo-Saxon England*, pp. 96–8, 112. Even where charters survive only in an interpolated form, their witness-lists may be genuine; Barlow, *Edward the Confessor*, pp. 244–5.

[44]Biddle, "Seasonal Festivals and Residence," pp. 58–9.

[45]Barlow, *Edward the Confessor*, pp. 36–49.

established in defensive lordships in Herefordshire, ostensibly to hold the frontier against the Welsh, but perhaps also to counterbalance the power of Earl Harold in that region.[46] Wulfstan would formerly have had little occasion to meet these men, although Harold no doubt briefed him on their activities during his visits to Worcester. Following Wulfstan's consecration and his ensuing attendance at the festive courts, he would come into contact with both laymen and clerics from the Continent, chiefly Normans and Lotharingians whom King Edward had raised to high office.[47] Their numbers were limited, and the court would remain predominantly English-speaking, but probably enough French would be heard to enable even the staunchest Englishman to acquire a few phrases, particularly in view of the thorough grounding which he would have in Latin. The more ambitious perhaps acquired a working knowledge of French. When Earl Harold campaigned in Brittany with Duke William of Normandy,[48] he was presumably able to understand, and to convey, shouted commands. Even though the English language remained the chief medium of communication at the court of King Edward, the presence of his influential Continental clerics would challenge the values of the environment in which Wulfstan had been raised. His consecration restored the total number of bishops to fourteen, of whom seven were monks, but they generally held the less important sees. The Continentals would find it strange that as many as half their fellow bishops were in monastic orders, but even in England there was now a growing trend to appoint bishops from among the secular clerks on the staff of the royal chapel.[49] The voices of these cosmopolitan clerks perhaps predominated in the king's counsels.

As in any age, the affluent and leisured were apt to be morally self-indulgent. Wulstan was concerned about the permissive, even debauched, lifestyle which seemed to him prevalent throughout most of England. He particularly deplored the fashion for men to wear long hair. Given the opportunity, he would trim back one lock with the little knife which he used to clean his nails or to scrape ink-blots from books. He would then order the culprit to have the rest of his hair cut short to

---

[46]Ibid., pp. 50, 94; M. W. Campbell, "A Pre-Conquest Norman Occupation of England?" *Speculum*, 46 (1971), pp. 21–31; C. Lewis, "The Norman Settlement of Herefordshire under William I," in *Anglo-Norman Studies VII* (1985), pp. 195–213, esp. pp. 202–3; Ann Williams, "Land and Power in the eleventh century: the estates of Harold Godwineson," in *Proceedings of the Battle Conference III. 1980*, ed. R. Allen Brown (1981), pp. 171–87, esp. pp. 174–5.

[47]Barlow, *The English Church 1000–1066*, pp. 77, 81–3.

[48]William of Poitiers, *Histoire de Guillaume le Conquerant*, ed. and transl. Raymonde Foreville (1952), pp. 104–14. Harold would have acquired some spoken French in the course of his travels among the "Franks" in "Gaul:" *Life of King Edward*, p. 33.

[49]Barlow, *The English Church 1000–1066*, pp. 65–6, 77.

match. If anyone began to object, he would accuse him of softness, and warn him of the evil consequences of such degeneracy. He argued that men who were ashamed to be what they were born, and instead imitated the flowing hair of women, would prove no more able than women to defend their homeland against aggressors from overseas.[50] Wulfstan's point was soon proved. The Bayeux Tapestry, a work of art commissioned to commemorate the Norman Conquest of England, sharply contrasts the closely cropped heads of the Normans with the luxuriant collar-length locks of the English.[51]

Wulfstan's urgent call for moral reform should be seen against a background of imminent political destabilization. At the time of his consecration, in 1062, the nation appeared superficially peaceful, but there were ominous undertones. Earl Harold, the eldest surviving son of Earl Godwin, had led the military defence of the kingdom since the 1050s, with some assistance from his brother next in age, Tostig, notably in 1063.[52] The propagandist *Life of King Edward*, commissioned by their sister Queen Edith, likened them to the classical heroes Atlas and Hermes, upholding the weight of the sky.[53] The analogy is appropriate, for when one "pillar" was removed, the other could not uphold the stability of the realm against mounting pressures within and without. The split between the brothers occurred when the Northumbrians rebelled against Tostig's rule. He had been appointed earl in 1055,[54] the first West Saxon to hold this position, since his predecessors belonged either to the native ruling house of Bamburgh or, more often, to the leading Anglo-Danish families of Yorkshire. The appointment of a complete outsider had a revolutionary impact, but Tostig established his rule while divisions persisted among the native leaders. By way of assimilating into the regional culture, he prudently became a benefactor of Durham cathedral, focus of the powerful cult of St Cuthbert. He secured his position by recruiting well over two hundred housecarls, more of a private army than a bodyguard. Housecarls were an effective fighting force, but expensive to maintain. Complaints arose of Tostig's oppressive government, and focused particularly upon his harsh taxation, which was probably designed to finance his housecarls. The

---

[50]*Vita Wulfstani*, p. 23.

[51]D. J. Bernstein, *The Mystery of the Bayeux Tapestry* (1986). Scenes II–IV, pp. 231–3, depict the fashionable hairstyles of Harold and his entourage, clearly contrasted with the current Norman fashion in scenes VIII–XIV, pp. 234–7.

[52]*The Anglo-Saxon Chronicle*, ed. Dorothy Whitelock, with D. C. Douglas and Susie I. Tucker (1961), *s.a.* 1055 (C); 1056 (C); 1063 (D, E); 1065 (C, D); *Florentii Wigorniensis monachi Chronicon*, I, pp. 221–3.

[53]*Life of King Edward*, p. 38 and note 1.

[54]*Anglo-Saxon Chronicle*, *s.a.* 1055 (D, E).

unpopular rule of the alien earl would inevitably foster support for a more acceptable ruler from among the local nobility.[55]

Gamel, son of Orm, and Ulf, son of Dolfin, were two such potential leaders. They were given safe conduct to visit Tostig in York in 1063, but were assassinated in the earl's own chamber.[56] They had been close associates of an eldery and eminent Northumbrian noble, Gospatric;[57] when he attended King Edward's Christmas court in 1064, he too was murdered. On grounds of lineage, Gospatric had the best claim to the earldom of Northumbria,[58] and it was believed at Worcester that Queen Edith arranged his death in the interests of her brother.[59] This culling of native leaders gave Tostig a free hand for the moment, but Gospatric's death, combined with the continued heavy taxation of a region which had traditionally rendered low dues, prompted the men of Northumbria and Yorkshire to join together against their earl. The earlier part of 1065 passed quietly, but in October, once the harvest was safely in, and Tostig was absent from the North, there was a violent popular rising. Tostig's housecarls were massacred, and the northerners marched to put their grievances to King Edward.[60] A respectable leader was needed to lend weight to their demands, and so they elected Morcar, the younger brother of Earl Edwin of Mercia. Edwin and his forces joined the northerners and King Edward was forced to accept Morcar as earl of Northumbria. Earl Harold, brother of the rejected Tostig, was in charge of the negotiations. He swore to recognize the *coup*, and renewed the "Law of Cnut," that is, the preferentially low rate of taxation due from Northumbria. Tostig went into exile, and the cumulative impact of the crisis caused a breakdown in the king's health.[61]

By Christmas 1065, King Edward was gravely ill, but plans went ahead for the consecration of his rebuilt abbey of Westminster. Dignitaries of

---

[55]W. E. Kapelle, *The Norman Conquest of the North: the region and its transformation 1000–1135* (1979), pp. 86–9, 94.

[56]*Florentii Wigorniensis monachi Chronicon*, I, p. 223.

[57]Kapelle, *The Norman Conquest of the North*, p. 95. This Gospatric is not to be confused with the young man who accompanied Tostig to Rome in 1061. The elder Gospatric was the youngest son of Earl Uhtred (d.1016), while his younger namesake was a son, or just possibly a grandson, of Earl Uhtred's daughter Aldgith: *Life of King Edward*, p. 36, note 1.

[58]Kapelle, *The Norman Conquest of the North*, p. 95.

[59]*Florentii Wigorniensis monachi Chronicon*, I, p. 223.

[60]Ibid., I, p. 223. *Anglo-Saxon Chronicle, s.a.* 1065 (C, D, E); Kapelle, *The Norman Conquest of the North*, pp. 94–8; *Life of King Edward*, p. 50, gives events from Tostig's viewpoint.

[61]*Anglo-Saxon Chronicle, s.a.* 1065 (C, D, E); *Florentii Wigorniensis monachi Chronicon*, I, p. 223; *Life of King Edward*, pp. 50–5; Kapelle, *The Norman Conquest of the North*, pp. 99–101.

church and state, including Bishop Wulfstan, were summoned to court for the seasonal and dedicatory festivities.[62] They found themselves witnessing a major political drama. The ailing king collapsed after attending the festivities on Christmas Day, and the solemn consecration of Westminster on 28 December went ahead in his absence.[63] The dying Edward had no son to succeed him. Earl Harold, as the leading lay magnate, was well placed to press his claims, although the court was not packed in his favour.[64] The country faced external threats from William, duke of Normandy, and Harold Hardrada, king of Norway, both of whom had designs on the throne. This was no time for the English magnates to recognize the claims of either of Edward's two young kinsmen, Edgar Etheling or Harold, son of the late Ralph, earl of Hereford. Both were great-grandsons of King Ethelred, Edward's father, but they were still young boys, unfitted to give military leadership in time of crisis.[65] King Edward's brother-in-law, Earl Harold, was a proven military commander experienced alike in politics and diplomacy.[66] The dying king accordingly commended the realm to him. In English custom, this was tantamount to designating Harold as successor to the throne, whatever Norman propagandists might later argue.[67] Edward's death probably occurred on the night of 4/5 January, 1066. The rebuilt Westminster had been intended as his mausoleum, and he was duly buried there on 6 January. The coronation of King Harold II followed on the same day. A nation under threat needed to have an acknowledged king as quickly as possible. It was convenient to conduct the ceremony while the magnates of church and state were still assembled, so that they could be seen to give public assent to Harold's rule.[68]

Bishop Wulfstan was now spiritual adviser to the king of England. Given a different turn of events in October 1066, he might have ended his days as Archbishop of Canterbury. It was probably Wulfstan's exceptional holiness of life which caused Harold to value his spiritual direction above that of other prelates. Moreover, the archbishops, and some of their episcopal colleagues, were very much political figures, in contrast to

[62]Barlow, *Edward the Confessor*, pp. 244–6.

[63]*Florentii Wigorniensis monachi Chronicon*, I, p. 224; *Anglo-Saxon Chronicle*, s.a. 1065 (C, D); Barlow, *Edward the Confessor*, pp. 246–7.

[64]Barlow, *Edward the Confessor*, p. 246.

[65]On the claimants to the throne, see ibid., pp. 219–20.

[66]*Life of King Edward*, pp. 30–3.

[67]Ibid., pp. 79–80. For the implications of the king's act, see Barlow, *Edward the Confessor*, pp. 249–53; Ann Williams, "Some Notes and Considerations on Problems connected with the English Royal Succession, 860–1066," *Proceedings of the Battle Conference on Anglo-Norman Studies I. 1978*, ed. R. Allen Brown (1979), pp. 144–67, esp. pp. 165–7.

[68]*Life of King Edward*, pp. 80–1; Barlow, *Edward the Confessor*, pp. 253–5.

Wulfstan, whose detachment from secular power struggles would ensure that his advice was impartial. No evidence survives to indicate that he guided Harold's actions during the succession crisis. Explicit mention of this would be considered out of place in Wulfstan's *Life*, designed as it was to focus on the bishop's qualities as a religious leader.

The considerations which led to the recognition of Harold as king had a wide appeal. Wulfstan's acknowledgement of a subsequent ruler who imposed law and order on a war-torn country[69] suggests that in January 1066 his voice was willingly lent to Harold's cause. It had been obvious from their early acquaintance that Harold aspired to the throne.[70] The plain-spoken Wulfstan would have dissociated himself from Harold if he had considered the earl's ambitions to be inordinate. Wulfstan's *Life* was composed some decades after the Norman Conquest, when the Norman line of kings was firmly established and a Norman bishop presided at Worcester. The work briefly mentions the tensions generated throughout England by the rival claims of Earl Harold and Duke William, adding only that Harold gained the crown and almost the whole realm "either by goodwill or by force."[71] The same might be said of the means by which many of King Harold's predecessors and successors came to the throne. Little sustained criticism would circulate, providing that the new ruler maintained himself in power; safeguarded the interests of the magnates of church and state, who were in effect the makers of public opinion, and maintained the peace of the realm.

Wulfstan's objections were voiced not against the king, but his subjects. His visits to the royal court had enlarged his awareness of decadence in high places. In plain tones, he told King Harold that it was his duty to impose a moral reform upon his wicked people, if England, and indeed the king himself, were to avoid a major disaster.[72] The same theme was echoed by a writer in the service of Edward's widow, the dowager Queen Edith,[73] and ultimately derives from Old Testament stories of how moral degeneracy, whether among Jews or Gentiles, earned retribution in the form of political catastrophe. It is reinforced in Wulfstan's *Life* by the writer's hindsight, although the views ascribed to the bishop are certainly of a piece with his known character. King Harold was by now well-accustomed to the views of his spiritual mentor. Opposites as they were in many respects, they yet shared common traits, resulting from the military discipline they might be said to have in

[69] *Florentii Wigorniensis monachi Chronicon*, I, p. 228.

[70] *Vita Wulfstani*, p. 13.

[71] Ibid., p. 22.

[72] Ibid., p. 23.

[73] *Life of King Edward*, pp. 5, 74–6. Since the work in its present form was completed after the Norman Conquest, an element of hindsight may be incorporated into the dying Edward's vision of disaster: Barlow, *Edward the Confessor*, pp. 247–51.

common, the king as the leading warrior of his nation, and the monk-bishop as a Soldier of Christ.[74] Regular military campaigning had accustomed Harold to endure physical hardship and to do without sleep and food.[75] If put to the test he might perhaps have matched the rigours of Wulfstan's Lenten observance. The king was intelligent, and an astute observer of human nature. He also had intellectual interests, and possessed a collection of books. Harold exercised complete verbal and mental self-control, listening to opposing views without revealing his own, let alone retaliating.[76] Far from taking offence at Wulfstan's rebuke, he determined to make use of his prophetic stature as a holy man in the tradition of the Northumbrian saints.

It was said of Harold that he could maintain total silence on his plans, too much so for his own good, at times, but on other occasions he would take into his confidence those on whose loyalty he believed he could rely.[77] Wulfstan was one of the favoured few. In Harold's view, the bishop was the very person to calm the restive northerners. Having disposed of their tyrannical earl, Tostig Godwinson, they were now in no mood to recognize his elder brother as their new king. Their recent success encouraged them to further resistance. They argued, for public consumption, that is was unfitting for the bold north to yield to the soft south.[78] Their real concern was perhaps rather that Harold, now that he was king, might withdraw his earlier concessions on taxation. From Harold's point of view, a campaign of repression, fought in midwinter over difficult terrain, with extended lines of communications, presented major problems even if he could ensure general support from the south and midlands. At best, successful military action woud provide only a temporary solution to the separatist tendencies of this region, and create as many problems as it solved. Given his other concerns, and in particular the anticipated Norman attack, Harold could not maintain substantial forces in the north on an indefinite basis. Moreover, repression in itself would give rise to further bitterness, perhaps prompting the northerners to make secret contact with Harold Hardrada of Norway.

Considerations such as these led Harold to discount military action and embark instead upon a hearts-and-minds campaign. Wulfstan was enlisted to accompany him upon this mission. We are told that "the fame

---

[74]On the analogies between the military and monastic disciplines, see Barbara H. Rosenwein, "Feudal War and Monastic Peace: Cluniac Liturgy as Ritual Aggression," *Viator*, 2 (1971), pp. 129–57.

[75]*Life of King Edward*, p. 31.

[76]Ibid., pp. 31, 33. On Harold's library, see C. H. Haskins, "King Harold's Books," *English Historical Review*, 37 (1922), pp. 398–400.

[77]*Life of King Edward*, p. 31.

[78]*Vita Wulfstani*, p. 22.

of his holiness had reached the most remote people, and it was believed that there was no arrogance that he could not soften."[79] King Harold was a realist, and the times were dangerous. Since he called on Wulfstan's help in this way, clearly he believed in the bishop's reputation as a holy man with great powers of persuasion, likely to make an impact upon the Northumbrians. Wulfstan had been compelled to spend some time in York just after his consecration[80] and local magnates were perhaps introduced to him at that time. It would be ironical if Wulfstan, while effectively detailed at Ealdred's pleasure, and obliged to act under his direction, then made contacts which were to render him of more use politically than the archbishop. Presumably Ealdred returned to his see after the eventful Christmas court of 1065, and no doubt he knew everyone of consequence in the north, but it was not he to whom King Harold turned in this new emergency. If the archbishop did play a key role, then we should expect to learn of it in the accounts of his own career, but these are silent.[81]

While the unrest might be quelled by identifying the ringleaders to whom an appeal should be made, prior acquaintance mattered less than an instinctive knowledge of how to approach them. Wulfstan, imbued as he was with traditional values, conveyed something of the aura of the old Northumbrian saints. These men, and perhaps even more their prede-cessors in the Celtic church, were believed to deploy their perceived spiritual powers to achieve political victory for their lay patrons.[82] Wulfstan's charismatic presence was certainly thought to be instrumental in quelling an attack which threatened his own diocese in later years.[83] By inference his appearance in the north, early in 1066, had a similar impact. The cultural heritage of the northerners would condition them to respond to the admonitions of an acknowledged holy man, while Wulfstan's own grounding in the values and activities of the northern saints[84] would have led him gradually and perhaps subconsciously to model his own conduct on theirs. Wulfstan was a good, gentle and kindly man, but he did not mince words when dealing with wrongdoers. A cleric

[79]Ibid., p. 22–3.

[80]Ibid., p. 19.

[81]Several accounts of Ealdred's life are included in *The Historians of the Church of York and its Archbishops*, ed. J. Raine, 3 vols (1879,1886, 1894).

[82]Saint Columba's career, in particular, illustrates this. See A. P. Smyth, *Warlords and Holy Men: Scotland A.D. 80–1000* (1984), ch. 3, and esp. pp. 96–7.

[83]*Florentii Wigorniensis monachi Chronicon*, II, pp. 24–6. See also *Anglo-Saxon Chronicle*, *s.a.* 1088 (E).

[84]The cults of several Northumbrian saints were venerated at Worcester, and also at Evesham, during Wulfstan's lifetime. *English Kalendars before A.D. 1100*, ed. F. Wormald, I, Texts (1934), Kalendars 16–18, pp. 200–34.

of his generation, imbued with the concepts of the Tenth Century Reform, would regard rebellion against the anointed king as a major sin. Wulfstan warned the northerners that if they did not end their revolt, retribution and suffering would follow. His words had the desired impact. The northerners responded to his appeal by yielding allegiance to King Harold "on account of the reverence which they bore towards the bishop." Wulfstan's wisdom was believed to extend to a real gift of prophecy, manifested both on this journey and on later occasions.[85] Thanks to his intercession, the king was able to return south by Easter (16 April).[86]

Harold II was an experienced politician who had played a dominant role in public life since the early 1050s. His younger brothers and his brothers-in-law monopolized the earldoms, while his own tenurial position was predominant, due to his continued tenure of the lands of his former earldom of Wessex together with the *terrae regis*, the estates held directly by the monarch.[87] Harold had the goodwill of the astute Archbishop Ealdred, and he cultivated the support of churchmen as a whole, whether bishops, abbots, clerks or monks, by his affable conduct towards them, and by being seen to be a patron of churches and monasteries. He ordered the expulsion of all malefactors, and took vigorous measures for the defence of the realm, both by sea and by land.[88] Given a free hand, Harold seemed likely to prove a strong and able ruler but, as his defensive measures indicate, he knew that trouble would soon come from overseas.

On 24 April a comet appeared in the skies over England and almost everywhere else in the known world. This portent was visible for a week, shining with great splendour. Shortly afterwards, Tostig Godwinson reappeared..[89] Late in 1065 he had been exiled "on account of his misrule," but in reality as a sop to the northerners. He spent the winter of 1065–6 in Flanders, at the court of his father-in-law, negotiating with potential allies, and planning a comeback.[90] Tostig's raids on the English coast were repelled, and he headed north, taking refuge in Scotland

[85]*Vita Wulfstani*, p. 23.

[86]*Anglo-Saxon Chronicle*, s.a. 1066 (C, D).

[87]Robin Fleming, "Domesday Estates of the King and the Godwines: a study in late Saxon politics," *Speculum*, 58 (1983), pp. 987–1007, esp. p. 1007.

[88]*Florentii Wigorniensis monachi Chronicon*, I, pp. 224–5. See also H. R. Loyn, *Harold son of Godwin* (1971), esp. pp. 12–13.

[89]*Florentii Wigorniensis monachi Chronicon*, I, p. 225; *Anglo-Saxon Chronicle*, s.a. 1066 (C, D).

[90]*Florentii Wigorniensis monachi Chronicon*, I, pp. 223–4. *Anglo-Saxon Chronicle*, s.a. 1065 (C, D, E); Barlow, *Edward the Confessor*, pp. 242–3.

during the summer of 1066. Meanwhile in the south of England, King Harold kept his forces on the alert, anticipating an invasion by Duke William of Normandy, but eventually supplies ran out, and both fleet and army were dismissed. In September, Tostig's forces, together with those of the Norwegian king, Harold Hardrada, landed in Yorkshire, where they decimated the troops of the young earls Edwin and Morcar at the battle of Fulford. Five days later, on 25 September, a relieving army led by King Harold routed the invaders at the battle of Stamford Bridge, outside York. Both Tostig and Harold Hardrada were killed. Mopping-up operations were still in progress when news came that the Normans had landed at Pevensey in Sussex. The two recent battles had taken a heavy toll of the English forces, and the king now summoned all available men to repel the Norman invasion. He marched his own troops south at top speed, without waiting for his reinforcements to assemble. On 14 October, at the strategic site on which now stands Battle Abbey, in Sussex, his forces defended the London road against the Normans. Throughout the day, the English army on the ridge stoutly resisted repeated attacks, but by evening Harold lay dead, together with his brothers Gyrth and Leofwin, and many of the English nobles.[91]

Continued English resistance seemed feasible at first. The earls Edwin and Morcar had recruited more troops, which they brought to London, although they prudently sent their sister, Queen Edith,[92] to the relative safety of Chester. Together with Archbishop Ealdred and certain leading Londoners, the earls planned to proclaim the young Edgar Etheling king, and to continue the military struggle. Once these plans were put into action, however, the earls had second thoughts, and decamped with their forces. Duke William meanwhile devastated one county after another, as his army circled around London at a distance, killing and burning. The remaining English leaders saw that total surrender was the only step which would halt the carnage. Archbishop Ealdred, together with Bishop Wulfstan; the Lotharingian Walter, bishop of Hereford; Edgar Etheling; and the earls Edwin and Morcar (who could not afford to remain in isolation), came with leading Londoners and others to William at Berkhamstead in Hertfordshire. They were compelled to give hostages as pledges of their good faith, but were then allowed to make formal submission and swear oaths of fealty. William promised in return that his

---

[91] *Anglo-Saxon Chronicle*, s.a. 1066 (C, D, E); *Florentii Wigorniensis monachi Chronicon*, I, pp. 225–7; William of Poitiers, *Histoire de Guillaume le Conquerant*, pp. 170–204.

[92] *Florentii Wigorniensis monachi Chronicon*, I, p. 228. Both Harold's sister, the wife of King Edward, and Harold's official wife, the sister of Earls Edwin and Morcar, were known as Edith. It is conjectural whether either was required to adopt this name, traditional in royal circles, on becoming queen-consort. Harold's handfast-wife was also named Edith.

army would now stop its burning and plundering.[93] These were the best terms which the English could hope to achieve, given the lack of reliable leadership for such troops as they could muster, let alone the lack of a convincing adult candidate for the throne. Ealdred was probably the instigator of this move, and he certainly had the force of character to persuade the others to see things from his viewpoint. Yet Wulfstan's response was perhaps far from passive, despite his long experience of taking orders from Ealdred. He himself was now a diocesan bishop of four years' standing, and the success of his recent mission to the north perhaps increased his public stature considerably. The example of his predecessor and namesake, Archbishop Wulfstan, on whose writings he placed such reliance, would prompt him to perceive that the interests of the English people could now best be served by co-operating with the man who now wielded power, and by doing so, help to restore stability to a war-torn country. On his own account, Wulfstan's practical approach to life, and his long-held belief that Divine retribution awaited the sinful English, would lead him to see the wisdom of submission.

The surrender of the English leaders appeared abject, but they were able to offer William something which would help safeguard both their position and also the values they held dear. It was William's claim to be King Edward's true successor. Given this premise, it would consolidate his hold on his new territory if he demonstrated that he ruled with the co-operation of the English leaders, largely following traditional practices. More even than this, the ingrained attitudes of the English clerical leaders would help him to establish his stature as king in the eyes of his French-speaking followers. His new status as the anointed king, raised above human criticism or challenge, was one which his English subjects might accept more readily than his Norman magnates. The influential clergy of the realm were to set a tone which his own followers might resent, but would find difficult to resist.[94]

The Christmas court of 1065 had witnessed the crisis surrounding the death of King Edward, while the Christmas court of 1066 was the setting for the coronation of King William. The ceremony was once again conducted in Westminster Abbey, in part for convenience, but as in the case of Harold II, specifically to associate the new ruler with King Edward, whose lawful successor each claimed to be. William declined to

[93]*Anglo-Saxon Chronicle*, s.a. 1066 (D, E); *Florentii Wigorniensis monachi Chronicon*, I, pp. 228–9; William of Poitiers, *Histoire de Guillaume le Conquerant*, pp. 210–22.

[94]Archbishop Ealdred's role was paramount: Janet L. Nelson, "The Rites of the Conqueror," *Proceedings of the Battle Conference on Anglo-Norman Studies IV, 1981*, ed. R. Allen Brown (1982), pp. 117–32; reprinted in her *Politics and Ritual in Early Medieval Europe* (1986), pp. 375–401.

accept unction from Stigand, in view of the dubious status of the Archbishop of Canterbury. Ealdred performed the office, and William was crowned on Christmas Day. Just at that moment, Ealdred had the upper hand, and before anointing the new king, he exacted from him an undertaking to safeguard the interests of his new subjects. Before the altar of the apostle St Peter (to whom the Abbey is dedicated), and in the presence of the clergy and people, William solemnly promised that he intended to defend the churches of the realm and their incumbents. He vowed also to rule justly over his subjects, and to uphold just laws, while forbidding looting and injustice. The detailed report of these promises which occurs in the Worcester Chronicle may derive from the eyewitness account of Wulfstan.[95] Less than a year had passed since he attended the coronation of his spiritual protégé, King Harold. Since then, he had been caught up in one traumatic episode after another. Any hopes which he now had of a respite were to be short-lived. The coming of the Normans to Worcestershire would bring troubles in plenty.

[95] *Anglo-Saxon Chronicle*, s.a. 1066 (D); *Florentii Wigorniensis monachi Chronicon*, I, pp. 228–9.

6

The Impact of the Norman
Conquest upon Wulfstan and
his Diocese

The Norman Conquest and settlement of England affected both the
ecclesiastical life and the secular concerns of Wulfstan's diocese. The
initial aim of William I, to rule as the lawful successor to his kinsman
King Edward, was undermined by mounting native resistance, culminating in the major crisis of 1068–9. Surviving natural leaders among the
English were viewed with growing hostility, but Wulfstan's exemplary
conduct as a diocesan bishop rendered him more acceptable than certain
of his English colleagues. Renewed recognition of his diocesan authority
is demonstrated in a letter sent to him by the visiting legates, John and
Peter, summoning him to attend a council at Winchester on 7 April,
1070. Wulfstan was instructed to show this letter to all the abbots of his
diocese, and to require them to accompany him to the synod.[1] Those
English prelates who attended this gathering found it an unnerving
experience, because the occasion served to remove from office several
Englishmen whose shortcomings were considered blatant. Bishop Leofwin of Lichfield, realizing that his deprivation was imminent, resigned
before the synod convened. Stigand, Archbishop of Canterbury, Ethelmer
Bishop of Elmham, the East Anglian see, and Ethelric Bishop of Selsey,
were all formally deprived. The deprivation of Bishop Ethelwin of
Durham followed in 1071.[2]

[1]*The Vita Wulfstani of William of Malmesbury*, ed. R. R. Darlington (1928), pp.
189–90; *Councils and Synods with other documents relating to the English Church, I. A.D.
871–1204*, ed. D. Whitelock, M. Brett and C. N. L. Brooke, 2 vols (1981), Part II, pp.
565–8.
[2]*Councils and Synods*, I, Part II, pp. 569–776; D. C. Douglas, *William the Conqueror*
(1964), p. 324. John Le Neve, *Fasti Ecclesiae Anglicanae 1066–1300: II. Monastic
Cathedrals*, compiled by Diana E. Greenway (1971), pp. 3, 29, 55.

Both provinces of the English church received new heads in 1070. Lanfranc, the Italian abbot of the Norman abbey of Bec, was nominated to Canterbury, while Thomas, a canon of Bayeux in Normandy, was nominated to York.[3] When the vacant suffragan bishoprics came to be filled, that of Lichfield presented a challenge. It covered Cheshire, Shropshire and Staffordshire, a region not yet settled by the Normans, and currently in an unpacified state. As a temporary solution, Lanfranc instructed Wulfstan to administer this diocese. Under the circumstances, an Englishman was best fitted to govern the see; Wulfstan accordingly governed the diocese from late 1070 to late 1072, when a new bishop of Lichfield was appointed.[4] Wulfstan's own diocese was compact, and presented no administrative problems, so that he could leave its routine administration to his subordinates.[5] Since the River Severn was navigable for much of its length, Wulfstan could make the outward part of any journey by boat, as far as Shrewsbury. He repeatedly passed through this town while making a visitation of the diocese. On each occasion, he kept vigil and prayed in the little suburban chapel of St Peter's, at that time the smallest of Shrewsbury's churches. The townspeople thought it odd that he ignored their major church, St Mary's, and asked him why he was so attracted to St Peter's. Wulfstan told them firmly: "Believe me, this chapel, so little esteemed, will in time become the most glorious place in all Shrewsbury, and the joy of the entire region. You will value it highly in your lifetimes, and rest there after your deaths." His prophecy was amply fulfilled by later events.[6]

The wooden chapel lay outside the east gate of Shrewsbury, close to the junction of the River Meole with the Severn. It was founded by a kinsman of King Edward, and after the Norman Conquest Roger de Montgomery, earl of Shrewsbury, granted it to a priest in his household, Odeler of Orleans.[7] The priest Siward had charge of the church, and from 1080 was entrusted with the education of Odeler's eldest son,

---

[3]F. Barlow, The English Church 1066–1154 (1979), pp. 59, 61.
[4]Vita Wulfstani, pp. xxx–xxxii, 26. It was later said that Archbishop Thomas (who claimed jurisdiction over this diocese) asked Wulfstan to make a visitation which he himself was reluctant to perform, whether on account of his fear of enemies or of his ignorance of the language: William of Malmesbury, De Gestis Pontificum Anglorum, N. E. S. A. Hamilton (1870), p. 285.
[5]Ailric, archdeacon of the Worcester diocese, is recorded in the Domesday Survey. The relevant entries show that his holdings were acquired after 1066 and in one case clearly after Archbishop Ealdred's time: Domesday Book 16: Worcestershire, ed. F. and C. Thorn (1982), 2: 20; 24; 57.
[6]Vita Wulfstani, pp. 27–8.
[7]The Ecclesiastical History of Orderic Vitalis, ed. and transl. Marjorie Chibnall, 6 vols (1969–80), III, p. 142.

Orderic, who acted as server there.[8] Earl Roger was later persuaded by
Odeler to estalish a monastery on the site, and its foundation can be
dated to Febuary 1083. Odeler himself became a monk in this new
abbey, to which he offered his youngest son, Benedict, as an *oblate*.[9]
Orderic was dispatched at the age of ten to the Norman monastery of St
Evroul, where he was given the additional name of Viel, or Vitalis. He
developed a talent for historical writing, and recorded the foundation of
St Peter's abbey in his major work, *The Ecclesiastical History*.[10] Earl
Roger acquired his lands in Shropshire in 1070 or 1071, and Odeler was
one of the clerks who administered his estates in that region.[11] In this
capacity he would probably meet Wulfstan during the bishop's pastoral
visits to Shrewsbury, and arrangements concerning the staffing of St
Peter's church also fell within the bishop's remit. Odeler was perhaps
prompted to conceive of St Peter's as a potential monastic site during
Wulfstan's visitation to the diocese, while the bishop's repeated visits to
pray in the church were most likely made with the intention of
interceding for this project.

In the ten or twelve years which elapsed between Wulfstan's visitation
of the Lichfield diocese and the fulfilment of his prophecy about St
Peter's, Shrewsbury, there were other pressing calls on his attention. The
two Archbishops, Lanfranc and Thomas, had scarcely assumed office
before they began to contest jurisdiction over the three bishoprics on the
frontiers of their respective provinces, namely Dorchester (the large
diocese in the east Midlands of which the seat was moved to Lincoln in
1072 or 1073),[12] Lichfield and Worcester. The moment seemed opportune for Wulfstan to renew his claims to those vills which Archbishop
Ealdred had retained, but which he himself had repeatedly declared on
oath to be the property of the diocese of Worcester.[13] Since Lanfranc was
claiming the diocese of Worcester for the province of Canterbury, he
would naturally support Wulfstan's claims over the alienated vills, while
Wulfstan was obliging him by administering the diocese of Lichfield. In
Wulfstan's *Life*, attention is focused on the conflict over the disputed
vills, as though this was the only point at issue. Lanfranc is introduced

---

[8] Ibid., III, pp. 6–8; VI, p. 552.

[9] Ibid., III, pp. 142, 146. For Odeler's role in the foundation and endowment of
Shrewsbury abbey, see also *The Cartulary of Shrewsbury Abbey*, ed. Una Rees, 2 vols
(1975), pp. x, xiv–xvi, xix, 6, 11, 30, 33, 39, 41, 255–6.

[10] *Ecclesiastical History of Orderic Vitalis*, III, pp. 6–8, 142–50; VI, pp. 552–4.

[11] J. F. A. Mason, "Roger de Montgomery and his sons," *Transactions of the Royal
Historical Society*, fifth series, 13 (1963), pp. 1–28, esp. pp. 3–4, 10.

[12] John Le Neve, *Fasti Ecclesiae Anglicanae 1066–1300: III. Lincoln*, compiled by Diana
E. Greenway (1971), p. ix.

[13] *Vita Wulfstani*, p. 24.

into the narrative simply as an ally of Wulfstan, in blatant disregard of the fact that it was Lanfranc's victory over Thomas which made possible Wulfstan's own triumph.

The dispute between the archbishops was taken to Rome in 1071, and pleaded before Pope Alexander II (1061-73), when the question of the vills was apparently raised by Lanfranc as a corollary. It is not said that Wulfstan himself went to Rome. The pope was a former pupil of Lanfranc, and was unwilling to offend him now. He was equally reluctant to reject the plea of Archbishop Thomas who would be left with a greatly truncated archdiocese, while that of Canterbury was aggrandized in territory and wealth, but a verdict in favour of York might run contrary to the political requirements of King William. To rid himself of an embarrassing dilemma, he referred the jurisdictional dispute, and hence also Wulfstan's grievance, to an English council. The dispute was considered in England first at Winchester, at Easter 1072, and then, after an adjournment, it was concluded at Windsor at Pentecost. Both the hearings took place within the context of seasonal Great Councils. Finally Lanfranc was awarded jurisdiction over all three bishoprics;[14] consequently he had a vested interest in supporting Wulfstan's plea over the vills. The bishop's *Life* indicates that the archbishop openly supported him, and that he was the only person to do so.[15] There was no doubt a general feeling that Archbishop Thomas should not be dismissed defeated on all counts.

In the matter of the vills, Thomas was supported by the rich and powerful Odo, bishop of Bayeux, the king's half-brother, together with many of the magnates, whom the writer of Wulfstan's *Life* alleged were recruited by flattery and bribery.[16] The writer omitted to mention that Wulfstan in turn enlisted the help of his astute neighbour, Abbot Ethelwig of Evesham, who knew how to handle both king and courtiers, and who deployed money and shrewd advice on Wulfstan's behalf.[17] King William listened attentively to the arguments which Lanfranc put forward in support of Wulfstan, but was inclined to favour the line taken by his brother, Bishop Odo, in support of Archbishop Thomas. When

[14]Ibid., pp. 24–5; Margaret Gibson, *Lanfranc of Bec* (1978), pp. 118–19; *The Letters of Lanfranc, archbishop of Canterbury*, ed. and transl. Helen Clover and Margaret Gibson (1979), no. 3. For accounts of the dispute as seen from the viewpoint of Archbishop Thomas, see *The Historians of the Church of York and its archbishops*, ed. J. Raine, 3 vols (1879, 1886, 1894), II, pp. 99–102, 243–4, 357–8; III, pp. 9–14.
[15]*Vita Wulfstani*, p. 25.
[16]Ibid., p. 25.
[17]*Chronicon Abbatiae de Evesham ad Annum 1418*, ed. W. D. Macray (1863), pp. 89–90.

both parties had made formal declarations of their positions, Thomas and his supporters withdrew to prepare a rejoinder, and Wulfstan meanwhile settled down to sleep. Thomas produced an incisive and fluent counter-attack when he returned. Wulfstan was woken up by his supporters and promptly began to recite psalms, and to pray, conduct which was disconcerting, if not downright exasperating, in a gathering of this nature. He was ordered to go outside the courtroom and give some thought to preparing his response to Thomas's arguments. But on withdrawing from the council chamber with his few supporters, Wulfstan promptly sang the monastic Office for the time of day. When his friends told him that he had more urgent concerns than psalm-singing, and that he should attend to the business in hand, he replied:

> Fools, don't you know what the Lord said? "When you are brought before kings and rulers, do not think about how you will speak, or what words you will utter. For you are to say whatever is given to you in that hour." (Mark 13: 9, 11). The same Creator, who said this, the Lord Jesus Christ, is able to give me today the words with which I can defend the righteousness of my cause, and destroy their deviousness.[18]

In scriptural terms, his answer was impeccable, but at that moment, his anxious and exasperated supporters would have other views on the matter. The go-getting clerks usually employed in an episcopal *familia* might find it difficult to work with a man of Wulfstan's temperament, and their opinion of his conduct was no doubt at variance, on this and other occasions, with the viewpoint which pervades his *Life*. But on this occasion the outcome demonstrated that Wulfstan's faith was fully justified. It is reported in his *Life* that his response was absolutely splendid. As he spoke, he was holding in his hands the *Lives* of Saints Dunstan and Oswald, two former bishops of Worcester whose lifestyles he imitated, just as he upheld their beliefs. He announced that he had perceived these saints there at his side, and he was confident that they had come to help him. On returning to the council room, so the *Life* relates, he won his case without difficulty. King William, evidently puzzled by Wulfstan's conduct, asked him on what grounds he based his case. Wulfstan replied, "My counsel is in you, because the heart of the king is in the hand of God" (Proverbs 21:1).[19] This response demonstrated Wulfstan's belief both in Divine Providence and in the theocratic

---

[18] *Vita Wulfstani*, p. 25. William of Malmesbury also gives two variant accounts of the episode: *De Gestis Pontificum Anglorum*, pp. 284–5; *De Gestis Regum Anglorum*, ed. W. Stubbs, 2 vols (1887, 1889), II, p. 354.

[19] *Vita Wulfstani*, p. 25.

justification for William's rule. The king, by virtue of his unction, was inspired by God to govern wisely. This sentiment was self-evident to a cleric of Wulfstan's generation, reared on the precepts of the Tenth-Century Reformation, and he had provided a timely lesson to the assembled magnates.[20] The proper reward ensued. The disputed vills were restored to Worcester as corollary to the assignment of the diocese to the province of Canterbury, while Archbishop Thomas was recompensed with equivalent estates by the king.[21] There is no reason to doubt Wulfstan's trust in Divine Providence, even though this was reinforced by the belief that Lanfranc had a vested interest in supporting his case. Wulfstan may have assumed from preliminary conversations with the archbishop that if Lanfranc won his suit, the vills would be assigned to Worcester automatically. Any misunderstanding on this point, or a presumption that the pleading of the articulate Lanfranc would serve for both of them, would account for Wulfstan's lack of preparation. This in turn might give rise to later allegations that Lanfranc had doubts about Wulfstan's fitness for episcopal rule because of his inadequate command of French.[22]

King William and his counsellors were no doubt perplexed, and perhaps irritated, by Wulfstan's conduct during the litigation, but he suffered nothing beyond a few sharp words. In the 1130s his dispute with Archbishop Thomas was used by Osbert de Clare, prior of Westminster, as the basis for a legend, incorporated in his *Life of King Edward*. According to this story, Wulfstan was ordered to surrender his pastoral staff, the symbol of his office. He replied that he would surrender it only to the king who had appointed him, and accordingly transfixed it in the masonry of King Edward's tomb. He then proved to be the only person who could dislodge it, upon which King William confirmed him in office.[23] This story, originally intended to glorify King Edward, quickly circulated as the most popular of Wulfstan's miracles. King John, disputing the papal appointment of Stephen Langton to Canterbury, interpreted the legend as demonstrating Wulfstan's belief that the right to

[20]*Regularis Concordia*, transl. and introd. T. Symons (1953), pp. 12–14, 20–2. On the assertion of theocratic kingship in this reign, see H. E. J. Cowdrey, "The Anglo-Norman *Laudes Regiae*," reprinted from *Viator*, 12 (1981), in his *Popes, Monks and Crusaders* (1984), VIII, pp. 37–78, esp. pp. 51–5; Janet L. Nelson, "The Rites of the Conqueror," reprinted from *Proceedings of the Battle Conference on Anglo-Norman Studies*, IV in her *Politics and Ritual in Early Medieval Europe* (1986), pp. 375–401, esp. pp. 399–401.

[21]*Vita Wulfstani*, p. 25.

[22]Emma Mason, "St. Wulfstan's Staff: a legend and its uses," *Medium Aevum*, 53 (1984), pp. 166–7.

[23]"La Vie de S. Edouard le Confesseur par Osbert de Clare," introd. and ed. M. Bloch, *Analecta Bollandiana*, 41 (1923), pp. 116–20.

appoint bishops pertained to the king alone. Accordingly he adopted
Wulfstan as his patron saint, a most appropriate choice given Wulfstan's
staunch support of the monarchy.[24]

Wulfstan made a written profession of obedience to Lanfranc, as his
metropolitan, perhaps at the conclusion of the lawsuit of 1072. In this
document he observed that all his predecessors had been suffragans of
Canterbury, but that Archbishop Stigand had incurred excommunication
by every pope from Leo IX (1049–54) to Alexander II (1061–73),
because of his unauthorized use of the pallium. Since they had prohibited
bishops-elect from accepting consecration at his hands, ordination was
therefore sought from others. He himself had been consecrated by
Ealdred of York, but had always refrained from making any profession
of obedience to that see.[25] Yet given the known character of Ealdred, it is
almost inconceivable that he did not exact a profession from Wulfstan,
whose activities in the York archdiocese in the earlier 1060s indicate that
Ealdred did regard him as suffragan. It was as well that Lanfranc
obtained Wulfstan's written profession, because there was a risk that in
practice the bishop of Worcester would continue to be regarded as a
suffragan of York. The reason for this was that the verdict in the lawsuit
between the two archbishops left Thomas with only one accredited
suffragan, the bishop of Durham. But Bishop Walcher (1071–80) had
charge of the insecure northern frontier, and from 1076 he was even
styled earl of Northumberland.[26] Given his urgent temporal responsibilities, he would have little time for ecclesiastical duties which called him
away from his own diocese. The lack of effective suffragans caused
Archbishop Thomas embarrassment towards the end of 1072, when the
cleric Radulf arrived, sent by Earl Paul of Orkney with a request that he
should be consecrated bishop. The Scottish dioceses were theoretically
under the jurisdiction of York, so it was desirable that Thomas should
reinforce his authority by being seen to perform the ordination. Since
canon law required the participation of fellow bishops, Thomas had to
request Lanfranc's help in providing temporary suffragans to assist at the
ceremony. Perhaps at the prompting of his cathedral chapter, jealous for
the alleged rights of the archbishopric, he specifically asked for two men
whom in happier circumstances he would have summoned himself:
Rémy of Dorchester and Wulfstan of Worcester. Rémy was suspicious of
Thomas's intentions, and did not act. Instead, Lanfranc wrote jointly to
Wulfstan and to Peter, the newly consecrated bishop of Lichfield who

[24]Mason, "St. Wulfstan's Staff," pp. 157–61.
[25]Vita Wulfstani, p. 190.
[26]W. E. Kapelle, The Norman Conquest of the North: the region and its transformation
1000–1135 (1979), pp. 137–8.

was apparently staying with him at the time, and instructed them to assist in the consecration. Lanfranc forwarded to them the letter he had received from Archbishop Thomas, in which he solemnly promised not to use this occasion as a precedent for reviving his claims to jurisdiction over them. The consecration of Bishop Radulf of Orkney took place on 3 March 1073, which necessarily involved Wulfstan in yet another difficult midwinter journey to York.[27]

The initiative did not always rest with Lanfranc. There were sound political arguments why King William should have enlarged the southern province at the expense of York, but he was aware of the pastoral problems which his verdict caused, and was willing to remedy them on a pragmatic basis. On one occasion, acting in consultation with Archbishop Thomas, he instructed Wulfstan to travel to York before Easter to bless the chrism (required for the traditional Paschal baptismal ceremony).[28] Long years of abstinence and self-discipline would build up the stamina which the ageing Wulfstan needed to make these winter journeys. Both his zeal for pastoral activities and his earlier acquaintance with the north rendered him the most appropriate of the southern bishops to be deputed with such duties. On the other hand, as his remaining English colleagues died, he was soon the only native bishop left in post.[29] In certain quarters it might be felt that Wulfstan was fortunate to be allowed to remain in office at all. Irksome taks which the incoming Continental prelates distained could therefore be assigned to him.

Wulfstan's continued involvement in the York diocese was necessitated by the employment at court of Archbishop Thomas, who was a highly-skilled administrator.[30] Yet reliance on Wulfstan as his deputy might establish precedents on which Thomas could revive his claims to jurisdiction over the see of Worcester. The danger was apparent to Lanfranc. When William of St Calais was consecrated as bishop of Durham, on 3 January 1081, the ceremony was held in the abbey of St Peter's, Gloucester, since his election had occurred at the Christmas court of 1080, which was held there. Archbishop Thomas officiated, assisted by Wulfstan (bishop of the diocese in which Gloucester lay), and the bishops of Exeter, Hereford and Wells. All four participated on instruc-

[27]*Letters of Lanfranc, archbishop of Canterbury*, nos. 12–13; Gibson, *Lanfranc of Bec*, pp. 125, 212.
[28]*Vita Wulfstani*, p. 28.
[29]Of those English bishops who survived the purge of 1070–1, Leofric of Exeter died in 1072, and Siward of Rochester in 1075. The last survivors of King Edward's Continental appointments were William of London, died in 1075; Walter of Hereford in 1079, and Giso of Wells in 1088.
[30]*Vita Wulfstani*, p. 30. On Thomas's clerical expertise, see *Historians of the Church of York*, II, pp. 99, 109, 355–6, 364, 520.

tions from Lanfranc.[31] This was one occasion which offered no grounds on which the jurisdictional claims of York could be reasserted.

Lanfranc and Wulfstan were contrasting characters in many respects, yet they also shared important values. They were among the handful of representatives of the monastic profession among the bishops.[32] Even when fellow monks joined their ranks, these were not necessarily congenial company. William of St Calais presents a case in point. He had formerly been abbot of St Vincent at Le Mans, but the qualities which recommended his appointment as bishop of Durham were not primarily those which were esteemed in a cloistered society.[33] Lanfranc and Wulfstan both believed strongly in their duty to support the monarchy, and they were natural allies in time of political crisis. Such unswerving loyalty might be ingrained in monks of their generation, but it was reinforced by their personal circumstances. Many of their fellow bishops enjoyed the support of a network of important family connections, whether in ecclesiastical circles or in lay society. In contrast, the Italian archbishop and his English suffragan had no such backing. Lanfranc was trusted with extensive political powers, and Wulfstan could preside over a see which was precariously close to the frontier with Wales, without a risk that either of them might be drawn by kinsmen into subversive political adventures.

Over the years, Lanfranc and Wulfstan seem to have developed a good working relationship. Wulfstan's trust in Lanfranc's good intentions is manifested in the willingness with which he accepted the archbishop's reforms of current monastic practice. His reception of these innovations is in contrast to his staunch retention of traditional English practices and values in other areas. Lanfranc introduced at Christchurch, Canterbury, a reinvigorated monastic discipline, expounded in his *Monastic Constitutions*. While his customs were not imposed uniformly on the other English monastic houses, they did circulate widely, and were observed in numerous monasteries, including several of the major houses.[34] The time-hallowed way of spreading disciplinary reforms was to invite each participating monastery to send a young monk to learn the customs of the house which was promulgating them, so that he could later instruct by his example the monks of his own house. Wulfstan accordingly sent to Canterbury the young monk Nicholas, to train for some time in the new

---

[31]*Acta Lanfranci*, in *Two of the Saxon Chronicles Parallel*, ed. C. Plummer and J. Earle (1892–9), I, pp. 289–90.

[32]Barlow, *The English Church 1066–1154*, p. 318.

[33]Le Neve, *Fasti Ecclesiae Anglicanae 1066–1300. II. Monastic Cathedrals*, p. 29; "Historia Dunhelmensis Ecclesiae," in *Symeonis Monachi Opera Omnia*, ed. T. Arnold, 2 vols (1882, 1885), I, 127–8, 170–95.

[34]Gibson, *Lanfranc of Bec*, pp. 146, 173–4.

monastic discipline under the guidance of Lanfranc. In later years, Nicholas became prior of Worcester (1116–24), and earned praise for his educative role, since he instilled into his monks high standards both of conduct and of scholarship.[35] It is arguable that he was not the only monk of his generation at Worcester sent to Canterbury for training, since the writer Eadmer, himself a monk of Canterbury, cited as one of his informants the Worcester monk Ethelred, who spent some time in Canterbury as sub-prior and *cantor* (precentor), but it has been suggested that this name is an alias of Nicholas.[36]

The adoption of revised and reformed monastic customs was accompanied by the provision of a new church in which to observe them. In the generations following the Norman Conquest of England, virtually all the cathedrals and major churches were rebuilt in the Romanesque style. Effectively, the new political regime was given visual expression. It was almost twenty years after the Norman conquest before Wulfstan conformed to the fashion for rebuilding. Eventually the growing size of the community constrained him to do so. As the work progressed, it became necessary to demolish the former cathedral church built by St Oswald, and this caused Wulfstan great distress. On the day the demolition began, he stood silently in the cemetery, gazing at the destruction, and eventually burst into tears. He was quoted as saying: "We wretches are destroying the work of the saints, pompously thinking we can do better. How superior to us was St. Oswald, who built this church. How many saintly monks have served God in it."[37] A variant report of this episode states that he deplored destruction for the sake of earning praise (for the replacement). While the men of old did not know how to construct pretentious buildings, they did know how to offer themseves to God under any kind of roof, and how to attract by their example those who followed after them. The men of his own generation, though, were straining to pile up stones while neglecting their souls.[38]

The destruction of St Oswald's church was necessitated by the limited space available for building. The cathedral and its precincts stood on commanding heights, on a steep and narrow ridge, part of which had

---

[35] *Vita Wulfstani*, p. 57.
[36] Eadmer, "Vita Sancti Dunstani archiepiscopi Cantuariensis," in *Memorials of Saint Dunstan, archbishop of Canterbury*, ed. W. Stubbs (1874), pp. 163–4. On the identification of Ethelred with Nicholas, see *Vita Wulfstani*, p. xxxviii, note 2. The list of Worcester monks recorded at Durham, *c*.1104, includes both Nicholas and Edred, possibly an abbreviation of Ethelred: *Durham Liber Vitae*, ed. A. H. Thompson (1923), in facsimile, folio 22 recto.
[37] *Vita Wulfstani*, p. 52.
[38] William of Malmesbury, *De Gestis Pontificum Anglorum*, p. 283.

been commandeered for the site of the new castle. While the complete rebuilding of a church, rather than its piecemeal enlargement, was normal practice on the Continent, the English custom was to retain any old church building as a relic of its founder (or in St Oswald's case, its re-founder). For Wulfstan, the quality of the monastic observance at Worcester mattered far more than the possession of a spectacular new building, and the destruction of the old church might appear as the negation of St Oswald's achievement. Yet the expanding community at Worcester urgently needed a larger church, and by the 1080s it was inevitable that any new building would be in the Romanesque style, in contrast to the simpler buildings to which Wulfstan had long been accustomed. His belief that this architecture was less in keeping with the disciplined lives of the monks than the pre-Romanesque of the late Anglo-Saxon era can be seen as foreshadowing the architectural puritanism of the twelfth-century Cistercians.[39]

Once Wulfstan was reconciled to the rebuilding of the cathedral, he saw it through to completion, so his *Life* relates. His new church was richly decorated with all imaginable types of ornamentation, and was wonderful both in every detail and in its overall impact. In a charter which he issued in May 1089, Wulfstan sounded positively enthusiastic both about the building and its decoration.[40] The brisk pace at which this costly rebuilding project was carried out required a steady flow of cash; the rapid completion of the project is a tribute to Wulfstan's efficient management of his extensive episcopal estates, which were organized in such a way as to maximize cash returns.[41] The work on the new church was begun in 1084,[42] and it is probable that both the crypt, and also the work above ground, from the east end to the choir, was completed by 1089, when the monks were able to move in. The dismantling of the older building suggests that this was the case.[43] The crypt, which still

[39]For a discussion of possible influences upon Wulfstan's architectural taste, see Richard Gem, "England and the Resistance to Romanesque Architecture," in *Studies in Medieval History presented to R. Allen Brown*, ed. C. Harper–Bill, C. J. Holdsworth and Janet L. Nelson (1989), pp. 129–39. The surviving work which dates from Wulfstan's episcopate is discussed by Richard Gem, "Bishop Wulfstan II and the Romanesque Cathedral Church of Worcester," in *Medieval Art and Architecture at Worcester Cathedral*, ed. Glenys Popper (1978), pp. 15–37.

[40]*Vita Wulfstani*, p. 52; *The Cartulary of Worcester Cathedral Priory* (Register I), ed. R. R. Darlington (1968), no. 3.

[41]J. D. Hamshere, "Domesday Book: Estate Structures in the West Midlands," *Domesday Studies*, ed. J. C. Holt (1987), pp. 168, 171.

[42]Annals of Worcester Cathedral Priory, *Annales Monastici*, ed. H. R. Luard (1864–9), IV, p. 373.

[43]Gem, "Bishop Wulfstan II and the Romanesque Cathedral Church of Worcester," pp. 17–19.

survives essentially as Wulfstan knew it, was the venue for a diocesan synod which he summoned in 1092.[44] Above ground, owing to successive phases of rebuilding, there are scarcely any visible remains of the church which he built, with the possible exception of some capitals in the south transept.[45] On the other hand, some of the masonry in the monastic precincts and passageways, including perhaps the refectory undercroft, and in particular the slype in the east wall of the cloister, can be dated to Wulfstan's time.[46]

The focus of any church was its collection of relics of the saints. The cathedral at Worcester possessed many such relics, for which a shrine had earlier been made by St Oswald. Wulfstan now enlarged this, so that it could also contain the relics of St Oswald himself. The shrine was intentionally a magnificent object, and Wulfstan accordingly contributed 72 marks (£48) towards its embellishment.[47] This splendid setting for the remains of his predecessor St Oswald, and the other holy ones commemorated there, was designed to reflect their spiritual glory. The formal translation (reburial) of St Oswald's relics took place on 8 October, in the presence of the bishop of Hereford, several abbots and a large crowd of people. Wulfstan ordered that this date should be observed annually as the Feast of the Translation of St Oswald. The anniversary of the deposition (burial) of St Oswald fell in the penitential season of Lent, whereas this new feast of their patron could be celebrated in a more fitting manner.[48] At this period, the papacy did not monopolize the recognition of deceased persons as saints. The designation of their remains as relics, and especially their solemn translation to a shrine designed to facilitate their veneration, were the means by which sanctity

---

[44]*Cartulary of Worcester*, no. 52. The crypt was probably the most convenient venue for formal gatherings in Wulfstan's episcopate, if further building work was in progress in the monastic precincts. The Romanesque chapter house appears to have been completed after Wulfstan's lifetime: Neil Stratford, "Notes on the Norman Chapterhouse at Worcester," in *Medieval Art and Architecture at Worcester Cathedral*, ed. Glenys Popper (1978), pp. 51–70. Two charters of Bishop Roger, dating from 9 April 1175, were also drawn up in the crypt: *Cartulary of Worcester*, nos 167, 178. Extensive rebuilding was perhaps in progress, since this was the year in which the crossing-tower of the cathedral collapsed: Annals of Worcester Cathedral Priory, *Annales Monastici*, IV, p. 383.

[45]G. Zarnecki, "The Romanesque Capitals in the South Transept of Worcester Cathedral," in *Medieval Art and Architecture at Worcester Cathedral*, pp. 38–50.

[46]N. Pevsner, *Worcestershire* (1968), pp. 305–7. For illustrations of slightly later Romanesque work in the claustral buildings, see Freda Anderson, "St Pancras Priory, Lewes: its Architectural Development to 1200," *Anglo-Norman Studies XI: Proceedings of the Battle Conference 1988*, ed. R. Allen Brown (1989), pp. 1–35, esp. pp. 12–13.

[47]*Vita Wulfstani*, p. 52.

[48]Ibid., pp. 52–3. Oswald died on 29 February 992: *Historians of the Church of York*, I, p. 472; II, p. 40.

was acclaimed. The presence of distinguished visiting clerics at a translation testified to widespread recognition of the merits of the new saint. In promoting the cult of St Oswald in this way, Wulfstan was making a stand for the traditional values of the English church in face of its infiltration by foreigners and their alien values.

With the passage of time, the incoming clerics increasingly saw themselves as the true heirs of their English predecessors in office. When the Italian Anselm was appointed to Canterbury in 1093, and wanted to know the scope of his jurisdiction, he appealed to Wulfstan as the one surviving native prelate with the knowledge to advise him. The bishop's response was most satisfactory from Anselm's point of view, particularly with regard to "the rights exercised by your excellent predecessor Stigand." Consequently, the archbishop's biographer, the English monk Eadmer, wrote in glowing terms of the knowledge and wisdom of the venerable English bishop: "the one and only [survivor] of the ancient fathers of the English; a man distinguished in all religious observance, and thoroughly imbued with knowledge of the ancient customs of England."[49]

The bishops met one another at the seasonal gatherings of the royal court. Sometimes they convened as a formal synod, to make decisions on such matters as the reform of the clergy; parochial organization; or recognition of Anglo-Norman saints. All vacancies in the episcopate were filled by men from the Continent in the generations after the Norman Conquest, and most bishops were now secular clerks rather than monks. By the end of William I's reign in 1087, Wulfstan was almost the longest-serving bishop, surpassed only by Giso, the physician from Lotharingia appointed to Wells by King Edward. Many of the new-comers, in contrast, were comparatively young men.[50] As the reign progressed, something of a cultural, as well as a generation, gap widened between Wulfstan and his episcopal associates, although conversely common pastoral and administrative problems would foster group solidarity. Little is known of his relations with the majority of his episcopal colleagues. Rather unexpectedly, one who was said to have some admiration for Wulfstan was a former royal clerk, Walkelin bishop of Winchester (1070–98).[51]

Mutual attestations to royal charters provide some indication of those whom he met formally, and when, but such records do not indicate

---

[49]Eadmer, *Historia Novorum in Anglia*, ed. M. Rule (1884), pp. 45–7. The quotation is taken from p. 46.

[50]H. R. Loyn, "William's bishops: some further thoughts," *Anglo-Norman Studies X*, ed. R. Allen Brown (1988), pp. 224–5.

[51]*Vita Wulfstani*, p. 26.

whether he was on friendly terms with his co-signatories. Evidence for this survives only in a few cases, and even of these, one is known only from one much-quoted exchange. Geoffrey, the incumbent of the Norman see of Coutances, presided over a lawsuit concerning lands which were adjudged to Wulfstan.[52] An ensuing celebratory dinner was perhaps the setting for a bantering exchange which is recorded between them, and which certainly took place in a convivial atmosphere. Geoffrey apparently believed that Wulfstan could the more easily claim his rights if his status was reflected in his dress. Now Wulfstan practised moderation in matters of clothes and footwear. He rejected anything which was showily expensive, or, conversely, shoddy, since he maintained that a false pride might be derived from dressing in rags. But Wulfstan's concept of moderation was that of a monk of the old school. The newcomers to the episcopal ranks had different ideas about what a bishop owed to his status. Geoffrey launched into a series of good-humoured witticisms on the subject of Wulfstan's dress sense, and eventually asked him why he persisted in wearing only lambskins as trimming to his robes, when he could, and should, use the pelts of sable, beaver or wolf. Wulfstan retorted that Geoffrey and other men skilled in worldly wisdom should wear the furs of crafty beasts, whereas he, who did not indulge in deviousness, was content with lambskins. Geoffrey said that at least he should wear the fur of cats, to which Wulfstan replied: "Believe me, we praise the Lamb of God more often than the cat of God." Geoffrey was delighted at this riposte, and burst out laughing, because the tables had been turned on him.[53]

In Wulfstan's later years, his closest episcopal friend was Robert of Lotharingia, bishop of Hereford from 1079 to 1095. He was a contrasting character to his predecessor, Walter (1061–79), who was reputedly stabbed to death with a pair of scissors when he tried to rape a seamstress.[54] Robert was a noted scholar; an astronomer and mathematician who was also skilled in chronology, the science of computing dates, and who introduced into his diocese the scientific learning of the Continent.[55] He was also instrumental in making Worcester an important centre of historical writing in this period. He brought to England the

---

[52]The suit is discussed in detail later in this chapter. For Geoffrey's role, see *Domesday Book 16: Worcestershire*, ed. F. and C. Thorn (1982), Appendix V, Worcester H.

[53]*Vita Wulfstani*, p. 46. See also William of Malmesbury, *De Gestis Pontificum Anglorum*, pp. 282–3. On Bishop Geoffrey, see J. Le Patourel, "Geoffrey of Montbray, bishop of Coutances," *English Historical Review*, 59 (1944), pp. 129–61.

[54]William of Malmesbury, *De Gestis Pontificum Anglorum*, p. 300.

[55]Ibid., pp. 300–3, 313; C. H. Haskins, "The Abacus and the King's Curia," *English Historical Review*, 27 (1912), pp. 101–6.

chronicle composed by an Irish monk, Marianus Scotus, who began the work after going into exile in the German lands in 1056, and ended it at Mainz in 1073. Robert obtained a text soon afterwards, and gave the manuscript, or a copy, to Wulfstan. He in turn saw its potential as the foundation for a locally based chronicle. He assigned to the young English monk, John, the task of editing and updating the work, which was continued at Worcester for several decades.[56] The friendship between Wulfstan and Robert dated from the time of the latter's consecration. They shared strong spiritual interests, and Robert was supportive in practical ways. He attended the Translation of St Oswald; and he maintained a tenancy on his own lands for Edric, the leader of Worcester's fighting force, when he was displaced from the episcopal estates by the tenurial revolution which followed the Norman Conquest. During Wulfstan's last illness Robert heard his confession, and later returned to officiate at his funeral. Their close friendship is exemplified in that, while in attendance at the royal court, he experienced a vision of Wulfstan, informing Robert of his death and urging him to come to Worcester to preside at the obsequies.[57]

In the years immediately after the Norman Conquest, Wulfstan still experienced the mixed blessings of frequent contact with Archbishop Ealdred and Abbot Ethelwig. Their actions might be overbearing at times, but Wulfstan's close association with these powerful men would afford him some protection at the start of the new reign. While pretexts of one kind or another were readily produced to remove other English prelates from office, the confessor and confidential adviser of the late King Harold remained securely in his bishopric. At the outset of the new reign, the archbishop continued to treat the diocese of Worcester as part of his own sphere of influence, but the limitations on his power became apparent when the new Norman sheriff of Worcester, Urse de Abetot, began building a castle on the high ground overlooking the Severn. This commanding site was already partly occupied by the cathedral precincts, and the building work encroached on the monastic cemetery. Wulfstan's reaction is not recorded, although he probably asked Ealdred to intervene. When Urse would not call a halt to the work on the castle, Ealdred

---

[56]*Ecclesiastical History of Orderic Vitalis*, II, pp. 186–8. See also M. Brett, "John of Worcester and his contemporaries," *The Writing of History in the Middle Ages: essays presented to R. W. Southern*, ed. R. H. C. Davis and J. M. Wallace Hadrill (1981), pp. 101–25; William of Malmesbury, *De Gestis Pontificum Anglorum*, pp. 300–1.

[57]Wulfstan ordained Robert to the priesthood before Lanfranc consecrated him bishop: *Florentii Wigorniensis monachi Chronicon ex Chronicis*, ed. B. Thorpe, 2 vols (1848–9), II, p. 13; *Vita Wulfstani*, pp. 52, 60, 62–3. William of Malmesbury, *De Gestis Pontificum Anglorum*, pp. 301–3. On Edric's tenurial position, see *Domesday Book 16: Worcestershire*, Appendix 5, Worcs. H. He is discussed in more detail later in this chapter.

finally had recourse to the ancient expedient of the ritual curse. This had
been employed by clerics in the early Middle Ages, following the collapse
of the Roman Empire, when secular government offered no effective legal
redress against predators on church property These citations to the court
of Heaven became less frequent over the centuries, as expanding royal
government provided legal sanctions against wrongdoers. By the Anglo-
Norman period, the sanction of anathema was largely confined to a
formal clause at the end of solemn charters, but the solemn invocation
against transgressors was still an option open to churchmen if the secular
power failed to offer protection. The elderly Ealdred, confronting the
ruthless young Norman, might feel that ritual cursing was the only way
to assert his rights. Ealdred's curse, a word-play on the name of the
sheriff, contained the sanction that his descendants would not long enjoy
the lands on which they had settled.[58] But the castle stood intact until the
thirteenth century, while the descendants of Urse's daughter long continued to dominate the region.[59] Ealdred was a deeply disappointed man
in his last years. Successive heavy gelds imposed by King William in 1067
and 1068 prompted the northerners to revolt. The rising of 1068 petered
out as the Normans advanced against them, but the renewed revolt in
1069 occurred in conjunction with a massive Danish invasion. The fleet
entered the Humber on 8 September; the city of York was devastated and
the minster burned. All that Ealdred had striven to achieve was now
ruined – both on the political front and in his own archdiocese. He died,
a broken man, on 11 September.[60]

The invaders withdrew, but the revolt of the English was brutally
suppressed by King William in a punitive expedition commonly known
as the Harrying of the North, in the winter of 1069–70. Several shires
were deliberately devastated, and the survivors fled away from the
region.[61] Among those who escaped were many who were very old or
very young, and women with little children; all of them starving.

[58]William of Malmesbury, *De Gestis Pontificum Anglorum*, p. 253. On the origin and
use of the ritual curse by ecclesiastics, see L. K. Little, "La morphologie des malédictions
monastiques," *Annales*, 34 (1979), pp. 43–66. The continued use of the anathema as a
sanction to protect rights guaranteed in writing is illustrated in Wulfstan's solemn Alveston
charter: *Cartulary of Worcester*, no. 3.

[59]On the lands of Urse and his descendants, see *The Beauchamp Cartulary: charters
1100–1268*, ed. Emma Mason (1980), pp. xviii–xxv; and for the shrievalty and castle of
Worcester, ibid., pp. xlviii–lii.

[60]*Historians of the Church of York*, II, p. 349; *The Anglo-Saxon Chronicle*, transl.
Dorothy Whitelock with D. C. Douglas and Susie I. Tucker (1961), 1069 (D, E); *Florentii
Wigorniensis monachi Chronicon*, II, pp. 3–4.

[61]*Anglo-Saxon Chronicle*, 1069 (D, E); *Florentii Wigorniensis monachi Chronicon*, II,
p. 4; Kapelle, *The Norman Conquest of the North*, pp. 112–19.

Evesham was inundated with people dying for lack of food. Some found refuge in the houses; others in the open; and some even in the cemetery. Every day, five or six at least, and often more, of them died, and were buried by the prior. Abbot Ethelwig arranged that, since there were many little boys among the fugitives, each sergeant or other lay employee of the abbey, and even some of the monks, should take responsibility for providing food for one of them. In course of time, some of these boys grew up to be responsible members of the abbey's lay staff. Meanwhile, the relief work was put in charge of the young and capable Prior Alfric, while the cellarer and the reeves – the lay foremen of the abbey's estates – were instructed to provide him with all the supplies he required for this famine relief.[62] Despite Ethelwig's unfavourable reputation at Worcester, he could be compassionate on his home ground. The measures which he took for the welfare of the refugees were presented by his biographer purely as an act of disinterested charity, without nationalistic overtones. Since Ethelwig was in effect King William's governor in western Mercia, he would not want it said that he had any sympathy for his outcast compatriots. It was tactfully recorded at Evesham that King William's Harrying of the North was carried out to suppress the outlaws and robbers who infested the woods in the northern shires.[63]

Evesham kept alive the traditions of the golden age of Northumbrian monasticism, and the feasts of the northern saints were commemorated there, just as they were at Worcester.[64] The Northumbrian religious houses were devastated during the Danish raids of the ninth century, and due to the turbulent politics of the region over the ensuing generations, monasticism had not revived. Its recovery in the 1070s was largely due to the inspiration of monks who were, or had recently been, under Ethelwig's rule. One of these was formerly a knight in the service of King William. Reinfrid had taken part in the brutal Harrying of the North, and was travelling through Northumbria when he turned aside to the ruined monastery of Streoneshalc (Whitby), where the desolation of the site, possibly combined with a reaction to the recent devastation, caused him to find a vocation for the monastic life. He found his way to Evesham, doubtless following the stream of refugees, since his choice of this particular monastery with its dominant English abbot is otherwise inexplicable. Reinfrid was admitted to the monastic life, and was soon inspired by the ambition of a visitor to Evesham, Prior Aldwin of Winchcombe, who had read Bede's *Ecclesiastical History of the English*

[62]*Chronicon Abbatiae de Evesham*, pp. 90–1.
[63]Ibid., p. 90; R. R. Darlington, "Aethelwig, abbot of Evesham," *English Historical Review*, 48 (1933), Part II, pp. 177–98.
[64]*English Kalendars before A.D. 1100*, ed. F. Wormald: I, Texts (1934), nos 16–18.

People, and longed to visit, and to live the monastic life, in the sites described in that book, even though these were now in ruins. The third member of the team, which set out in 1073–4, was Elfwy, deacon and monk of Winchcombe. The Bede-age monasteries of Jarrow, Wearmouth and Whitby were directly revived as a result of this mission. Whitby colonized St Mary's, York, while monks from Jarrow and Wearmouth were used to inaugurate the monastic life in Durham cathedral.[65] Abbot Ethelwig would have known the Winchcombe monks, since he had custody of that house in 1066–9.[66] Prior Aldwin's subsequent visit to Evesham was perhaps made in the hope of enlisting Ethelwig's help in obtaining permission for the venture from the new French abbot of Winchcombe. Reinfrid, as a monk of Evesham, would certainly need his own abbot's permission to travel, but Ethelwig's biography makes no comment on the project. Several years went by before the success of the mission became apparent, and by that time Ethelwig had died.

Abbot Ethelwig was a more complex character than he is depicted by the Worcester writers. His biographer readily admitted that Ethelwig's prompt submission to King William in 1066 paid off. The abbot faithfully served the king, and William in turn was well disposed towards him for the rest of his life. While other abbots were losing their lands and possessions, Ethelwig retained all his property, while his status greatly increased. The king, astutely recognizing his ability, appointed him in effect governor of Worcestershire, Gloucestershire, Oxfordshire, Warwickshire, Herefordshire, Staffordshire and Shropshire, which together comprised almost the whole of Earl Edwin's earldom of Mercia, apart from Cheshire where the bulk of the earl's family lands lay. The abbot's knowledge of the law rendered him an expert relied upon by French and English alike in those difficult times. The Evesham chronicler became quite lyrical on the whole subject of Ethelwig's influence.[67] One Worcester writer, in contrast, morosely commented on Ethelwig's expertise in the secular law – after all, he studied no other. He was so powerful, and

[65]*Cartularium Abbathiae de Whiteby,* ed. J. C. Atkinson, 2 vols (1878–9), I, pp. 1–2; "Historia Dunhelmensis Ecclesiae," in *Symeonis Monachi Opera Omnia,* I, pp. 108–9. See also R. H. C. Davis, "Bede after Bede," in *Studies in Medieval History presented to R. Allen Brown,* pp. 103–16; Anne Dawtry, "The Benedictine Revival in the North: the last bulwark of Anglo-Saxon monasticism?" in *Religion and National Identity,* ed. S. Mews (1982), pp. 87–98.
[66]*Chronicon Abbatiae de Evesham,* p. 90.
[67]Ibid. For a wide-ranging discussion of Aethelwig's activities, see Darlington, "Aethelwig, abbot of Evesham," pp. 1–22.

so eloquent, that he could silence any criticism of his actions, even intimidating the Frenchmen.[68]

At Evesham it was said that whenever their abbot was going to hear pleas, or attend the shire court, people flocked to him in droves. So did all those who, in their hour of need, came to petition for his advice and assistance against their enemies.[69] In the wake of the Norman Conquest there were many bitter disputes about property, and a powerful patron such as Ethelwig was much in demand. Many men commended themselves to his protection, with the result that their lands came to be regarded as Evesham's property. Some of these alienated estates were rightfully held of the bishop and cathedral priory, and after Ethelwig's death, Wulfstan needed to rally the more influential Normans and English of the diocese to declare the true facts on oath, before he could obtain a verdict awarding him lands retained by Evesham.[70] Meanwhile it was triumphantly noted at the abbey that earls, sheriffs and barons, conscious of Ethelwig's worldly wisdom, venerated him almost as their lord. Whenever he came to the royal court, or acted in a judicial capacity elsewhere, crowds of obsequious notables flocked around him. He was even able to oblige Archbishop Lanfranc over a lawsuit concerning lands alienated from his cathedral church. Within the diocese of Worcester itself, the newly appointed Abbot Serlo of Gloucester (1072–1104) succeeded to an abbey which was in an extremely impoverished state. He humbly petitioned Ethelwig's help, and Gloucester's troubles were steadily alleviated.[71] A state of affairs in which one abbot of the diocese was effectively regional governor, while another was his client, could only militate against the status of the bishop himself. To the Worcester writers, Ethelwig's conduct was deplorable, particularly in the matter of their alienated estates. Any unavoidable mention of him in their works was unfavourable. The monks of Worcester saw the abbot as a sharp practitioner in the land market, whereas at Evesham it was maintained

---

[68]*Hemingi Chartularium ecclesiae Wigorniensis*, ed. T. Hearne, 2 vols (1723), I, pp. 269–71. Judicial verdicts given by Ethelwig throughout this region perhaps formed the basis of the Mercian law, the existence of which is first recorded in the reign of Henry I: *Leges Henrici Primi*, ed. and transl. L. J. Downer (1972), c. 6, 1; c. 6, 2, p. 97. This text dates from 1114–1118: ibid., pp. 35–6. See also Darlington, "Aethelwig, abbot of Evesham," pp. 12–18.

[69]*Chronicon Abbatiae de Evesham*, p. 89.

[70]*Domesday Book 16: Worcestershire*, Appendix V, Worcs. H; Darlington, "Aethelwig, abbot of Evesham," pp.11–12,18; *Hemingi Chartularium*, I, p. 271.

[71]*Chronicon Abbatiae de Evesham*, pp. 89–90. Gloucester was impoverished because Archbishop Ealdred had taken much of its land in order to recoup his expenses in rebuilding its church: *Historia et Cartularium Monasterii Sancti Petri Gloucestriae*, ed. W. H. Hart, 3 vols (1863, 1865, 1867), I, p. 9; II, p. 119.

that he exchanged estates with the bishop by mutual agreement.[72] Wulfstan himself realized that he needed an ally in those difficult times. Conscious of Ethelwig's influence with the king and the lay magnates, he often consulted him and requested his help, sometimes summoning the abbot, but on other occasions going to visit him. Wulfstan reciprocated with spiritual advice, since he was Ethelwig's confessor.[73]

Throughout the whole of his life, Ethelwig suffered intermittently from attacks of gout in his feet, an ailment which caused him great distress towards the end of his life. He died on 16 February 1077 "full of years" (but age unspecified), and fortified by the Sacraments. Wulfstan decided he ought to intercede for his soul, but he was immediately stricken by the same illness. It was then revealed to him in a vision that he did wrong to pray for someone who had harmed the interests of the church of Worcester. He ceased his prayers for Ethelwig, and was promptly cured.[74] The moral of this story may seem hard-hearted, but to medieval monks, one of their prime duties was to safeguard the inheritance of their patron saint. Ethelwig was regarded at Worcester as a predator on the patrimony of St Mary, hence his unfavourable reputation there, and hence, too, Wulfstan's own guilt-induced physical reaction, even though he had been fulfilling a religious duty in praying for his former penitent.

The death of Ealdred and more especially that of Ethelwig removed from the scene two men who, while they overshadowed Wulfstan in some respects, also acted as his worldly champions and cleared his way through the ramifications of secular politics. The removal of dominating, quasi-parent figures would be a mixed blessing for anyone who had spent many years in a subordinate position, but the withdrawal of their political support and temporal wisdom was amply counterbalanced by Wulfstan's growing reputation as a spiritual leader, while his jurisdictional authority in the region would stand out more sharply in the absence of Ethelwig. Local writers at Evesham, as well as at Worcester, were impressed by Wulfstan's simplicity and goodness.[75] These qualities, joined to the growing belief in his power to work miracles, ensured his

---

[72]*Chronicon Abbatiae de Evesham*, p. 90.

[73]Ibid., pp. 89–90.

[74]The pious end of Ethelwig, recorded by his own biographer (ibid., p. 95), should be contrasted with his wretched demise as seen from Worcester, where it was claimed that he died neither at peace with Wulfstan nor absolved by him, hence Wulfstan's "error" in praying for him: *Hemingi Chartularium*, I, pp. 272–3.

[75]*Chronicon Abbatiae de Evesham*: A religious man, simple and upright," p. 89; "a good man," p. 90; *Hemingi Chartularium*, II, p. 406: "the simplicity of the dove;" *Florentii Wigorniensis monachi Chronicon*, II, p. 24: "a man of great piety and the simplicity of the dove."

reputation as a holy man. With the removal of native secular leadership, the English of Mercia would be more inclined to look to their bishop for authoritative leadership. This enhancement of Wulfstan's stature was perhaps not perceived by those clerics and laymen who had designs on the lands of his church, but his own assimilation of the conduct of the old Celtic and Northumbrian saints would foster in him unconsciously the attitudes and conduct of a charismatic patriarch.

Throughout the diocese, Wulfstan came to be surrounded by Continental abbots, as the English heads of the religious houses gradually died off. At Evesham, Ethelwig was succeeded by Walter (1077–1104), formerly a monk of Caen in Normandy. He had been a chaplain of Archbishop Lanfranc, hence no doubt his promotion. Walter was an erudite young man, but lacked worldly prudence and relied on the advice of certain youthful kinsmen, circumstances which the monks of Evesham thought were largely to blame for the territorial losses which ensued.[76] Winchcombe, from which the outspokenly patriotic Abbot Godric was removed in 1066, was held by Abbot Ethelwig for about three years before Abbot Galand's succession, and again after his death in 1075. The death of Ethelwig in 1077 was followed by a new appointment at Winchcombe, where Ralph (1077–93) inauguarated a line of abbots of Continental stock.[77] Pershore's English abbot Edmund died in 1085,[78] and Wulfstan's former colleague Wilstan, latterly abbot of Gloucester, died in 1072 while on a pilgrimage to Jerusalem.[79] His successor, the Norman Serlo, was on good terms with Wulfstan, and even visited him during his last illness.[80] Close contact between them probably accounts for the artistic influences of Worcester origin which can be traced in the architecture at Gloucester, and even in the abbot's seal.[81] During Wulfstan's lifetime, Tewkesbury probably had minster status and re-

[76]*Chronicon Abbatiae de Evesham*, p. 96.

[77]Ibid., p. 90; *The Heads of Religious Houses England and Wales 940–1216*, ed. D. Knowles, C. N. L. Brooke and Vera C. M. London (1972), p. 79.

[78]*Florentii Wigorniensis monachi Chronicon*, II, p. 18; Winchcombe Annals 1049–1181, ed. R. R. Darlington, in *A Medieval Miscellany for Doris Mary Stenton*, ed. Patricia M. Barnes and C. F. Slade (1962), p. 118.

[79]*Historia et Cartularium Monasterii Sancti Petri Gloucestriae*, I, p. 9.

[80]*Vita Wulfstani*, pp. 37–8, 61.

[81]On the probable influences of Wulfstan's new cathedral upon the abbey church, see Christopher Wilson, "Abbot Serlo's church at Gloucester (1089–1100): its place in Romanesque architecture," in *Medieval Art and Architecture at Gloucester and Tewkesbury*, ed. T. A. Heslop and V. A. Sekules (1985), pp. 52–83. On the abbey's seal, which appears to date from after Wulfstan's death, see T. A. Heslop, "Seals," in *English Romanesque Art 1066–1200*, ed. G. Zarnecki, Janet Holt and T. Holland (1984), no. 350.

mained a dependency of Cranborne in Dorset.[82] Abbot Gerald evidently made frequent visits to Tewkesbury, since his acquaintance with Wulfstan was close enough for him to visit Wulfstan as he lay dying.[83] The new monasteries founded in the adjacent diocese at Shrewsbury, c.1083[84] and Chester in 1092–3[85] had Norman heads from the outset.

One of the largest of the monastic landholders in the diocese was the abbot of Westminster, thanks to King Edward's expropriation of much of Pershore's property so that it could be used to enlarge the endowments of his designated mausoleum.[86] Evidence from the latter part of Henry I's reign shows that the abbot of Westminster was then accustomed to make an occasional tour of his properties in the West Midlands, including the cell of Great Malvern.[87] But this house was founded only in the later eleventh century,[88] and since Westminster's lands in the region were largely held at farm (held by tenants on long leases) in this period, the Norman successors of Abbot Edwin (d. 1068) had little reason to visit Wulfstan's diocese.[89] During his lifetime, only the small houses, Great Malvern, and Westbury-on-Trym, which was dependent on Worcester, retained English heads.[90] The English bishop of Worcester might strive to lessen the impact of the Norman Conquest upon the monastic life of his diocese, but Benedictine abbots exercised considerable autonomy. The abbeys retained their pre-existing complement of English monks who would prefer to observe traditional practices. Such inclinations might be uncongenial to a new and alien head of house. At Glastonbury, in the neighbouring diocese of Wells, the monks persisted in conducting the liturgy according to native traditions, whereupon the Norman Abbot,

[82] D. Knowles and R. N. Hadcock, *Medieval Religious Houses England and Wales* (1971), pp. 63, 77–8; Knowles et al., *Heads of Religious Houses*, pp. 73, 87.

[83] *Vita Wulfstani*, p. 61. Gerald is styled abbot of Tewkesbury, presumably an editorial amendment by William of Malmesbury.

[84] *Ecclesiastical History of Orderic Vitalis*, III, p. 146; cf. Knowles et al., *Heads of Religious Houses*, p. 71.

[85] *Heads of Religious Houses*, p. 39.

[86] Barbara Harvey, *Westminster Abbey and its estates in the Middle Ages* (1977), pp. 26–7, 344–5, 360–4.

[87] *Westminster Abbey Charters 1066–c.1214*, ed. Emma Mason assisted by the late Jennifer Bray, continuing the work of the late Desmond J. Murphy (1988), no.248a.

[88] *Vita Wulfstani*, pp. xli–xlii, 26; Annals of Worcester Cathedral Priory, *Annales Monastici*, IV, p. 373.

[89] Late and questionable evidence depicts the Westminster monks Hugh and Warner perambulating lands adjoining Powick (Worcs), given to Great Malvern by Abbot Gilbert Crispin of Westminster: *Westminster Abbey Charters*, no. 243, note.

[90] *Vita Wulfstani*, pp. 26, 51.

Thurstan, installed archers in the choir loft, with orders to shoot down the disobedient brethren. A massacre ensued.[91]

In Worcester cathedral itself, the English bishop and his brother, Prior Alfstan, could ensure continuity in the liturgy as in other matters. But when the prior died, some time between 1077 and 1080,[92] his successor was Thomas. This man was probably a Frenchman, conspicuous among the English *seniores* when they witnessed an episcopal charter.[93] It may be that the king insisted on an outside appointment so that a watching brief could be maintained on this centre of English sympathies. Even in Worcester itself, there were some changes in the religious observance, notably in the introduction of the feasts of the Blessed Virgin. Whether these would have been adopted without the impetus of the Normans is conjectural. In the event, they were perhaps among the new ideas which Nicholas brought back from Canterbury.[94]

The marked increase in the numbers of monks in the diocese, notably at Worcester and Evesham, can more confidently be attributed to the effects of the Norman Conquest. At Evesham, the increase from twelve monks to thirty-six took place before Ethelwig's death in 1077,[95] while in 1089 Wulfstan declared that during his time at Worcester, its monastic inmates had risen from twelve to fifty.[96] These two men, eminent in their different ways, were likely to attract a steady flow of recruits. Monasteries governed by notable Englishmen would have a special attraction for members of dispossessed English families. Both Wulfstan and Ethelwig presided over chapters which were largely English in composition, but since Wulfstan survived Ethelwig by nearly eighteen years, it is not surprising that there is some evidence of Norman recruitment towards

[91]There are several accounts of the Glastonbury massacre, including *Anglo-Saxon Chronicle*, 1083 (E); William of Malmesbury, *The Early History of Glastonbury*, ed. J. Scott (1981), pp. 156–8; 209; *Florentii Wigorniensis monachi Chronicon*, II, pp. 16–17; *Ecclesiastical History of Orderic Vitalis*, II, p. 270. See also D. Hiley, "Thurstan of Caen and Plainchant at Glastonbury: Musicological Reflections on the Norman Conquest," *Proceedings of the British Academy*, 72 (1986), pp. 57–90.

[92]Prior Alfstan's *obit* was commemorated on 16 August: I. Atkins, "The Church of Worcester from the Eighth to the Twelfth Centuries," Part II, *The Antiquaries Journal*, 20 (1940), p. 32. For the year of his death, see John Le Neve, *Fasti Ecclesiae Anglicanae 1066–1300. II Monastic Cathedrals*, p. 102 and note 3; *Cartulary of Worcester*, no. 304 and note.

[93]The Alveston charter, dated 20 May 1089, was attested by the senior monks, and the lay officials of the bishop. Almost all the witnesses had English names, apart from Prior Thomas, and Urse the sheriff, although Fritheric the chaplain was perhaps of Continental origin: *Cartulary of Worcester*, no. 3.

[94]Gibson, *Lanfranc of Bec*, p. 171 and note 1.

[95]*Chronicon Abbatiae de Evesham*, p. 96.

[96]*Cartulary of Worcester Cathedral Priory*, no. 3.

the end of his episcopate.[97] On a smaller scale, a new wave of recruitment can also be discerned at Gloucester. When Abbot Wilstan died in 1072, the Norman Serlo succeeded to a house where there were two monks of full age and "about eight little young ones."[98] Gloucester was a newer and poorer foundation than either Worcester or Evesham, and Wilstan, whatever his merits, did not enjoy the reputation of Wulfstan or Ethelwig. Yet the presence at Gloucester of the eight little *oblates* provides the clue to the success of the other houses. The real impact of the Norman tenurial settlement in Mercia was felt after the revolts of 1068 and 1069. By the early 1070s, many English families, driven from their estates, would see a monastic life as the only viable future for their sons. At Worcester, this increase in the numbers of monks in the wake of the Norman Conquest called for tenurial readjustments. The one-hide manor of Knightwick was among those lands whose revenues were assigned to providing food for the monks. In the reign of King Edward, while monastic numbers were low, this estate was leased to the nun Edith, to hold for as long as it suited the brethren, and they had no need of it. But when the community grew in the reign of King William, she restored it.[99] This first wave of English recruits would be supplemented, from the 1080s and 1090s, by increasing numbers of French, as the new settlers raised families of their own. They too would have younger sons for whom the monastic life was the obvious choice, if small fiefs were not to become overburdened.

The changes resulting from the Norman Conquest also had an impact on Wulfstan's secular activities, although in many respects his position remained unchanged. He was still expected to attend the royal court, and along with neighbouring magnates, he was required to take some part in the administration of his own region. Since his *Life* is written from a spiritual standpoint, it contains little evidence on activities which would in practice occupy a good deal of his time. The pro-English sentiment prevailing at Worcester was a subsidiary reason why minimal treatment should be given to Wulfstan's activities on behalf of the Norman regime. The reader is told that William I never did anything to annoy Wulfstan. He treated the bishop with great reverence, loving him as a father, and

[97]The lists of monks of Evesham and of Worcester, sent to Durham *c.*1104, may be compared with the names of Evesham monks (virtually all of them English), compiled *c.*1077; Atkins: "The Church of Worcester from the Eighth to the Twelfth Centuries," Part II, pp. 215–16, 218–19.
[98]*Historia et Cartularium Monasterii Sancti Petri Gloucestriae*, I, p. 10.
[99]*Domesday Book 16: Worcestershire*, 2:67. It is likely that the priory's estates were largely managed so as to provide food rents: see Hamshere,"Domesday Book: Estate Structures in the West Midlands," pp. 168–9.

speaking of him as one. The practical consequence of this was that Wulfstan was able to recover lands which had earlier been appropriated by Danish settlers, by Earl Leofric of Mercia and his kindred, or by Archbishop Ealdred.[100] But the *Life* does not discuss in any detail the working relationship between king and bishop. Inevitably it was not a close one, as it had been in Harold's brief reign. The very fact that Wulfstan had been so close to the man whom William regarded as a ursurper meant that the onus was now on the bishop to prove himself conspicuously loyal and diligent. Wulfstan's conduct while he was actually at the royal court is not discussed in his *Life*, but there are accounts of sensational incidents which occurred when he was on his way there.

On one such journey, Wulfstan was travelling towards London (perhaps actually to Westminster, which lay outside the walls of the city). He stopped overnight with his retinue at Wycombe in Buckinghamshire, where the whole party, baggage animals included, were lodged in one old building, its roof on the point of collapse. Just as they were preparing to leave in the morning, the whole house began to creak, and the roof-posts and beams started to give way. The panic-stricken servants rushed out, forgetting that Wulfstan was left alone inside. When they realized where he was, instead of going back in, they stood in the doorway, shouting to him to escape before the whole building fell down. Not one of them was prepared to risk his own life by going in to save the bishop. But Wulfstan stayed calm, saying, "You haven't any faith: do you think I will be engulfed in this ruin?" He refused to go outside until he had supervised the rescue of the tethered packhorses. As soon as he came out himself, the whole house crashed down with a terrible noise, its walls and roof collapsing on one another in a heap of rubble.[101] This episode says more for Wulfstan's presence of mind than it does for the devotion of his retinue, and is one of several stories which suggest that his entourage of clerks and secular servants was less devoted to him than was the inner circle of his monastic community. This story also demonstrates the inconveniences to which travellers were exposed. In the absence of a handy monastery in which they might lodge overnight, they – and their animals – had to take whatever accommodation was available. Even when the outcome was not so sensational, conditions must often have been cramped and squalid.

On another occasion, Wulfstan and his retinue were travelling to Winchester for the Easter court and its solemn crown-wearing. They came across a Frenchman lying in the road, suffering agonizing abdom-

---

[100]*Vita Wulfstani*, p. 24.
[101]Ibid., pp. 31–2.

inal pain. Passers-by were sympathetic, but could offer no remedy. When Wulfstan noticed him he dismounted from his horse. His companions also jumped down, crowding round the sick Frenchman, who could hear their horses snorting but could not see what was happening. He asked those who understood French what was going on, and was told that Bishop Wulfstan and his entourage had arrived. Since even the French had heard of Wulfstan, the man immediately asked him for a blessing. Wulfstan offered him some consecrated water from a drinking-horn, and prayed for him at the same time. When the man recovered and stood up, Wulfstan continued on his way to Winchester.[102] The distress of the ailing Frenchman, and the gist of his request, would have been apparent even if the bishop's own French was minimal. Yet as a regular habitué of the seasonal royal courts, Wulfstan probably heard enough French to use that language in a basic conversation. By analogy, the twelfth-century English hermit, Godric of Finchale, acquired conversational French at a mature age, despite lacking Wulfstan's educational background.[103]

When in attendance at the royal court, Wulfstan joined other magnates in witnessing grants and mandates which were recorded in writs and charters. The chances of survival of such documents are variable: those received by ecclesiastics had a better chance of preservation in this period than those issued to laymen. Churchmen, on the other hand, were more likely to perceive the legal and financial advantages to be gained from tampering with such texts, and also possessed the skills to make the desired amendments. Bearing in mind such uncertainties about the extent and reliability of the surviving evidence, it can be shown with reasonable confidence that Wulfstan witnessed charters and writs of King William I at Windsor at Pentecost 1072[104] (when Wulfstan's dispute with Archbishop Thomas was also heard), and Winchester on 31 May 1081.[105] He also witnessed one charter of William Rufus issued at Lincoln in May 1090[106] and another issued at Dover in January 1091.[107]

[102]Ibid., pp. 34–5.

[103]Reginald of Durham, *Libellus de vita et miraculis Sancti Godrici, heremitae de Finchale*, ed. J. Stevenson (1847), pp. 203–4, 206; Victoria Tudor, "Reginald of Durham and Saint Godric of Finchale: learning and religion on a personal level," in *Religion and Humanism*, ed. K. Robbins (1981), p. 46. See also I. Short, "On Bilingualism in Anglo-Norman England," *Romance Philology* 33:4 (1980), pp. 467–79, esp. pp. 474–7.

[104]*Regesta Regum Anglo-Normannorum, 1066–1154: I. 1066–1100*, ed. H. W. C. Davis with R. J. Whitwell (1913), nos 64–5.

[105]Ibid., I, no. 137.

[106]Ibid., I, no. 328, to be read in conjunction with *Regesta Regum Anglo-Normannorum II: Regesta Henrici Primi: 1100–1135*, ed. C. Johnson and H. A. Cronne (1956), p. 400, where a date of 24 September 1090 is suggested.

[107]*Regesta Regum Anglo-Normannorum*, I, no. 315.

Wulfstan is also named as a witness to several documents of doubtful authenticity. Whereas some clerical archivists would enlarge the substance of a grant, leaving the original witness-list, place and date of issue (where given) intact, others tried to antedate grants, or to gain credibility for dubious texts, by adding these crucial details, including a witness-list, which might be taken from another, genuine, charter. Wulfstan's attestation appears on ten documents which are suspect for one such reason or another. All of these purport to have been issued by William I, and where a place of issue is named, this is most often London or Westminster.[108] So far as any conclusions can be drawn from Wulfstan's attestations as a whole, these are that he attended the court of William I, and was believed by monastic archivists to have attended it, only at the major seasonal festivals. It seems that he was not summoned to attend the king at other times of the year, nor at places other than those where the solemn courts were customarily held. This pattern of attendance is what might be expected of an ageing English prelate. His presence was required on formal occasions, but he was not a chosen counsellor required to advise on the ongoing problems of government. Similarly those charters of William Rufus which he attested were clearly issued in large formal gatherings. It is a tribute to Wulfstan's stamina that he was still physically capable in this reign of attending courts far away from his diocese. The gathering at Dover in January 1091 was perhaps his last such major expedition. All available magnates of church and state were summoned to take formal leave of the king before he embarked on a campaign in Normandy, but there was no intention that Wulfstan or numerous other venerable dignitaries should risk the Channel crossing.[109] The journeys to Lincoln and Dover in this reign would be the more taxing for Wulfstan in that his health was already failing by 1090.[110]

While attendance at the royal court was physically taxing, a regular and perhaps increasingly uncongenial demand on Wulfstan's time and energies, the summons to attend was a recognition of his status, and attendance was a duty he owed not only to the king but also to the dignity of his bishopric. Formal gatherings of the royal court also

---

[108]Ibid., I, nos 11, 34, 90, 95, 141, 144, 148, 196, 197, 262.

[109]On the circumstances in which this charter was issued, see F. Barlow, *William Rufus* (1983), pp. 277–80.

[110]In the account of the vision in which Wulfstan announced his death to Robert, bishop of Hereford, the latter's response was that Wulfstan was then (January 1095) looking fitter than he had done for the past five years: *Vita Wulfstani*, p. 63. In a charter of 1092, Wulfstan stated that he believed he was approaching the end of his life: *Cartulary of Worcester*, no. 52. Ill-health caused his absence from the consecration of Archbishop Anselm in 1093, and from the ensuing Christmas court; Barlow, *William Rufus*, p. 326.

afforded an opportunity to petition the king for favours, but the surviving evidence suggests that Wulfstan's success in this area was limited. Two royal grants date from early in William I's reign. The king assigned to Wulfstan and the monks the vill of Cookley in Worcestershire,[111] and issued another charter in this period, presumably at Wulfstan's request, confirming to Prior Alfstan and the monks all their customary rights in their properties as they held them in previous reigns.[112] Royal grants were only to be obtained at a price, usually a high one.

Three further documents which Wulfstan received from the king, or on his authority, relate to his major dispute with Abbot Walter of Evesham concerning their respective rights in Hampton (Warwicks) and Bengeworth (Worcs). This dispute was the latest, but as it transpired, the last, in a series of conflicts waged intermittently between Worcester and Evesham over several generations. In the aftermath of the anti-monastic reaction of the late tenth century, the fortunes of Evesham were slow to rally and their successful revival dated only from the reign of Cnut. In an attempt to secure those lands which they claimed as their own, the monks of Evesham produced a number of forged charters during the earlier eleventh century.[113] The powerful position of Abbot Ethelwig enabled Evesham both to withstand Worcester's claims to disputed lands and jurisdiction and to attract the commended service of many men who were in reality tenants of Worcester. After the death of Ethelwig in 1077 the rights of Worcester were reasserted. The earlier documents relating to the re-opened dispute date from between 1079 and 1083. The first of these is a writ of William I, addressed to Archbishop Lanfranc and Geoffrey, bishop of Coutances, ordering them to settle the dispute over jurisdiction (*sac* and *soc*) between Bishop Wulfstan and Abbot Walter. Matters were to be arranged as they were in the reign of King Edward, when the tax was last levied for the building of (Worcester's) ship. Bishop Geoffrey was to do justice in the king's place, and to see that Bishop Wulfstan had those houses in Worcester which he claimed against the abbot. Geoffrey was specifically instructed to ensure that all tenants of the bishop of

---

[111]*Regesta Regum Anglo-Normannorum*, I, no. 10; *Cartulary of Worcester* no. 23. It is argued (ibid., pp. xix–xx) that either William I issued two charters relating to Cookley, or that the monks forged the version which apears in this Cartulary.

[112]*Regesta Regum Anglo-Normannorum*, I, no. 252; *Cartulary of Worcester* no. 2.

[113]The texts of almost all of Evesham's charters dating, or purporting to date, from before 1066 have been amended to some extent, and several are blatant forgeries. The most dubious documents include: *Anglo-Saxon Charters: an annotated list and bibliography*, compiled P. H. Sawyer (1968), nos 78–81, 83, 112, 122, 226, 957, 1174–5, 1214, 1250–1, 1398, 1479. See also D. C. Cox, "The Vale Estates of the Church of Evesham *c*.700–1086," *Vale of Evesham Historical Society Papers*, 5 (1975), pp. 25–50.

Worcester were prepared to render the service they owed to Wulfstan and to the king.[114] The real issue, therefore, was less the actual possession of the land than the enforcement of services due to Worcester.

A narrative account of the proceedings made at Worcester named the prominent English and French men of the region who testified on Wulfstan's behalf as reliable witnesses concerning the position in King Edward's reign. The first-named of these was Edric, formerly leader of the bishop's military contingent. In his capacity as the former steersman of the episcopal ship, he would know what service was due from each tenancy in the shipsoke of Worcester. The other witnesses included Kyneward, the last English sheriff of Worcester; Siward, "a rich man from Shropshire" – a grandson of the notorious Edric Streona and great-grandson of King Ethelred; and Osbern Fitz Richard – this narrative discreetly omits to mention that he was also a judge in the case. Osbern, although "French," was in a position to give evidence since he was a descendant of a Norman marcher lord introduced by King Edward, and not one of the recent wave of immigrants. Osbern had assimilated to the extent of marrying a Welsh wife, and he was also a benefactor of the cathedral priory. The last of the named witnesses was Thorkell "of Warwickshire," one of the few major English landholders to survive the Norman settlement with their estates largely intact. Wulfstan himself held estates in Warwickshire, which was one good reason for enlisting the help of this influential man, although circumstantial evidence suggests that Thorkell was also his kinsman.[115] Many other, unnamed "elders and nobles" supported the bishop. Even at the preliminary hearing, it was apparent that virtually everyone of consequence in the diocese supported Wulfstan. Abbot Walter, lacking support among the living, obtained permission to bring relics to vindicate the rights of Evesham, but in the event, not even the body of St Egwuin sufficed to

---

[114]*Regesta Regum Anglo-Normannorum*, I, no. 184.

[115]*Domesday Book 16: Worcestershire*, Appendix V, Worcester H 2, is a narrative account of the trial. On Siward see Ann Williams, "'Cockles among the Wheat:' Danes and English in the Western Midlands in the first half of the Eleventh Century," *Midland History*, 11 (1987), p. 17, note 17. For Osbern Fitz Richard, see *Cartulary of Worcester*, pp.xxxiii–xxxiv. For Thorkell's extensive lands see *Domesday Book 23: Warwickshire*, ed. J. Morris (1976), no. 17. Thorkell's paternal grandfather Beorthtwine can be identified with the Bricstuin who held 7.5 hides in Alveston in King Edward's reign (ibid., 3:4); Ann Williams, "A Vice-Comital family in pre-Conquest Warwickshire," *Anglo-Norman Studies XI*, ed. R. Allen Brown (1989), pp. 279–95, esp. pp. 280, 282, 293. The jurisdiction over this land pertained at that time to Archbishop Ealdred, but Bricstuin served Earl Leofric, and his sons afterwards held this estate from the earl. This alienation of an estate claimed by the church of Worcester suggests that Bricstuin can be identified with Wulfstan's brother Byrcstan, the man whose kinship with the bishop was discreetly recorded in cypher: cf. Atkins, "The Church of Worcester from the Eighth to the Twelfth Centuries," Part II, p. 30.

uphold his case. On the day of the formal trial, at the point when the solemn oaths were to be taken, testifying to the rights of the respective claimants, Walter's advisers persuaded him to concede the whole case. Wulfstan was also assured of the support of the men at arms who served the cathedral church. During the trial, they observed Abbot Walter's brother Ranulf, a co-litigant against the bishop. They declared that if Ranulf tried to contest the verdict, they were ready to wage judicial combat against him. Similarly, several of the clergy loyally announced that they were prepared to take an oath on the Blessed Sacrament, to uphold the bishop's rights.[116] This widespread support, combined perhaps with the fact that two of the judges, Urse de Abetot and Osbern Fitz Richard, were themselves holding lands claimed by Abbot Walter,[117] ensured Wulfstan's resounding victory. Walter did not have the stature to maintain Abbot Ethelwig's position.

On the conclusion of the case, Wulfstan obtained a second writ from the king, notifying the sheriff of Worcestershire, Urse de Abetot; the prominent local magnate, Osbern (Fitz Richard) Fitz Scrob; and the French and English men of Worcestershire of the adjudication in favour of the bishop. Wulfstan was to have *sac* and *soc* (rights of local jurisdiction), with the services and customary rights pertaining to his hundred of Oswaldslow, as he held them in the time of King Edward. He was also to have the service of the four hides at Bengeworth and the houses in the city of Worcester which he proved that the abbot of Evesham held of him. Wulfstan had also proved his right to certain dues from fifteen hides in Hampton: namely *soc*, geld, *expeditio* (the levying of military service), church-scot and burial fees. No-one was to hold these rights in defiance of his own. All the foregoing were to be held as he proved his right, by witness of the suitors of the shire court, before Bishop Geoffrey of Coutances, together with Urse and Osbern themselves. The royal writ was witnessed by Bishop Geoffrey.[118] While the recipients were fully acquainted with the outcome of the lawsuit, this formally worded document would serve as an official guarantee of the

---

[116]*Domesday Book 16: Worcestershire*, Appendix V, Worcester H 2. Abbot Walter's brother Ranulf was probably the man of that name who held land of the church of Evesham in Abbot's Morton (ibid., 10:13); and in Kinwarton (*Domesday Book 23: Warwickshire*, ed. J. Morris (1976), 11:4). The proceedings in this plea may be compared with those in another celebrated lawsuit of the period over which Geoffrey of Coutances also presided: D. R. Bates, "The Land Pleas of William I's Reign; Penenden Heath Revisited," *Bulletin of the Institute of Historical Research*, 51 (1978), pp. 1–19.

[117]*Regesta Regum Anglo-Normannorum*, I, nos 185–6; cf. *Domesday Book 16: Worcestershire*, 10:12; *Domesday Book 23: Warwickshire*, 37:5.

[118]*Regesta Regum Anglo-Normannorum*, I, no. 230.

bishop's rights, in the event of any revival of the dispute. The support of so many powerful interests had ensured Wulfstan's victory, but the tenants of the disputed lands did not perceive the issue in quite the same light.

When the Domesday Survey was made in 1086, the evidence given concerning both Hampton and Bengeworth effectively revived the earlier claims of the abbot.[119] It was probably for this reason that Wulfstan petitioned for the issue of a certificated summary of the earlier verdict. Bishop Geoffrey accordingly addressed the Domesday commissioners for Worcestershire: Rémy, bishop of Lincoln; Walter Giffard; Henry de Ferrers and Adam de Port, formally notifying them that he had heard the dispute between bishop and abbot. Bishop Wulfstan had proved his title to the contested three hides of land in Bengeworth, and houses in the city of Worcester. Consequently Abbot Walter owed service for them like any other vassal of the bishop. Wulfstan had also proved his claim that *sac* and *soc* over Hampton pertained to the episcopal hundred of Oswaldslow, and that the men of Hampton ought to pay their share of geld and host-service and other lawful charges from the fifteen hides there. They also owed church-scot and burial dues at the bishop's vill of Cropthorne. The bishop's title to all the foregoing was proved on oath before Bishop Geoffrey, Urse de Abetot, Osbern (Fitz Richard) Fitz Scrob and other barons of the realm, as the verdict of the shire court.[120] The Domesday commissioners considered this written submission, and then negotiated a compromise between Bishop Wulfstan and Abbot Walter. This was publicly confirmed by the commissioners before the whole monastic community of Worcester (probably in the chapter house of the cathedral), together with many of the monks of Evesham. The fifteen hides of land in Hampton were declared to pertain to the bishop's hundred of Oswaldslow. Royal dues and services should therefore be rendered from this land, and the bishop should be invited to hold pleas there. These requirements also pertained to the four hides in Bengeworth. In addition to the dues and services, the bishop was now claiming all the actual land as his lordship, and the abbot humbly acknowledged Wulfstan's rights. At the request of the commissioners, Wulfstan granted the land to the abbot and monks of Evesham, but on condition that Walter gave him as honourable an acknowledgement (of his overlordship) as he required, and rendered the services for as long as he required. This compromise was witnessed by Abbot Serlo of Gloucester, together with several of the

[119]*Domesday Book 16: Worcestershire*, 2: 74–5; cf. 10:11–12.
[120]Ibid., Appendix V, Worcester H, no. 4; *Regesta Regum Anglo-Normannorum*, I, no. 221.

staff of Bishop Rémy, Archdeacon Ailric, and several substantial lay tenants.[121]

Wulfstan's assertive tactics throughout this dispute, and his enlistment of such powerful allies, both at national and regional level, appear somewhat out of keeping with the image of his simplicity which was so assiduously projected by the Worcester writers. Yet persistence in upholding the rights of his church was a duty he owed both to his monastic community and to his predecessors. To the monks of Worcester, the success with which Wulfstan defended their patrimony was a guarantee that he was a worthy bishop, whose efforts were sustained by Divine approval. There need be no inconsistency between simplicity of life and a concern for the pastoral welfare of his diocese, on the one hand, and on the other a determination to enlist all possible support in defending the temporal interests of his church.

As diocesan bishop, and a major landholder, Wulfstan himself was required to take some part in supervising the routine secular administration of Gloucestershire, Warwickshire and Worcestershire. He is addressed with other eminent men in a number of writs in which the king announced that he had granted or restored land to named individuals, sometimes with specific rights of local jurisdiction, or with fiscal exemptions.[122] In the event of these rights, or of actual possession, being challenged, it was the responsibility of those addressed in the document to see that the beneficiary's entitlement was upheld. Some of Wulfstan's colleagues in this task were fellow prelates, but an increasing preponderance of laymen is found in the later writs. The full range and time-span of Wulfstan's activity in this field is uncertain, given the variable survival rate of such documents. Occasionally he is one of those notified in writs which, in their present form, are of doubtful authenticity, but in several cases where genuine royal grants have subsequently been amended by the beneficiary, the list of those notified is genuine.[123]

During the earlier years of Wulfstan's episcopate, the shire court was the venue for both ecclesiastical and secular lawsuits. It is known that on one occasion, in the earlier part of William I's reign, Wulfstan acted as adjudicator in a suit in which estates in the region were awarded to the abbot of Westminster.[124] In comparison with ecclesiastical cases, secular litigation is said to have held little interest for Wulfstan. It was reported that when a secular suit began, Wulfstan disdainfully fell asleep.[125]

---

[121]*Domesday Book 16: Worcestershire*, Appendix V, Worcester H, no. 5.
[122]*Regesta Regum Anglo-Normannorum*, I, nos 9, 32, 186, 252 (this writ concerned Prior Alfstan).
[123]ibid., I, nos 36, 104, 106 (all probably forgeries); 245, 282 (both questionable).
[124]Ibid., I, no. 213.
[125]William of Malmesbury, *De Gestis Pontificum Anglorum*, p. 282.

Possibly he did, given his extended round of prayer late at night and early in the morning, combined with his advancing years. Since he could fall asleep in the king's court, even when lands of the church of Worcester were at stake, no doubt he could readily doze off in the shire court when the case held no interest for him. What is more certain is that the writer of a work of hagiography would want his readers to believe that Wulfstan did not waste his energies on secular wrangling. In due course, William I issued a writ ordering that ecclesiastical cases should be heard only in church courts.[126] But it did not relate to the secular proceedings in shire courts, so that even after his ruling, the bishop was still involved in major matters of secular administration, and some of the writs in which he is addressed appear to date from quite late in the reign of William I.[127] Wulfstan's obligation to participate in secular government was inherent in his status as a diocesan bishop, and not a task newly imposed after the Norman Conquest. Yet there is little evidence for his work in this field before 1066, so that any discussion of it necessarily focuses on the later period.

The biggest single administrative task imposed by William I on his servants was the compilation of the Domesday Survey in 1086. The king made his decision to conduct this enquiry after much deliberation at the Christmas court of 1085, which convened at Gloucester,[128] in Wulfstan's own diocese, and a mere boat-trip downriver from his cathedral. It is highly probable that he participated in this celebrated gathering, and given his own lengthy experience in documenting and recovering the lands of the church of Worcester, he was well-equipped to contribute some worthwhile observations. The Worcester writers do not say that he was actively involved in the compilation of the Survey, as a commissioner, although the selective bias in their works renders it unlikely that they would in any case have recorded his participation.[129] Those chosen as commissioners were always required to serve well away from the region where they held their estates. For the most part, the names of the

---

[126]*English Historical Documents, II. 1042–1189*, ed. D. C. Douglas and G. W. Greenaway, second edn (1981), no. 79. this writ dates from 1072–6, and probably from April 1072.
[127]*Regesta Regum Anglo-Normannorum*, I, no. 186, which probably dates from 1079–83, and the questionable no. 282, apparently dating from 1080–7.
[128]*Anglo-Saxon Chronicle*, 1085 (E). For a review of recent literature on the Domesday Survey, see W. E. Kapelle, "Domesday Book: F. W. Maitland and His Successors," *Speculum*, 64 (1989),pp. 620–40.
[129]The question of Wulfstan's participation in the making of the Survey is discussed by H. R. Loyn, "William's bishops: some further thoughts," *Anglo-Norman Studies X*, ed. R. Allen Brown (1988), pp. 223–35, esp. 229. Dr Ann Williams has pointed out in conversation that Wulfstan would be admirably qualified to preside over the York circuit.

commissioners are not known: those who served in Worcestershire are identified only from the documents arising out of Wulfstan's lawsuit against Abbot Walter of Evesham. If Wulfstan was required to act as a commissioner his previous knowledge of the north would make him a particularly suitable choice for Yorkshire (the Survey did not extend beyond the Tees). By 1086 the bishop was in his late seventies, but thanks to his disciplined lifestyle, he was capable of travelling long distances for years to come, as shown by his attestations to charters drawn up at the royal court.

Whether or not the bishop's age excused him from taking part in the Domesday Survey, he still shared responsibility for the military defence of his cathedral city. During the rebellion of 1075, when Wulfstan was already about sixty-seven years old, he, together with Abbot Ethelwig, Urse de Abetot, sheriff of Worcester, and Walter de Lacy, held the line of the Severn against the dissident Earl Roger of Hereford, to prevent him from crossing eastwards to link up with his ally, the earl of East Anglia. As sheriff, Urse had overall responsibility for the military readiness of the shire, but the bishop and the abbot both held extensive franchises outside his control. Wulfstan is said to have participated with a large fighting force (*cum magna militari manu*), and Ethelwig also led a contingent. While the abbot owed the crown the service of only five knights, as against Wulfstan's *servitium debitum* of fifty, both would have additionally mustered those of their other tenants capable of serving as footsoldiers. Some of the thegns of Oswaldslow were probably still active, and would also have been summoned in this dire threat to the diocese.[130] As churchmen, Wulfstan and Ethelwig were debarred from wielding the sword, and neither is known on other occasions to have been among those fighting prelates who recur in eleventh-century history. There is no account of any military engagement in this region, so that once the bishop and abbot had deployed their troops, they had perhaps only to join in discussions on defensive tactics. Given the threat to their own lands, they had every reason to co-operate in this campaign. Moreoover, while they were both known to be loyal to the government of William I, it was as well that they were seen to be so zealous, especially in view of the inadvertent involvement in the conspiracy of the last

<hr>

[130]*Florentii Wigorniensis monachi Chronicon*, II, p. 11, *sub an.* 1074. *Anglo-Saxon Chronicle* correctly dates the revolt to 1075 (D, E). While the D text is vague about Earl Roger's activities in the Welsh Marches, the E text states that "Roger went west to his earldom, and assembled his people for the king's undoing, but he was prevented." The military forces commanded by Wulfstan and Ethelwig are discussed below.

surviving English noble, Waltheof earl of Northampton. His failure to disclose the plot cost him his head.[131]

In 1088 there occurred a widespread rebellion, in support of Duke Robert Curthose, the elder brother of King William Rufus. In the Welsh marches, the ringleaders were Bernard of Neufmarché, Roger de Lacy and Ralf de Mortimer who, with their sworn associates and the men of Roger, earl of Shrewsbury, invaded Worcestershire with a great army of English, Normans and Welsh. As they advanced, they devastated the rural settlements in their path, until they reached the gates of Worcester. Their declared intention was to burn the city, taking a great revenge on its loyal inhabitants, loot the cathedral and seize the royal castle.[132] Wulfstan had overall charge of the defence. The sheriff, Urse de Abetot, is not mentioned in any of the accounts of this attack, and was probably involved in military operations further afield.

The approach of the large rebel force was very worrying for Wulfstan – by this time aged about eighty. When his military experts pointed out the gravity of the situation, he was at first distressed in case he proved unable to fulfil his obligation to maintain the defences satisfactorily. Two accounts state that he had been formally entrusted with the defence of the castle.[133] In his hour of need, he invoked God in intense prayer, prostrating himself before the altar.[134] Then, "like a second Moses," and trusting in the Divine Mercy, he took active measures to defend his people and city. Arms were prepared for deployment against the enemy, while at the same time the bishop urged his men to put their trust in God, who fights neither with sword nor spear. While he was still addressing his own men, the royal troops entered the council chamber, and begged the bishop to go across from the cathedral to the castle, saying that they would feel safer if he was with them, for they loved him dearly.[135] By this date Wulfstan's reputation as a holy man was evidently as strong among the French as among the English. The request of the garrison might be seen as a ploy to ensure the safety of the venerable bishop, since the sanctuary of his cathedral would offer little protection once looters broke in. Yet the request was evidently made, and understood, on the premise that Wulfstan's sanctity, and his wonder-working powers., would ensure

[131]For Earl Waltheof, see *Anglo-Saxon Chronicle* (D, E), for 1075 and 1076, and for a more sympathetic account of his activities, *Ecclesiastical History of Orderic Vitalis*, vol. II, pp. 312–14, 320–2.
[132]*Florentii Wigorniensis monachi Chronicon*, II, p. 24; William of Malmesbury, *De Gestis Regum Anglorum*, II, p. 361; Henry of Huntingdon, *Historia Anglorum*, ed. T. Arnold (1879); *Anglo-Saxon Chronicle*, 1087 (E).
[133]*Anglo-Saxon Chronicle*, 1087 (E); William of Malmesbury, *De Gestis Regum Anglorum*, II, p. 361.
[134]Henry of Huntingdon, *Historia Anglorum*, p. 214.
[135]*Florentii Wigorniensis monachi Chronicon*, II, p. 25.

both his own safety and that of those around him. Since the castle was the ultimate objective of the rebels, he would be scarcely any safer there than in his cathedral. Wulfstan certainly understood the garrison's request as a plea for help and it was said that he agreed to the move because of his great gentleness, his loyalty to the king, and his affection for the troops.

While this exchange with the royal troops was taking place, the warriors of his own household continued arming and then joined forces with the garrison. All the able-bodied citizens declared that they too were ready to do battle with the enemy from the region beyond the Severn, if the bishop would allow this. These civilian volunteers were equipped and given some instruction in the use of their weapons, and then trooped off to the castle to request Wulfstan's permission to join in the counter-attack.[136]

In practical terms, his decision was a hard one. Given the inexperience of the citizen-volunteers, their sally might well end in disaster. If Wulfstan's own retinue and the castle garrison were then decimated, the city, cathedral and castle would be helpless in the face of the rebels. But Wulfstan did not hesitate to authorize the defending force to go on to the attack. His speech to the troops is recorded in these words:

> Go, my sons. Go in peace, go safely, with God's blessing and our own. I trust in the Lord, and I promise you that today the sword will not harm you, neither will any misfortune, nor any adversary. Be faithful to the king, strive manfully for the safety of the citizens and the city.

When Wulfstan finished his speech, emergency repairs were made to the bridge, which had evidently been deliberately damaged by the defenders to prevent the rebels from storming the city. The loyal troops crossed quickly, and as soon as they caught sight of the enemy in the distance, rushed to attack them. The rebels, meanwhile, became utterly reckless. Disregarding an earlier proclamation of the bishop, they set fire to his lands. Wulfstan was grief-stricken on hearing that the property of his church was being destroyed. He consulted all those gathered around him and then pronounced an anathema – a ritual curse – on the malefactors. The amazing consequences were seen by the monks as demonstrating the power of God and the stature of Wulfstan as a holy prophet. As the enemy moved through the fields, many of them experienced a sudden paralysis in their limbs, or a rapid onset of blindness. They were scarcely able to wield their weapons, or to recognize their comrades, let alone distinguish their allies from their opponents, which combined to ensure

[136]Ibid., II, p. 25.

their defeat. They could neither see any way of escape nor organize an effective defence. Their senses were stricken by Divine command, so it was later said, and they were easily cut down by the men of Worcester, who were heartened by their trust in God and by the blessing they had received from Wulfstan. Footsoldiers were killed out of hand, Normans, English and Welsh alike, while knights (who might be ransomed) were taken prisoner, and others barely escaped by fleeing. The loyal men of the king's garrison and the bishop's household troop returned home exulting in their victory, which had occurred without losses on their side. They even retrieved some of the goods of the church, undamaged, for which thanks were rendered to God, while their safe return was ascribed to the mediation of Wulfstan.[137]

This long account is taken from the Worcester Chronicle. Its author, John of Worcester, was a member of the community from boyhood.[138] The wealth of circumstantial detail in his narrative suggests that he experienced these events at first hand. His comparison of Wulstan with Moses reflects the Old Testament parallels which would be readily apparent to the monks. To John, and to his brethren, the victory was due to Divine Providence, invoked by Wulfstan's intercession. His pronouncing of the anathema was perceived to cause the downfall of the enemy. Because of its solemnity, and anticipated impact, this ritual curse was laid only after careful deliberation. It was deemed necessary not because of the rebels' political stance, but because they had blatantly disregarded the bishop's earlier prohibition to leave unharmed the property of the Blessed Virgin, dedicatee of the cathedral. Monastic communities were well experienced in dramatizing the liturgy, and the participants themselves, the assembled chapter of Worcester, would be impressed by the solemnity of this occasion, culminating in the extinguishing of the lighted tapers.[139] To the young John, the grave ritual, and the subsequent defeat of the rebels, would be perceived as cause and effect.

All the sources are agreed that the victory was a resounding one. Estimates of rebel casualties varied from five hundred to five thousand,[140] the medieval way of saying that they ran into large numbers. The sudden affliction of the enemy would most likely derive from the smoke – possibly toxic fumes of some kind – coming from the material which they set alight, but the rebels knew of the bishop's prohibition and some might be stricken by a psychosomatic paralysis, if the warcry of the bishop's force invoked his name. Conversely the defending forces were fortified by

[137]Ibid., II, pp. 25–6.
[138]Ecclesiastical History of Orderic Vitalis, II, p. 186.
[139]Little, "La morphologie des malédictions monastiques," pp. 49–51, 54–5.
[140]Anglo-Saxon Chronicle, 1088 (E); Henry of Huntingdon, Historia Anglorum, 214.

the bishop's blessing, which spurred them on to the victory they believed was assured. Among the monks of Worcester, grounded as they were in the Scriptures and especially the Psalms, Wulfstan's actions that day might well have seemed those of a second Moses. A further analogy which might occur to the Worcester chronicler was that of the Celtic Saint Columba, whose prayers were believed to bring victory in a righteous cause.[141] Whatever the balance between spiritual and temporal forces in determining the outcome, the monks of Worcester would readily believe that their cathedral and city had experienced a miraculous escape.

The military retinue of the bishop which took part in the defence of Worcester was a long-standing institution, although its composition had changed since the Norman Conquest. Wulfstan's predecessors, and he himself in King Edward's reign, would certainly have travelled with an armed escort. Before 1066, the men of the church of Worcester owed military service in time of national emergency. The last designated leader of this force, Edric, was accustomed to lead his troop as required, either on land, or on sea as captain of the bishop's warship. After the coming of the Normans, he lost the land which he had held of the bishopric of Worcester; but he was a tenant of Robert, bishop of Hereford, when he witnessed on Wulfstan's behalf in the suit against Abbot Walter of Evesham.[142] This Edric, a man of proven military experience, may be identical with the post-Conquest resistance leader Edric "the Wild", alias *Silvaticus* (or in French, *Salvage*), a cognomen derived from his habit of living in the open, often in woodlands. The Worcester chronicler, well-informed about his activities, relates that Edric, a nephew of Edric Streona, had been a powerful official (*praepotens minister*). As a guerrilla leader, he was active in Herefordshire from 1067 to 1070, when he made his peace with King William.[143] Edric was then restored to some of his lands, but his tenurial position was inferior to what it had formerly been. The Domesday Survey records Edric as a former tenant of six manors in Shropshire and one in Herefordshire.[144]

---

[141]*Adomnan's Life of Columba*, ed. and transl. A. O. and M. O. Anderson (1961), pp. 199–201; *Acta Sanctorum*, ed. J. Bollandus, G. Henschenius et al. (reprinted Brussels, 1969), June, II, pp. 195b–196a; *Early Sources of Scottish History A.D. 500 to 1286*, collected and transl. A. O. Anderson, 2 vols (1922), I, p. 96.

[142]*Domesday Book 16: Worcestershire*, 2:52; Appendix V, Worcester H, no. 2.

[143]*Florentii Wigorniensis monachi Chronicon*, II, pp. 1, 7, 9. See also *Anglo-Saxon Chronicle*, 1067 (D); *Ecclesiastical History of Orderic Vitalis*, II, pp. 194–5 and notes, 228.

[144]*Domesday Book, seu liber censualis*, ed. A. Farley, 2 vols (1783), I, folio 183v (Herefordshire); folios 253v, 256, 256v, 258 (Shropshire). The land which Edric the steersman held of the bishop of Hereford is not readily identifiable, although he may be one of the bishop's various unnamed *miles*.

The activities of English guerrillas were widespread during the late 1060s, when the band of Edric the Wild which devastated Herefordshire was one of several which threatened to destabilize the new Norman regime throughout England.[145]

Edric was a common name in late Anglo-Saxon England, so that the identity of the bishop's military commander with the freedom fighter cannot easily be proved. In support of the identification, it is obvious that Wulfstan's captain-general would be a man of some tenurial status. This, combined with his official post, would readily designate him as *praepotens minister*, while his military experience would develop some of the skills later deployed when a guerrilla leader. Firmer support for identification comes from an account of the descent of the episcopal manor of Little Witley, which was leased to Ernwy, the priest of Edric the Wild (*Silvaticus*) by Bishop Ealdred and Prior Wulfstan, i.e. not later than the early months of 1062. This estate was later taken from Ernwy by Ralph of Bernay (sheriff of Hereford), presumably during Edric the Wild's rebellion, but was not returned to the church of Worcester when Ralph was imprisoned (for his implication in the revolt of Roger earl of Hereford, in 1075).[146] Edric the Wild is not named as a tenant of the church of Worcester, yet it is odd that his chaplain held land in the diocese if he himself did not. Edric the Steersman was a tenant of the church of Worcester in respect of one Worcestershire manor, that of Hindlip and Offerton, an estate later occupied by Urse de Abetot.[147] Arguably the bulk of the steersman's family lands lay in the shires of the Welsh March, like those of Siward (the cousin of Edric the Wild) who with Edric the Steersman supported Bishop Wulfstan against Abbot Walter.

Those Englishmen who were prompt to recognize William I in 1066 had to be seen to dissociate themselves from such vehement patriots as Edric the Wild, hence the care taken by the Evesham writer to describe the rebels as "outlaws," even while recounting Abbot Ethelwig's relief efforts on behalf of their dependants.[148] If Wulfstan's former military commander established himself as the leader of a successful resistance unit, that was a pressing reason why he should no longer hold land of the

---

[145]Susan Reynolds, "Eadric Silvaticus and the English Resistance," *Bulletin of the Institute of Historical Research*, 54 (1981), pp. 102–5. There are points of resemblance between the activities of Edric the Wild in the Welsh Marches, and those of Hereward the Wake in the Fenlands: John Hayward, "Hereward the Outlaw," *Journal of Medieval History*, 14 (1988), pp. 293–304.

[146]*Domesday Book 16: Worcestershire*, 2:8; Appendix V, Worcester, G12. *Hemingi Chartularium*, I, pp. 256–7.

[147]*Domesday Book 16: Worcestershire*, 2:52.

[148]*Chronicon Abbatiae de Evesham*, p. 90. The word *exules* was used to denote "exiles" in classical Latin, but by *c*.1100 normally meant "outlaws."

church of Worcester. Evidently there were no hard feelings, since he later testified on Wulfstan's behalf against the abbot of Evesham. It was perhaps at Wulfstan's request that Edric then held lands of the bishop of Hereford. The example made of Abbot Godric of Winchcombe in 1066 was a warning to other monastic leaders that English nationalism must no longer find expression in political action. They could justify their discretion both on the practical grounds that by this means they could best save the patrimony of their houses, and on the scriptural grounds that the will of Divine Providence had been manifested in the military victory permitted to the Normans.

What cannot readily be determined from the surviving evidence is the extent to which Wulfstan and Ethelwig were in contact with the leaders of the English resistance during the late 1060s. Ethelwig probably gleaned intelligence of their movements from the refugees who struggled through to Evesham. As governor of Mercia, he had a vested interest in using such information to maintain law and order, even though his practical actions indicate that he retained some sympathy with the dispossessed English. The very fact that these outcasts arrived at his abbey in such numbers suggests that he was already well known to wield secular authority, and that it was widely believed that he would use his powers to protect the dispossessed. On the question of possible contact between Wulfstan and Edric the Wild, there is the circumstantial evidence that the Worcester chronicler described his activities in an informed and sympathetic way; that there are strong arguments for identifying the guerrilla leader with the bishop's dispossessed steersman, and that the latter was evidently on amicable terms with Wulfstan in later years as well as being a tenant of Wulfstan's friend, the bishop of Hereford. But Wulfstan's position was highly delicate, since he had been such a close associate of King Harold II, and during the early years of the Norman settlement his activities would be closely scrutinized. Several powerful Mercian laymen who had close connections with Evesham or Worcester suffered the loss of their lands at this time, and it might seem that the Sword of Damocles even hung over Wulfstan.

The displacement of Englishmen from the lands of the bishop of Wocester and of other magnates in the West Midlands did not occur as an immediate result of the Battle of Hastings, but rather as a consequence of the rebellions of 1068 and 1069. The rapid submission of Wulfstan, Ethelwig and the Mercian nobles in the autumn of 1066 ensured both their own continued possession of their estates and also the rights of their tenants. To the magnates of the West Midlands, it must have seemed that events were about to take the same course as in 1016, with a few changes at the top of the political hierarchy, but things continuing much as before in all essential respects. Yet those Continental adventurers who had supported William I's conquest of England expected some return for their efforts. Greedy eyes were cast on the prosperous lands of the West Midlands. The chronicler Orderic Vitalis, who was born of mixed parentage and raised in Shropshire, later alleged that certain of the newcomers deliberately goaded Earl Edwin into rebellion so that his estates would be forfeit.[149] From a Mercian point of view, the death of Edwin in 1071 was as important as that of King Harold just over four years earlier. The lands of those who rebelled in 1068 and 1069, whether tenants-in-chief or under-tenants, were seized and granted to King William's supporters. These newcomers were collectively known as "Frenchmen," since French was their common language. While there were many Normans among them, others came from various provinces of northern France, Brittany and Flanders. By 1086 only a small proportion of the tenants of the see of Worcester were men with Anglo-Saxon or Anglo-Danish names.[150]

This tenurial revolution is not discussed in the *Life* of Wulfstan, although this work does occasionally mention his dealings with specific Normans. In general, events appear to occur in a political vacuum, as required by the hagiographical format. The impact of the coming of the French to the lands of the bishopric has to be pieced together from the cartulary which Wulfstan ordered his monk Hemming to compile, and from accounts of the descent of individual manors in the Domesday Survey. One such account relates that in the reign of King Edward the manor of Croome was held of the bishop by Sigref. When he died, Wulfstan gave this land to one of his knights, together with Sigref's daughter, so that he might support her mother and render the bishop the service due from it.[151] Anecdotes such as this are presented in laconic fashion in the Domesday Survey, because it was the business of the clerks employed on this massive project to reduce the narratives of such personal tragedies to usable records. By the time the hundred-jurors gave their evidence, the new French hierarchy was well established, while old and bitter memories had begun to blur with the passing of time. The

---

[149]The most detailed account of the rising of Earls Edwin and Morcar and other English nobles is given in *Ecclesiastical History of Orderic Vitalis*, II, pp. 214–36.

[150]The coming of the Normans to Wulfstan's diocese is discussed in "An Introduction to the Worcestershire Domesday," in *Domesday Book: Worcestershire*, ed. R. W. H. Erskine and A. Williams (1989), pp. 27–31; and "An Introduction to the Gloucestershire Domesday," in *Domesday Book: Gloucestershire*, ed. R. W. H. Erskine and A. Williams (1989), pp. 33–6. See also C. Dyer, *Lords and Peasants in a Changing Society: the estates of the bishopric of Worcester, 680–1540* (1980), p. 45. The survival of Englishmen as landholders is perhaps rather higher than is indicated in this work if full account is taken of under-tenants, cf. *Domesday Book: Gloucestershire*, p. 31.

[151]*Domesday Book 16: Worcestershire*, 2:33.

Worcester monk Hemming, on the other hand, had a vested interest in keeping alive the burning indignation and bitter grievances generated by the tenurial upheaval. Even though his sentiments are those of the monastic chapter, his stories of violent dispossession hint at the cruel dislodgement experienced by tenants of the church of Worcester, whether they were ousted by Normans in the reign of William I, or by Danes in that of Cnut.

The dispossession of English tenants of the church of Worcester was justified legally only on the grounds that they were rebels, but in practice the new dispensation also provided the bishop with men better able to fulfil the military service required by the Norman kings. The English tenants of the bishopric had owed service on occasional campaigns; the majority were in no sense professional soldiers. Yet Bishop Oswald's leases clearly imposed a military role upon certain tenants and their heirs. Several lessees were styled "warrior," and others had duties which included both those of escort-rider and courier.[152] Such services continued to be exacted by Oswald's successors, because the bishop of Worcester, like all men of consequence, travelled with an armed escort, and also maintained contact with his associates among the other magnates, both ecclesiastics and laymen.

The debate over the introduction of feudalism to England, and in particular to the estates of the bishop of Worcester, encompasses a range of issues. First among these is the question of continuity in the tenurial obligations from estates of a given size.[153] Another debate has focused on the distinction between the weapons and the tactics of the English and those of the Normans. Warriors of both races are described in the sources by the Latin term *miles*, but it is generally agreed that whereas the Norman knight was a cavalryman, his English counterpart fought on foot, even though he rode to war. Following the imposition of knight service by King William I, Englishmen were therefore unable to fulfil the

---

[152]Several of Bishop Oswald's leases were made to men variously addressed as *cniht*, *miles* and thegn: *Anglo-Saxon Charters*, compiled Sawyer, nos 1305, 1326, 1332, 1341, 1343, 1346, 1366, 1373.

[153]There has been extensive debate on the question of whether the recruiting of warriors from units of five hides of land continued to be maintained on the estates of the bishopric in the Norman era. The evidence is summarized by Dyer, *Lords and Peasants in a Changing Society*, pp. 39–46. See also C. Warren Hollister, *Anglo-Saxon Military Obligations on the Eve of the Norman Conquest* (1962), pp. 54–5, 96, 98–102, 105, 111–12, and his *The Military Organization of Norman England* (1965), pp. 61–7; Richard Abels, "Bookland and Fyrd Service in late Anglo–Saxon England," *Anglo-Norman Studies VII*, ed. R. Allen Brown (1985), pp. 1–25; John Gillingham, "The Introduction of Knight Service into England," *Proceedings of the Battle Conference on Anglo-Norman Studies IV: 1981*, ed. R. Allen Brown (1982), pp. 53–64.

requirements for this service.[154] The king wanted to ensure that his major landholders would help to maintain the permanence of the Norman Conquest. He did so by imposing on them quotas of knight service, perhaps even before they received commensurate lands, which they were granted as these became available. The extent of the endowment of the church of Worcester was determined long before William's accession, and Wulfstan's quota of knight service was probably set at fifty.[155] Attempts have been made to correlate the basis on which the military service of the diocese was now calculated with that pertaining before the Conquest, but this hypothesis depends on the selective use of late evidence, and cannot be demonstrated satisfactorily.[156] In order to provide his quota of knights, Wulfstan gradually changed the basis on which his tenants held land from him. The old pattern of *laen* tenure, the holding of land on a lease for three lives in return for specified but not necessarily military duties, was replaced by sub-infeudation, that is, the granting out of land in return for a specific amount of knight service. The change-over took some time to complete, and it is likely that some *laen* tenures were converted into fiefs.[157] Under the new system, substantial tenants owed the service of several knights, and it was up to the landholder whether he retained these men as regular members of his household, or chose to settle them on individual knights' fees. The latter option came to be generally adopted, for the mutual convenience of lord and man. Long before this process was completed, each tenant-in-chief, holding directly of the crown, had still to provide his requisite quota of knights when the king demanded it. Abbot Ethelwig, in his capacity as administrator of western Mercia, supervised the muster of the feudal levy throughout the region. A royal writ, probably dating from 1072, ordered the abbot to summon each tenant-in-chief with all the knights he owed

[154]See, for instance, N. Hooper, "Anglo-Saxon Warfare on the eve of the Conquest: a brief survey," *Proceedings of the Battle Conference on Anglo-Norman Studies I. 1978*, ed. R. Allen Brown (1979), pp. 84–93; and D. R. Cook, "The Norman Military Revolution in England," in ibid., pp. 94–102.

[155]On the establishment of feudal tenure, see J. C. Holt, "The Introduction of Knight-Service in England," *Anglo-Norman Studies VI*, pp. 89–106, esp. p. 105. The earliest firm evidence on the knight service owed by the bishop of Worcester dates only from 1166. It was then recorded that forty-eight and a half fees, with a further four-fifths of a fee, had initially been created on the lands of the bishopric: *Liber Niger Scaccarii*, ed. T. Hearne, 2nd edn (1774), p. 174. Following the death of Bishop Wulfstan in 1095 a feudal relief was levied upon the lands of the diocese by William Rufus, *Hemingi Chartularium*, I, pp. 79–80. the sum demanded was £250, which probably relates to an official quota of fifty knights: J. H. Round, *Feudal England*, 2nd edn (1964), pp. 241–5. See also Dyer, *Lords and Peasants in a Changing Society*, pp. 45–6.

[156]Dyer, *Lords and Peasants in a Changing Society*, pp. 41–2.

[157]Ibid., p. 47.

the crown. They were to assemble before the king at Clarendon (Wilts) a week after the feast of Pentecost, and the abbot was to bring the five fully-equipped knights whose service he himself owed the crown.[158]

Wulfstan's own contingent would, of course, be required to answer any such summons, besides helping to ensure the defence of their own region, as in 1075 and 1088. Their loyalty is demonstrated by their willingness to wage judicial combat against Abbot Walter's brother Ranulf, in defence of Wulfstan's rights, even though they cannot have known at first hand the tenurial arrangements in the diocese during the reign of King Edward. Such loyalty perhaps resulted from a degree of racial and cultural assimilation. A young adventurer, once settled on a knight's fee of his own, would probably marry a local woman. English would be the language of the household and English values would be maintained there.[159] Such an environment would foster respect for the saintly bishop. A few of the knights may even have been English by birth. When knight service was first imposed, adult Englishmen would not have been able to acquire the techniques of cavalry warfare, which had to be taught from early boyhood, but some might contrive to secure a training for their sons, who would be young adults by the 1080s. Just such processes of intermarriage and racial assimilation can be traced among the military tenants of the abbess of Shaftesbury.[160]

The loyalty of Wulfstan's knights was encouraged by what would now be termed good employer-staff relations. Wulfstan regularly dined either with his monks in their refectory or else with his knights in the hall. He considered it unfitting and below his dignity to eat alone, and moreover his household would get into the habit of grumbling if he was habitually absent.[161] Yet problems arose from having to balance two roles, the monastic and the baronial. Wulfstan used to have edifying books read to him at the dinner table (in accordance with the practice in the monastic refectory). Silence was kept, so that everyone could hear, because he wanted them to receive spiritual, as well as temporal, nourishment. When they had all finished eating, he expounded the passage in English (books were normally written in Latin, although at Worcester itself some vernacular texts were produced in his day). After dinner, ale or mead was placed before everyone else in the English fashion, but Wulfstan drank only water. Only his servant knew this, and everyone else thought he had

[158] *English Historical Documents* II, no. 218, p. 960.

[159] On the question of linguistic and cultural assimilation in the Anglo-Norman period, see Cecily Clark, "Women's names in post-Conquest England: observations and speculations," *Speculum*, 53 (1978), pp. 223–51.

[160] Ann Williams, "The Knights of Shaftesbury Abbey," *Anglo-Norman Studies VIII*, ed. R. Allen Brown (1986), pp. 217–18, 221–2, 228–9, 232.

[161] *Vita Wulfstani*, pp. 46–7.

some expensive drink. He drank only water throughout his earlier years, but as he aged he drank diluted ale or wine. The convivial drinking which followed the meal went on for hours in the English manner, one result of cultural assimilation which the bishop could well have done without. Wulfstan felt obliged to remain for the duration, pretending to drink and murmuring to himself the appropriate psalms for the monastic Office. Everyone else had foaming tankards in front of them, while Wulfstan kept to one small goblet. The Norman knights of his retinue are not said to have developed a drink problem, but they did consume huge quantities of food every day, to which they were entitled in addition to their annual stipends.[162] When drink did lead to trouble, it came about after King William ordered each of his magnates to admit additional knights to his household because of a rumoured Danish invasion, which in the event did not materialize. This measure had been proposed by Lanfranc in a meeting of the Great Council, and met with unanimous approval. If the invasion did take place, it was intended that these household troops could be quickly mobilized as a national defence force. Wulfstan consequently recruited a number of such knights, keeping them appeased with plenty of pay, and satiated with luxurious meals. One day they had more to drink than usual. At first they became increasingly jovial, but then, as often happens at such times, the jokes turned to abuse. There was a heated quarrel and they came to the brink of fighting. Wulfstan became angry. He told the cupbearers to stop clattering about, and said that no-one on the premises should have any more strong drink that day. The previously raucous knights were shocked into compliance.[163] It was well known that disastrous consequences ensued for anyone who disobeyed a holy man.

The arrival of numbers of French-speaking warriors on the territory of the church of Worcester was counterbalanced by the removal of English notables, such as the military commander, Edric, or the sheriff, Kyneward. Many lesser men, dislodged from their holdings, chose to seek a living abroad. Englishmen found employment in the service of the Byzantine emperor, and a large contingent of these recruits travelled to Constantinople from west Mercia.[164] Of the Normans who succeeded them the most conspicuous within Worcestershire was the new sheriff,

[162]Ibid., p. 94; William of Malmesbury, *De Gestis Pontificum Anglorum*, p. 281.
[163]*Vita Wulfstani*, pp. 55–6. In order to meet the invasion threat, King William brought over large numbers of knights and infantry, recruited in France and Britanny. He ordered this force to be dispersed throughout the country, to be maintained by his vassals in proportion to the extent of their fiefs: *Anglo-Saxon Chronicle*, 1085.
[164]K. N. Ciggaar, "L'Émigration anglaise à Byzance après 1066: un nouveau texte en Latin sur les Varangues à Constantinople," *Revue des études Byzantines*, 32 (1974), pp. 301–42.

Urse de Abetot. His confrontation with Archbishop Ealdred over the construction of Worcester castle cannot have occurred later than the summer of 1069, since Ealdred died in the following September. The English sheriff, Kyneward, was probably replaced after the outbreak of unrest in 1068. Urse remained in office until his death in 1108.[165] His name dominates the tenurial records of the church of Worcester dating from the later eleventh century because of the extent of the estates which he effectively controlled, and the aggressive means by which he acquired them. He held only a moderate amount of land in chief, that is, directly from the king, but most of this lay in Worcestershire. The Domesday Survey of 1086 shows that his lands there were modest compared to those of other lay lords, notably Roger de Montgomery, earl of Shrewsbury, William Fitz Ansculf of Dudley, Ralf de Tosny and Osbern Fitz Richard, but whereas the dominant interests of these men lay in other shires, those of Urse were much more localized. He was also a major tenant of the great ecclesiastical landlords in Worcestershire: by far the greatest tenant of the bishop and cathedral priory, and a major tenant of both Evesham and Westminster. The Domesday Survey shows that by 1086 his under-tenancies greatly outweighed his tenancies-in-chief, both in monetary value and in geographical extent. This consolidation of under-tenancies was perhaps encouraged by the king, on the grounds that Urse must be seen to be a commanding figure if he was to be effective in his political role.[166] The monks of Worcester resented the aggressive means by which Urse acquired certain of his tenancies, and his misappropriations were documented in the contemporary cartulary compiled by the monk Hemming.[167] To the monks, the wrongful occupation of lands of their church was a grave offence, to be described in terms in which emotion predominated over accuracy.[168]

Yet Urse in turn had a grievance against the ecclesiastical landlords. As sheriff, he expected to control the financial, legal and military administration of the shire, but the existence of the wide franchisal rights of the great ecclesiastical landholders, the churches of Worcester, Evesham,

[165]Winchcombe Annals, 1049–1181, p. 122.

[166]For the estates held by Urse, see Beauchamp Cartulary, pp. xviii–xx; Judith Green, "The Sheriffs of William the Conqueror," Anglo-Norman Studies V, ed. R. Allen Brown (1983), pp. 137, 141, 144; Hamshere, "Domesday Book: Estate Structures in the West Midlands," p. 179.

[167]Domesday Book 16: Worcestershire, Appendix V, Worcester G, nos 2, 7, 13, 16.

[168]N. R. Ker, "Hemming's Cartulary: a description of the two Worcester cartularies in Cotton Tiberius A.XIII," reprinted from Studies in Medieval History presented to F.M. Powicke, ed. R. W. Hunt, W. A. Pantin and R. W. Southern (1948), pp. 49–75, in N. R. Ker, Books, Collectors and Libraries: Studies in the Medieval Heritage, ed. Andrew G. Watson (1985), p. 49.

Pershore and Westminster, diverted substantial resources from his control, and consequently prevented him from fulfilling his commitments to the crown. Nearly twenty years after his arrival in Worcestershire he was still voicing frustration of these franchises, and his blunt comments were recorded by the Domesday Commissioners.[169]

Given these sources of disagreement, relations between Wulfstan and Urse cannot have been easy, and a generation gap of some thirty years, combined with their differing cultural backgrounds, would foster misunderstanding. On the other hand, no overt clash is recorded, perhaps because the bishop was able to collect some at least of the service due from the lands held by Urse. Wulfstan's lack of interest in secular power struggles would also make it easier for him to reach a demarcation of interests with the sheriff. Wulfstan was philosophically adjusted to the Norman Conquest from the outset and since the military victory must inevitably be followed by the arrival of Norman settlers, he might experience less difficulty than others in accepting them in his neighbourhood. Powerful conquerors of any nationality would behave in much the same way, as indeed had the native-born Earl Leofric.[170] Since Wulfstan had witnessed the assimilation of the Danes earlier in the century, he might have the equanimity to face even the mightiest of his Norman tenants. Any tensions which continued to be generated by close proximity would diminish after the accession of William Rufus in 1087, when Urse became a pivotal figure in the day-to-day running of the royal government.[171] He would necessarily spend less time in the shire, leaving Wulfstan with a free hand. Since Urse acted as an auxiliary judge when Bishop Geoffrey of Coutances pronounced in favour of Wulfstan at the conclusion of his plea with Abbot Walter,[172] it is unlikely that by the 1080s a state of hostility persisted between bishop and sheriff. Urse is not known to have become a benefactor of the cathedral priory, although the land held by his English chaplain, Alfred, was later confirmed to the

---

[169]*Domesday Book 16: Worcestershire*, C (Worcestershire Customs); 3. Urse's duties included also the management of almost all the royal demesne in the shire: Hamshere, "Domesday Book: Estate Structures in the West Midlands," p. 166.

[170]Even before the Danish invasions English notables were liable to withhold ship-scot from clerical landlords: *Anglo-Saxon Writs*, ed. F. E. Harmer (1952), no. 63. For forcible alienation of estates of the church of Worcester both by Danes and by English magnates, see *Domesday Book 16:Worcestershire*, Appendix V, Worcester G, nos 4, 8, 11, 14–17, 19–20, 28–30.

[171]F. West, *The Justiciarship in England 1066–1232* (1966), pp. 11–13; Barlow, *William Rufus*, pp. 202, 209–11, 217, 244, 279–80, 360, 365, 399.

[172]*Domesday Book 16: Worcestershire*, Appendix V, Worcester H, no. 3.

chapter.[173] When Wulfstan issued his solemn Alveston charter in 1089, increasing the endowment of his growing monastic community, Urse was one of the dignitaries present, attesting "with all the knights of his shrievalty."[174] This may or may not indicate cultural assimilation, but certainly implies peaceful co-existence.

The name of the formidable sheriff, *Ursus* (the Bear), carried connotations of remorseless strength and ferocity. These qualities probably earned him his appointment to the shrievalty in the first place, combined with the support at court of his brother Robert, Dispenser (or steward) of William I. The occupation of church lands was probably completed within a few years of acquiring the shrievalty. Consequently it is this aspect of his activity, that of the aggressive young-man-in-a-hurry, which has been transmitted through the writers of Worcester and Evesham. With the passing of time, he would merge into a long line of those who exercised domineering, yet legitimate, secular lordship in West Mercia, a line which stretched back through Earl Leofric, Edric Streona and Ealdorman Alfhere, and which counterbalanced that of the great ecclesiastical lords. Since Urse lacked any substantial base in Normandy, his territorial status, power and prestige rested on the position which he could establish in Mercia. There was no going back, so that some measure of mutual accommodation with the other authorities of the region would become inevitable.

[173]*Cartulary of Worcester*, no. 338. The cathedral priory also held the tithe of wine from Elmley Castle, "by the gift of William de Beauchamp and his ancestors," ibid., nos 73, 77. This plural noun should indicate that the donation was originally made either by William's grandfather, Urse, or else by Urse's brother, Robert Dispenser, who occupied Elmley Castle in the time of Bishop Wulfstan: *Domesday Book 16: Worcestershire*, 2:72; Appendix V, Worcester G, no. 25. The chaplain is identified in an episcopal charter dating from about 1131; its scribe cites the form "Elfred."
[174]*Cartulary of Worcester*, no. 3.

7

The Pastor of his Flock

Wulfstan's great strengths lay in his dedication to his religious vocation and his concern for the welfare of the monks, clergy and laity under his jurisdiction. His commitment to these responsibilities, which took priority over all other concerns, is reiterated throughout his *Life*. By implication, Wulfstan is sharply contrasted to his successor, Samson, a very different kind of bishop.[1] Wulfstan lived long before the era when it became the practice for bishops to keep a register of their activities, and few of his charters now survive, so that knowledge of his pastoral activities largely depends on anecdotes recorded by Coleman. These stories are related as *exampla*, tales with a moral, which are presented so as to highlight Wulfstan's virtues. Many of the episodes are narrated in such a way as to recall Biblical stories from the life of Christ, or those of the prophets, but there is no reason to doubt their essential veracity. Several of these anecdotes convey a hint of the miraculous, but the events can be interpreted as natural phenomena, either physical or psychological. The monks of Worcester perhaps shared this view, since they accused Coleman of trying to boost Wulfstan's reputation by repeating tall stories about him.[2] Coleman himself would have believed that any reputable work of hagiography should contain elements of a miraculous nature, to enrich the faith of those who already accepted the merits of its subject.[3] Wulfstan himself, as will be shown, repeatedly squashed the efforts of others to depict him as a wonder-worker.

In several instances, anecdotes depict Wulfstan's conduct as embodying the precepts of the Rule of St Benedict. These episodes also owe

---

[1]V.H. Galbraith, "Notes on the career of Samson, bishop of Worcester (1096–1112)," *English Historical Review*, 82 (1967), pp. 86–101, reprinted in his *Kings and Chroniclers, essays in English medieval history* (1982), pp. IV 86–101.
[2]*The Vita Wulfstani of William of Malmesbury*, ed. R. R. Darlington (1928), p. 42.
[3]By way of analogy, see J. T. Rosenthal, "Bede's use of miracles in the 'Ecclesiastical History'," *Traditio*, XXXI (1975), pp. 328–35, esp. pp. 330, 333.

something to deliberate selection and presentation, but they are sufficiently consistent with one another to indicate that they are a true
reflection of the bishop's habitual conduct. His prayer life, in particular,
is shown as underlying and sustaining all his other actions.[4] The
depiction of his spiritual activities is based upon the recollections of those
who knew him in his later years, when he was less active physically and
would probably devote more of his time to prayer and contemplation
than he had done either as a busy prior or as a recently consecrated
bishop. In Wulfstan's day, personal prayer largely comprised recitation
of the Psalms. It is said that whatever he was doing, there was always a
psalm on his lips. When he was worn out from excessive prayer, he
would fall asleep, but as soon as he awoke, or someone woke him up, he
began a psalm such as "Look after me, God, I take shelter in you" (Psalm
16) or "I love you, O Lord my strength" (Psalm 18). In summer, after
dinner, he would often rest on his bed, but fell asleep only when someone
read to him. So long as the reader continued, Wulfstan appeared to sleep,
but woke up at once if he stopped. On such occasions he ordered a
reading from the *Lives of the Saints*, or some similar work.[5] Every day,
Wulfstan heard two Masses, and made an oblation at each of them. He
then sang a third Mass himself.

   His prayers were not disrupted by travel. As he mounted his horse he
began to recite the Psalter, and said it right through. He continued with
Litanies, Collects, and then Vigils and Vespers of the Dead. If the journey
was still in progress, he repeated the psalms of the appropriate liturgical
hours. His clerks and monks rode with him, ready to take up the
alternate verses, or to jog his memory if he seemed to hesitate. He
ordered their participation so that they would have no opportunity for
the casual talk in which travellers usually indulge when there is so much
to attract their attention and call for comment.[6] This discipline which
Wulfstan imposed upon himself and his companions admirably fulfilled
the precepts of the Rule of St Benedict concerning the conduct of monks
while travelling,[7] but his clerks, who were in secular orders and therefore
not bound by the Rule, perhaps chafed under these constraints. Much of
Wulfstan's time would be taken up in travel, given his need to attend the
royal court at major festivals; supervise his own diocese; undertake
pastoral tasks by request occasionally in other dioceses, and also visit his
own episcopal manors. Whenever Wulfstan went on a journey his

[4]*Vita Wulfstani*, p. 49.
[5]Ibid., p. 49. There still survives a collection of Lives of the Saints, written at Worcester
in the mid-eleventh century: N. R. Ker, *Catalogue of Manuscripts containing Anglo-Saxon*
(1957), no. 29, p. 41.
[6]*Vita Wulfstani*, pp. 48–9.
[7]*The Rule of St. Benedict*, ed. and transl. J. McCann (1951), chs 50, 67.

chamberlain Coleman rode beside him, carrying a purse so that alms could be given to all those who asked for them. When they reached their lodgings, at the end of the day's journey, Wulfstan always went first to pray in the church, before going to his room. On arrival, he would order a priest to purge every room of the lodgings with holy water and the sign of the cross, so that hostile powers should be driven away, and friendly ones invoked.[8] On long-distance journeys, Wulfstan and his entourage had to make the best of whatever lodgings they could find. They might have to share communal and uncomfortable accommodation, in circumstances which made contemplative prayer almost impossible.

Within the diocese of Worcester, though, arrangements could readily be made to give the bishop some privacy. In every one of Wulfstan's manor houses, he had a small room into which he would lock himself after Mass. Here there was nothing to disturb his contemplation, except when a clerk knocked on the door to warn him that it was time for dinner, or for one of the monastic Offices. Private prayer was important to him, but he did not want to make a show of religious practices, and so the passage leading from his audience-chamber to his private oratory was known only to his servants. The existence of these hidden rooms enabled him to find solitude even when he was surrounded by his entourage, and to snatch an hour away from his worldly concerns. This privacy was important to him, especially in Lent. He prayed in earnest, concentrating upon the meaning of each successive verse of the Psalms. When he reached any verse which carried a particular spiritual plea, such as: "Listen to me, O Lord, and answer me, poor and needy as I am" (Psalm 86) he would repeat the verse two or three times, raising his eyes to heaven.[9]

The prime duty of all monks was to engage in a regular cycle of prayer, and Wulfstan kept his own community up to the mark in this respect. He is depicted as dealing with defaulters according to their individual circumstances, in a gentle but firm manner. If he noticed that one of the monks was not at Matins (in the early hours of the morning), he said nothing at the time, but when the others returned to their beds, he woke the defaulter gently, not frightening him with kicks or threats. The erring monk was then made to say the Office. As he chanted, Wulfstan himself said the responses. He was not prepared to condone any neglect of this

---

[8]*Vita Wulfstani*, p. 49.

[9]Ibid., pp. 50–1. On Wulfstan's religious observances, see also William of Malmesbury, *De Gestis Pontificum Anglorum*, ed. N. E. S. A. Hamilton (1870), pp. 281–2.

spiritual duty, but made the monk earn pardon for his fault in this way.[10] Monks were perceived as the "soldiers of Christ" engaged in spiritual combat against the powers of darkness.[11] Any shortcomings in their observance was as much a dereliction of duty as a sentry who slept at his post.

Wulfstan imposed as strict a monastic observance upon himself as he did upon others. Whenever he was in residence at Worcester, he said High Mass almost daily, usually from his own choice rather than because he was asked by the monk whose duty it was that week. He frequently remarked that since he himself was a monk of the community, he owed his week's duty to the cathedral church like the other monks, and because his episcopal commitments prevented him from filling a regular slot in the rota, he must perform his share when he was actually there. Wulfstan's aspiration to combine the roles of bishop and abbot derives from the writings of Pope Gregory the Great, whose works were well represented among the books known to have been at Worcester during the eleventh century. The monastic Rule prescribed readings from Scripture in the refectory while the monks ate lunch, and Wulfstan frequently joined them.[12] Afterwards, he made his confession in the church, and gave his blessing to the community before returning to his own quarters. His own cycle of prayer began in the church at the crack of dawn, while the other monks went back to sleep after the night Office. Each monk in priest's orders had an obligation to say Mass daily, and if any of them was short of a server, Wulfstan himself took on the task.[13] The implication is that he was demonstrating the scriptural precept of Our Lord that he who wants to be the greatest must also be servant of all (John 13:15). His concern for correct monastic observance encompassed the *oblates*, and if he noticed that one of them was untidily dressed, he himself straightened out the child's habit.[14]

Wulfstan's authoritarian concern for the spiritual welfare of his monks, and his rigorous insistence upon their proper observance of the monastic discipline, were entirely in accordance with the Rule of St Benedict.[15] Wulfstan's care for his monks ought to have been comple-

[10]*Vita Wulfstani*, p. 51. A much harsher episcopal reaction is described by William of Malmesbury, *De Gestis Pontificum Anglorum*, p. 282, more on a par with Wulfstan's treatment of his erring household staff, which is described below. See also *Rule of St. Benedict*, ch. 43.

[11]Barbara H. Rosenwein, "Feudal War and Monastic Peace: Cluniac Liturgy as Ritual Aggression," *Viator*, 2 (1971), pp. 129–57, esp. pp. 45–6.

[12]*Vita Wulfstani*, p. 54. On the readings prescribed in the monastic refectory, see *Rule of St. Benedict*, ch. 38.

[13]*Vita Wulfstani*, p. 54.

[14]Ibid., p. 54.

[15]*Rule of St. Benedict*, chs 2, 63–4.

mented by their equal regard for him. There is evidence that he was regarded with affection,[16] but it is questionable whether all the inmates of the cathedral priory were equally unhesitating in their affection for their bishop, or even in their deference towards him. The rapid increase the size of the community, combined with Wulfstan's unavoidable absences on other duties, meant that the monastic community would be less close-knit towards the end of his life than it had been when he was one of only a dozen or so. As in the case of other monastic cathedrals, a division came to be made between the lands of the bishop and those assigned to the monks. It was clearly in existence by 1086 when the Domesday Survey recorded it in operation. The division of the estates assigned the majority of the land, including virtually all of those manors which generated the most income, to Wulfstan. This division gave him the resources to sustain the role of a feudal magnate, which he undoubtedly was. The monks' estates, in contrast, were largely administered as demesne holdings, producing food rents for the support of the chapter.[17] Wulfstan made several grants of land to his monks, including properties in Alveston (Warwicks), Cookley (Cullacliffe), Tappenhall (Worcs) and Westbury (Gloucs),[18] but circumstantial evidence suggests that by 1092, when Wulfstan's health was failing, the monks were asserting their own economic and jurisdictional interests. The celebrated charter *Altitonantis*, purportedly granted by King Edgar in 964, was probably composed in the late eleventh century in order to support the alleged historicity of their claims.[19] The effective spokesman for the interests of the chapter

[16]*Vita Wulfstani*, p. 61. An affectionate regard is also suggested by the riddle which was a play on his name: *Hemingi Chartularium ecclesiae Wigorniensis*, ed. T. Hearne, 2 vols (1723), I, p. 217. The riddle was: "Sic pariter lupo pax, vita longa salusque. Jungere gaudemus lapidem disjungere nec ne laxatur pius his vinctis, nostri memor et sit." This may be translated, literally, as "Thus [we wish] peace, long life and health alike to the Wolf. We are pleased to join the Stone and not separate [them]. And the worthy person is not demeaned once these [two] are bound. May he [i.e. Wulfstan] be mindful of us."

[17]C. Dyer, *Lords and Peasants in a Changing Society: the estates of the bishopric of Worcester, 680–1540* (1980), p. 36; J. D. Hamshere, "Domesday Book: Estate Structures in the West Midlands," in *Domesday Studies*, ed. J. C. Holt (1987), pp. 155–82, esp. pp. 167–8.

[18]*The Cartulary of Worcester Cathedral Priory (Register I)*, ed. R. R. Darlington (1968), nos 3–4; *Hemingi Chartularium*, II, pp. 413–14, 418–19, 421–5.

[19]*Anglo-Saxon Charters: an annotated list and bibliography*, compiled P. H. Sawyer (1968), no. 731. P. H. Sawyer, "Charters of the Reform Movement: the Worcester archive," in *Tenth Century Studies: essays in commemoration of the Millennium of the Council of Winchester and Regularis Concordia*, ed. D. Parsons (1975), pp. 84–93, esp. pp. 85, 87; E. John, *Orbis Britanniae and other studies* (1966), pp. 238, 240–1, 245, 259–63. Wider issues underlay the dispute of 1092 over the church of St Helens: *Cartulary of Worcester*, no. 52.

was the prior, whose rights, exercised in the person of the bishop's brother, Alfstan, were extended after the Norman Conquest.[20]

Wulfstan's imposition of religious discipline encompassed not only the monks, but also the clerks and laymen of his household. He insisted that every man should attend Mass daily, and all the canonical Offices, a ruling which would cause inconvenience to the dispatch of urgent business. The lay officers had not bound themselves to the disciplined round of prayer which was the duty of professed monks; accordingly the bishop's orders met with resistance, and he found it necessary to appoint attendants to enforce the command. Offenders were either deprived of alcohol for the day, or were caned on the hand. Even a lay official, when he was sent out on business, was ordered to pray seven times a day, for Wulfstan argued that since those in clerical orders offered to God the Offices of the seven canonical hours, laymen should offer seven prayers. This was not an onerous obligation, since the recital of the Lord's Prayer would probably have sufficed. Any man who swore in the bishop's presence was immediately beaten. Wulfstan considered that habitual swearing could lead to the unintentional uttering of curses, and he frequently preached on this topic. Yet although a strict discipline was imposed, he became angry if anyone in his presence told tales about someone else, or criticized his lifestyle. The bishop considered backbiting of this sort to be very wicked.[21]

Wulfstan imposed high standards on those around him, but was also prepared to be hard on himself. At night, after he had slept a little, he got up and recited the Psalms, or else read from a book of prayers which he used as much as the Psalter, and always carried about with him.[22] At other times he recited the hours of the Blessed Virgin. He often prayed alone, so as not to deprive the others of their sleep, but if someone was awake Wulfstan prayed in company with him. One night his companion was a certain Edric.[23] Wulfstan continued without a break for some time,

[20] The circumstances surrounding the composition of *Altitonantis* are discussed in the following chapter; the scope of the writ of King Edward for Alfstan (*Anglo-Saxon*) Writs, ed. F. E. Harmer (1952), no. 116), should be compared with that of King William (*Cartulary of Worcester*, no. 2). Some extension of monastic rights is apparently implied; John, *Orbis Britanniae*, note on pp. 241–2. See also F. Barlow, *The English Church 1000–1066* (1979), p. 241.

[21] *Vita Wulfstani*, pp. 94–5.

[22] Ibid., p. 95. The most likely candidate for the book of prayers is *The Portiforium of Saint Wulfstan* (Corpus Christi College, Cambridge, MS 391), ed. Dom Anselm Hughes, 2 vols (1958–60). See also Laurentia McLachlan, "St Wulstan's Prayer Book," *The Journal of Theological Studies*, 30 (1929), pp. 174–7.

[23] *Vita Wulfstani*, pp. 47, 95. The monk Edric is among those listed *c*.1104: *Durham Liber Vitae*, ed. A. H. Thompson (1923), folio 22 recto. He is also mentioned, perhaps posthumously, in a charter of Bishop Simon, which probably dates from 1125–39: *Cartulary of Worcester*, no. 87.

and Edric grew tired of the long psalms and prayers, so tired that he actually dared to signal the bishop to stop. Wulfstan gave him a withering look, and Edric reluctantly sat down again, but he kept nodding off, and eventually fell asleep. At once he began to dream that he was being soundly beaten and scourged, and it was only when he solemnly promised never to prevent or hinder a good man from doing a good deed that he was delivered from the perils of his dreadful nightmare.[24]

Wulfstan took a stern line against the continuing existence of married priests in his diocese, even though his own father had been one. The bishop's insistence upon clerical celibacy stemmed from several diverse considerations. Both as prior and afterwards he was faced with the practical task of recovering alienated lands of the church of Worcester, including tenancies which on occasion had been acquired by a cleric who treated it as a family fief.[25] Secondly, the reform of the Church promoted by the papacy from the middle decades of the eleventh century created a moral and disciplinary climate in which clerical marriage was censured.[26] In England, there had been intermittent attempts to suppress clerical marriage in earlier times,[27] but renewed insistence upon clerical celibacy was maintained by Lanfranc, archbishop of Canterbury (1070–89), a Benedictine monk, like Wulfstan himself.[28] Wulfstan's own monastic education, and his later social and professional situation, would pre-dispose him towards celibacy, even before he took monastic vows. Understandably he would come to believe that what was best for himself was also best for all those with whom he had dealings, far beyond the confines of the cathedral priory. A lifetime spent among professional celibates would further help to explain his incomprehension, both of marriage as a mutually supportive relationship, and of the difficult position of an isolated priest or a clerk, who lacked both the support of a marital relationship and also that deriving from the regimented and communal life of Benedictine monks. Wulfstan's negative view of marri-age is heightened by the transmission of his *Life* through the medium of the monastic writer William of Malmesbury, who himself had a dismiss-ive attitude towards women. He described the importunate *femme sole* of

[24]*Vita Wulfstani*, pp. 47, 95.

[25]*Hemingi Chartularium*, II, p. 335.

[26]See, for instance, *The Epistolae Vagantes of Pope Gregory VII*, ed. and transl. H. E. J. Cowdrey (1972), pp. xvii, xxvi, nos 6, 8–11.

[27]*Councils and Synods, with other documents relating to the English Church I, A.D. 871–1204*, ed. D. Whitelock, M. Brett and C. N. L. Brooke, 2 vols (1981), Part I, pp. 13, 289–90, 299n.

[28]*The Letters of Lanfranc, archbishop of Canterbury*, ed. and transl. Helen Clover and Margaret Gibson (1979), p. 8; nos 41, 43.

Worcester who propositioned Prior Wulfstan as a *muliercula*, or "little woman,"[29] and used the identical term in his *De Gestis Pontificum*, when recounting the sorry end of Bishop Walter of Hereford at the hands of the seamstress.[30] Salutary warnings of misadventure resulting from dealings with women are only to be expected in lives of clerics, written by celibate clerics for their own kind.

Wulfstan abhorred sin arising from sexual relationships. He approved of chastity in all men, but especially in clerics in holy orders. If he found one who was wholly committed to chastity, he took him into his circle, and loved him like a son. He issued an edict ordering all married priests either to renounce their sexual relationships or their churches. They were told that if they loved chastity, they were welcome to remain in their livings, but if they were slaves to sensuality they must go away in disgrace. The majority of the married priests preferred to renounce their churches rather than their "little women." Some of these men wandered about until they starved, while others looked for, and eventually found, other employment. A minority, those who were deemed wisest in the official view, remained in their benefices to an honourable old age. In order to avoid any future scandal, the bishop subsequently refused to ordain to the priesthood anyone who was not vowed to celibacy.[31] The audience for whom Wulfstan's *Life* was first intended would approve of the episcopal drive against clerical marriage, regardless of any consideration either for the displaced priests who remained loyal to their family commitments, or for those women and children who were turned out of their homes to fend for themselves, while their husbands stayed safely in their livings. Even if Wulfstan felt any compassion for the displaced clerical families, this would not be reflected in his *Life*, given its hagiographical format. Wulfstan's ruling on the dismissal of clerical wives was in line with earlier Continental practice, but was more drastic than the decree on this subject issued at the Council of Winchester, 1076.[32] His stern imposition of celibacy upon his parochial clergy, as with his enforcement of discipline upon his household, presents a side of his character which is in sharp contrast to that usually depicted in his *Life*. From the viewpoint of the hagiographer, though, Wulfstan's disciplinary measures were aspects of his efforts to improve the religious

[29] *Vita Wulfstani*, p. 12.
[30] William of Malmesbury, *De Gestis Pontificum Anglorum*, p. 300
[31] *Vita Wulfstani*, pp. 53–4.
[32] *Councils and Synods*, I, Part II, pp. 616–17, 619. The only early copy of the canons of this council comes from Wulfstan's archives: ibid., pp. 617–18. See also *Letters of Lanfranc*, nos 41, 43. Wulfstan probably recalled that King Canute had legislated against clerical marriage: I Canute ch. 6: *The Laws of the Kings of England from Edmund to Henry I*, ed. and transl. A. J. Robertson (1925), pp. 162–3.

and moral life of those in his care, and to enforce ideals of perfection. The effects of Wulfstan's reform did not long survive his death, and Bishop Roger (1163–79) found it necessary to launch a new drive against married priests.[33]

In his personal behaviour towards members of his household, those whom he had chosen to have around him and who, presumably, conformed to the standards he decreed, Wulfstan displayed a different side of his character, one in which humility predominated. When he was criticized for exercising humility to a degree which was beneath the dignity of a bishop, Wulfstan's reply was: "He that is greater among you shall be your servant (Matthew 23:11). I am your bishop and master, and so I ought to be servant of you all, according to the precept of Our Lord." It was said that Wulfstan never followed his own inclination but in every respect was guided by the teachings of Christ. He was uniformly good-natured, never distressing the members of his household by any harshness[34] – not a viewpoint which would be shared by those of them who had suffered from his disciplinary measures. The writer of his *Life* was concerned to demonstrate how the bishop's conduct exemplified the virtue of *humilitas*, and also repeatedly made the point that all of Wulfstan's actions contributed towards the general good. Anyone who incurred the bishop's censure did so deservedly. Wulfstan never shamed, by a display of ingratitude, those who genuinely tried to serve him. He often drew on things which had been set aside for his own use in order to make provision for the well-being of his people, but at the same time he spoke and acted in every respect as befitted the office of a bishop.[35]

Wulfstan's humility was particularly manifested in his zeal for pastoral work of all kinds – he was the servant of his diocese as well as its governor. Whenever he received an invitation to visit a religious house, he did not keep its inmates waiting for an answer, nor did he make excuses for any delay in coming to see them. Such visits were often combined with a mass confirmation of the children of the locality, and on these occasions his response was immediate, taking priority over any other business then in hand, and even over his own need for rest.[36] A third call frequently made on his time was that of re-dedicating altars. Since the early years of Christianity in England the vast majority of altars had been made of wood, but Wulfstan ordered the abolition of wooden altars throughout his diocese and their replacement by stone ones,

---

[33]Mary G. Cheney, *Roger, bishop of Worcester 1164–1179* (1980), pp. 66–77, 219, 348.

[34]*Vita Wulfstani*, p. 54.

[35]Ibid., p. 54.

[36]Ibid., p. 54.

probably following the decreee to this effect issued at the Legatine
Council at Winchester in April 1070. This major project caused Wulfstan
to dedicate two altars in one day in one village – presumably both in the
same church; two more the day after, apparently elsewhere in the
vicinity, and more on the third day elsewhere in the neighbourhood. This
made many calls on his time, to all of which he responded with great
speed.[37] Wulfstan also made regular formal visitations of all parts of his
diocese, inspecting a different section each year, both to avoid overtaxing
his own health and out of consideration for the stamina of those who
were to meet him. His archdeacons would give advance notice of his
route, and great crowds would then gather to meet him as he travelled.
These visitations imposed a considerable strain on him, but his willpower
enabled him to bear the burden and to accomplish all he had set out to
do. His administrative load was eased by the activities of his archdeacons, who exercised a deputed administrative oversight of his diocese.[38]

The later eleventh century experienced a new wave of church-building,
caused in part by the replacement of ancient structures by new ones in the
Romanesque style, and partly by the gradual phasing out of the old
territorial minsters and their replacement by a network of parishes, a
movement which received considerable impetus from the wish of territorial lords to establish churches at the centre of their own lands.[39]
Wulfstan himself was one such lord. He built parochial churches on his
own estates, and also instructed them to be built elsewhere. This
church-building programme took precedence over secular architectural
projects, and he never built new halls or banqueting rooms for his manor
houses. His taste was always austere, whether in respect of ecclesiastical
or of secular buildings.[40]

As Wulfstan aged, his determination to continue his pastoral activities
placed an increasing strain on his stamina, but it was said that he took
care to control his temper and his language when he was vexed by the
shortcomings of his flock. If he did flare out at people, it was for a good
reason. One such episode occurred when he was invited by a former
officer of King Edward, a man named Ailsi, to consecrate a church in his

[37]Ibid., p. 54. See also *Councils and Synods*, I, part ii, p. 575.
[38]*Vita Wulfstani*, pp. 51–2. The text mentions archdeacons, although only Ailric has
left any record of his activities. It is possible that Wulfstan had another, whose name is now
lost. This man perhaps served before Ailric took up office, but they may have worked
together. There were certainly two archdeacons by the time that William of Malmesbury
translated Wulfstan's *Life*: *Cartulary of Worcester*, pp. lxiii–lxiv; John Le Neve, *Fasti
Ecclesiae Anglicanae 1066–1300: II. Monastic Cathedrals*, compiled by Diana E. Greenway (1971), p. 104.
[39]J. Blair, "From Minster to Parish Church," in *Minsters and Parish Churches: the Local
Church in Transition 950–1200*, ed. J. Blair (1988), pp. 1–19, esp. pp. 7–8, 10.
[40]*Vita Wulfstani*, p. 52.

village of Longney-on-Severn.[41] Wulfstan came, and so did great crowds of people – far too many for the confined space. In the churchyard there was a nut tree which had not been pruned, so that its wide, shady branches darkened the church. Wulfstan sent for Ailsi and told him to cut down the tree. If Nature had not allowed room for the church, then this must be provided by human handiwork. Besides, it was unfitting that what Nature had provided should be used by man as a place of debauchery. Evidently Wulfstan and Ailsi were long-standing acquaintances, because the bishop knew that he used to sit under this tree, especially in summer, drinking, throwing dice and amusing himself with other games. Ailsi stubbornly refused to cut down the tree and said that sooner than do so, he would rather not have his church consecrated at all. Wulfstan became irate, and cursed the tree, afflicting it so that it gradually became barren, ceased to bear fruit, and withered from the roots. Ailsi then became tired of it, and he himself gave orders for it to be cut down. He related this sequel to Coleman, the bishop's chancellor and future biographer, when he was next in Longney on business, and concluded that nothing was more bitter than Wulfstan's curse and nothing was sweeter than his blessing.[42]

Readers of this story of the cursed nut tree would be intentionally reminded of Our Lord's treatment of the fig tree (Matthew 21:18–22). An incident which occurred after another dedication was seen to have a parallel with an Old Testament miracle. Archdeacon Ailric had recently built a church, probably at Cutsdean, although he also held other estates in Worcestershire.[43] When news reached Wulfstan that the church was ready to be dedicated, he sent for Ailric one evening saying, "Go and get everything ready for the consecration of the church. I will come at dawn, and be with you for the ceremony." This short notice shocked Ailric, who turned pale. The only excuse he could think of was that he had not prepared enough refreshments. A great crowd was likely to attend, and these people would need a good deal of food and drink. Ailric said he

[41]Ibid., p. 40. Ailsi (Alfsi) held Longney in chief as a king's thegn, and can probably be identified with the thegn of that name who also held land in chief in Windrush, was tenant of a royal demesne estate in Great Barrington, held another estate in Windrush of Winchcombe abbey and wrongfully occupied land in Bourton-on-the-Water which belonged to Evesham abbey (*Domesday Book 15: Gloucestershire*, ed. and transl. J. S. Moore (1982), 1: 66; 11: 14; 78: 1; 12).

[42]*Vita Wulfstani*, pp. 40–1.

[43]For Ailric, see J. Le Neve, *Fasti Ecclesiae Anglicanae: II*, p. 104. The archdeacon was a tenant of the church of Worcester at Bradley Green, Cutsdean (where he had a priest) and Huddington (*Domesday Book 16: Worcestershire*, ed. F. and C. Thorn (1982), 2:20; 24; 57). For a summary of further information on Ailric, see *Vita Wulfstani*, pp. xxxv–xxxvi.

would not want much himself, but he was sure his friends would expect more. Wulfstan told him: "Go and do what you have to do. God will find food for His servants. Since we are near the place, we will do God's work."

Ailric had no choice but to hurry away to get everything ready for the consecration. He prepared generously for a feast, but there was a problem in that the only mead he could obtain – the most appropriate drink for the dignitaries he was expecting – was one small jar which he begged from his friends. Wulfstan duly came the next morning, dedicated the altar and then made preparations to set off again, but Ailric and his friends managed to prevent him from leaving, and persuaded him to stay there for the rest of the day. After dinner, Ailric hospitably offered his friends mead from the borrowed jug. The quantity proved quite adequate for the number of drinkers. It flowed as if from a spring, and the more they drew from the jug, the more mead was available. Our Lord's miracle of the feeding of the five thousand offers an analogy, but the event seemed to Wulfstan's circle more reminiscent of the Old Testament story of the barrel of meal and the cruse of oil from which the prophet Elijah was fed by the widow when he asked for food (1 Kings 17:10–16). In fact, said Ailric, it might be said that the present episode manifested a greater work of grace, for in the scriptural story only three people were kept alive, whereas here a multitude had enough and to spare. Not only that: three days after the celebrations the jug was discovered to be still half full, even though initially it had scarcely seemed to hold enough for so great a gathering. This interpretation of events was spread around by Ailric, as proof of Wulfstan's tender care for his people.[44] The archdeacon was a man of consequence in the diocese. He would be relieved that his dedication feast had passed off in style, without embarrassment to his distinguished guests, or loss of face to himself. His clerical education would prompt him to draw on a Biblical analogy, even though his actual plight was not remotely as grim as that of the poor widow and her son. Ailric's concept of hospitality was no doubt lavish, and his fears about the drink running out were most likely proportionate to the generous scale on which he planned the catering. The small supply of mead would be reseved only for the most prominent guests in any case. Ailric and his closest friends would draw very sparingly on the jug, while Wulfstan himself was abstemious. Over-caution most likely saved the day, rather than any intervention on the bishop's part.

Besides presiding over an extensive programme of church-building, Wulfstan was also instrumental in the establishment of two monasteries within his diocese. An uneducated man named Aldwin became a monk,

[44]*Vita Wulfstani*, p. 55.

and then tried to live as a hermit at Malvern, below the range of ancient hills lying to the south-west of Worcester. It proved difficult to establish a monastery on any secure basis, and after a few years he was on the brink of giving up the project, especially when his one companion, Guy, decided to travel to Jerusalem in the hope of visiting the Holy Sepulchre or at least meeting the death of a martyr at the hands of the Muslims. Yet Aldwin thought it would be ill-advised to relinquish his vocation without consulting Wulfstan. He went to the bishop and complained about the difficulties he faced, and the shortage of funds. Aldwin said that if he was unable to help others, he might at least dedicate himself to the service of God by making a pilgrimage to Jerusalem. Wulfstan stopped him with the most solemn oath he ever used, saying, "Believe me, you would be absolutely delighted if you knew the extent to which it is Divinely preordained that the religious life will be observed there in the future." Aldwin had faith in Wulfstan's prophecy and persevered in his efforts to establish a monastery. Recruits began to arrive until there was a monastery with thirty inmates. By the time Wulfstan's *Life* came to be written, Malvern priory was in a flourishing condition.[45] Although Wulfstan encouraged the establishment of this house, it is doubtful whether it was ever legally subject to Worcester. It lay within the bounds of an estate which King Edward had given to Westminster Abbey, and by the middle of Henry I's reign Great Malvern was formally recognized as a dependency of that monastery.[46]

But another monastic house was subject to Worcester cathedral priory during its brief reincarnation in Wulfstan's episcopate. At Westbury-on-Trym (Gloucs) there was an ancient church which was greatly in need of repair – in fact half of its roof was off. Wulfstan rebuilt it right from the foundations, repairing the walls with hewn stone and the roof with lead. In order to give it some financial support, he endowed it with glebe-land and tithes, and even provided Office books for the church. When everything was complete, Wulfstan presented Westbury by formal deed of gift to the church of Worcester; placed monks in it, and appointed his chancellor, Coleman, as its prior.[47] Westbury's earlier history had been chequered. It was believed to have been founded as a minster early in the eighth century, and the church of Worcester gained possession of it a century later. The Danes destroyed it, but it was revived by Bishop

[45]Ibid., p. 26; William of Malmesbury, *De Gestis Pontificum Anglorum*, pp. 285–6; D. Knowles, C. N. L. Brooke and Vera C. M. London, *The Heads of Religious Houses England and Wales 940–1216* (1972), p. 90.
[46]*Westminster Abbey Charters, 1066–c.1214*, ed. Emma Mason assisted by the late Jennifer Bray, continuing the work of the late Desmond J. Murphy (1988), no. 164; see also nos 166, 171, 248A; and *Cartulary of Worcester*, nos 300–1.
[47]*Vita Wulfstani*, p. 52.

Oswald, who is said to have taken twelve of its monks to help colonize his new foundation of Ramsey. Westbury itself then lapsed, hence its ruinous condition when Wulfstan took it in hand. Coleman is known to have been active as prior in 1093, but he returned to Worcester when the monastery was disbanded by Wulfstan's successor, Bishop Samson (1096–1112).[48]

Wulfstan was a famous orator, who delighted the crowds which flocked to hear him whenever he was going to preach after he had dedicated a church. His sermons focused the attention of the congregation upon Christ and His works, and Wulfstan's zealous prayers and preaching were considered the more effective because of his own intensive fasting and vigils.[49] He always neglected his physical comfort in performing his spiritual duties. On his travels throughout his diocese he habitually celebrated Mass for the crowds besides preaching to them. The day's duties were completed by his confirming all the children who were brought in from the surrounding countryside, and this might continue until dusk, even on long summer evenings. Witnesses stated that often he confirmed two thousand, and occasionally three thousand, in a single day. The medieval manner of reckoning crowds renders these figures an exaggeration, yet it does imply that large numbers were involved. Since each part of the diocese was visited cyclically only once in several years, numbers would build up. These mass confirmations were usual not only in Wulfstan's earlier years as bishop, but even when he was a frail old man. There was an occasion when eight clerks bearing the chrism wilted from weariness, while Wulfstan continued vigorously. It was believed that in his old age he was sustained by the love of God, which enabled him to continue in this work despite his increasing infirmities. These mass confirmations were performed throughout his dioceses – the use of the plural noun in his *Life* is intentional, and refers to similar activity in the York diocese in the 1060s and early 1070s.[50]

When Wulfstan was engaged in confirming children, he would normally carry on without a break for a meal, and there was trouble once at Gloucester when Abbot Serlo (1072–1104) persuaded him that he needed a rest. Following the celebration of the preceding Masses, Wulfstan was about to go out to the children when Serlo induced him to take a much needed break. Anticipating resistance, he begged Wulfstan to honour the monastic refectory with his presence, arguing that he

[48]D. Knowles and R. N. Hadcock, *Medieval Religious Houses England and Wales*, 2nd edn (1971), p. 79; Knowles, Brooke and London, *Heads of Religious Houses*, p. 97.

[49]*Vita Wulfstani*, p. 20. See also William of Malmesbury, *De Gestis Pontificum Anglorum*, p. 281.

[50]*Vita Wulfstani*, p. 36. For his dedication of the chrism at York, ibid., p. 44.

should not be seen to reject the goodwill of the monks, who were themselves the servants of God. Probably paraphrasing the bishop's recent sermon, he supported his entreaty by citing Christ's consideration for others. He argued that while they were dining, the children could be lined up in an orderly way, so that Wulfstan could move about among them more easily. Serlo's reasoning, and the pleas of the assembled monks, persuaded the bishop to give way. Meanwhile, outside in the cemetery, the change in his schedule caused people to wonder what was the matter. The crowd, which was in an excited and anticipatory state, was easily swayed by the first persuasive speaker who opened his mouth. One brash young man began to taunt them mockingly, "Why are you waiting for the bishop, who is filling his belly with the monks? Come on, if anyone wants his child signed with the cross, he can come to me." He took some mud, and smeared the face of the nearest child, muttering some obscene words in parody of the blessing. His mood spread among the crowd, and those who saw what he had done shouted "Bind up that one's forehead" (that is, to cover the supposed chrism) and there were gusts of coarse laughter. But the young man who had begun it all soon began raving, as his blasphemy turned to frenzy. He tore his hair, grimaced, and beat his head against the wall. His reaction was no doubt triggered by his awareness that he had committed an outrage, and tension would be heightened by the shocked disapproval of the children's parents. Those who saw the change in him acclaimed it as a miracle, praised God and drove the maniac away. He stumbled about in a crazy way, and then plunged into a well or pit next to the cemetery. He could easily have choked to death, but his kinsmen hauled him out with ropes and carried him to the inn. When Wulfstan was told of the episode, he grieved both for the young man's wrongdoing and for his punishment. He sent his blessing to the culprit, who became rational again, but he died a few days later, "either in consequence of his blasphemy or of his injuries."[51]

On another occasion when the abbot of Gloucester invited Wulfstan to dedicate a church in his city, there was a sensational happening of a different kind. A crowd of people thronged around the bishop, pleading, as they usually did, for remission of the penances they had incurred, and also for his blessing. Wulfstan was encouraged to see the people flocking in to the service of God, "like a mighty river," and he responded to them wholeheartedly. He spent most of the day in preaching to them, instilling into them the things they most needed to learn. The theme of his sermon was that they shoud live peacefully, that peace was the most precious

[51]Ibid., pp. 37–8.

thing that people could strive to obtain. It was peace which brought salvation and is God's final purpose for mankind:

Peace was chanted by the angel choir at the Nativity. Peace was given by the Lord to the disciples before the Crucifixion. Peace was what He brought back to them at His Resurrection.

Wulfstan continued in similar vein, and as a result, many people who had been bitterly opposed to one another agreed on that day to be reconciled. People urged one another to make peace, and if any were still in dispute they appealed to the bishop to mediate.[52] Wulfstan took the opportunity offered by the church dedication to suppress a whole spate of personal conflicts then being waged in and around Gloucester. Their causes are not known, but probably many of them sprang from the tenurial revolution caused by the Norman settlement.

William the Bald was a resident in the city of Gloucester, where he held a house at a rent of 12d,[53] but he is not readily identifiable as a property-holder elsewhere in Wulfstan's diocese. He took the opportunity of Wulfstan's visit to explain the grave danger he was in since he had accidentally killed a man without any malicious intent.[54] The Old English laws permitted someone in this situation to offer compensation, the *wergild* (man-price), to the kindred of the victim.[55] William had tried to do so, but the man's family were bent on vengeance. The abbot of Gloucester had repeatedly tried to mediate, without success. William explained to Wulfstan that there were five brothers, all threatening to avenge the death of their kinsman, and that was enough to frighten any man. Who would not be terrified at the sight of five strong, fierce men who were out to take the life of one? The gang of five were brought before Wulfstan, who asked them to pardon William's wrongdoing, but they vehemently refused. They said angrily that sooner than fail to avenge their brother, they would accept excommunication – the abbot, or perhaps Wulfstan, had evidently hinted at this. Wulfstan was still robed in his full episcopal vestments, worn in honour of the church dedication, but that did not deter him from prostrating himself at their feet, begging them again to put aside their vengeance. If they would accept a settlement, he promised that he would have Masses said for the soul of the dead man, both in Gloucester and at Worcester itself.

[52]Ibid., p. 38.
[53]*Domesday Book 15: Gloucestershire*, G4.
[54]*Vita Wulfstani*, p. 38.
[55]This ruling on *wergild* was reiterated in a post-Conquest compilation of Old English Law, the so-called "Laws of William I," chs 7–8: *Laws of the Kings of England from Edmund to Henry I*, pp. 256–7.

Wulfstan's public act of humility had no effect. The five still declared that they would never be reconciled to William, and that the death of their brother had so enraged them that they had lost any humane feelings. Their rejection of the moving plea of the elderly bishop was an act which they knew to be a grave wrong before God. Wulfstan's humiliation of himself in public, in his attempt to end the vendetta, would cause a great stir of emotion among the crowds of clerics and laity. The expected response in such dramatic circumstances would be for the aggrieved men to humble themselves in return, and accept a reconciliation. Their failure to do so was an insult to Wulfstan, and a rejection of his episcopal authority. Despite his well-known personal humility, he was fully conscious of what was due to his episcopal office. Even more ominously, the men had rejected his mediation of the peace of God.

Wulfstan now took a sterner line. He said that it was easy to distinguish between the children of God and the children of the Devil. Citing the saying of Our Lord: "Blessed are the peacemakers, for they shall be called the children of God" (Matthew 5:9), Wulfstan said that those who make peace impossible are self-evidently children of the Devil, since men are the offspring of those whose work they do (John 8:44). The crowd started shouting that the bishop was right, and that they believed what he said. They all began to harangue the vindictive brothers – probably telling them that they were accursed. This concerted verbal battery produced sensational results. The fiercest of the five broke down. He wallowed on the ground, gnawing the earth, clawing at it with his fingers, and even foaming at the mouth. He was evidently sweating heavily so that his perspiration condensed in the cool air, because the bystanders saw what seemed to be smoke coming from his limbs, and the air around him was polluted with the foul stench. The other four brothers were shattered. Their pride and insolence vanished, and they frantically started pleading for the reconciliation which they had earlier rejected. They offered peace and begged for mercy. Their cringing terror was all for themselves, but their sudden submission was prompted by love of their brother, or so it seemed to the bishop's circle. Since all five were guilty of the same crimes (of hatred and obduracy), they were frightened that the wrath of God was about to fall on them, too. Wulfstan took pity on their new-found humility. Mass was said, and afterwards he granted healing to the demented brother, relieved the others from their fears, and brought them all to accept peace.[56]

After such sensational events, no-one dared to contradict Wulfstan when he preached reconciliation. He in turn was glad that his flock was

[56] *Vita Wulfstani*, pp. 38–9. William of Malmesbury, *De Gestis Pontificum Anglorum*, pp. 283–4.

growing wiser and better, and that his ministrations resulted in their increased spiritual well-being. The gradual improvement encouraged him to continue with his preaching, using all possible arguments, and at some physical cost to himself. In his last years he suffered pain in his legs – probably from arthritis – and he used to order Coleman to preach in his place. Wulfstan valued Coleman for his chaste lifestyle, his dignified presence, his fluent speech and his considerable learning. But the people did not care for his preaching as much as they did for Wulfstan's. When the bishop himself preached reconciliation everyone hung on his words, but when Coleman preached, they started muttering, or drifted away. Coleman, the narrator of this story, claimed that he was then vindicated by Heaven, so that everyone should learn to honour the bishop in honouring his ministers. There was a workman in Worcester called Ermer, a mason by trade, specializing as a plasterer, who had a murderous hatred of someone else in the town. Whenever he heard Coleman start preaching on reconciliation, he immediately went out of the church, without waiting to hear the rest of the sermon. His excuse to himself was that the preacher was not Wulfstan. Since Coleman was only a monk his advice coud be ignored. But Coleman noted with satisfaction that God did not see things in that way. Not long after Ermer had begun walking out of Coleman's sermons, he was working up on a scaffold, laying stones, when the timbers broke. He fell, and was lamed in both legs. He was bedridden for a whole year, and never walked properly again. This taught a lesson to many other people, and subsequently no one dared to refuse when he was ordered in Wulfstan's name to accept reconciliation with his neighbour.[57]

Another occurrence of Divine displeasure striking someone who disobeyed Wulfstan happened when the bishop arrived on the Sunday after Easter at Blockley (Gloucs). This episcopal manor on the Cotswold Edge had been the site of an early minster.[58] There was a parish church there, since its priest is recorded in the Domesday Survey, but it seems that there was also a chapel in the compound of the episcopal manor house, and that it was supervised by the resident chamberlain. When the bishop was ready to say Mass, he was vexed to find that the altar furnishings were in a deplorable condition. The guttered candles were in common candlesticks, and the altar-linen had clearly not been washed for a long time. Such slovenliness was unworthy of the service of God. Wulfstan sent a young server to run to the chamberlain with orders to

[57] *Vita Wulfstani*, pp. 39–40.
[58] In 1086, Wulfstan held in demesne 25.5 hides, some two-thirds of the total estate there: *Domesday Book 16: Worcestershire*, 2:38; Dyer, *Lords and Peasants in a Changing Society*, pp. 11, 15n, 23.

put things right. But this man had often presumed on the kindly bishop's good nature, and now he was outraged at the unexpected censure. He boxed the ears of the boy, who burst into tears and ran to tell Wulfstan. Those who were standing round the bishop noticed the change in his expression which reflected his anger at this defiance, but he did not say anything, and passed over the matter for the moment. Meanwhile the chamberlain's anger at Wulfstan's criticism turned to fear as he realized the outrage he had committed in defying the bishop's orders. He had a seizure, collapsed unconscious to the floor of his room, and scarcely seemed to breathe. He looked as though he was on the point of death, with his ashen complexion and chilled limbs. When he regained consciousness, he could not speak. The people who ran to help could not think at first what was the matter, until they recalled that he was afflicted at the very moment when Wulfstan grew angry because he had struck the innocent child. They decided that the chamberlain was now paying for his sacrilege in rejecting Wulfstan's orders and attacking his messenger. The only hope for the man was to obtain Wulfstan's pardon for him. The intermediary was an unnamed monk – evidently Coleman. Wulfstan at once granted his blessing to the chamberlain, and as soon as he expressed penitence for his sin, he recovered.[59]

Just as these stories reflect a widespread belief that Wulfstan mediated the anger of God at human sin, so another series of incidents reflects the bishop's reputation as the mediator of His loving and saving powers. Wulfstan willingly acted as mediator in cases of mental illness, where the underlying spiritual malaise fell within his proper sphere. Two such incidents occurred in quick succession, during a visit which he was making to his manor of Bishop's Cleeve (Gloucs).[60] One of his well-off peasant farmers there suffered from bouts of violence, during which he would destroy anything that came within reach, tearing it apart with his hands, or gnawing it to pieces with his teeth. When his destructive attention fell on anything out of reach, he would grind his teeth, hurl curses and spit at it. Perhaps he suffered from a form of epilepsy, but to his contemporaries he would appear to be possessed by an evil spirit. His medical symptoms were most likely augmented by some form of mental collapse, when he met with the repeated hostility – as he saw it – of his neighbours. Eventually the local people agreed to take steps to deal with his dangerous habits. His friends and immediate neighbours took the lead, and despite his resistance, they bound him with thongs of rawhide. But he seized these in his teeth, and bit them through or burst them as

---

[59]*Vita Wulfstani*, pp. 41–2.

[60]Ibid., p. 28; *Domesday Book 15: Gloucestershire*, 3:7; Dyer, *Lords and Peasants in a Changing Society*, pp. 15n, 23, 44–5.

though they were merely threads of cotton. The neighbours then managed to bind him with iron chains to the post, or the frame, of his bed. He shouted at them, and continued to bellow in a confused way when he was securely bound. This roaring terrified people even at a distance, and sounded like the discordant yelling of an army.

When Wulfstan came to Bishop's Cleeve, the demented man's relations brought their troubles to him. They begged him to come to see the wretched fellow, since it was physically impossible to haul him before the bishop. Wulfstan did not hesitate for a moment, although he sighed deeply as he accompanied them to the house. The demented man recognized Wulfstan. When he caught sight of the bishop, he started to tremble, and to shout out insults, grimaced, and spat out a torrent of saliva. His torments grieved Wulfstan, who raised his hands in prayer, and said: "Lord Jesus Christ, who through Your death delivered mankind from the power of the Devil; Who also permitted the demon Legion, cast out from a man, to enter into the swine (Luke 8:26–39); deliver this man from the Devil and restore him to his right mind." Then, turning to the deranged man, he said: "Unclean spirit, depart from this image of God, and render honour to the Holy Spirit." Amazingly, the man was cured at once. He shook off his savage mood, stopped rolling his eyes, and returned to his senses. His mental state improved by the hour, and by the time the bishop left the village, the man was completely cured of his madness. He survived for some years after this, outliving Wulfstan, and testified to the bishop's miracles the more convincingly in that he had personally experienced their blessings.[61]

The rituals involved in the healing of the mentally ill would be those used in exorcism, a practice which had an ancient tradition in the Church. Mental illness of any kind would be perceived as demonic possession, and its treatment therefore fell within the bishop's proper sphere of activity. Mental illness is by no means solely a phenomenon of modern urban and industrial society, and medieval clergy were probably often summoned to deal with cases comparable to that which confronted Wulfstan. Those who gained a livelihood from agriculture would frequently be subjected to stress caused by anxieties about crop failure, disease among livestock, and other natural hazards for which there was no remedy, quite apart from the tensions generated by disputes arising from the tenurial revolution of the eleventh century, or from a breakdown in personal relationships. But an exorcizing ritual such as that which Wulfstan performed would work only in certain cases – hence his sighs as he approached the man. The recital of familiar-sounding words, and the recalling of a comparable healing performed by Our Lord would

[61]*Vita Wulfstani*, pp. 28–9.

reassure the kinsfolk of the sufferer and reduce their anxiety. This would be sensed by the patient, and to the extent that he himself was conscious of the words being used, his own tensions would also lessen. The cessation of his violent conduct would ease the tense atmosphere among those around him, causing him to relax still further, and this in turn would contribute towards the return of his mental equilibrium.

A second healing of mental illness occurred a few days after the first, while Wulfstan was still on this same tour. His dapifer, or steward, needed to let him know about some necessary expenditure on the episcopal estate. He sent word of it by a squire, who had not gone far on his way when he was seized by a disturbing mental affliction – possibly a form of agoraphobia – which caused him to flee from all human company and take refuge in the forest nearby, where he stayed night and day. It was believed that his odd behaviour was the result of Divine judgement. The country people were uneasy at the idea of some reprobate lurking in their area in this eccentric way. They captured him, and bound him tight with cords, but he was put in the charge of a careless keeper, managed to get rid of his bonds, and escaped to the woods again. The people of the neighbourhood were scared to go anywhere they believed him to be lurking, whether because he had injured some of them, or because it was natural to shun anyone who avoided human contact. Wulfstan had been travelling more slowly than was advisable, and it was dusk when he reached the settlement which was troubled about the fugitive. The bishop was just about to go to bed when he heard of the man's wretched condition, which was a great cause of agitated talk among the servants. Wulfstan immediately pointed out to them that it was their religious duty to offer up prayers for the sufferer, and that they should particularly say the Lord's Prayer – one of the few which they would know by heart. It was a regular habit of Wulfstan's that, wherever he was, or whatever time of day it was when he heard of anyone's illness or death, he immediately ordered all those present to pray, whether that the sick person might be cured, or that the dead might rest in peace. The young man's mind cleared the same evening, and he returned to the village of his own accord. That very night he mingled with the members of the household, and never again gave the slightest sign of madness.[62] The disturbance created on the road by the bishop's retinue as it passed by would be readily heard, and perhaps seen, by anyone lurking in the woods. This in turn would prompt the young man both to recall his mission to Wulfstan, and to sense that the bishop could protect him from his persecutors. As he approached the house, he would gather from the prayers being offered aloud by the assembled household that they had his

[62]Ibid., pp. 29–30.

welfare at heart, and that he was acceptable among them. His calm reappearance would then make this acceptance a reality. Everyone had prayed for the squire, but it was Wulfstan's instigation of this corporate act which was perceived to have ensured the Divine intervention which restored the young man to health. Those who had charge of other sufferers would now confidently turn to their bishop as the mediator of healing.

Wulfstan achieved a considerable reputation as a healer during his lifetime. Medieval churchmen frequently pointed out to the families of sufferers that scientific medicine alone was less efficacious than the healing of the spirit mediated through the prayers of churchmen. The intercessions of Wulfstan were widely believed to be the most effective of all. This proved to be the case when a young girl in Evesham became mentally ill. Her family was well off but had unspecified troubles of one sort or another which perhaps contributed to her distress. Her condition worsened until she abandoned the family home and took to wandering aimlessly down country lanes, or wherever else her whim led her. Her parents, who thought this quite unacceptable, seized her and bound her with chains. This harsh treatment was followed by growing compassion as her condition worsened. First they tried bringing doctors to treat her, and then priests, in the hope that she could be healed by exorcism. One of these was the unnamed prior of Evesham who is the source for this story, but he, like the other clerics, and the doctors, went away disappointed that he could achieve nothing. Neither medicine nor exorcism produced any result, while the family spent much of their wealth on these useless remedies. When they were utterly discouraged they went back to the prior of Evesham, knowing that he was a good-living man, to see whether he had any more advice for them. They said that if he knew of anything they might try, he had only to tell them and they would certainly do it, provided it was humanly possible. He thought for a while, and then advised that they should take her to Wulfstan. They should put their trust in the bishop, as he himself did, since no sickness dared to exist in the presence of a man who delighted in submitting himself to the commands of his Creator. The girl's parents thought this suggestion a good one; they went to the bishop and everything turned out well. As soon as Wulfstan saw the girl, he was greatly moved by the wretchedness of her sufferings. He groaned at her misery, but then found a cure. He stretched out his hand and blessed her, murmuring what the onlookers understood to be a mysterious and special prayer. The deranged girl immediately came to her senses, recognized her family and blessed the bishop. He gave her this valedictory advice: "Go home in peace; bless God, not Wulfstan. Love virtue; reject sinful ways. Do not lose your modesty in case something worse happens to you." This sounds as though her alienation from her family resulted from an urge to go down the primrose path. Any plans the parents had made for the girl's future would be thwarted if she gained a reputation for promiscuity, and chaining her up might seem the only answer. Wulfstan's advice sank in, and soon after the girl's recovery, she entered a nunnery, where she remained for the rest of her life.[63] For a monastic writer, there could be no happier ending to her story.

Wulfstan was more reluctant to try to mediate cures of physical illness, but people approached him as he travelled about the diocese visiting his scattered manors, which served as staging posts on his regular tours during which he combined ecclesiastical and secular duties. In this way the food rents due from each estate in turn would support him and his retinue.[64] Wulfstan's route would be easily discovered by those who wanted to see him, including beggars who thought it worthwhile to track him down. On one occasion when Wulfstan's schedule included a visit to Kempsey, in the valley of the Severn, alms were distributed every day to a group of beggars who sat outside his residence. Among them was a man who had come all the way from Kent, and was suffering from the disfiguring complaint termed "the King's Evil," identified in later centuries as scrofula.[65] All his limbs had gradually become infected, so that it could scarcely be said that he still had a body. He went around like a living corpse, a horrible sight, running with slimy pus. Even his speech was disgusting to hear, because he could communicate only in a hoarse shriek. The beggars received alms distributed by Arthur, the bishop's steward at Kempsey.[66] He was repelled by the appearance of the poor man from Kent, who repeatedly begged him not to despise talking to him, and not to shun him for once. Finally the man implored him to turn back to him in the name of God. Arthur stayed, and gave him the chance to tell him all he wanted to, even though the man's mumbling and panting made it difficult to understand him. The beggar said he had been born in Kent, and he was now riddled with a foul disease, as Arthur could see. Three times he had had a revelation in a dream that he should present himself to Wulfstan in the hope of obtaining healing, and that

[63]Ibid., pp. 27–8.
[64]On the economic management of the episcopal estates, see Dyer, Lords and Peasants in a Changing Society, pp. 11, 28–30, 36–7.
[65]Vita Wulfstani, p. 30. See also F. Barlow, "The King's Evil," reprinted from English Historical Review, 95 (1980), pp. 3–27, in F. Barlow, The Norman Conquest and Beyond (1983), pp. 24–47, esp. p. 26.
[66]Vita Wulfstani, p. 30. On Kempsey, see Domesday Book 16: Worcestershire, 2:2. The personal name Arthur is uncommon in this period. The bishop's steward is perhaps identical with Arthur the Frenchman (probably a Breton), who in 1086 was a tenant of Westminster Abbey in Powick (Worcs): Domesday Book 16: Worcestershire, 8:10e.

was the reason he had come there. He asked Arthur to request Wulfstan to intercede for him with God. The steward presented his request, but this displeased Wulfstan, who did not want to be exposed to human adulation as a wonder-worker. He replied, "It is not for me to attempt any miracle, especially something of this sort. Go out and give him food and clothing, so that at least he has the consolation of some human kindness to recompense him for his exhausting journey." Arthur's intervention would have come to nothing, if Eilmer the priest had not now become involved.[67]

Next to Wulfstan himself, Eilmer could be esteemed as the holiest man among the bishop's circle, except that he was so oppressively severe. It was well known that Wulfstan would often break off an amusing conversation if Eilmer would not smile, or if he actually reproached him with a frown. In all other respects, his lifestyle was just as it should be, chaste and temperate, so that no-one who envied him could find any fault, and his friends could not praise him too much. Wulfstan greatly admired his good qualities, and every day he devoutly heard Eilmer say Mass. Each of them vied with the other in their religious observance, so that they never let a day go by without the celebration of the Blessed Sacrament. Eilmer now took the sick man into his lodging, and spoke to him in a kindly and comforting way. What is more, he thought of a way to win from Wulfstan surreptitiously the miracle which could not be obtained openly. Everything hinged on the fact that Eilmer always accompanied the bishop at the daily Mass. One day, when Wulfstan had been celebrant, Eilmer contrived to take away the water in which the bishop afterwards performed the ritual hand-washing. The priest gave this water to Arthur, and ordered him to pour it into a bath which had been prepared. The sick man bathed, a sight which was horrible to watch, since his flesh was full of sores. But amazingly the swollen boils went down at once, the deadly matter ran away, and all his flesh was restored so that it was pure as that of a little child. Even the scabs and mange on his head vanished, and his hair grew thick and handsome again. Poor hygiene and vitamin deficiency had no doubt contributed to his condition in the first place. A thorough bathing, faith in the water purloined from Wulfstan, good food provided by the steward, and the

[67]*Vita Wulfstani*, pp. 30–1. The *obit* of Elmer, priest and monk, on 26 November, is among those listed in the Kalendar of Wulfstan's homiliary, but it has been suggested that this man is identical with a witness to Worcester charters down to 1017; I. Atkins, "The Church of Worcester from the Eighth to the Twelfth centuries," Part II, *The Antiquaries Journal*, 20 (1940), pp. 1–38, and 203–28, esp. p. 29. On the zealous Eilmer, see also William of Malmesbury, *De Gestis Pontificum Anglorum*, p. 282 (where his name is given as Egelric).

interest taken in his plight by Eilmer and Arthur, all combined to restore the Kentish man to health.[68] Readers of this story would understand that the cure had been effected by the combined faith of these three men in Wulfstan's innate powers as a mediator of healing.

In other cases of physical healing Wulfstan mediated intentionally. In each case his intervention took the form of a simple prayer. One such episode occurred as he was travelling from Worcester to one of his manors, riding last in the company, as he always did, so that no-one interrupted him with casual talk as he recited the Psalms. Coleman, the direct witness of this incident, was riding near him. When Wulfstan noticed a blind man at the roadside, shouting out to them, he signalled to Coleman to give alms to the man, because he thought that was what he wanted. But the blind man was asking for something far more worthwhile than that. He walked alongside Coleman's horse, and explained his request, asking Coleman to beg Wulfstan, in the name of God, to stop for a little while, since it had been revealed to him in a dream that the bishop could cure his sight, if he chose. Coleman agreed to intercede for the man, repeated his request to Wulfstan and added his own entreaties. Wulfstan resisted for some time, pleading that he was unworthy to work miracles, but Coleman could usually persuade the kindly bishop to do as he asked, and continued pestering him until he dismounted from his horse. Wulfstan repeated Psalm 25: "I lift up my soul to You, O Lord my God" and made the sign of the cross over the eyes of the blind man. The episcopal party then continued on its way. A week later, Coleman was travelling back to Worcester when he found the man again, now seeing clearly. Coleman himself, and all those who heard of this incident, gave thanks to God, and spread the news of what had occurred.[69]

Coleman would have seen blind people before this, and he is unlikely to have been mistaken about the man's former condition. A beggar might pretend to be blind, but he had no incentive to claim a cure when the bishop himself firmly rejected the role of miracle-worker. The man perhaps suffered from cataracts, which might respond to rudimentary treatment of the kind which was practised in later centuries,[70] yet Coleman does not say that such treatment took place. Without further evidence it would be doing Coleman an injustice to argue that he simply

[68] *Vita Wulfstani*, p. 31.
[69] Ibid., pp. 33–4.
[70] For the treatment known in the nineteenth century as couching, in which the cataract film was pressed below the line of vision, see Elizabeth Gaskell, *Mary Barton*, ed. and introd. E. Wright (1987), pp. 464, 493. Worcester was not conspicuous among those Benedictine houses which retained some knowledge of classical medical works in this period: Anne F. Dawtry, "The *Modus Medendi* and the Benedictine Order in Anglo-Norman England," in *The Church and Healing*, ed. W. J. Sheils (1982), pp. 25–38.

omitted such details, or falsified events entirely, in order to heighten the drama of his story, but in another instance his fellow monks accused him of precisely that.[71] Two points clearly emerge. First, the man did not claim an instant cure, his recovery took place over several days. Secondly, his waylaying of Wulfstan testifies to the bishop's growing reputation as a mediator of the healing of physical diseases, despite his own firm discouragement of this role, in contrast to his acceptance of his duty of mediating spiritual healing, which fell within his remit by virtue of his clerical status.

On one occasion when Wulfstan was asked to assist in the curing of a physical disease, his own response was minimal, but a cure still occurred, thanks to the faith of the sufferer in his powers of mediation. In the salt-producing vill of Droitwich (Worcs)[72] there was a well-off couple whose comfortable lifestyle was shattered when the woman suddenly developed arthritis, which afflicted each of her limbs, and stiffened and knotted all her joints. She grew worse each day, and became bedridden. The couple called in physicians, who did their best with such skills as they had, and made up the difference with promises. But these medical consultations achieved nothing. The couple spent all their available money, but just when the woman was despairing of human help, she had a vision that she would be delivered from her illness if she could obtain a letter from Wulfstan. She had a son who was in the bishop's household, and who was being trained as a clerk by Coleman. This young man took a message from his mother which eventually reached Wulfstan, who responded by sending the succinct reply, "May Jesus Christ heal you, Segild." This note was conveyed to the invalid by the deacon Frewin, an honest, cheerful man who later became a monk. Segild received the bishop's gift with faith. The scroll was first placed where the pain was most severe, and her discomfort was eased. Soon she was altogether rid of her illness, and regained her strength.[73]

Coleman, as chancellor, or head of Wulfstan's writing-office, naturally supervised the trainee administrators, who would generally be young men from well-off families like that of Segild and her husband. She was evidently impressed by the administrative skills which her educated son was acquiring, and had probably heard him describe how the bishop's

[71] *Vita Wulfstani*, p. 42.
[72] The Domesday Survey contains numerous references to salt production in Droitwich. For the involvement of the church of Worcester in this lucrative manufacture, see *Domesday Book 16: Worcestershire*, 2:7, 2:15, 2:48, 2:68, 2:77, 2:78, 2:82, 2:84; Dyer, *Lords and Peasants in a Changing Society*, p. 25.
[73] *Vita Wulfstani*, pp. 35–6. See also M. L. Cameron "Anglo-Saxon Medicine and Magic," *Anglo-Saxon England*, 17 (1988), pp. 191–215, esp. pp. 210–15 on the part played in healing by the patient's confidence in the healer.

orders were conveyed by tersely worded writs. Since the bishop's written instructions were promptly obeyed in temporal matters, it might seem to her that he could also mediate healing in this way. The analogy of Our Lord's healing of the centurion's servant (Matthew 8:5–13) would not be lost on a monastic readership, even if this did not occur to the sufferer herself. Visions were often experienced by those who were ill, helping them to formulate in visual terms ideas which they could not otherwise articulate;[74] Segild, like the blind man and the Kentish beggar, was helped by her dreams to grasp the idea that Wulfstan could heal her. In her case, as in the other two, the supernatural connotations of the revelation would generate the faith needed to effect a cure. From Wulfstan's standpoint, he had simply sent a kindly note expressing the hope that Christ would heal the woman, but for Segild the letter itself was the means of her cure.

The cheerful deacon Frewin, who brought Wulfstan's message to Segild, was one of the bishop's clerks, active towards the end of Wulfstan's episcopate. This honest intermediary is introduced into the story to provide circumstantial detail and as a corroborative witness. Throughout his episcopate, Wulfstan, like his predecessors, would have maintained a household staff of secular clerks, besides a hierarchy of lay officers, including chamberlains, stewards and reeves. Some of these individuals are mentioned, by name or by office, in Wulfstan's *Life*, but the episodic nature of this material, combined with the infrequent survival of the bishop's charters, precludes any systematic survey of his administration. Coleman, Wulfstan's future biographer, would be in constant attendance on the bishop during Wulfstan's later years, in his capacity as chancellor, in charge of the bishop's personal chapel, and his writing-office,[75] but it is uncertain whether he relinquished these duties when he was made prior of Westbury-on-Trym.

Wulfstan's mediation of the healing of mental and physical illness was the more welcome throughout his diocese in that conventional medical care was available only to limited groups in society. Even those who could afford scientific medicine discovered, like Segild and her husband,

---

[74]C. J. Holdsworth, "Visions and Visionaries in the Middle Ages," *History*, 48 (1963), pp. 141–53, esp. pp. 143–4, 146.
[75]On Frewin see *Hemingi Chartularium*, II, pp. 421–4. Frewin is among the monks of Worcester listed *c*.1104: *Durham Liber Vitae*, folio 22 recto. Some of Wulfstan's late charters, dating from between 1089 and 1092, each list several of his officials: *Cartulary of Worcester*, nos 2–3, 52.

1. *The Portiforium of Saint Wulfstan:* a prayer-book which probably belonged to him. It includes this full page portrait of King David playing upon the harp. (MS 391 f.24 is reproduced by kind permission of The Master and Fellows of Corpus Christi College, Cambridge)

2. *Charter B. 1680: The Alveston Charter* This is the original version of a grant which St Wulfstan made and witnessed. Reproduced by kind permission of the Dean and Chapter of Worcester Cathedral (Photograph: J. R. Thoumine)

3. 'Hemming's Cartulary' This is a composite manuscript, the second part of which was composed under the direction of St Wulfstan and is an important illustration of his activities. There are three folios reproduced here: MS Cotton Tiberius A. XIII, folios 119, 131v and 144. (Reproduced by kind permission of the British Library)

4. *Dialogues:* Clare College MS 30 Gregory the Great (produced at Worcester in the late eleventh century). Five splendid historiated initials. (Reproduced by kind permission of Cambridge University Library)

5. MS *Cotton Claudius A.V.* folios 160v–199v comprise a late twelfth-century text of the *Life* of St Wulfstan. Illustrated here is the first page, 160 verso. (Reproduced by kind permission of the British Library)

6. MS *Latin Theol. d, 33 folio 1r Augustine, Enchiridion* (Reproduced by kind permission of the Bodleian Library, Oxford)

VM·INhERE·Mo·
SCIThIE·VBI·
MONAChOʒ₧·
PROBATISSiMI·

PATRES· ETOMNIS COMMORATUR PERFECTIO·ABBATE
MOỳSEN qui INTER illoS EGREGIOS floRES SuaviuS NON
Solum acruali neru eria theorica intuire flagrabat

7. *MS Hatton 23, folios 3v and 18v Cassian, Collations* (Reproduced by kind permission of the Bodleian Library, Oxford)

EGVS
ITA(
MXIϝ
SOP(
cym ortū lyc:
NOBIS CLARI

- dentes repmissam narratione reposcere co(
beatus moyses ita exarsis est. Cū uideā uo

8. *King John's Tomb in Worcester Cathedral*. King John adopted St Wulfstan as his patron saint and insisted upon being buried beside him. The tomb covering is a mid-thirteenth-century sculpture, depicting the king flanked by miniature figures of St Wulfstan and St Oswald. (Reproduced by kind permission of A. F. Kersting)

9. *A Writ of King Edward (The Confessor) appointing Wulfstan to the bishopric of Worcester*. (BL Additional Charter 19802. Reproduced by kind permission of the British Library)

10. *Worcester Cathedral from the river*. The exterior of the cathedral is now largely a Victorian restoration. (Reproduced by kind permission of the Dean and Chapter of Worcester Cathedral) (Photograph: J. R. Thoumine)

11. *A Panoramic View from the Tower of Worcester Cathedral*, viewing towards the Malvern Hills. St Wulfstan's chief political role in the area was to guard the Severn fords in time of insurrection in the Welsh Marches. (Reproduced by kind permission of the Dean and Chapter of Worcester Cathedral) (Photograph: J. R. Thoumine)

12. *The Crypt of Worcester Cathedral* is reproduced by kind permission of the Dean and Chapter of Worcester Cathedral (Photograph: J. R. Thoumine)

or the couple at Evesham, that the high fees of physicians were not always matched by effective treatment. A monastic writer such as Coleman had a vested interest in extolling the superior quality of healing effected by spiritual means. This required the exercise of religious faith on the part of the sufferer, or, in cases of mental affliction, on that of his kindred, but this is not to deny that such healing could, and did, take place. Wulfstan himself firmly rejected the role of miracle-worker, but he had a widespread and growing reputation as such, and it may be that he really did possess the gift of healing hands.

Faith in Wulfstan's spiritual powers led to a spectacular event of another kind being ascribed to his intervention. Once again, Coleman is the informant. As the foregoing episodes indicate, the bishop's chancellor frequently travelled throughout the region. When he first brought this particular story back to Worcester from the seaport of Bristol, on the estuary of the river Severn, he was widely disbelieved by those who said it was untrue, and that he was only citing it to enhance Wulfstan's reputation. Eventually, though, he produced enough credible witnesses who swore by all that was holy to the truth of the following episode. They claimed that some Bristol men and other Englishmen were sailing on a trading voyage to Ireland when they ran into a violent storm. All the elements seemed in disarray. There was a howling gale, and torrential rain, and the force of the wind was overwhelming. The ropes snapped; the mast broke and the oars were swept away. The ship drifted completely out of control. For three days and nights the sailors went without food or sleep, expecting annihilation. On the fourth day, when their morale was sinking fast, one of them had an inspiration, and said, "Those of you who come from the diocese of the holy Bishop Wulfstan, try praying to God's mercy that through Wulfstan's intercession He may bring us out of this danger." The others took up his suggestion, and they all began to pray heartily. Then they saw a vision of Wulfstan, going around the ship fastening the tackle, splicing the ropes, encouraging one man here and another there, and eventually the whole crew, saying to them: "Cheer up. Hoist the sails, belay the halliards and sheets, and by God's good will and my help you will soon reach land." Soon after this they reached a harbour in Ireland. After a short stopover, they returned to England with fair winds, and began to spread the story of their miraculous rescue. Coleman concluded this episode in Wulfstan's *Life* by arguing that, since God had often worked such wonders in ancient times, it was not impossible that He should do similar things in the present. Coleman knew of accounts of holy men who helped people over a great distance, sometimes knowingly but on other occasions unconsciously, appearing to them in visible form even though they were present only in spirit. He insisted that although he knew of such stories, he was not borrowing from them.[76]

Coleman claimed that it was Wulfstan's supernatural rescue of the storm-tossed trading vessel which made the Bristol people obedient to him, so that he was eventually able to eradicate an evil custom of long standing in that town, one which was practised in defiance both of the laws of God and the prohibition of King William.[77] Traders from Bristol used to buy men from all over England, and transport them for sale in Ireland. They even sold women, whom they themselves had made pregnant. These young men and girls, bound together in long rows, were openly sold in the market in Bristol. Wulfstan's eradication of this long-established trade took some time to complete. He knew how entrenched the Bristol men were in their ways, so he would stay in the neighbourhood for two or three months at a time. This could be conveniently arranged, since the church of Worcester possessed lands in the south of Gloucestershire, within a few miles of Bristol, including the big demesne manor of Westbury-on-Trym, where the bishop founded his priory. Each Sunday Wulfstan would come into the city of Bristol and preach to its inhabitants. They responded gradually, and in ending their trade in slaves, the Bristolians set an example for the rest of England. When almost all the traders had been converted by his preaching, one slave merchant held out against him and continued in business, until his fellow citizens blinded him and expelled him from the city. Coleman thought they meant well, even though they over-reacted, but then, the Bristolians always were a rough lot, given to extremes.[78]

Slavery had been a feature of life in Anglo-Saxon England since the earliest times. The majority of slaves, both male and female, were employed in agricultural and allied work on the estates in the neighbourhood in which they had been born and bred. The manumission, or freeing, of slaves earned spiritual merit for the owner, and was a frequent provision in wills. In the course of time, many of the slaves in private

---

[76] *Vita Wulfstani*, pp. 42–3. The writer perhaps had in mind episodes such as occur in *Adomnan's Life of Columba*, ed. and transl. A. O. Anderson and M. O. Anderson (1961), pp. 204–5, 302–3. Coleman could have heard of the sailors' rescue while he was prior of Westbury-on-Trym near Bristol, and the monastic community of Worcester perhaps had commercial interests in the seaport. The church of Worcester was granted exemption from toll on two ships at London as early as some uncertain date between 743 and 745: *Anglo-Saxon Charters*, compiled Sawyer, no. 98.

[77] *Vita Wulfstani*, p. 43. The sale of Christian slaves overseas, and especially to heathen lands, had been forbidden by King Cnut, and the prohibition recurs in the so-called "Laws of William the Conqueror," *Laws of the Kings of England from Edmund to Henry I*, pp. 176–7, 270–1.

[78] *Vita Wulfstani*, pp. 43–4.

ownership were given their liberty and joined the poorest ranks of the peasants. The institution of slavery survived mainly on the big ecclesiastical estates, owned by self-perpetuating corporations whose individual members could not legally alienate the property of their community, while a collective act of manumission would deplete the possessions of the patron saint for whom they were trustees.[79] In 1086, there were still 155 slaves on the estates of the bishopric of Worcester, although Wulfstan, like other major landholders at this time, was gradually settling his permanent labour force of ploughmen, dairymaids and the like on individual smallholdings. The immediate impetus behind this trend was economic, since these people now became responsible for their own maintenance, while their conditions of tenure would still provide all the necessary labour for the estate. By the twelfth century, no slaves remained on the lands of the church of Worcester.[80]

The traffic in slaves from Bristol could draw on regular supplies from various parts of Britain. Prisoners of war, and perhaps even civilians, abducted from Wales or Scotland, would be the one regular source of supply. But many of the slaves would have been native English, who had fallen into slavery through poverty, or as a result of incurring the penalty of penal servitude. When anyone was to be designated as a slave, the law required that this should be done, in accordance with the jurisdictional competence of the master taking possession of him, either in the hallmoot (the court of the lord of the manor) or in the court of the hundred (an administrative division of the shire) or in the village court, in the presence of witnesses. The new slave's master paid toll for him, so that the slave had no opportunity of denying his servile status at a later date. Poverty and imminent starvation would drive some people to this desperate course, either in person or by selling their children. In particular, many people were reduced to starvation in, and for years after, 1070, following the Harrying of the North. In preaching against the sale of slaves overseas, Wulfstan was once more following the example of his namesake, the archbishop. Their objection to the traffic was grounded in a fear that transported slaves would eventually be bought by infidels.[81] The Irish economy is unlikely to have generated a demand for a large and constantly replenished servile workforce in this period, but Irish seaports

[79]D. Pelteret, "Slave raiding and slave trading in early England," *Anglo-Saxon England*, 9 (1981), pp. 99–114; J. S. Moore, "Domesday Slavery," *Anglo-Norman Studies XI*, ed. R. Allen Brown (1989), pp. 191–220.

[80]Dyer, *Lords and Peasants in a Changing Society*, pp. 28, 33, 37, 97, 104; see also Hamshere, "Domesday Book: Estate Structures in the West Midlands," pp. 158–9, 170–1.

[81]Pelteret, "Slave raiding and slave trading in early England," pp. 109–110, 112. On the legal process by which people were formally reduced to slavery, see *Leges Henrici Primi*, ed. and transl. L. J. Downer (1972), 78:2, and 78:2 a–c, pp. 242–4.

perhaps served as trans-shipping bases for contingents of slaves from both Scotland and England. Their eventual destination would be the great agricultural estates of the Iberian peninsula – not only in the Muslim lands of the south, but also in the Christian kingdoms. Archbishop Lanfranc, as well as Wulfstan, is believed to have been instrumental in stopping the shipment of slaves overseas.[82]

The welfare of the souls of the dead was another concern of Wulfstan's. He was continually forbidding men to ride through churchyards just as they pleased, pointing out to them, "Many bodies of the saints lie there, and we should pay reverence to their souls, which are with God." But all his efforts achieved little, since even after his death horsemen still trampled irreverently over graves.[83] He would be particularly concerned at the habitual desecration of the former monastic graveyard in Worcester itself, part of which had been commandeered for the site of the castle.[84] Whenever Wulfstan heard of the death of anyone, he immediately ordered those present to say the Lord's Prayer. On these occasions, Wulfstan himself would recite three psalms: "Praise the Lord all you nations" (Psalm 117); "From out of the depths I call you, O Lord" (Psalm 130); and "Praise the Lord in His Temple on Earth" (Psalm 150), besides appropriate prayers. After he had prayed for the soul of the deceased person, he would speak about him, for a longer or shorter time, as circumstances permitted. He had a Mass sung for the dead every day except Sundays and the greater feasts, when he relaxed this pious duty out of respect for the festival, trusting that he would be heard more readily on other occasions because he refrained from interceding at a time of rejoicing.[85]

Wulfstan enjoyed a considerable reputation as a confessor and spiritual mentor. He gladly received those who came to him to confess their sins, dealing tenderly with them, hearing their confessions in a kindly way and without any sense of rejection. He was willing to weep over their sins, but did not shrink from them on the grounds that these were too grave. As a result, men from all over England did not hesitate to confess to him what they would have entrusted to no other confessor, and were not ashamed to tell him things they had done which they now bitterly regretted. He treated his penitents with goodwill, earnestly advising them not to despair. He taught them how to atone for the sins

---

[82]William of Malmesbury was uncertain whether it was Wulfstan, or Archbishop Lanfranc, who took the dominant role in persuading King William I to ban the sale of slaves overseas: William of Malmesbury, *De Gestis Regum Anglorum*, ed. W Stubbs, 2 vols (1887, 1889), II, p. 329.

[83]*Vita Wulfstani*, p. 53.

[84]William of Malmesbury, *De Gestis Pontificum Anglorum*, p. 253.

[85]*Vita Wulfstani*, p. 53.

they had committed, and also how to avoid sin in the future. As a result of all this, his penitents were among his closest friends.[86] As titular head of the cathedral priory, Wulfstan perhaps considered it his duty to act as confessor to the monks, but the growing numbers at Worcester, combined with his other pressing commitments, would make this impracticable on the weekly basis prescribed in the Rule.[87] In the early years of Wulfstan's episcopate, his penitents had included some of the most prominent men in the realm, notably Harold Godwinson and Abbot Ethelwig. Those who later flocked to Wulfstan from all parts of the country were probably Englishmen who had retained some degree of territorial status. In their defensive position after the Norman settlement, they would prefer an English spiritual director, particularly if their grievances had led to involvement in vendettas with their new "French" neighbours.

Among Wulfstan's regular penitents was a merchant called Sewulf. On one occasion, when the bishop gave him absolution, he added some advice, saying, "You persistently fall back into those sins you confessed before, as the proverb says, 'Opportunity made the robbery possible.' That is the reason I am now advising you to become a monk. If you do, you will avoid those situations which lead you to commit these sins." Sewulf answered that he was unwilling to become a monk because of the strictness of the vows. This made Wulfstan rather angry, and he replied, "Go away. You will become a monk, whether you like it or not, but this will happen only when your capacity for sin is failing." Later on, the prophecy was fulfilled. Sewulf did convert to the religious life when his health was broken with age, and his eventual conversion was prompted by illness. Meanwhile, every time he expressed penitence he recalled Wulfstan's words, and his resistance to his vocation was gradually weakened.[88] In this account of Sewulf's eventual conversion, found in William of Malmesbury's *De Gestis Pontificum Anglorum (Deeds of the English Bishops)*, the reader is told "we saw this [prophecy fulfilled] because he became a monk in our monastery." If William is the speaker, then the implication is that Sewulf became a monk of Malmesbury, but logically it is more likely that he joined the community at Worcester. The story occurs in the middle of a long section of material derived directly

[86]Ibid., pp. 49–50.
[87]*Rule of St. Benedict*, ch. 7: the fifth degree of humility. Already by the time of the Tenth Century Reform provision was made for a substitute confessor: *Regularis Concordia*, ed. and transl. T. Symons (1953), pp. xxxix and n. 2; 18; while by the later eleventh century, when the numbers in monastic houses were increasing, a hierarchy of confessors – abbot, prior and appointed deputies – was prescribed: *The Monastic Constitutions of Lanfranc*, transl. and introd. D. Knowles (1951), pp. 107, 116.
[88]William of Malmesbury, *De Gestis Pontificum Anglorum*, pp. 286–7.

from informants at the cathedral priory, and appears to be a verbatim account, in which the speaker would be a monk of that house, and not William himself. This story is presented as an *exemplum* of the value of confession and the inevitable acceptance of a religious vocation by those for whom it was intended.

Sewulf himself can probably be identified as one or other of two contemporaries with similar names. In 1095, shortly after Wulfstan's death, King William levied a relief on the lands of the vacant bishopric. Among the tenants of the see who are listed as contributors to this exaction are Saulf, who paid £15 and was clearly among the most affluent of them, and also Siward, who contributed £2.[89] A Worcester *obit* list associated with Wulfstan includes the anniversary of the death, on 15 May, of Saulf alias Saewulf (both forms are given), a layman, the father of Clement, but even a deathbed conversion should have earned for Wulfstan's penitent the title of monk. The same *obit* list adds, in a later hand, the anniversary on 25 November of the death of Siword, monk and *conversus* (that is, someone who had come to the monastic life as a mature adult). Among the monks of Worcester included in a list recorded at Durham *c.*1104 are Clement (presumably the son of Saulf alias Saewulf, but not identified as such) and Saeuuold. Several names added to this list in a later hand include that of Saeuuard.[90] The variations in the forms of these personal names (owing to changing practices in the transliteration of distinctive Anglo-Saxon letters) make identification uncertain, but on balance it seems likely that the Sewulf of the story was a rich tenant of Worcester, with a son who was already a monk there, and whose own conversion can be dated to within a few years of Wulfstan's death. Sewulf has been identified with the man of that name who made an adventurous pilgrimage to the Holy Land in 1102–3; later he composed a detailed account of his travels, and more especially of the Holy Places which he visited in various parts of the Latin Kingdom which was established in the wake of the First Crusade. New traditions rapidly grew around old sites, including the former mosque of Al-aqsa in Jerusalem, which now housed the royal palace. Here, Sewulf's Syrian guide showed him what he claimed to be "the bedroom of the Virgin Mary, that of Jesus Christ, and His bathroom."[91]

[89]*Hemingi Chartularium*, I. p. 80.

[90]Atkins, "The Church of Worcester," Part II, p. 32. It is arguable that both entries relate to the same man and that the belated inclusion of the *conversus* Siward was an attempt to rectify the status of Clement's father. *Durham Liber Vitae*, fol. 22 recto.

[91]A. Grabois, "Anglo-Norman England and the Holy Land," *Anglo-Norman Studies VII*, ed. R. Allen Brown (1985), pp. 132–41, esp. pp. 138–40. The narrative has been published as *Relatio de peregrinatione Saewulfi ad Hierosolymam et Terram Sanctam*, ed.

Wulfstan's household, like that of other magnates, admitted young boys of noble family who received an education which included the deportment and conduct appropriate to their future rank in life. Given the great depletion in the ranks of native landholders, it is likely that most of the boys trained in this way at Worcester would be of "French" race. One of the *obit* lists associated with Wulfstan includes the names of two English boys, Ethelgeat, who died on 17 June, and Aldred, who died on 14 October,[92] but from the context it is unclear whether these were *oblates*, probably pupils from his time as novice-master, or sons of English aristocratic families. The young boys educated at Worcester served their lord at table, as was usual in such cases, but the education offered by the bishop added to their duties a moral and humanitarian aspect which would not often be found elsewhere. Wulfstan taught his pupils to substitute humility for pride and, especially while they were still young, to live pure lives, in case they should thoughtlessly lose their chastity. To drive home the importance of humility, Wulfstan made his pupils wait upon the table of the poor men for whom he regularly made generous provision. The boys were to serve them on bended knee, and pour water on their hands for washing, as servants did. If any of the boys felt disgust at the task, and betrayed his pride in his noble blood by so much as a glance, he was rebuked for his insolence. Wulfstan could forgive any offence more readily than a contemptuous look which might hurt a poor man. He insisted that the boys must observe the teaching of Our Lord that one should serve the poor, because the person who gives to the poor also shows reverence to Him, who said: "To the extent that you did this for one of the least of these brethren, you did it for Me" (Matthew 25:40).

Wulfstan pointed out to the boys that they had many advantages: they were young, and the sons of rich men, with the added blessing of health to make them happy. But they might be cast down by a change of fortune, and then they would be glad if anyone came near them, and condescended to have dealings with them. Wulfstan's wise words were aimed at reducing their youthful haughtiness and making them grow up to respect the needy.[93] The bishop's efforts to instil compassion into his aristocratic pupils would be uphill work at times, since the ethos of the landed classes excluded all sympathy for the poor and humble.[94] Some

---

T. Wright, M. d'Advenzao and A. Rogers (1896), pp. 31–52. A new edition and study by R. B. C. Huygens and J. Prior is now in preparation.
[92]Atkins, "The Church of Worcester," Part II, p. 30.
[93]*Vita Wulfstani*, p. 50.
[94]Mary Hackett, "Le climat moral de Girart de Roussillon, " in Études de Philologie Romane et d'Histoire Littéraire offerts à Jules Horrent, ed. J. M. D'Heur and Nicoletta Cherubini (1980), pp. 165–74; P. Noble, "Attitudes to Class as revealed by some of the older chansons de geste," *Romania*, 94 (1973), pp. 359–85.

pupils, whether *oblates* or not is unclear, evidently did respond to the bishop, who caressed the handsome boys, embracing the beauty of God's handiwork in them. Wulfstan drew an analogy from their good looks, and said that the Creator Himself must be lovely, since He makes such lovely creatures.[95] Contemporaries would support his view that physical beauty reflected spiritual perfection, and social conduct was generally more demonstrative then than now, but monastic discipline forbade any caressing of the boy *oblates*.[96] Presumably this applied to lay pupils too, yet no-one would have dared to criticize the bishop.

Wulfstan's well-known care for the poor intensified during Lent. On every single day of this season, he washed the hands and feet of poor men, and gave them an allowance of food.[97] His zeal in this respect was inspired by the precepts of the Rule of St Benedict and those of the *Regularis Concordia*.[98] The latter text presupposed that each monastery supported a considerable number of poor people on a regular basis. In Worcester, St Wulfstan's Hospital, for the poor and infirm, is believed to have been founded by the bishop himself, about 1085. A second hospital St Oswald's, was initially a leper-house, said to have been founded by Archbishop Oswald, but it later became a hospital for the poor and sick.[99] Wulfstan's own generous almsgiving was reserved for the evening rather than performed in the daytime, in order to avoid worldly judgements, which are always inclined either towards excessive adulation or towards equally unrestrained criticism. There is no reason to doubt that Wulfstan's generous almsgiving occurred on the scale, and in the manner, described in his *Life*, even though other saints' lives of the period contain comparable passages. If any one of the poor men brought forward for washing was afflicted with the disease called the King's Evil, Wulfstan would handle his feet longer than he did those of the others, kiss him more tenderly, and keep his eyes on the man's sores.[100] Sufferers from this disease, with its revolting physical symptoms, experienced

[95] *Vita Wulfstani*, p. 50.
[96] *Regularis Concordia*, pp. xli, 7–8.
[97] *Vita Wulfstani*, p. 57.
[98] *Rule of St. Benedict*, ch. 53; *Regularis Concordia*, pp. xxxvii, 61–2.
[99] *Regularis Concordia*, p. 61. On the Worcester hospitals, see Knowles and Hadcock, *Medieval Religious Houses*, p. 406.
[100] *Vita Wulfstani*, p. 57. Wulfstan's almsgiving and Maundy devotions may be compared with those of Queen Margaret of Scotland, as described by Turgot. His Durham associations make the comparison particularly apposite, especially as this work is so near in date to Wulfstan's *Life*. The *Life* of Queen Margaret, attributed to Turgot, prior of Durham, is printed in *Symeonis Dunelmensis Opera et Collectanea*, ed. H. Hinde (Surtees Soc., 51, 1868), I, pp. 234–54. esp. pp. 246–9. On the attribution of this work, see Antonia Gransden, *Historical Writing in England c.550 to c.1307* (1974), p. 116 and note 71.

violent rejection from most of those who caught sight of them, so that Wulfstan's actions compensated by acknowledging a common humanity. On Maundy Thursday, Wulfstan would spend the whole day, until nightfall, in good works. He always gave priority to God's service, but on Maundy Thursday he took great care that no worldly concerns should intrude at all. When he had sung Matins with his monks in choir (at the crack of dawn), he went back to his own quarters, where, by pre-arrangement, his servants had hot water and napkins all ready. Wulfstan would immediately wash the feet of many poor men, and with his own hands clothe them from head to foot. After this, he took a short rest, and his servants meanwhile filled the great hall with poor people, sitting them in ranks as closely as possible. Then Wulfstan personally handed each of them shoes and food. If anyone respectfully suggested that he had done a good job, and deserved a rest, Wulfstan answered, "I have done only a little, but I have the will to do my Lord's command." When this distribution was completed, he went into church and spent time in contemplation until the late afternoon Office of Nones. Following this Office came the Maundy liturgy of the reconciliation of the penitents, the celebration of Mass and the blessing of the chrism (for the Easter Eve baptisms).[101]

Wulfstan's original biographer, Coleman, described these rituals in great detail, but his account was drastically reduced by the later writer William of Malmesbury when he translated Wulfstan's *Life* into Latin, on the grounds that he was writing a biography, not simply repeating the liturgical rituals prescribed for every bishop by virtue of his office.[102] It was said that Wulfstan's expression, as he reconciled his penitents on Maundy Thursday, was so compassionate that observers thought they were looking at an angel of God, since instinct teaches mankind to hope for remission of sins through someone in whom no wrongdoing can be found. On completion of this communal liturgy of reconciliation, Wulfstan customarily dined with the penitents. After dinner, he then washed the feet of all the monks – a re-enactment of Our Lord's washing of the feet of His disciples (John 13:3–15). This last ritual of the day concluded with Wulfstan serving cups of wine to his monks with the kiss of peace. This taxing Maundy ritual, in all its stages, occupied Wulfstan from the early hours of the morning until late into the night – focusing his attention entirely upon spiritual concerns.

In Holy Week 1094, Wulfstan was recalled as having performed the Maundy ceremony so thoroughly that his diligence in former years

[101]Ibid., pp. 57–8.
[102]Ibid., p. 58. On the Maundy Thursday rituals, see *Regularis Concordia*, pp. 36–41; *Monastic Constitutions of Lanfranc*, pp. 27–38.

seemed as nothing in comparison. It was as though he foresaw that he was doing it for the last time, and in his care for the task he excelled all his servants. He ordered each of his reeves to provide from every vill under his control a complete outfit for one man, shoes for ten men, and food for a hundred. He gave similar instructions to his chamberlains, so that his household should supply anything which his estates could not. On that Maundy Thursday, the great hall was filled with poor people in three successive sittings. They were so closely packed that there was scarcely room to move forwards, because all the approaches were blocked by long confused lines of those who were seeking alms, and the building reverberated with the noise. The clerks and the monks were busy washing the feet of the people, while Wulfstan sat on the episcopal chair in the middle of the throng. The immense task had exhausted his strength, but even though he could no longer take his share in the washing, he wanted to say the appropriate psalms. He was full of compassion for those assembled there, wanting all of them to be satisfied, so that no-one should go away hungry.

The first and second contingents of paupers were dismissed well fed and cheered with gifts of clothes, shoes and money. But as a third great intake was being lined up, a monk whispered to Wulfstan that all the money and clothes had been distributed, and there was not much food left. The steward and the chamberlains could find no more. What was the good of washing men's feet if there was nothing to give them afterwards? The implied suggestion was that the whole ceremony should be called off. But Wulfstan would not hear of this, saying: "No. Let the will of the Lord be done. His bounty will not fail to provide food for His servants. My officers do not want to carry out my instructions, but they will, after I am gone." He had scarcely finished speaking when three messengers rushed in, almost falling over one another in their hurry. The first announced that he had brought money, the second had brought a horse, and the third had arrived with a gift of some oxen. Wulfstan raised his eyes and his hands to Heaven, rejoicing in the miracle not so much for his own sake as for that of the paupers. The monks wept for joy, thankful that they had such a lord. Everyone blessed God, Who would not deny the prayers of those who trusted in Him, and would not permit Wulfstan to be distressed even for an hour. The horse and the oxen were sold, and the money they fetched, together with that brought by the first messenger, provided alms for the needy.[103]

---

[103] *Vita Wulfstani*, pp. 58–9. Coleman probably wanted to draw a deliberate parallel with St Oswald's observance of this Maundy ritual, and in particular his final enactment of it: *Historians of the Church of York and its archbishops*, ed. J. Raine (Rolls Series, 1879, 1886, 1894), I, pp. 471–2; II, p. 37.

This detailed account of the Maundy rituals performed at Worcester in the late eleventh century illustrated Wulfstan's compassion and generosity towards the poor, and demonstrated that his faith in Divine Providence was justified by an occurrence reminiscent of Our Lord's miracle of the loaves and fishes (Matthew 14:13–21). Incidentally, it also provides glimpses of the economic management of the estates of the church of Worcester, the administration of the episcopal household, and the relationship between the cathedral priory and the poorer inhabitants of the city and its environs. The "visible" members of the church of Worcester comprised the bishop, the fifty or so monks in residence during the last years of his episcopate, and his clerks, of whom there were perhaps ten or a dozen. There would also be fluctuating numbers of *oblates*, and of boys receiving an education for the secular world (whose aristocratic parents presumably paid for their keep in both cash and goodwill in practical matters such as lawsuits over contested lands).

These assorted residents of the cathedral precincts were sustained by the great estates of the church of Worcester, worked by large numbers of slaves and peasants. The monastic establishment itself would employ many domestic servants, at least in a ratio of one to every choir monk and probably more, besides the bishop's personal servants and armed retinue. One way and another, large quantities of foodstuffs would be consumed daily. The monks, and those domestic servants who ministered to their needs, would be supplied from the food rents due from those lands assigned to the monastic chapter, but there would still remain large numbers of employees to be fed from the episcopal estates. These lands also supplied the means by which Wulfstan provided regular doles of food for the poor, quite apart from the massive Maundy distribution. The episcopal manors also generated cash from the sale of surplus produce, and some of this money was distributed in alms to beggars as the bishop travelled round the diocese. Given all these demands on Wulfstan's estates, it is not surprising that their overseers, and for that matter the household officers in charge of domestic management, were at times unable or unwilling to respond to extraordinary demands on the produce which they controlled. Wulfstan's annoyance at his steward and chamberlains perhaps arose simply from his belief that they were dragging their feet, but he may also have suspected that somewhere along the line large quantities of estate produce were being diverted for the private profit of his employees and their families. In this context, his preference for an all-celibate household, subject to a quasi-monastic discipline, takes on a new relevance.

The church of Worcester, as a great corporate landholder, would have a dominant effect on the economy of the region. Surplus produce from its estates would be sold in local markets, where its availability would affect the price of commodities both for buyers and for other sellers. Bishop and monks were landlords of large numbers of peasants and were both landlords and employers of a considerable proportion of the urban population. The lifestyle of the monks, although disciplined, was comfortable in other respects, conspicuously more so than that of the urban and rural poor. At times of hardship due to famine or to seasonal unemployment, there would be an undercurrent of resentment at the continuing exactions of the monastic landlords. Even the better-off peasants and labourers in regular employment, such as those engaged in the ongoing building works in the cathedral precincts, would know that in course of time failing health or advancing years would render them unable to earn a livelihood. The regular dispensation of alms would alleviate the worst effects of economic hardship, although the bishop's redistribution of some fraction of the substantial income of his estates was not only a humanitarian duty but also one dictated by prudence as a means of curbing potential unrest. In particular, the large-scale almsgiving on Maundy Thursday would be a real help to those whose plight regularly worsened towards the end of the winter months, when food supplies ran low. The preceding foot-washing ritual would have little relevance for peasants who did not indulge in personal hygiene at other times, and any therapeutic benefit would count for little in their estimation in comparison with the alms which they expected to receive afterwards. Such anticipation would be heightened among the last batch of recipients in 1094 if they had glimpsed the good things distributed to those who had attended the earlier sittings. This annual disbursal of alms would be regarded as an entitlement by the urban and rural poor of the neighbourhood,[104] and the disappointed expectations of a large crowd in a confined space could easily turn to fury. It is no wonder that the bishop's household staff advised against proceeding with the footwashing if sufficient alms for the crowd were not available. The account in the Life of the timely arrival of new supplies perhaps glosses over frantic efforts behind the scenes to fend off a looming disaster.

Wulfstan's own attitude towards the poor, at the end of his life, was markedly more altruistic than that of his household staff. Following the account of his last Maundy distribution, his Life describes the bishop's remarkable banquet which he gave on Easter Day 1094. He gave his officers advance notice of this, telling them that he wanted to dine with good men, but his staff did not understand whom he had in mind, and invited a number of rich guests. On Easter Day, Wulfstan brought into

[104]An ordinance of King Athelstan had decreed that the king's reeves were always to provide food for any destitute Englishman, either in their own district or elsewhere: The Laws of the Earliest English Kings, ed. and transl. F. L. Attenborough (1922), pp. 126–7.

the hall as many poor men as it would contain, sat down among them, and gave orders for the banquet to be served. His steward became extremely angry, and upset Wulfstan by saying that it was more fitting for the bishop to dine with a small number of rich men than with a great crowd of the poor. Wulfstan answered:

Those people are rich who know the will of God and can do it. We must serve those who have no means of repaying us. Since the needy cannot invite us to feasts in their turn, God will recompense us. It gives me more joy to look at this gathering than if I was sitting down with the king of England, as has often been the case.[105]

The steward had expected Wulfstan to use the Easter feast to entertain influential landholders of the neighbourhood. The regular exercise of hospitality of this kind was important for maintaining social links with those who exercised patronage and carried political weight. By 1094, however, Wulfstan's health was failing, and he was determined to assert those priorities which carried weight in the Heavenly court.

[105] *Vita Wulfstani*, p. 59.

8
Wulfstan's Transmission of English Values to the Anglo-Norman World

The values of English monasticism were transmitted through Wulfstan's *Life* to successive generations of the monks of Worcester. His English biographer, Coleman, wrote within a few years of the bishop's death, when most of the chapter would still have known Wulfstan personally, but by the time that William of Malmesbury translated this *Life* into Latin, at some time between 1125 and 1135, only the older generation would have known the bishop. The younger monks had only an indirect knowledge of his acts, beliefs and objectives.[1] The hagiographical format of Coleman's *Life* leads to emphasis on Wulfstan's spirituality and his monastic and pastoral activities, but excludes any discussion of his reaction to major social and political changes.

Wulfstan's long survival after the Norman Conquest enabled him to inculcate traditional values into the first wave of "French" recruits to the cathedral priory, and his lessons would be reinforced posthumously by readings from his *Life*. The ethos of this work would be upheld by Wulfstan's devoted pupil Nicholas, during his time as prior (*c*.1113–24), and the continued transmission of its values may be gauged by the commissioning of William's translation by the "French" Prior Warin (*c*.1124–42), to make it more readily accessible to the younger generation at Worcester, and, probably, elsewhere.[2] William of Malmesbury's pride in his English ancestry led him to appreciate Coleman's work, which he claimed to have translated without any substantial alteration.[3]

[1]*The Vita Wulfstani of William of Malmesbury*, ed. R. R. Darlington (1928), p. 2.
[2]Ibid., pp. 1–3.
[3]Ibid., pp. viii–ix, 23–4, 58; R. Thomson, *William of Malmesbury* (1987), p. 20.

It would be a pleasure for him to recount the activities of an eminent Englishman because, as William complained in other works, in his own day his compatriots had no chance of attaining to high office in church or state.[4] Yet by the time that he translated the *Life* of Wulfstan, the "French" heads of the major monasteries were promoting the cults of their English saints, as a means of defending the rights and furthering the interests of their churches.[5] His commissioned translation was probably intended to publicize Wulfstan's cult more widely during the middle and later years of Henry I's reign.

Wulfstan himself believed that he was supported and vindicated by the former bishops of Worcester, Saints Dunstan and Oswald, when the rights of the church of Worcester were threatened by Archbishop Thomas I of York.[6] The interests of the church of Worcester were consciously promoted when Bishop Wulfstan ordered the translation of St Oswald in the presence of local notables.[7] This act would be designed to publicize throughout the region the cult of the bishop who had secured the "liberty" of the church of Worcester, and by implication to reassert that liberty and the rights of the church. The presence at this ceremony of Bishop Robert of Hereford shows that it took place after 1079.

Some years earlier Wulfstan had already found another means by which traditional English monastic values could be sustained. He was the instigator of a confraternity association which drew together the surviving heads of several major English houses, together with their "French" counterparts in others. This association included Ethelwig, abbot of Evesham; Wulfwold, abbot of Chertsey; Alfsige, abbot of Bath; Edmund, abbot of Pershore; Ralph, abbot of Winchcombe; Serlo, abbot of Gloucester; and Alfstan, prior of Worcester, together with the monks of their respective houses. They solemnly committed themselves to earnest obedience to God, the Blessed Virgin and St Benedict. They all undertook to maintain a course of action which was as near to righteousness as possible, being, in the words of Scripture, "as though of one heart and one mind." They would also be faithful to King William and Queen Matilda before God and before the world.

After consulting together as to what was necessary for the well-being of their own souls, and those of the monks committed to their charge,

[4]William of Malmesbury, *De Gestis Regum Anglorum*, ed. W. Stubbs, 2 vols (1887, 1889), I, 278.
[5]Susan J. Ridyard, *The Royal Saints of Anglo-Saxon England: a study of West Saxon and East Anglian cults* (1988), pp. 251–2; Susan J. Ridyard, "Condigna Veneratio: Post-Conquest Attitudes to the Saints of the Anglo-Saxons," *Anglo-Norman Studies IX*, ed. R. Allen Brown (1987), pp. 179–206.
[6]*Vita Wulfstani*, p. 25.
[7]Ibid., p. 52.

they decided to maintain a unity as though all seven monasteries were one. Every week, in each monastery, Mass was to be sung for all the brothers (of all seven houses) on both Mondays and Fridays. The brother celebrating the Mass was to do so on behalf of the living, and commemorate the dead, as though they were all members of the same monastery. The abbots acknowledged the obedience they owed both to God and to their respective bishops. Each abbot was to provide and pay, at his own expense, for a hundred Masses; wash a hundred needy men, and provide food and shoes for them. He was also to sing seven Masses in person, "and for thirty days set their meat before them, and a penny on their meat." The text of the agreement concluded with an invocation to God for Divine assistance in performing these obligations. There followed lists of the monks of each house, headed by their abbots, in the order in which they were given in the text. Next after Ethelwig there is listed Abbot Godric, the deposed abbot of Winchcombe who was now in Ethelwig's custody, and then Ethelwin the dean, followed by the names of twenty-eight others. Almost all were English, although Regnold and Ulf were probably of Danish stock. Abbot Wulfwold of Chertsey was followed by the names of twenty monks, all English apart from Benedict, which was probably a name adopted on profession, rather than a baptismal name. Abbot Alfsige of Bath was followed by seventeen monks of his own house, all of them seemingly English; followed, in a later hand, by the names of Godric the monk of Malmesbury, "also another one" (not named), and Wulfwerd Pices, a brother of Taunton.[8] The text survives only as a copy, in English, and the names of the brethren of the other houses were probably omitted due to lack of space.

The agreement can de dated to shortly before the death of Abbot Ethelwig of Evesham, on 16 February 1077. The most recent newcomer to the abbatial ranks among those listed was Ralph of Winchcombe. He is said to have been appointed abbot in 1077, but the textual evidence for this year is late and questionable.[9] It was perhaps the appointment of

---

[8]*Diplomatarium Anglicum Aevi Saxonici*, ed. and transl. B. Thorpe (1865), pp. 615–17; *Two Chartularies of the Priory of St. Peter at Bath*, ed. W. Hunt (1893), pp. 3–4, N. R. Ker, *Catalogue of Manuscripts containing Anglo-Saxon* (1957), no. 35. Abbot Ethelwig's biographer claimed that there were 36 members of the monastic community by 1077, a figure which may include novices and *oblates*: *Chronicon Abbatiae de Evesham ad annum 1418*, ed. W. D. Macray (1863), pp. 95–6.

[9]D. Knowles, C. N. L. Brooke and Vera C. M. London (eds), *The Heads of Religious Houses England and Wales 940–1216* (1972), pp. 47, 79. The date of Ralph's appointment follows that given in the annals of his abbey. On the reliability of these, with particular reference to Ralph's accession, see Winchcombe Annals 1049–1181, ed. R. R., Darlington, in *A Medieval Miscellany for Doris Mary Stenton*, ed. Patricia M. Barnes and C. F. Slade (1962), pp. 111, 118.

Ralph which prompted Bishop Wulfstan to devise the agreement. Five of the seven participating monasteries lay within his diocese, and the confraternity association would bind Ralph and the other "French" abbot, Serlo of Gloucester, into an observance of traditional English practices. The two outsiders among the native heads of houses, Wulfwold of Chertsey and Alfsige of Bath, respectively from the dioceses of Winchester and Wells, would be glad of the moral support which the association would give to them and their monks. Alfsige was based near to the borders of Wulfstan's see, although the normal routine of their respective dioceses would not have thrown them together. Since Englishmen were a dwindling minority in high office, both the "outside" abbots would naturally gravitate to the circle of Wulfstan and Ethelwig when attending either the royal court or a synod, and were perhaps recruited to the league on some such occasion. Abbot Alfsige subsequently enlisted kindred spirits from elsewhere in his diocese. Godric the monk of Malmesbury and his unidentified associate came from a house which was now governed by its second successive "French" abbot.[10] Brother Wulfwerd Pices is something of a mystery man, since there had never been a Benedictine abbey in Taunton. He was probably a member of the secular collegiate church which preceded the Augustinian priory there,[11] although his English name suggests that he might have been an anchorite attempting to follow the religious life. The west of England certainly produced a number of such recluses at a later date.[12] The surviving lists of monks indicate that there was as yet little "French" recruitment to those houses which retained English heads, and these monasteries would therefore retain an ethos which owed more to the tenth-century *Regularis Concordia* than to Lanfranc's *Monastic Constitutions*. The seven monasteries were bound together by their loyalty to the Blessed Virgin, to whom Worcester cathedral was dedicated, although her cult was observed with greater solemnity at Evesham than at Worcester in this period.[13]

[10]Knowles, Brooke and London, *Heads of Religious Houses*, p. 55. The names of Abbot Alfsige's additional recruits are added in a later hand.

[11]D. Knowles and R. N. Hadcock, *Medieval Religious Houses England and Wales* revised edn (1971), pp. 175, 418, 555.

[12]H. Mayr-Harting, "Functions of a Twelfth-Century Recluse," *History*, 60 (1975), p. 337.

[13]The feast of "the Dedication of the Basilica of St Mary" was observed at Worcester on 13 May: *English Kalendars before A.D. 1100, I*: Texts, ed. F. Wormald (1934), pp. 216, 230. The feasts of the Assumption (15 August) and the Nativity (8 September) of the Blessed Virgin were observed both at Worcester and at Evesham in the later eleventh century, but were celebrated with greater solemnity at Evesham (ibid., pp. 205–6; cf. pp. 219–20, 233–4).

The values promoted by the agreement were those of the late Anglo-Saxon church, exemplified both in the prayers for the monarch and his consort, and in the extensive commitment to almsgiving, features which were minimized in the *Monastic Constitutions*.[14] The prayers which the *Regularis Concordia* prescribed on behalf of the king and queen were in effect a reciprocal offering of spiritual support in return for the royal guarantee of the extensive monastic endowments of that period. In the wake of the Norman Conquest, many monastic communities waged an anxious and sometimes losing struggle to defend their title to their lands against the newcomers.[15] A king who perceived that the stability of his realm was maintained by the prayers of his loyal monks might listen more attentively to their pleas and less to those of his predatory magnates.

At Worcester, almsgiving was observed to exacting standards.[16] The participants in the association were in effect restating the value of their conservative monastic tradition in the face of the revised practices which Archbishop Lanfranc introduced.[17] The strength of Wulfstan's association depended on the goodwill of the heads of the various houses; as Englishmen were replaced by French, the impetus to uphold the older traditions would dwindle, and even while it lasted such unity as there was existed primarily on the spiritual plane. It did not deter Hemming from including in his cartulary barbed diatribes against Abbot Ethelwig's misappropriations,[18] nor did it inhibit Wulfstan from embarking on his celebrated lawsuit against Ethelwig's French successor at Evesham.[19]

[14]*Regularis Concordia*, transl. and ed. T. Symons (1953), pp. xxxvii; 5, 12–14, 16, 20–3, 61–2. Lanfranc's Monastic Constitutions prescribed every move a monk was to make in the course of his duties, but lacked the concern with wider issues reflected in the provisions of Wulfstan's confraternity league. In effect, the Monastic Constitutions were the most up-to-date form of the customs of the great Burgundian monastery of Cluny: Margaret Gibson, *Lanfranc of Bec* (1978), p. 173.

[15]P. Hyams,"'No Register of Title:' the Domesday Inquest and Land Adjudication," *Anglo-Norman Studies IX*, ed. R. Allen Brown (1987), pp. 127–41, esp. pp. 132–4.

[16]*Vita Wulfstani*, pp. 50, 57–9.

[17]*The Monastic Constitutions of Lanfranc*, transl. and introd. D. Knowles (1951). Confraternity links which the new community at Durham later established on an individual basis with Chertsey, Evesham, Gloucester and Worcester probably did not carry the same connotations: *Durham Liber Vitae*, ed. A. H. Thompson (1923, in facsimile), folios 21 verso, 22 recto, 33 verso, 48 recto, especially since direct links were also established at an early date between Durham and both Westminster and Winchester (*Durham Liber Vitae*, folio 48 recto); *Westminster Abbey Charters, 1066–c.1214*, ed. Emma Mason, assisted by the late Jennifer Bray, continuing the work of the late Desmond J. Murphy (1988), no. 235. The agreement with Westminster was made at some uncertain date between 1080 and 1085.

[18]*Hemingi Chartularium ecclesiae Wigorniensis*, ed. T. Hearne, 2 vols (1723), pp. 270–2.

[19]*Domesday Book 16: Worcestershire*, ed. F. and C. Thorn (1982), Appendix V, Worcester H.

WULFSTAN'S TRANSMISSION OF ENGLISH VALUES

After Thomas succeeded Alfstan as prior of Worcester, another confraternity agreement was made between Wulfstan, Thomas and their monks, and Abbot Elfwin and the monks of Ramsey, in Huntingdonshire. The text survives only in a summarized form in a Worcester cartulary. It recalled that Ramsey had been built and dedicated by Bishop Oswald of Worcester. The brethren of either house were to pray for thirty days for any brother of the other house who died, and a monk's "prebend," or sustenance, was also to be given in alms for thirty days. On the death of the bishop or the prior of Worcester, or that of the abbot of Ramsey, his "prebend" was to be given in alms for a whole year. In case of need, each brother of either house was to be allowed refuge, and a guaranteed place, in the other monastery.[20] This last clause would not be designed to encourage monks to break their vow of stability, nor to renounce the obedience they owed to the head of their house. Most likely it was included as a safeguard in the event of the inmates of either monastery being harassed by predatory French settlers, or by political unrest.[21] In the text as it now survives there is no mention of the obligation found in the earlier agreement to offer prayers for the king and queen, nor of the cults of the Blessed Virgin and of St Benedict. It is arguable that the full version did include clauses on these points, which are also omitted from the Worcester memorandum of the earlier confraternity bond.[22] The confraternity agreement with Ramsey was probably made soon after the earlier one, since Abbot Elfwin died in 1079 or 1080. Despite the general Normanization of the clerical hierarchy, he was succeeded by another Englishman, Elfsige, formerly abbot of St Augustine's, Canterbury.[23]

In the decades after the Norman Conquest, virtually every major church was rebuilt on a grander scale in the new Romanesque style. Wulfstan's architectural taste appears to have been austere,[24] while other

[20]*The Cartulary of Worcester Cathedral Priory (Register I)*, ed. R. R. Darlington (1968), no. 304. There is no record of this agreement in Ramsey's cartulary. One charter of William I for Ramsey, dated 29 December 1077, is attested by Wulfstan. Alone among the witnesses he added the sanction of anathema to be invoked on transgressors of the abbey's privileges: *Chronicon Abbatiae Ramesiensis*, ed. W. D. Macray (1886), p. 204. The authenticity of this text is questionable: Dr David Bates, in a personal communication.
[21]During the crises of 1068–9 and 1075, the inmates of religious houses manned and headed by Englishmen perhaps anticipated harassment.
[22]*Cartulary of Worcester*, no. 305.
[23]Knowles, Brooke and London, *Heads of Religious Houses*, pp. 61–2.
[24]*Vita Wulfstani*, p. 52; William of Malmesbury, *De Gestis Pontificum Anglorum*, ed. N. E. S. A. Hamilton (1870) p. 283; R. Gem, "England and the Resistance to Romanesque Architecture," *Studies in Medieval History presented to R. Allen Brown*, ed. C. Harper-Bill, C. J. Holdsworth and Janet L. Nelson (1989), pp. 132–5.

men of English origins were openly scathing of the ostentatious buildings commissioned by the newcomers.[25] The rebuilt Canterbury cathedral, and those major English churches which followed its design, derived their plans from St Etienne, Caen. But Rouen Cathedral and the abbeys of Mont-St-Michel and Saint-Wandrille shared another plan which culminated in a complex east end, combining ambulatory, radiating chapels and crypt. This design influenced a small group of important English churches, including St Augustine's at Canterbury (begun c.1073), Winchester cathedral (begun in 1079), the abbey church of Bury St Edmunds (begun in 1081), Worcester cathedral (begun in 1084) and Gloucester abbey (begun in 1089).[26] St. Augustine's, Bury St Edmunds and Worcester all staunchly upheld English traditions, and it has been suggested that the plans which houses such as Winchester and Worcester followed would be better suited than the Canterbury-Caen model to accommodate the dramatic liturgical practices prescribed by the *Regularis Concordia*.[27] Winchester's adoption of this plan was presumably the personal choice of Bishop Walkelin, although it had perhaps special liturgical requirements emanating from its large collection of early royal relics. Walkelin was apparently on good terms with Wulfstan,[28] and perhaps led him to see that he could conform to the pressures to rebuild in the fashionable Romanesque style while retaining cherished traditions. Wulfstan would also have seen for himself the potential of Winchester, when attending the Easter court there.[29] Wulfstan in turn provided inspiration for his close associate Abbot Serlo. The new work at Worcester was already well under way when a major fire at Gloucester in 1088 necessitated the rebuilding of the abbey. Serlo had been a monk of Mont-St-Michel, and probably derived some additional ideas directly from his former monast-

[25]William of Malmesbury, *De Gestis Regum Anglorum*, pp. 306, 334.

[26]C. Wilson, "Abbot Serlo's church at Gloucester (1089–1100): its place in Romanesque architecture," in *Medieval Art and Architecture at Gloucester and Tewkesbury*, ed. T. A. Heslop and V. A. Sekules (1985), pp. 52–83, esp. pp. 52–4.

[27]A. W. Klukas, "The Architectural Implications of the *Decreta Lanfranci*," in *Anglo-Norman Studies VI*, ed. R. Allen Brown (1984), pp. 136–71, esp. pp. 140, 167. The essential argument put forward by Klukas, that other heads of house were generally constrained to rebuild in conformity with the plan of Lanfranc's Canterbury, has met with considerable disagreement.

[28]*Vita Wulfstani*, p. 26.

[29]In the reign of William I, the Easter court usually convened at Winchester when the king was in England. On one occasion in his reign the Pentecost court is known to have met there: M. Biddle, "Seasonal Festivals and Residence: Winchester, Westminster and Gloucester in the tenth to twelfth centuries," in *Anglo-Norman Studies VIII*, ed. R. Allen Brown (1986), pp. 51–72, esp. p. 64. Wulfstan certainly attended the court at Winchester on occasion: *Vita Wulfstani*, pp. 34–5.

ery.[30] Gloucester and Winchester were two of the increasingly regular venues for the solemn crown-wearings,[31] while the lavish rebuilding of Gloucester in the reign of William II was supported by royal patronage, perhaps with the intention that it should become the royal mausoleum.[32] Wulfstan had no such grandiose inducements to rebuild his church. His distress at the destruction of the old church to make way for the new suggests that it was only pressure of growing numbers which led him to accept that a replacement was essential.[33]

Liturgical practice at Worcester in Wulfstan's day can be largely reconstructed from two manuscripts which were formerly there. One is a *Pontifical*, a compendium of liturgical rites which required the participation of a bishop. The earlier part of this manuscript was probably written in the Old Minster at Winchester, but it was at Worcester in the late eleventh century and the early twelfth, when substantial additions were made, and the name of St Egwuin (an early bishop of Worcester) was added to that of the Winchester saint, Ethelwold.[34] The other liturgical manuscript is a collection of texts, now published under the name of the *Portiforium of Saint Wulfstan*.[35] It was written at Worcester in Wulfstan's time, and contains a kalendar (i.e. a table of saints' feasts which were to be celebrated); psalms and canticles in the Gallican version; hymns; and a book of collects. It included the *incipits*, or opening words, of antiphons; hymns and other chants for the day hours; private prayers; full service for saints' days; for Sundays after Trinity Sunday; and for weekdays. Among the saints invoked in prayer two former bishops of Worcester are prominent, Oswald and Egwuin.[36] This small, thick book

[30]While Worcester and Mont-St-Michel were important models, other influences can also be deduced: Wilson, "Abbot Serlo's church at Gloucester," pp. 53–66.

[31]Biddle, "Seasonal Festivals and Residence," pp. 53, 64; *Westminster Abbey Charters*, no.58.

[32]F. Barlow, *William Rufus* (1983), pp. 114–15, 428; D. Bates, "The Building of a Great Church: The Abbey of St. Peter's, Gloucester, and its early Norman Benefactors," *Transactions of the Bristol and Gloucestershire Archaeological Society*, 102 (1984), pp. 129–32.

[33]*Vita Wulfstani*, p. 52. On the increase in the number of monks during his episcopate, see *Cartulary of Worcester* no. 3.

[34]Ker, *Catalogue of Manuscripts Containing Anglo-Saxon*, no. 37.

[35]*The Portiforium of Saint Wulfstan* (Corpus Christi College, Cambridge, MS 391), ed. A. Hughes, 2 vols (1958, 1960).

[36]Ker, *Catalogue of Manuscripts containing Anglo-Saxon*, no. 67. The manuscript is discussed in three of the contributions to *Learning and Literature in Anglo-Saxon England: studies presented to Peter Clemoes on his sixty-fifth birthday*, ed. M. Lapidge and H. Gneuss (1985): (1) H. Gneuss, "Liturgical Books in Anglo-Saxon England and their Old English terminology," pp. 112–13; (2) Susan Rankin, "The Liturgical Background of the Old English Advent Lyrics: a reappraisal," p. 324; (3) M. McC. Gatch, "The Office in Late Anglo-Saxon Monasticism," pp. 349–50.

provided most of the liturgical material which Wulfstan would be likely to need on his travels, hence the title of *Portiforium* or portable breviary, which it has latterly acquired.[37] It was probably written early in Wulfstan's episcopate and is a major source for the English monastic liturgy on the eve of the Norman Conquest.[38] A comparison of the liturgy and monastic chant, as it appears in these manuscripts, with the contents of a Worcester antiphonary of the thirteenth century indicates that the traditions observed by Wulfstan long continued to be maintained in his cathedral.[39]

Following the Norman Conquest, and probably as a result of the adoption of Lanfranc's monastic customs, a new order of chants was adopted at Worcester. The older practice there derived ultimately from Corbie, one of the Continental centres of the tenth-century monastic reform, and had probably been transmitted through Winchester. In the later eleventh century the practices of Corbie gave way to those of Bec to a considerable extent, at Worcester as well as at Canterbury. The reformers were more concerned with the texts of what was sung, in what order and on what day, than with the music which was used. Therefore Worcester, and other houses which retained English cantors, continued to observe their pre-Conquest musical traditions. Uhtred, a cantor appointed by Wulfstan, died only 1132.[40] At Glastonbury things turned out differently. The writer John of Worcester gives one of the fullest accounts of the outrage committed there when, in 1081 or 1083, Abbot Thurstan compelled the monks to abandon their ancient musical traditions, which they claimed to have learned from the disciples of Gregory the Great, and to learn instead a new and alien chant. Their resistance caused Thurstan to lose his temper in chapter. He summoned his armed retainers, who hounded the monks into the abbey church, where two were killed and fourteen others wounded. One of the monks seized a silver crucifix, which he clutched in front of him as a shield. An arrow was fired at him and the aggressors were astonished to see that it

[37]Gneuss, "Liturgical Books in Anglo-Saxon England and their Old English terminology," pp. 112–13; Laurentia McLachlan, "St. Wulstan's Prayer Book," *The Journal of Theological Studies*, 30 (1929), pp. 174–7.

[38]Rankin, "The Liturgical Background of the Old English Advent Lyrics," p. 324; "The office in Late Anglo-Saxon Monasticism," pp. 349–50.

[39]Laurentia MacLachlan, Introduction to the *Antiphonaire Monastique XIIIe siècle: Codex F 160 de la Bibliothéque de la Cathedrale de Worcester* (1922).

[40]D. Hiley, "Thurstan of Caen and Plainchant at Glastonbury: Musicological Reflections on the Norman Conquest," *Proceedings of the British Academy*, 72 (1986), pp. 57–90, esp. pp. 63, 65, 81, 84–5, 89. Uhtred, who from his name was clearly an Englishman, was in office at Worcester in 1092: *Cartulary of Worcester*, no. 52. For the date of his death, see *The Chronicle of John of Worcester*, ed. J. R. H. Weaver (1908), p. 36.

appeared to wound the image of Our Lord below the knees. A stream of blood began to flow from the altar to the steps, and from the steps to the floor, striking the abbot's retainers with the fear that Divine vengeance was about to fall on them. The man who had shot the arrow rushed frantically out of the church, fell to the ground, broke his neck and died.[41] News of the massacre would quickly spread throughout the Benedictine network. John's circumstantial account, reflected in the work of other monastic writers, indicates the sense of outrage felt at traditionalist Worcester.[42]

Wulfstan's long survival permitted the cathedral priory to retain and perhaps even enhance many of its ancient traditions. An early eleventh-century kalendar (a kalendar indicates saints' days to be observed) which is possibly from Worcester contains little observance of cults of saints who were native to the British Isles, whereas a Worcester kalendar of the later eleventh century includes the feast of St Chad (2 March) and that of St Cuthbert (20 March) together with those of several later insular saints. But Evesham additionally observed the Translation of St Cuthbert (4 September) and the Translations of Saints Aidan and Ceolfrith (8 October) during the later eleventh century. It may be that Worcester, during Wulfstan's episcopate, responded to the influence of Abbot Ethelwig and the monks of Evesham in their observance of insular cults.[43] This concern on the part of the community of Evesham to uphold English cults was also manifested in the lead taken by some of its monks in the revival of Northumbrian monasticism, discussed in an earlier chapter. Since the initiators of this project comprised only monks of Evesham and of Winchcombe, recently under Ethelwig's rule, it can be argued that Ethelwig was quite as concerned to preserve Anglo-Saxon traditions as was Wulfstan himself. The plentiful source material surviving from Worcester has ensured Wulfstan's reputation as an upholder of English values. It may be that Ethelwig was not merely a loyal supporter of his diocesan bishop in this activity, but perhaps even its instigator. Yet,

---

[41]*Florentii Wigorniensis monachi Chronicon ex Chronicis*, ed. B. Thorpe, 2 vols (1848–9), II, pp. 16–17; *The Early History of Glastonbury*, ed. John Scott (1981), pp. 156, 209; *The Anglo-Saxon Chronicle*, transl. and ed. Dorothy Whitelock with D. C. Douglas and Susie I. Tucker (1961), *sub an.* 1083; *The Ecclesiastical History of Orderic Vitalis*, ed. and transl. Marjorie Chibnall, 6 vols (1969–80), II, pp. 270–1; Hiley, "Thurstan of Caen and Plainchant at Glastonbury," esp. pp. 57–60.

[42]The Worcester Chronicler influenced the narrative of William of Malmesbury, in his *Early History of Glastonbury*: Hiley, "Thurstan of Caen and Plainchant at Glastonbury," p. 58. Worcester influence, whether deriving from its Chronicle or from its oral tradition, also influenced Orderic Vitalis, Shropshire-born, but writing at St Evroul, in Normandy, *Ecclesiastical History of Orderic Vitalis*, II, p. 271, note 1.

[43]*English Kalendars before A.D. 1100*, I: Texts, nos 16–18.

just as the Northumbrian mission would surely have gone ahead only with Wulfstan's approval, so he can be seen to have sanctioned other manifestations of Anglo-Saxon monasticism throughout and beyond his diocese.

English traditions were also reflected in the contents of the library at Worcester in Wulfstan's day. A substantial proportion of the manuscripts copied there in the later eleventh century were written in the English language, and an English script also continued to be used. The contents of the library at this time, in so far as they can traced, show a strong bias in favour of homiletic literature together with several manuscripts of works by Gregory the Great, who was himself a monastic bishop. The nature of these Worcester manuscripts reinforces the reiterated message of Wulfstan's *Life* that he gave priority to pastoral concerns, and that he maintained monastic practices of a traditional kind. It was inevitable that major changes would occur after his death, but to judge from the nature of the surviving manuscripts copied at Worcester in the early twelfth century, this zeal for pastoral activity lived on among the monks there. Wulfstan's immediate acceptance of the Norman Conquest, and his co-operation with the new rulers, safeguarded his community from major changes in its culture or its religious practices in the late eleventh century. Worcester was not in the forefront of intellectual development at that time, but the bishop was able to maintain the priorities in which he had been reared.[44]

The cultural and mental world of the monks of Worcester can be glimpsed through the scriptural and literary works which they are known to have possessed in Wulfstan's day. There survives from the middle of the eleventh century a short list of books which were probably intended for use in the schoolroom. These included: a *Legendary* in English, possibly a copy of Elfric's *Lives of the Saints*; two copies of the *Dialogues* of Gregory the Great, in the English translation by Werferth; a book "belonging to Odda," who was probably the mid-eleventh century Worcester monk of that name; a copy of the so-called *Old-English Martyrology*, that is, a book containing short entries on the lives and sufferings of both martyrs and confessors; two Psalters, either in English translation, or with extensive interlinear glossing in English; two copies of King Alfred's English translation of Gregory the Great's *Pastoral Care*; Bishop Ethelwold's English translation of the Rule of St Benedict,

---

[44]For a full discussion of Worcester manuscripts surviving from the time of Wulfstan and his immediate successors, see Elizabeth A. McIntyre, "Early Twelfth-Century Worcester Cathedral Priory, with special reference to the manuscripts there" (Oxford University D.Phil. thesis, 1978), esp. pp. 91–3, 98–101, 109, 114, 195, 198.

and finally the *Vision of the Holy Monk Barontus*, a work which was probably in Latin. Of these works, the *Legendary*, both copies of the *Dialogues* and also of the *Pastoral Care*, together with the English translation of the Rule of St Benedict, can be identified with manuscripts which still survive.[45] In Wulfstan's early days as novice-master, he probably taught his pupils from these very books. The fact that so many of these English-language works have survived testifies to the onward transmission of the cultural traditions maintained by Wulfstan.

Worcester perhaps also owned the books which occur in a much longer list dating from the late eleventh century. This list, which occurs in a copy of the *Dialogues* of Gregory the Great made early in the century, is chiefly of works intended for use in a schoolroom, since it includes multiple copies of several texts which were commonly used for teaching. Gregory the Great is represented by several of his works. Most of the other authors represented, ranging from the Classical to the early medieval, also worked on the Continent. The eminent English scholar, Bede, is represented by two, and possibly three, copies of his *Ecclesiastical History* as well as his *De Temporibus*. British writers also account for a *Life of St Wilfrid*, and a copy of the *Life of St Kyeran*. The list concludes with a variety of liturgical works.[46] Whereas English texts predominated in the earlier and shorter list, those contained in this one are all in Latin. During Wulfstan's lifetime, English translations of standard works continued to be made at Worcester, while Latin works were frequently annotated in the vernacular, sometimes by the chancellor, Coleman.[47] This English-language output virtually ceased after the bishop's death.[48] The prominence given both in the lists of Worcester manuscripts and in Coleman's *Life* to Bede and to Gregory the Great suggests that these writers were among those who most influenced Wulfstan and his monks. The bishop's first dedication of a church was to Bede, which Coleman thought appropriate since he was the writer who

---

[45]M. Lapidge, "Surviving Booklists from Anglo-Saxon England," in *Learning and Literature in Anglo-Saxon England*, ed. Lapidge and Gneuss, pp. 33–89, esp. pp. 62–4.

[46]Lapidge,"Surviving Booklists from Anglo-Saxon England," pp. 69–73.

[47]N. R. Ker, "Old English Notes Signed Coleman," reprinted from *Medium Aevum*, 18 (1949), pp. 29–31, in N. R. Ker, *Books, Collectors and Libraries: studies in the medieval heritage*, ed. A. G. Watson (1985), pp. 27–30. For manuscripts at Worcester in Wulfstan's time which were either written, or annotated, in English, see Ker, *Catalogue of Manuscripts containing Anglo-Saxon*, nos 23, 29, 30, 35, 37, 41, 48, 53, 64, 67, 73, 166, 169, 171, 178, 182, 190, 192, 248, 250–1, 324, 327, 330–3, 338, 343, 399, 412.

[48]McIntyre, "Early Twelfth-Century Worcester Cathedral Priory, with special reference to the manuscripts there," p. 92. On the other hand, some members of the community at Worcester still made use of English-language texts in the early years of the thirteenth century: Ker, *Catalogue of Manuscripts containing Anglo-Saxon*, p. xlix; nos 30, 331.

was most esteemed among the English people.[49] Bede's *Ecclesiastical History* was valued not only for its literary merits but because its historical scholarship could be put to practical use. Ecclesiastics cited his authority when contending against one another in jurisdictional disputes during the late eleventh century. His work was well-known on the Continent, and hence was used by newcomers to England, including Archbishop Lanfranc, who found in Bede proof of the traditions both of the whole English Church and also of individual monasteries.[50]

Wulfstan's education at Peterborough perhaps included some training in the decoration of manuscripts,[51] but when he became bishop he did not establish his cathedral as a major centre of Romanesque illumination. His *Portiforium*, or prayer book, contains a full-page portrait of King David playing the harp, which closely resembles a similar illustration in a Canterbury manuscript. This reflects Norman influence, which can also be discerned in an individual decorated initial in this volume, and also some further initials in other Worcester manuscripts produced during his episcopate.[52] Overall, the emphasis is on content, rather than on outward show, which reinforces the inference that book production was seen there primarily as an adjunct to pastoral activity, but it may be that pastoral books have survived better than others.

The contents of the library at Worcester inevitably shaped both Wulfstan's own concept of his role and the way in which he was depicted by the writers of his church. In particular, the text of the Rule of St Benedict and the writings of Gregory the Great[53] would make him aware not only of the duties, but also of the rights of the head of an autonomous Benedictine house, which in turn would account for his imposition of high standards of conduct.[54] The continuing production at Worcester in the late eleventh century of English translations of the works of Gregory

---

[49]*Vita Wulfstani*, p. 20.

[50]Antonia Gransden, "Bede's Reputation as an Historian in Medieval England," *Journal of Ecclesiastical History*, 32 (1981), pp. 397–425, esp. 409–10, 412. See also R. H. C. Davis, "Bede after Bede," in *Studies in Medieval History presented to R. Allen Brown*, ed. Harper-Bill, Holdsworth and Nelson, pp. 103–16.

[51]*Vita Wulfstani*, p. 5.

[52]C. M. Kauffmann, "Manuscript Illumination at Worcester in the Eleventh and Twelfth Centuries," in *Medieval Art and Architecture at Worcester Cathedral*, ed. Glenys Popper (1978), pp. 43–50, esp. pp. 44–5. Yet the influence of the Anglo-Saxon style may be perceived at Worcester as late as *c*.1130, in a drawing of the Crucifixion in the Chronicle of Florence of Worcester: F. Wormald, "The Survival of Anglo-Saxon Illumination after the Norman Conquest," *Proceedings of the British Academy*, 30 (1944), pp. 127–45, esp. pp. 141–2, and Plate 7.

[53]Lapidge, "Surviving Booklists from Anglo-Saxon England," p. 51; Ker, *Catalogue of Manuscripts containing Anglo-Saxon*, nos 41B, 64, 182, 324, 327–8.

[54]*Vita Wulfstani*, pp. 11, 17, 20, 36, 47–9, 51, 54.

the Great was most likely intended to facilitate pastoral work in the diocese.[55] Earlier collections of homilies were also preserved, and some of these were re-copied, including that which was probably used by the bishop himself.[56] Wulfstan's thorough grounding in the *Lives* of the leaders of the Tenth Century Reform,[57] and in the *Lives* of early saints,[58] would help to condition his approach to his role. The later reporting of his activities would be shaped not only be personal knowledge of his doings, but also by the impact upon the Worcester monks of the works which they, too, read and absorbed. His *Life* seems to depict him as a saint in the mould of the leaders of the tenth century reform movement. Saint Ethelwold, as depicted by Elfric, has been suggested as the chief model,[59] but Wulfstan is consciously likened both to St Jerome and to Bede.[60] Elements from the lives of St Cuthbert and St Columba perhaps also influenced the selection and presentation of material in Wulfstan's biography, but may equally have influenced the bishop himself, given his commitment both to physical austerity and to sustained recital of psalms and prayers.

Wulfstan's zeal as a pastor was matched by that of his concern for the rights of his cathedral church. One of the best-known Worcester manuscripts of the late eleventh century is that commonly known as *Hemming's Cartulary*. By inspiring the production of this work, Wulfstan kept alive the traditions of his monastery in a different way, but one which was at least equally important to its inmates, the preservation of their title to their endowments. This cartulary, or charter-register, had an early eleventh-century predecessor with which it is now bound together.[61] Throughout the century the endowments of the church suffered from repeated encroachments, whether from Danish settlers,

[55]McIntyre, "Early Twelfth-Century Worcester Cathedral, with special reference to the manuscripts there," pp. 97–8.

[56]Ker, *Catalogue of Manuscripts containing Anglo-Saxon*, nos 41, 48, 331, 332; McIntyre, "Early Twelfth Century Worcester Cathedral, with special reference to the manuscripts there," p. 100.

[57]*Vita Wulfstani*, p. 25.

[58]Lapidge, "Surviving Booklists from Anglo-Saxon England," pp. 63, 70–3; Ker, *Catalogue of Manuscripts containing Anglo-Saxon*, nos 23, 29, 251.

[59]Antonia Gransden, *Historical Writing in England c.550 to c.1307* (1974), p. 88.

[60]*Vita Wulfstani*, pp. 15, 20. Worcester possessed manuscripts of works by Bede including the *Ecclesiastical History of the English People: Catalogue of Manuscripts containing Anglo-Saxon*, no. 23; Lapidge, "Surviving Booklists from Anglo-Saxon England," pp. 70–3.

[61]N. R. Ker, "Hemming's Cartulary: A description of the two Worcester cartularies in Cotton Tiberius A.XIII," *Studies in Medieval History presented to Frederick Maurice Powicke*, ed. R. W. Hunt, W. A. Pantin and R. W. Southern (1948), pp. 49–75, reprinted in Ker, *Books, Collectors and Libraries*, pp. 31–59, esp. pp. 31–46.

from Earl Leofric, his kinsmen and clients, or from Normans. By Wulfstan's later years there seemed little hope of recovering many of these lost properties. He believed that some of the losses were due to the negligence of his predecessors, and frequently urged the monks to document their claims to properties rather than simply to rely on fallible memory. He ordered the muniment chest to be opened in his presence, and a thorough examination to be made of all the ancient charters relating to the privileges and estates of the church, in case they had been kept so carelessly that they had decayed, or been pilfered. His suspicions were justified and he went to some lengths to ensure that damaged documents were repaired, and stolen ones recovered.

Wulfstan then arranged the collection into two volumes. In the first were grouped all the early privileges and title deeds which set out how, and by whom, the estates were first given to the monastery. His second group comprised the deeds by which Archbishop Oswald, with the help of King Edgar, established the title of the church of Worcester to lands which had at various times been wrongfully seized by magnates. The archbishop had set out in writing, for the benefit of his successors that, by order of King Edgar and with the sanction of the Witan, and the testimony of the nobles of the realm, the lands which were held at lease were to be restored to the control of the church of Worcester after a period of two or three lives. Each leaseholder was bound by the terms of his charter, copies of which were kept in the cathedral's deed-box.[62] Wulfstan ordered all these deeds, both groups, apparently, to be transcribed in the same order as in the earlier cartulary and bound into the cathedral's *bibliotheca*, probably its great Offa Bible.[63] He knew that individual deeds might go astray, but at least the copies would remain as evidence of title.[64] This collection as a whole is now lost, although fragments from it have been identified.[65] What remains intact is the last stage of the project. Once the ancient deeds of the cathedral had been

[62]*Hemingi Chartularium*, I, pp. 283–5. Archbishop Oswald's letter to King Edgar is transcribed in this work, I, pp. 292–6; calendared by P. H. Sawyer, *Anglo-Saxon Charters: an annotated list and bibliography* (1968), no. 368. A translation of the letter is printed by R. Allen Brown, *Origins of English Feudalism* (1973), no. 42, pp. 133–5.

[63]*Hemingi Chartularium*, I, p. 285; Ker, "Hemming's Cartulary," pp. 49–52.

[64]*Hemingi Chartularium*, I, pp. 285–6. Worcester was by no means alone in attempting to reclaim alienated lands for which few, if any, title deeds survived. The problem was shared by many religious houses and lay lords: Hyams, "'No Register of Title:' The Domesday Inquest and Land Adjudication," pp. 127–41.

[65]Where original charters survive, their endorsements indicate that they were carefully examined in the time of Bishop Wulfstan. The quality of transcription of the surviving leaves of the late eleventh-century manuscript is poor. Fortunately copies of most of the texts had been included in the early eleventh-century cartulary which is now bound together with this one. Ker, "Hemming's Cartulary," pp. 49–51.

registered in this way, Wulfstan ordered that all the privileges and leases relating to those lands specifically reserved for the support of the monks should be brought together separately, and arranged in two volumes.[66] By the last decade of the eleventh century, the laymen who had wrongfully occupied estates of the church of Worcester were well entrenched, while the older monks, who preserved memories of the rights of the church in King Edward's reign, would be a dwindling minority. It is natural that when instigating the project Wulfstan should give priority to the recording of those early documents which related to the endowments of the church of Worcester as a whole.

The division of the *mensa*, that is the assignment of certain estates of the church to the bishop, and others to the monks, which is reflected in *Hemming's Cartulary*, can be firmly documented from the last years of King Edward's reign, probably from soon after Wulfstan's consecration in 1062. Some such division is implicit in the king's grant to Alfstan (the dean or prior) of *sac* and *soc*, and toll and team (various judicial and financial rights) over his land and his men within town and without.[67] These rights of the prior and monks were confirmed and expanded by King William I.[68]

The tenure of the bishopric of Worcester in plurality with the archbishopric of York gave rise to the initial division of lands between the monks of Worcester and their bishop. The wording of King William's writ was: *sicut tenuerunt temporibus antecessorum meorum regum* (as they held in the times of the kings [who were] my predecessors). This is a common form of phrase, but if it is intended to be strictly interpreted, it either tacitly acknowledges Harold II to have been a legitimate ruler,[69] or else implies that the estates were divided no later than the reign of Harthacnut (1040–2). By the late eleventh century, perhaps no-one recalled just when a division had been made. There is no evidence to indicate that a division existed in the time of Oswald or Wulfstan I. Any such development during either of their episcopates would greatly

[66]*Hemingi Chartularium*, I, p. 286. Charters which have survived include one batch relating to the monks' demesne: II, pp. 319–46; and another group concerning lands recovered by Ealdred and Wulfstan: II, pp. 395–425. See also Ker, "Hemming's Cartulary," pp. 39–46.
[67]Sawyer, *Anglo-Saxon Charters*, no. 1157. By way of analogy the division of the *mensa* at Canterbury can be traced from the reign of William I: F. R. H. Du Boulay, *The Lordship of Canterbury* (1966),pp. 52–65.
[68]*Cartulary of Worcester*, no. 2.
[69]Early writs of William I did occasionally acknowledge the legitimacy of Harold II's rule: G. Garnett, "Coronation and Propaganda: some implications of the Norman claim to the throne of England in 1066," *Transactions of the Royal Historical Society*, fifth series, 36 (1986), pp. 91–116, esp. pp. 98–100.

antedate comparable divisions in the lands of other religious communities. Ealdred, on the other hand, effected a partition around the time of Wulfstan's consecration. It will be recalled that after appropriating the lands of the church, he initially conceded seven villages to Worcester, but that over a period of time Wulfstan persuaded him to return more.[70] The writ of King Edward in favour of Prior Alfstan would therefore have secured the monks' possession of the first seven vills to be released, while that of William I would ensure title to those which Ealdred relinquished later. The archbishop could justify his retention of a further twelve vills by regarding Wulfstan as a mere suffragan. Similarly Archbishop Thomas's initial retention of these twelve would be consequent upon his claim to hold Worcester together with York. Only when Wulfstan was finally declared quit of formal subjection to him were these villages restored.[71] They were probably identical with demesne manors held by the bishop in 1086. Their distinctive management, designed to maximize cash returns,[72] was probably initiated to meet the requirements of the archbishop of York. This interpretation of the recent history of the estates of Worcester would explain why it was primarily Wulfstan himself, rather than his monks, who saw the need to record all surviving title deeds of the church of Worcester. Despite his personal lack of acquisitiveness, he wanted to transmit to his successors their rightful due.[73] In this he followed his namesake the archbishop, who probably commissioned the early eleventh-century cartulary.[74] Ironically, by ensuring that the monks' needs took priority when estates were recovered from Ealdred, he secured the most profitable estates for himself and his successors.

The misappropriation of old charters which Wulfstan brought to light was probably due in part to the activities of Ealdred, but since Wulfstan was able to recover some documents, it is likely that these had been taken by high-handed obedientiaries.[75] Lay marauders were unlikely to have had access to the archives, and sheet brute force often sufficed to establish their control over lands which they coveted. This long history of alienations and depredations accounts for a tendency on the part of Hemming and his associates to incorporate fictitious circumstantial

---

[70]*Vita Wulfstani*, p. 20.
[71]Ibid., pp. 24–5.
[72]Cf. J. D. Hamshere, "Domesday Book: Estate Structures in the West Midlands," in *Domesday Studies*, ed. J. C. Holt (1987), pp. 155–82, esp. pp. 168–70.
[73]*Hemingi Chartularium*, I, pp. 283–4.
[74]Ker, "Hemming's Cartulary," pp. 52–6.
[75]*Hemingi Chartularium*, I, p. 285. Before succeeding to the bishopric Wulfstan had earlier recovered some land misappropriated by senior monks: ibid., II, p.335.

detail when recording their title to some estates.[76] Wulfstan was already "a man of venerable old age" when he initiated this major project,[77] which was completed only after his death.[78] The first stage of the work, relating to the lands of the church as a whole, is shown by its surviving fragments to have been of inferior workmanship, when specific texts are compared with their counterparts in the early eleventh-century cartulary.[79] Hemming, anticipating unfavourable comment, stated that he was not writing for the over-critical, but he hoped that those who took pleasure in his work would remember him in their prayers.[80] A number of the estates which Hemming recorded had been appropriated by Danes, English or French, from whom there was little hope of redress. To that extent the cartulary reflects the landed wealth enjoyed by the church of Worcester in previous generations, rather than that effectively controlled by Wulfstan and his monks. Yet it is a valuable record both for its documentation of the endowments claimed by the monks, and for its series of vignettes detailing the violent or dishonest circumstances in which lands were misappropriated, which make plain the turbulence of the society surrounding the monastic community at Worcester.

Bishop Wulfstan's instigation of Hemming's cartulary would enhance the credibility of the completed record. The monks themselves might be slow in seeing the advantage of making this compilation, and slow in completing it, but when their immediate interests were under threat, they were quick to produce evidence in support of their claims. This is apparent from the sequence of events arising from a dispute over their ecclesiastical possessions which arose in Wulfstan's last years. In 1092 his health was failing, and he believed that his end was near. He determined to put the ecclesiastical affairs of his see in good order, and convened a diocesan synod at which any necessary reforms might be debated. Its proceedings were disrupted by a long dispute between Alfnoth, priest of St Helen's church, and Alam, priest of St Alban's. Wulfstan appointed a panel of senior men of the diocese, who were expected to have the greatest knowledge of the long-standing rights and customs of the churches and parishes of Worcester, and to be able to pronounce on the ancient rights of all the churches in the city. The monks of Worcester then intervened to protest that the dispute was causing them to lose rents due to them from St Helen's, which was their church. Wulfstan consequently instructed the investigating panel to pronounce additionally upon the rights of the cathedral church itself. The team

[76]Ker, "Hemming's Cartulary," p. 49.
[77] *Hemingi Chartularium*, I, p. 284.
[78] Ker, "Hemming's Cartulary," p. 45.
[79] Ibid., p. 50.
[80] *Hemingi Chartularium*, I, p. 286.

comprised Prior Thomas, Alfhere (Elfer) the sacristan (*secretarius*), Godric Wirl, the chamberlain of the cathedral priory, Uhtred the precentor (cantor), Ailric (Agelric) the archdeacon and his brother Edwin, Frideric, and the priest Eilmer (Egelmer), with other, unnamed, participants. Following their deliberations, they delivered the ensuing verdict to the synod:

> The only parochial church in the whole city is that of the cathedral itself. The church of St Helen has been a vicarage of the mother church ever since the days of King Ethelred [of Mercia, 675–704] and Archbishop Theodore [of Canterbury, 668–90], who founded the see, and established Bosel as its first Bishop in 680. The bishopric was served continuously by clerks from the episcopate of Bosel to that of Archbishop Oswald, who, with the help of King Edgar and the sanction of Archbishop Dunstan, replaced the clerks by monks in 969. Wynsige (Winsius), the vicar of the cathedral church, was priest of St Helen's, and when St Oswald persuaded him and the other clerks to adopt the monastic life, he surrendered the keys of the church, together with the lands, tithes and other rents. His fellow converts did likewise, and the properties which they had each held individually were now put to common use. In 972 St Oswald appointed Wynsige as prior, with the title of dean over the churches possessed by the monks, and over their priests. The prior, in his capacity as dean, rendered to the bishop the ecclesiastical dues payable from the monastic churches.

Wulfstan himself confirmed that he had been taught these things by his predecessors, and had seen matters administered in this way both in Bishop Ealdred's episcopate and in his own. Approving the testimony of the panel, he concluded the dispute between the priests, sealed the record of the panel's findings and concluded with an anathema against anyone infringing the settlement.[81]

St Alban's was not one of the churches possessed by the monks. It belonged to Evesham abbey by virtue of a grant made by Ethelbald of Mercia in 721, and it was a visible representation of Evesham's interests within the cathedral city. Consequently the dispute between the two priests probably arose from the ongoing rivalry beween Worcester and Evesham.[82] Wulfstan's terse statement that he had ended the dispute between the priests is given without further comment, but since he was satisfied that St Helen's pertained to his monks, he could dismiss any

---

[81]   *Cartulary of Worcester*, no. 52.
[82]   I. Atkins, "The Church of Worcester from the Eighth to the Twelfth Centuries," Part II, *The Antiquaries Journal*, 20 (1940), pp. 1–38 and 203–28, esp. pp. 206–7.

claim which Alam was making against it. The monks' own intervention about the loss of their rents indicates that these had formerly been diverted to Alam.

The record of this case conveys a superficial but misleading impression that the bishop's reforming synod was entirely preoccupied with the dispute between the two priests. In fact the account was selectively worded in order to serve as the monks' title deed to their churches. The diocesan synod is mentioned simply to establish the solemn and public occasion on which the dispute was adjudicated, and the testimony and episcopal verdict were declared. This record has survived because it was copied from the original deed into a mid-thirteenth century cartulary concerning the monks' possessions.[83] Since bishops did not keep registers of their *acta*, or formal decisions, in this period, there is no extant summary of the administrative and disciplinary rulings of Wulfstan's synod. Papal legates and archbishops occasionally convened synods in the late eleventh century, but there is no authentic record of English diocesan bishops' synods before that convened by Wulfstan in 1092, although there are passing references to such synods having been convened in other dioceses earlier in the Anglo-Norman period.[84]

Wulfstan's ratification of the findings of his commission of inquiry implies that he accepted an early date for the division of the *mensa*, since the report declared that not only the churches but also the lands formerly held by the clerks who served Worcester cathedral were transferred to the communal possession of the monks in the time of Bishop Oswald. Wulfstan could certainly testify to the existence of a divided *mensa* throughout his own episcopate, and the actions of his predecessor in 1062 indicate that Ealdred also acknowledged some such division. But although Wulfstan had been a monk of Worcester since the 1030s, he does not claim to have seen the division in operation during the episcopates of Brihtheah, Lyfing and Elfric Puttoc. Oswald and Wulfstan I were pluralists, and inevitably absentees for much of their episcopates. Whether or not the material interests of the monks actually suffered, they would inevitably develop aspirations to manage independently the property which was supposed to sustain them. Oswald and Wulfstan I were formidable characters, unlikely to make any such formal concessions, and they were followed by three resident bishops, Leofsige,

---

[83]   *Cartulary of Worcester*, no. 52, note 1.
[84]   Ibid., p. xlvi. *Councils and Synods, with other documents relating to the English Church, I. A.D. 871–1204*, ed. D. Whitelock, M. Brett and C. N. L. Brooke, 2 vols. (1981), Part II, 1066–1204, no. 100, pp. 635–9. The Councils of Winchester, of 1070, ch. 14, decreed that diocesan bishops should hold two synods yearly: ibid., no. 86, p. 576. On diocesan synods between 1066 and 1092, see M. Brett, *The English Church under Henry I* (1975), pp. 156–9.

Brihtheah and Lyfing. The crisis at the time of Lyfing's deprivation and the temporary substitution of Elfric Puttoc in 1040–1 is the most likely period when claims by the monks for a divided *mensa* were articulated. At that time, Wulfstan was a young monk, and it is most likely that he was then taught by his seniors how the clerks' prebends were surrendered in Oswald's day, and how these properties "ought" to be collectively administered by the monks as their common property. The advantages of such an arrangement would be obvious to the monks. In his capacity as prior, Wulfstan administered the estates assigned to the monks, but it is conjectural whether he had previously joined fellow *seniores* in negotiations with one or another bishop which resulted in the formal division of the *mensa*.

The one certain point is that it was not established in the way claimed in the commissioners' testimony. Bishop Oswald's clerks were not converted instantaneously to monasticism, and Wynsige certainly retained personal property after he became a monk.[85] Monastic jursidiction over the churches was not included in the writ granted by King Edward for Prior Alfstan, although it was incorporated in that which the prior later obtained from King William. Yet these identical ecclesiastical rights were granted by William to Bishop Wulfstan, and were perhaps disputed between bishop and monks until Wulfstan gave his verdict in 1092.[86] Since his acceptance of the testimony of his commissioners guaranteed the rights of the monks over their churches, the public dispute between the two priests occurred most opportunely from the monastic viewpoint.

The most striking feature of the report conveyed to Wulfstan by his commissioners is its parallels with the famous Worcester forgery *Altitonantis*, a document purporting to record the establishment of monasticism at Worcester in 964, but which is now generally accepted as a product of the later eleventh century. This document supports the claims which were made by the monastic community at that period, and it was perhaps in existence before the dispute over the churches was heard in 1092.[87] Wulfstan's acceptance of the testimony of his commissioners implies that he also accepted the substance of *Altitonantis*. Given his interest in the archives of his cathedral, it is open to conjecture that he authorized the production of this document, even though the suggestion

[85]   The question of when, and by what stages, monasticism was introduced to Worcester, is discussed in detail in ch. 1.
[86]   E. John, "An alleged charter of the reign of Edgar," *Bulletin of the John Rylands Library*, 41 (1958), pp. 54–80, esp. pp. 77–9. E. John, *Orbis Britanniae and other Studies* (1966), pp. 241–2, 262. For an opposing view, see *Cartulary of Worcester*, p. xlv; and for the view that St Helen's alone was the point at issue, see McIntyre, "Early Twelfth-Century Worcester Cathedral Priory," pp. 160–3.
[87]   *Anglo-Saxon Charters*, compiled Sawyer, no. 731; John, *Orbis Britanniae*, pp. 240–1.

appears incompatible with his reputation for "simplicity." He was a staunch defender of the rights of his church, and to a monk of his generation, forgery carried no reprehensible implications. The production of such a charter would be seen to set out in detail, for posterity, the rights which his church had exercised from early times, but which were supported by little explicit documentation. The charter is not entered either in the early eleventh century Worcester cartulary, nor in the late eleventh century one. When work on the latter was under way, it would become clear to Hemming and his associates that their collection lacked a full-scale foundation charter which both guaranteed the "triple hundred" and detailed the titles to individual manors. The substance of the charter represents the rights of the church of Worcester as they were asserted and exercised in the late eleventh century so that the composition may represent the combined inspiration of the *seniores*, with or without the connivance of Wulfstan himself. Among those who are likely to have had an interest in its composition are the chancellor, Coleman (his duties as prior of Westbury permitting) and Hemming. A third, and perhaps the most likely, candidate is the scholarly Nicholas, who trained at Canterbury in Lanfranc's time.[88] The monks there embarked on a programme of forgery production in the early 1070s, when, in the course of compiling a dossier of privileges for their new archbishop, they composed a letter supposedly written by Pope Boniface IV to King Ethelbert of Kent (560–616) establishing monks perpetually in his cathedral.[89] Nicholas, in his later years, wrote persuasively in defence of the interests of his monastic community, and was fully aware of the importance of preserving documentation to support his case.[90] Wulfstan's verdict in 1092 shows that the premises which underlay *Altitonantis* were accepted at Worcester during his episcopate, but the charter was perhaps composed in anticipation of his death or else shortly after that event, when there was a likelihood that his successor would be unaware of the traditions of his church, and unsympathetic towards its monastic community.

The substantial narrative content of *Hemming's Cartulary* allows it to be depicted as a product of the historical activity which Wulfstan inspired, and which also included both his *Life*, written by Coleman, and the universal history which he ordered his monk John to undertake.[91]

---

[88] *Vita Wulfstani*, p. 57.
[89] Gibson, *Lanfranc of Bec*, pp. 168–70, 231–7.
[90] D. L. Bethell, "English Black Monks and Episcopal Elections in the 1120s," *English Historical Review*, 84 (1969), pp. 673–98, esp. pp. 681–3, 694–8.
[91] M. Brett, "John of Worcester and his contemporaries," in *The Writing of History in the Middle Ages: essays presented to R. W. Southern*, ed. R. H. C. Davis and J. M. Wallace-Hadrill (1981), pp. 102, 104.

The latter work was based on the chronicle of Marianus Scotus, which in turn was introduced to Worcester by Wulfstan's friend Robert, bishop of Hereford.[92] John co-operated with fellow historians working on projects of their own in Canterbury, Durham and Malmesbury. Although his own work is one of synthesis rather than of real perception, it includes many valuable details which would otherwise have been lost. The activities of John and his fellow Benedictine historians were motivated in part by their desire to reassert the continuity of their experience, despite the traumas of the Norman Conquest and settlement, and to defend the long-standing titles of their houses to lands and rights threatened by the newcomers.[93] But there were new dangers threatening Benedictine houses in the early decades of the twelfth century. Their management of their external affairs was progressively threatened by the expanding activities of diocesan bishops and their subordinates; the newly intro-duced Order of Canons, and the increasingly articulate secular clergy challenged the monks' exercise of authority beyond their own precincts, while the new ascetic orders, following a more austere version of the monastic rule, attracted public esteem at the expense of the Benedictines, whose way of life had gathered so many accretions since the days of their founder. The political and tenurial upheaval of the later eleventh century, combined with the inrush of new spiritual and intellectual ideas in the early twelfth, compelled the monks to restate their own values, and in doing so, to inaugurate a major school of historical writing.[94] In setting the young John of Worcester to work, Wulfstan made a significant contribution to historical studies in England.

Two of the leading English monastic historians also acknowledged their debt to another monk of Worcester. Nicholas, the devoted disciple of Wulfstan, held the office of prior from some uncertain date between 1113 and 1116 until 1124;[95] he supplied important information to the Canterbury monk Eadmer, and advised him in his difficulties during the latter's traumatic spell as bishop-elect of St Andrews, in 1120–1. At that time, Eadmer was harassed by the canons of York, and Nicholas provided him with a wealth of historical evidence to prove that they had

---

[92]   Brett, "John of Worcester and his contemporaries," p. 110; *Ecclesiastical History of Orderic Vitalis*, II, pp. 186–8.
[93]   Brett, "John of Worcester and his contemporaries," pp. 117, 119, 125; R. W. Southern, "Aspects of the European tradition of Historical Writing: 4. The Sense of the Past," Presidential Address, *Transactions of the Royal Historical Society*, fifth series, 23 (1973), pp. 243–63, esp. pp. 246–56.
[94]   Brett, "John of Worcester and his contemporaries," pp. 125–6.
[95]   John Le Neve, *Fasti Ecclesiae Anglicanae 1066–1300: II. Monastic Cathedrals*, compiled by Diana E. Greenway (1971), p. 102.

no claim over the Scottish clergy.[96] Much earlier, and probably before 1109, Nicholas had written to Eadmer with information on the descent of King Edward the Martyr, which he stated he had gathered from ancient authorities, chiefly chronicles and songs compsed by learned men in the vernacular, but also from other, unspecified writings.[97]

William of Malmesbury received some of his most perceptive anecdotes concerning Wulfstan's spirituality from Nicholas, even though the latter's own intrusion into the narrative of the bishop's *Life* is unpropitious. On the occasion when Wulfstan banned all alcohol for the day, to stop the heated arguments of his hired knights from degenerating into a free-for-all fight, Nicholas was the one person who defied the order. Presuming on his favoured position, he dared to go into the cellar late at night, and helped himself to a drink. On falling asleep, he was plagued with terrible nightmares, and began to shout out, disturbing Coleman who was sleeping nearby. He woke up Nicholas, to find out what was the matter, but was shocked to hear him say that he had been grievously tormented by a devil, and could find no rest because he had disobeyed the bishop's order. Coleman persuaded him that he could dispel the nightmare by making the sign of the cross, and by praying. Nicholas fell asleep again, but twice more he was woken by nightmares, even worse than the original one. As last he realized that the only way to stop them was to obtain pardon from Wulfstan, whom he had disobeyed to his own cost. As usual at that time of night, Wulfstan was praying alone in the church. Nicholas found him there, fell at his feet and confessed his disobedience. Wulfstan, no doubt thinking he had learned his lesson and been punished enough already, restored his peace of mind and gave him a blessing.[98] The story is introduced into the *Life* to show that Wulfstan's orders could not be defied with impunity, even by a privileged young man who presumed upon his favoured status.

This unique and privileged position of Nicholas's was not due solely, or even primarily, to Wulfstan's affection for him. They were undoubtedly close but their relationship was that of father and son, not that of lovers. William of Malmesbury gives some information about Nicholas which he must have heard directly from him. He came from one of the most famous of the English dynasties, and his parents had an immense reverence for Wulfstan, doing a great deal to win his friendship.[99]

---

[96] Brett, "John of Worcester and his contemporaries," p. 113; R. W. Southern, *Saint Anselm and his Biographer: a study of monastic life and thought 1059–c.1130* (1966), p. 369.

[97] *Memorials of Saint Dunstan*, ed. W. Stubbs (1874), pp. 422–4; Brett, "John of Worcester and his contemporaries," p. 113; Southern, *Saint Anselm and his Biographer*, p. 369.

[98] *Vita Wulfstani*, p. 56.

[99] Ibid., p. 56.

William does not spell out the name of this family. It may be that he was never told in so many words; perhaps he thought that the name would mean little to his readers by the third decade of the twelfth century or, more likely, he appreciated the need for discretion even then. For the writers of the church of Worcester, even at that period, one English dynasty was pre-eminent above all others, the house of Godwin, and Harold was by any reckoning the greatest of its sons. His role in ensuring Wulfstan's election, and the latter's support of his rule in the north are expressly stated in Wulfstan's *Life*.[100] Harold's younger brothers held land elsewhere than in Mercia, and are unlikely to have had a close relationship with Wulfstan, while the turbulent career of Sweyn Godwinson ended too soon for any son of his to have been educated from infancy by Wulfstan. The other dynasty which the monks of Worcester would perceive as pre-eminent was that of Earl Leofric of Mercia, whose son Earl Alfgar was also active in furthering Wulfstan's election.[101] The identification of this family as the kindred of Nicholas is possible, even though its members and their associates were often predators upon the lands of the church of Worcester.[102]

The chronicler John of Worcester was well informed about King Harold's descendants, relating that three of his sons, Edwin, Godwin, and Magnus landed in Somerset in 1068; suffered military defeat; looted in Cornwall and Devon, and then returned to Ireland.[103] On chronological grounds, these young men are presumed to have been the sons of Harold's handfast wife, Edith Swanneshals (Swan-neck). It is likely that Harold's son Ulf was also the offspring of this union. Ulf was held hostage by William I, but on the king's death in 1087 he was released by Duke Robert of Normandy, given the arms appropriate to knightly status, and freedom to go wherever he chose.[104.]

[100]   Ibid., pp. 13, 18, 22–3.
[101]   Ibid., p. 18.
[102]   *Domesday Book 16: Worcestershire*, ed. F. and C. Thorn (1982), Appendix V, Worcester G, nos 14–15, 17, 20.
[103]   *Florentii Wigorniensis monachi Chronicon*, II, pp. 2–3. Another account of this expedition of King Harold's sons names its leaders as Godwin and Edmund, together with Tostig (their cousin), son of Sweyn: *Lestorie des Engles solum la Translacion Maistre Geffrei Gaimar*, ed. T. D. Hardy, 2 vols (1888–9), I lines 5046–9. Two unnamed sons of Harold made a further unsuccessful landing at the mouth of the River Tavy in June 1069: *Florentii Wigorniensis monachi Chronicon*, II, p. 3. Varying accounts of the expeditions of these young men are given in the *Anglo-Saxon Chronicle*, *s.a.* 1067, 1069 (D); *Ecclesiastical History of Orderic Vitalis*, II, p. 224 and n. 2. See also B. Hudson, "The Family of Harold Godwinsson and the Irish Sea Province," *Journal of the Royal Society of Antiquaries of Ireland*, 109 (1980 for 1979), pp. 92–100.
[104]   *Florentii Wigorniensis monachi Chronicon*, II, p. 21. Ulf was more fortunate than his uncle Wlnoth, brother of King Harold, and Earl Morcar. They were released by the dying William I, but returned to custody by William II: ibid., p. 20.

John of Worcester also mentions briefly Harold's son Harold, whose mother was Edith, the daughter of Earl Alfgar of Mercia. Before her marriage to Harold Godwinson, she had been the wife of the Welsh king, Gruffyd ap Llywelyn, who died in 1063. The younger Harold can have been barely two years old at his father's death in 1066. He was educated as a layman, and took part in the expedition against Anglesey in 1098.[105] Since his paternal lands, and those of his maternal uncles, had been forfeit, his tenurial status would be constrained. Any younger son of the marriage between Harold Godwinson and Edith would have very limited prospects in the secular world, and the life of a Benedictine *oblate* might appear to offer the best alternative. Even so, a younger son of this marriage might well be given the name of Ethelred, the last wholly English predecessor of Harold II.

The children, especially the sons, of any formerly prominent English family would face a sharp reduction in their status, which would account for Nicholas, whatever his parentage, having been reared in the cloister from virtually his earliest years. Wulfstan himself baptized the boy, who was said by William of Malmesbury to have been the bishop's "special foster child," and arranged that he should have a first-class education, progressing in stages according to his age. He always kept Nicholas by his side, until he sent him into Kent, in order to complete his training by serving for a while under the discipline of Lanfranc.[106]

This final phase of Nicholas's education would give him the opportunity of extending his academic education beyond that which Worcester itself was equipped to provide. It would also enable him to learn the new monastic customs introduced by Archbishop Lanfranc, so that he in turn could teach them to the monks of Worcester. The Canterbury historian Eadmer, when mentioning those who provided him with information for his *Life of St Dunstan* (bishop of Worcester before his elevation to Canterbury), singled out "Ethelred, who held the office of sub-prior and cantor most energetically for a long time, and who later, because of his monastic knowledge, and his knowledgeable practice of the monastic discipline, was a dignitary of the church of Worcester under Bishop Wulfstan of blessed memory."[107] This Ethelred, scholar and obedientiary of Worcester, is not readily identifiable, and it has been suggested that

---

[105] *Florentii Wigorniensis monachi Chronicon*, I, p. 276. For his participation in the Anglesey expedition, see William of Malmesbury, *De Gestis Regum Anglorum*, II, pp. 318, 376.

[106] *Vita Wulfstani*, pp. 56–7; William of Malmesbury, *De Gestis Pontificum Anglorum*, p. 287.

[107] *Memorials of Saint Dunstan*, pp. 163–4.

Eadmer's informant was Nicholas.[108] Eadmer, an Englishman himself, might have known him by his given name, rather than by his name in religion, especially if the former name was used at Canterbury to avoid confusion with any other Nicholas in that large community. In the mid-eleventh century, Nicholas would not have been the baptismal name of a child of English stock, but it was a suitable name for a monk of Worcester to adopt on making his monastic profession, especially for the bishop's protégé, because it was Pope Nicholas II whose insistence on the separation of the sees of Worcester and York had ensured Wulfstan's accession to the episcopate.[109] The witnesses to the few surviving charters of Bishop Wulfstan are, apart from Prior Thomas, all men with English or Anglo-Scandinavian names, but as that of Nicholas himself indicates, it was becoming common in Wulfstan's later years for monks to adopt a name "in religion" when they made their professions. A comprehensive list of current and recently deceased monks of Worcester, recorded at Durham c.1104, reveals the changing pattern. Apart from entries in a later hand, there are thirty-one names, including that of Wulfstan himself, which are English or Anglo-Scandinavian; eight members of the Worcester community, including Bishop Samson and Prior Thomas, had "French" names, while the remaining twenty-three on the list are variously scriptural, Patristic and Classical.[110] Given the English cultural bias at Worcester throughout Wulfstan's episcopate, it is likely that the new practice was introduced either by Prior Thomas, who perhaps considered the English personal names uncouth, or even unpronounceable,[111] or else was an innovation brought back from Canterbury by Nicholas himself.

The careful education bestowed on Nicholas, and his special relationship with Wulfstan, are indications that from an early age he was destined for high office. Thomas remained prior from c.1080 to his death in October 1113, and no successor is recorded before Nicholas, who is known to have been in office in August 1116.[112] According to his friend

---

[108] *Vita Wulfstani*, p. xxxviii. The list of Worcester monks recorded in 1104 includes two men named Nicholas, and one Edred, possibly an abridged form of Ethelred: *Durham Liber Vitae*, folio 22 recto. An identification of the future prior Nicholas with the Ethelred named by Eadmer suggests the further possibility that Wulfstan's protégé was a son of Siward, the "rich man from Shropshire" who supported Wulfstan in his lawsuit against Abbot Walter of Evesham, and was a great-grandson of King Ethelred II.

[109] *Vita Wulfstani*, p. 16.

[110] *Durham Liber Vitae*, folio 22 recto.

[111] The Shropshire-born chronicler Orderic was given the additional name of Vitalis (Viel) when he was admitted as an oblate to Saint-Evroul in Normandy, because his English name was considered uncouth: *Ecclesiastical History of Orderic Vitalis*, VI, p. 554.

[112] John Le Neve, *Fasti Ecclesiae Anglicanae 1066–1300. II. Monastic Cathedrals*, p. 102.

William of Malmesbury, he was made prior "in the time of Bishop Theulf,"[113] and his appointment probably dates from soon after that of the bishop himself.[114] Some fifty or so years after the Norman Conquest, there was no practical reason why Theulf, as titular abbot, should hesitate to promote an Englishman as prior. Within the monastic chapter there was still a large proportion of English monks likely to support a candidate of their own race, especially given his superior monastic education, and the self-confidence which derived from his special position. William was particularly impressed by the high standard of scholarship which Nicholas imposed on the monks of Worcester during his time as prior. As a result of his teaching, and the example he set, the monks of the cathedral priory were as learned as those in even the largest monasteries.[115]

William met Prior Nicholas when he visited Worcester to research on major historical projects of his own, the *De Gestis Regum* (*Deeds of the Kings*) and the *De Gestis Pontificum* (*Deeds of the Bishops*).[116] He discovered that the prior loved to recount Wulfstan's sayings and doings, and considered it a pity, perhaps even a fault, that Nicholas himself had not written the bishop's biography. No-one, William thought, could have recorded his activities more accurately, because no-one was closer to him.[117] Evidently William preferred Nicholas's perceptive anecdotes, which illuminated Wulfstan's spirituality, to some of the episodes included by Coleman which reflect a predominant urge to sensationalize in standard hagiographical vein. William of Malmesbury considered that even the most casual sayings of Wulfstan had some weight. At an early age, the hair on Nicholas's brow began to recede. Once, when Wulfstan was affectionately stroking his head Nicholas said jokingly, "You are certainly taking good care of my hair, but it is thinning out all the same." Wulfstan answered, "Believe me, you will not turn bald as long as I live." Sure enough, in the very week that Wulfstan died, Nicholas lost all his remaining hair.[118] Where the modern reader sees only the progressive onset of baldness, the twelfth century discerned a minor prophecy.

The position of the young Nicholas was undoubtedly privileged, and his careful education was designed to equip him for a leading role in the church of Worcester at a later date. His appreciation of Wulfstan's loving

---

[113] *Vita Wulfstani*, p. 57.
[114] Bishop Theulf was appointed on 28 December 1113, but consecrated only on 27 June 1115: Le Neve, *Fasti Ecclesiae Anglicanae 1066–1300. II. Monastic Cathedrals*, p. 99.
[115] *Vita Wulfstani*, p. 57.
[116] Ibid., p. ix.
[117] Ibid., p. 57.
[118] Ibid., p. 57. For a variant on this story, see William of Malmesbury, *De Gestis Pontificum Anglorum*, p. 287.

care for him is reflected both in his own affectionate response and by his concern to preserve memories of the bishop for others. Nicholas, rather than Thomas, was probably "the prior" who gave Wulfstan's lambskin-lined riding cloak to Robert of Hereford when he arrived to conduct the bishop's funeral.[119] The sensitive disciple glimpsed in the *Life* of Wulfstan matured into an effective prior. Given the prejudice against Englishmen in high office by the twelfth century,[120] it is a reflection of the impact which Wulfstan himself had upon the chapter that his protégé could succeed to this office in the second decade of the reign of Henry I. Following the death of Bishop Theulf on 20 October 1123, Nicholas led his chapter in a struggle to obtain free election of a monastic successor, an aspiration which ran contrary to all the rising forces in the Church at that time. In this battle, he deployed all his learning and literary skills, heedless of a warning from his friend Eadmer that excessive zeal would end in failure. Wulfstan would have approved of his protégé's aims, even though his methods reflected nothing of the bishop's reputed simplicity.[121] Wulfstan perhaps had hoped that this son of a pre-eminent English noble house would be his eventual successor. The bishop accepted the political defeat of the English, but led the struggle to preserve the values of their monasticism; undoubtedly he caused Nicholas to be trained to exercise leadership in transmitting these to the succeeding generation. The success of this earned Nicholas in turn the recognition which was due, but the failure of his energetic struggle to secure a free election at Worcester probably hastened his death, which occurred on 24 June 1124.[122] His zealous leadership of a struggle to sustain traditional values, against mounting odds, recalls in a very different context an English leader whom Wulfstan had known at an earlier time. The resemblance is perhaps not fortuitous.

King Harold's daughter Gunnhild was living in the nunnery of Wilton (Wilts), one of the most prestigious of the women's religious houses founded before the Norman Conquest. An account of a visit which Wulfstan made there was studiously vague as to whether he called on purpose, or whether his route just happened to pass that way;[123] it might easily have done so if he was travelling to or from a gathering of the royal court at Winchester. This one visit is recorded only because on this occasion he was perceived to mediate a healing miracle. There is no way

---

[119] William of Malmesbury, *De Gestis Pontificum Anglorum*, p. 302. William would have met Nicholas when he was already prior.
[120] William of Malmesbury, *De Gestis Regum Anglorum*, p. 278.
[121] Bethell, "English Black Monks and Episcopal Elections," pp. 681–3, 694–8.
[122] Le Neve, *Fasti Ecclesiae Anglicanae 1066–1300. II. Monastic Cathedrals*, p. 102.
[123] *Vita Wulfstani*, p. 34.

of knowing whether he called regularly on the daughter of his old friend when he happened to be travelling in that direction. The nuns (probably Englishwomen for the most part), were delighted to see him, and he sat down to talk to them. He learned that Gunnhild was suffering from a malignant tumour which had swollen her eyelids so that their weight blocked her sight. When he heard of her distressing ailment, he ordered them to fetch her. He was greatly moved by her suffering, and did what he could to alleviate it, saying that he owed a good deal to her father's memory. He made the sign of the cross before her eyes, and immediately she was able to raise her eyelids and see the light. Even if her ailment was not in fact a tumour, but simply a bad attack of the infection known as styes, its cure would be a great relief. The pain and discomfort would have dissuaded her from even trying to open her eyes, but the bishop's compassionate approach encouraged her to make full use of her faculties.[124] In the last few years of Wulfstan's life, failing health is likely to have prevented him from travelling any great distance, so that the episode probably dates from the previous decade if not before.

The nunnery of Wilton dated from the ninth century, and subsequently enjoyed the patronage of several of the English kings. Its church was rebuilt by Edith, the wife of King Edward, who visited it again in her widowhood.[125] Although she died in 1075,[126] the status of patron's kin would continue to ensure favourable treatment there for her niece Gunnhild. The latter's position at Wilton was somewhat ambiguous. Englishwomen of noble families were often educated as secular pupils in nunneries, and many more took refuge in religious houses in the wake of the Norman Conquest and settlement. Even though they did not take the veil, questions were raised about their religious status if they later chose to leave in order to marry. Some French settlers were only too willing to acquire an English wife, by reason of whose presence their tenants might more readily acquiesce in their occupation of their newly acquired lands. Consequently the more eligible parlour-boarders were apt on occasion to

---

[124] Ibid., p. 34. An effective antibiotic treatment for styes was known at this time: M. L. Cameron, "Anglo-Saxon Medicine and Magic," *Anglo-Saxon England*, 17 (1988), pp. 191–215; see esp. pp. 201–3. The patient's confidence in the healer would also help to effect a cure: ibid., pp. 210–15. The account of this incident may be influenced by an episode in the *Life of St Edith*, who was credited with healing Abbess Elfgiva of Wilton (1065–7), whose right eye was swollen by the royal sickness. For this miracle, see A. Wilmart, "La légende de Sainte Edith en prose et vers par le moine Goscelin," *Analecta Bollandiana*, lvi (1938), pp. 5–101, 265–307; see esp. pp. 294–5.

[125] *The Life of King Edward who rests at Westminster*, attributed to a monk of St Bertin, ed. and transl. Frank Barlow (1962), pp. 46–9, 100; Knowles and Hadcock, *Medieval Religious Houses*, pp. 268–9.

[126] *Anglo-Saxon Chronicle, s.a.* 1075 (D, E).

leave their nunneries with a dramatic flourish. The issue was raised at the highest level, and Archbishop Lanfranc spoke for the king as well as for himself when he stated that professed nuns, and those who had been formally presented as *oblates*, were obliged to remain in the religious life. Those who were simply boarders should be dismissed, unless and until further investigation proved that they truly wished to become nuns. Women who had fled to nunneries for fear of the French were free to leave, provided that senior nuns testified unambiguously that they had entered solely as refugees.[127]

Wilton was the residence not only of King Harold's daughter Gunnhild but also of Edith, the daughter of King Malcolm Canmore of Scotland and his wife Queen Margaret, a great-granddaughter of King Ethelred. Gunnhild and Edith both compromised their secular status by wearing the veil, but each later insisted that she had never become a professed nun. Gunnhild had expectations of becoming an abbess – it is not certain where – but these hopes were dashed. In the summer of 1093, an entirely different future opened before her. The marriage which King Malcolm had planned between Edith and Count Alan the Red, lord of Richmond (Yorks), was forbidden on political grounds by King William II. Malcolm angrily left the royal court at Gloucester and took Edith back to Scotland with him. It is likely that Alan travelled with him, and found at Wilton a substitute for his thwarted ambitions. It soon became known that Gunnhild was living under his protection. Alan was well into his fifties, and Gunnhild at least thirty – considerably more than that if her mother was Edith Swan-neck rather than King Harold's official wife. Whether or not theirs was a romantic elopement between two mature adults, their union had political implications. Count Alan's extensive lands in the Danelaw and eastern England absorbed many estates which are believed to have been formerly held by Edith Swan-neck. Gunnhild, as the daughter of Harold, and perhaps also the daughter of this Edith rather than of the other, was well suited to foster the loyalty of the tenants of these estates towards Count Alan.[128]

Lanfranc's pragmatic ruling on women who left the cloister was not shared by his successor Anselm, consecrated in December 1093.[129] The new archbishop firmly believed that salvation was to be found only within the confines of a religious house. The very fact that Gunnhild and

---

[127]   *Letters of Lanfranc*, ed. and transl. Helen Clover and Margaret Gibson (1979), no. 53. See also Eleanor Searle, "Women and the legitimization of succession at the Norman Conquest," *Proceedings of the Battle Conference on Anglo-Norman Studies III. 1980*, ed. R. Allen Brown (1981), pp. 159–70, and 226—9, esp. pp. 165–6.
[128]   Searle, "Women and the legitimization of succession," pp. 166–9, 229.
[129]   Le Neve, *Fasti Ecclesiae Anglicanae 1066–1300. II. Monastic Cathedrals*, p. 3.

Edith had once worn the nun's habit, even though neither had taken vows, marked them in his view as irrevocably committed to what he perceived as the one true way of life. Anselm was pleased to learn that William II would be glad if Edith could be persuaded to return.[130] The king, for his part, would be displeased that these daughters of two rival dynasties had fled from their nunnery. Either woman might at any moment be used by an adventurer as a pretext for raising unwelcome territorial claims, or even rebellion or invasion. Anselm's zealous efforts to restore them to the cloister were motivated by spiritual considerations, and he was not consciously representing the king's interests when he turned his attention to Gunnhild. There have survived two letters from the archbishop in which he tried to persuade her to return. The earlier one is respectful, and even tender. After receiving it, Gunnhild met him amicably. He understood from a letter which she later sent to him that she would not abandon the life of the cloister.[131] When Count Alan died, she changed her mind, and the archbishop's subsequent letter is written in a bitter tone:

> You loved Count Alan Rufus, and he loved you. Where is he now? What has become of the lover whom you loved? Go now and lie with him in the bed where he now lies; gather his worms into your bosom; embrace his corpse; kiss his bare teeth from which the flesh has fallen. . .[132]

This horrible imagery reflects the fact that from Anselm's viewpoint Gunnhild had deserted her destined vocation. She, on the other hand, had been deprived of the status she would have had as an abbess, while the subordinate and monotonous life of a choir nun would seem a dreary prospect after life as Count Alan's chatelaine.[133] She was spared the ignominy of surrending to the archbishop's demand because the count's brother, Alan the Black, succeeded both to his estates and to Gunnhild.

---

[130] *Sancti Anselmi Opera Omnia*, ed. F. S. Schmitt, 6 vols (1940, 1946–61), no. 177; Southern, *Saint Anselm and his Biographer*, p. 183; Barlow, *William Rufus*, pp. 312–13.
[131] *Sancti Anselmi Opera Omnia*, ed. F. S. Schmitt, IV, no. 168; Barlow,*William Rufus*, p. 313 and note 219. See, however, Southern, *Saint Anselm and his Biographer*, pp. 186–7 for a different view of the dating and consequently the significance of Anselm's two letters to Gunnhild.
[132] *Sancti Anselmi Opera Omnia*, IV, no. 169. The translation is that of Southern, *Saint Anselm and his Biographer*, p. 186. See also Barlow, *William Rufus*, p. 314.
[133] Gunnhild's prospects at Wilton would seem particularly dreary compared with those of Gytha, the wife of Vladimir, prince of Kiev, who is believed to have been another daughter of Harold Godwinson: F. Dvornik, "The Kiev State and its Relations with Western Europe," reprinted from *Transactions of the Royal Historical Society*, fourth series, 29 (1947),pp. 27–46, in *Essays in Medieval History*, ed. R. W. Southern (1968), pp. 1–23, see esp. pp. 17, 23.

This relationship, too, was without benefit of formal matrimony.[134] This sequence of events was played out during Wulfstan's last years. He is likely to have heard of it, whether through his contacts in the archbishopric of York, or those at Canterbury. The daughter of his old friend chose a path which was diametrically opposed to that which he would have advised. The best that could be said of her now was that her presence in the north helped to maintain the peace of that region.

The presence in nunneries of marriageable Englishwomen raises the possibility that Wulfstan occasionally conveyed messages between the surviving families of native stock and their cloistered kindred. He was certainly in touch with King Malcolm and his wife Margaret,[135] who transmitted to her own descendants the consciousness that they were now the representatives of the Old English kings.[136] The queen and her sister Christina probably met Wulfstan during their girlhood years at the court of King Edward, so that the bishop's visit to Wilton might equally be occasioned by the presence there of Christina and her niece Edith as by that of Gunnhild. Just as Wulfstan's inauguration of the confraternity agreement upheld the values of English monasticism, so the social contacts maintained in the course of his travels would help to keep surviving English families in touch with one another. In the absence of native political leadership, the surviving English bishop took on a focal and patriarchal role extending far beyond the confines of his own diocese.[137] This is demonstrated by the requests he received from English landholders in other bishoprics to consecrate the churches which they built on their lands.[138] Yet while he represented a focus for ethnic loyalties, his role was in no sense that of an opposition leader, given his belief in the unswerving loyalty due to the anointed king. The very fact of Wulfstan's longevity would enable him to place recent political events in their proper perspective. From his vantage-point, many of the changes of

---

[134] Searle, "Women and the legitimization of succession," pp. 167–9.
[135] *Vita Wulfstani*, pp. 59–60.
[136] William of Malmesbury was commissioned to write the *De Gestis Regum Anglorum* by Queen Edith Matilda, daughter of Queen Margaret. Copies were sent by William to King David of Scotland (Margaret's son), and to the Empress Matilda, daughter of Edith Matilda: Thomson, *William of Malmesbury*, pp. 15, 34–6, 154. See also A. Squire, "Aelred and King David," *Collectanea Sacri Ordinis Cisterciensium Reformatorum*, 22 (1960), p. 368.
[137] Unstable or destabilized societies of many kinds experience an instinctive need to recognize a charismatic spiritual leader who stands above and apart from political and economic conflict. On the role of the specifically Christian holy man, see P. R. L. Brown, "The Rise and Function of the Holy Man in Late Antiquity," *Journal of Roman Studies*, 61 (1971), pp. 80–101.
[138] *Vita Wulfstani*, pp. 32, 45.

the later eleventh century could be matched by developments which had occurred in his region several decades earlier.[139] Within Wulfstan's own household a reconciliation of political values might be achieved if the "sons of rich men" being educated there included those of some of the surviving English families.[140] Since certain "French" customs were selectively adopted in Wulfstan's household,[141] any English pupils could be encouraged to adapt to the new ways, while those of "French" stock would be taught to value what was best in English practice. This would foster the development of a unified social order within the diocese, which would be to the advantage both of the next generation of episcopal tenants and to the church of Worcester itself. In monastic circles it was received wisdom that the secular pupils, however wayward their conduct during their schooldays, were likely to further the interests of the house later in life.[142] Probably the majority of the secular pupils at Worcester were the sons of "French" fathers, even if in some instances their mothers were English. Those surviving Englishmen formerly of thegnly status were now only mesne tenants, but might still retain considerable influence at shire level, since the great magnates, as in earlier times, would frequently be away from the region on business of one kind or another.[143] Probably, therefore, some Englishmen could still afford to have their sons educated as secular pupils at Worcester, and would be the more eager to do so in view of Wulfstan's stature among their race.

Together with the transmission of cultural values, Wulfstan handed on those pertaining to ecclesiastical and spiritual matters. By the early 1090s his was the one voice which could pronounce authoritatively on traditional rights for the benefit of the newcomers. On points for which little

---

[139] Emma Mason, "Change and Continuity in Eleventh-Century Mercia: the experience of St. Wulfstan of Worcester," *Anglo-Norman Studies VIII*, ed. R. Allen Brown (1986), pp. 154–76.

[140] *Vita Wulfstani*, p. 50. Throughout his episcopate, Wulfstan regarded the lands of the church of Worcester as inalienable *dominium*, to be held by tenants only for lease of one life, and not as *feudum*, to be held in heredity: V. H. Galbraith, "An Episcopal Land-Grant of 1085," *English Historical Review*, 44 (1929), pp. 353–72; esp. pp. 354, 366–8. Englishmen, accustomed to such a conservative tenurial policy, might be more willing than Normans to hold such tenancies in good faith. Normans did acquire leaseholds, but usually treated them as hereditary fiefs.

[141] William of Malmesbury, *De Gestis Pontificum Anglorum*, p. 281.

[142] This opinion was voiced by a tenth-century abbot of Ramsey, when his monks urged him to punish pupils who climbed among the bells of his church, set them swinging, and cracked one: *Chronicon Abbatiae Ramesiensis*, ed. W. D. Macray (1886), pp. 112–14.

[143] "An Introduction to the Gloucestershire Domesday," in *Domesday Book: Gloucestershire*, ed. R. W. H. Erskine and A. Williams (1989), p. 39.

if any documentation survived, customary rights were those which he recalled, and what he proclaimed them to be.[144] Eadmer was gratified when Wulfstan's pronouncement on "the rights exercised by your excellent predecessor Stigand" upheld Anselm's claim to consecrate churches outside the diocese of Canterbury. It was self-evident to the Canterbury historian that Wulfstan was "the unique survivor of the ancient fathers of the English; the one especially imbued with the knowledge of the ancient English customs."[145]

But overall memory played a lesser part in assisting Wulfstan to preserve traditional values than did the intellectual and spiritual resources on which he drew. Worcester's selectively well-stocked library enabled him to make good use of the spiritual writings of earlier generations. In particular, it can be demonstrated that during his episcopate the homilies of his namesake the archbishop, and those of Elfric, were put to good use, probably by the bishop in person.[146] It was not only others who perceived Wulfstan as the repository of traditional English wisdom: rather it was a role which he consciously filled. His grounding in older values, combined with his intensive prayer life, raised him to a unique position in late eleventh century England.

The depiction of Wulfstan in his *Life* as a patriarchal figure, not only in his own diocese but also among his compatriots throughout England, reflects him as he was perceived in the last ten to fifteen years of his life, but this status was acquired gradually over a long period of time. The extinction of the claims of the archbishop of York over the see of Worcester, the disappearance of the last English secular leaders, and the successive deaths of Ealdred and Ethelwig all contributed to bring Wulfstan's position into sharper focus. His longevity increasingly underlined the fact that he was a living embodiment of the values of an earlier generation. Once the newcomers in church and state were established in office, they would want to enhance their authority by drawing on the best of the older traditions. Attention has rightly focused on the work of Archbishop Wulfstan, and of Ealdred, in helping successive royal

---

[144] For discussion of analogous selective memorizing of facts, see J. Goody and I. Watt, "The Consequences of Literacy," reprinted from *Comparative Studies in Society and History*, 5 (1963), pp. 304–45, in *Literacy in Traditional Societies*, ed. J. Goody (1968), pp. 27–68, esp. pp. 29–30, 32–4, 48, 50–1.

[145] For Anselm's letter of enquiry to Wulfstan, and the bishop's reply, see *Sancti Anselmi Opera Omnia*, IV, nos 170–1; and for comment at Canterbury on this correspondence, see Eadmer, *Historia Novorum in Anglia*, ed. M. Rule (1884), pp. 45–6.

[146] Ker, *Catalogue of Manuscripts containing Anglo-Saxon*, nos 41, 331–2, 338. See also nos 48, 178, 333.

dynasties to establish their position in the eyes of the English.[147] Bishop Wulfstan, their successor in the see of Worcester and inheritor of the traditions which moulded their actions, performed an equally important service in reconciling the newcomers to older monastic and spiritual values.

Archbishop Wulfstan had defined the episcopal role as that of "Christ's sheriff."[148] In the absence of those who may be termed spiritual ealdormen, his namesake emerged as the counterpart of the new breed of secular sheriff, no longer answerable to the predominant local magnate. The disappearance of the major English landholders was followed by the fragmentation and redistribution of their estates. This deprived Englishmen lower down the tenurial ladder of their traditional patrons, who might be succeeded by two or more alien, and even rival, lords.[149] The resulting sense of insecurity would generate a widespread impulse to seek out a compatriot who could mitigate the new evils. A climate of anxiety would generate a belief in someone with the spiritual power to allay fears of many kinds, and who was perceived by some to command supernatural forces. In this way, Wulfstan emerged as a "holy man" who mediated healing of body and mind for those faithful believers who obeyed his teachings, but whose rebuke to the recalcitrant brought disastrous consequences. In certain respects, Wulfstan's activities can be compared to those of the numerous English and Anglo-Scandinavian hermits living in the century after the Conquest, who eased the lot of their compatriots by helping them adjust to the social effects of the Norman settlement.[150] The traditional holy man was so influential because he was perceived to be detached from the ambitions of worldly society. At the core of Wulfstan's influence lay the simplicity with which he was attributed: the simplicity of the dove, which tempers the cunning of the serpent. In scriptural exegesis the dove perceives with an eye which is simple but spiritual, penetrating the mysteries of God and the secrets of the human heart. A man who possessed this spiritual insight would see far more quickly and clearly than others in any given case what was right,

---

[147] Dorothy Whitelock, "Archbishop Wulfstan, Homilist and Statesman," *Transactions of the Royal Historical Society*, fourth series, 24 (1942), pp. 25–45; "Wulfstan and the laws of Cnut," *English Historical Review*, 63 (1948), pp. 433–52; and her "Wulfstan's authorship of Cnut's laws," ibid., 70 (1955), pp. 72–85; Janet L. Nelson, "The Rites of the Conqueror," *Proceedings of the Battle Conference on Anglo-Norman Studies, IV. 1981*, ed. R. Allen Brown (1982), pp. 117–32, esp. pp. 126–7.

[148] *Die "Institutes of Polity, Civil and Ecclesiastical," ein Werk Erzbischof Wulfstans von York*, ed. K. Jost (1959), pp. 144–5.

[149] Robin Fleming, "Domesday Book and the Tenurial Revolution," *Anglo-Norman Studies IX*, ed. R. Allen Brown (1987), pp. 87–102.

[150] Mayr-Harting, "Functions of a Twelfth-Century Recluse," pp. 337–52.

and what was the proper course of action.[151] In Wulfstan's day disorientation was endemic. The surviving but demoted English, and perhaps also Frenchmen who were uprooted from their old homes yet had difficulty in adjusting to a new and alien environment, would turn to Wulfstan for guidance towards peace of mind.

[151]   Ibid., p. 339.

9

Wulfstan and the Wider World

Wulfstan's activities as a conscientious diocesan bishop necessitated extensive travel throughout his own see, and because of the involvement of Archbishop Thomas I of York in the royal service, he was also required to exercise deputed episcopal authority in the north, on the instructions of Ealdred, Lanfranc and Thomas himself.[1] Until failing health curbed his mobility in his last years, Wulfstan also attended the seasonal royal courts at centres widely scattered throughout southern England. There is a strong implication in Wulfstan's *Life* that throughout England he was increasingly regarded as a patriarchal figure, to whom English penitents flocked from all over the country.[2] His services were also in demand by Englishmen in other dioceses who wanted him to dedicate their newly built parish churches. It is conjectural how often he performed such tasks, since the accounts of Wulfstan performing extra-diocesan dedications are incorporated in his *Life* only when the occasion provided the setting for some dramatic incident. Some of his fellow bishops were perhaps all too ready to have him perform dedications in out-of-the-way corners of their dioceses, especially when an English patron had built the church. Wulfstan's reputation for humility and simplicity would safeguard him from any allegation of eroding a fellow bishop's authority, while his unswerving loyalty to the king precluded any risk that he might become a focus for political unrest among the English. It was said that the king and his nobles showed great honour to Wulfstan; invited him to their tables, and respected his advice, especially those of them who acted justly. It was tartly observed in his *Life* that some men instinctively admire in others what they cannot hope to attain to themselves, and that many of the magnates fell into this category.[3] Just

---

[1]*The Vita Wulfstani of William of Malmesbury*, ed. R. R. Darlington (1928), pp. 19, 26, 44.
[2]*Vita Wulfstani*, p.50.
[3]Ibid., p. 59.

as the English saints came to be venerated by the newcomers, so the genuine goodness of the surviving native bishop would be appreciated by the more perceptive of them. The others would at least have the good sense not to show disrespect towards someone reputed to be a prophetic and wonder-working holy man.

On one occasion when King William and Archbishop Thomas I of York (1070–1100) jointly instructed Wulfstan to travel to York in order to bless the chrism before Easter (when it would be required for baptisms), his route took him through Nottingham, which was already an important town, lying on a crossing point of the Trent, a major river.[4] If Wulfstan set out from his own diocese, he and his retinue would first travel east, across country, or, more conveniently, south-east, on the saltway leading from Droitwich to link up with the Foss Way, one of the four royal roads. Their route would then take them north-east towards Nottingham, but they would need to leave the road to reach this town, from which another road led north to York.[5] Accommodating the bishop and his retinue could present problems. Some stages of a journey could be planned so that halts would occur at sizeable religious houses, but few journeys would ensure a comfortable billet at every halt, as shown by the ignominious retreat from the ruinous building at Wycombe.[6] A bishop would naturally expect to receive official hospitality wherever possible. Wulfstan was travelling on the king's orders, and called on the services of the sheriff of Nottingham.[7] After the crisis in the early years of William I's reign, most English sheriffs were replaced by Normans, but some sheriffs with English names are recorded as late as the reign of William II. The English-sounding sheriff Ernwig was active in the north Midlands after 1075, probably as a successor to HughFitz Baldric, sheriff of Nottingham.[8] The bishop of Worcester would be doubly sure of a good reception in an English household.

---

[4]Ibid., p. 44. On Nottingham in the earlier Middle Ages, see M. W. Beresford and H. P. R. Finberg, *English Medieval Boroughs, a Hand-List* (1973), p. 146. After the Norman Conquest, a separate "French borough" was founded for the new settlers, and this area retained traces of its distinctive organization for centuries: Susan Reynolds, *An Introduction to the History of English Medieval Towns* (1977), pp. 43, 49, 191.
[5]D. Hill, *An Atlas of Anglo-Saxon England*, 2nd edn (1984), p. 116, map 199.
[6]*Vita Wulfstani*, pp. 31–2.
[7]Ibid., p. 44.
[8]*Regesta Regum Anglo-Normannorum 1066–1154: I. Regesta Willelmi Conquestoris et Willelmi Rufi 1066–1100*, ed. H. W. C. Davis, with R. J. Whitwell (1913), nos 333, 335, 337; Judith Green, "The Sheriffs of William the Conqueror," *Anglo-Norman Studies V*, ed. R. Allen Brown (1983), pp. 129–45, esp. p. 131. Since the source for the ensuing story is Frewin, active as an episcopal clerk in Wulfstan's later years, it may be assumed that it was the English sheriff, Ernwig, whom the bishop proposed to visit.

Wulfstan sent some of his men ahead, to arrange lodgings for his whole retinue. The sheriff happened to be away from home, but his wife received the messengers honourably, and the more so because they were from Bishop Wulfstan, of whose reputation she had heard. She neither entirely believed, nor altogether disbelieved, what she had heard about him. In fact, she hardly knew what to believe, so she closely questioned his advance party, asking them in the name of God to resolve her doubt as to whether the bishop's holiness truly matched his reputation. The clerk Frewin answered truly and with moderation, neither undervaluing anything about the bishop nor exaggerating. He said that Wulfstan gave himself to the service of God gladly and simply. That was what he himself aspired to, and what he liked others to do. The lady then questioned him more intensively, obviously expecting some sign from Heaven which would confirm what she had heard of the bishop's reputation. She privately considered that Wulfstan's reputation as a holy man would be proven if fish came to the nets to augment the food which would be offered to him, because no fish at all had been caught at Nottingham for the past three months. Christ, who confirmed the faith of Doubting Thomas (John 20:24–9 – an analogy which would come more readily to the writer of Wulfstan's *Life* than to the lady herself) would resolve her uncertainty. She entertained the messengers most hospitably, then sent her servants to fish, and waited to see how things turned out. The lady's secret test of Wulfstan's stature as a wonder-worker was one which might naturally occur to her, but the writer of the bishop's *Life* doggedly persevered with allusions to scriptural analogies of miraculous catches of fish (cf. Luke 5:4–7; John 21:3–12). The fishermen had caught nothing in their previous sustained efforts, but at this attempt they immediately landed five huge salmon in their nets.

Given the previous dearth of fish, they had hopes of making a profit out of their unexpected catch, and were quite prepared to lie about their success. They appropriated the three largest salmon, and took the other two to the sheriff's wife. She went to Wulfstan, positively dancing with joy, and told him the whole story. She no longer doubted that he really was a holy man. Signs and wonders obviously impressed her far more than her perception of the bishop's real spiritual qualities, but most of her contemporaries would have been similarly biased. In view of this manifestation (as she understood it) of Wulfstan's supernatural powers, she earnestly begged him to remember her in his prayers. On the next day the malpractices of the fishermen were discovered, and the remaining three salmon were produced, which made the marvel seem all the greater. The lady insisted that the discovery of the theft must also be ascribed to Wulfstan's holiness, in that God manifestly would not permit the bishop to be cheated of any part of this Divine bounty. She herself then gave

Wulfstan a handsome present.[9] On one level this was a token of gratitude, because the "miraculous" catch of salmon enabled her to offer worthy hospitality to her distinguished guest. On another level, her gift was made in the hope of ensuring the goodwill of so powerful a holy man.

Wulfstan's gift of prophecy was also considered to have been demonstrated in another, but altogether more sombre, episode which occurred in Nottinghamshire. A rich man named Sewy built a church on his estate in Ratcliffe-upon-Soar.[10] As an Englishman, and a king's thegn, he was eager to have the dedication performed by Wulfstan. He asked the archbishop of York to permit Wulfstan to act, and this was agreed.[11] Archbishop Thomas was normally only too willing for Wulfstan to perform routine tasks – and in any case bishops apparently functioned outside their own dioceses on occasion before such activity was curbed by the expansion of canon law in the twelfth century.[12] News went round that Wulfstan was to perform the dedication, and people flocked to the church. The arrival of this eminent and venerable Englishman, and his celebration of the elaborate ritual, would make a welcome change from the drudgery of the daily round. As usual, Wulfstan took the opportunity offered by the big congregation to preach a long sermon – probably a novelty in itself to most of those present – and he expounded his favourite theme of peace and goodwill. This encouraged a certain poor man to come forward. He earnestly asked the bishop to make peace between him and a rich man who was standing nearby. Both names were omitted from the original *Life*, either because Coleman did not know them or, as is hinted, out of discretion. What he did say was that the rich man was a priest, who had betrayed his calling for love of increased wealth. Wulfstan called this man forward, and asked him repeatedly – three times in all– to make peace with the poor plaintiff, but the rich

[9]*Vita Wulfstani*, pp. 44–5.

[10]Ibid., p. 45. In 1086, Sewy, alias Sawin, a king's thegn, held in addition to his substantial estate in Ratcliffe-upon-Soar, lands in Barton-in-Fabis, Gotham, and Kingston: *Domesday Book, sive liber censualis*, ed. A. Farley, 2 vols (1783), I, f. 292 verso, col. b.

[11]*Vita Wulfstani*, p. 45. This aside is perhaps the work of the translator, William of Malmesbury, writing in a more legalistic age than that of Coleman.

[12]Hugh, bishop of Lisieux, dedicated the chapel of St Évroul in the diocese of Evreux, c.1060, at the request of Abbot Robert, but seemingly without obtaining the permission of the diocesan bishop, perhaps a reflection on the informal conditions of the early stages of the reorganization of the church in Normandy: *Ecclesiastical History of Orderic Vitalis*, ed. and transl. Marjorie Chibnall, 6 vols (1969–80), II, pp. 76, 78 and note 1.

priest scornfully ignored all the bishop's entreaties. With the priest still standing before him, Wulfstan then prophesied:

> You are determined not to have peace. I tell you truly that the time is coming, and is almost here, when you will want to be merciful to this man, and to others, but you will not be able to do so. You yourself will ask for mercy, and it will be denied to you.

Wulfstan would know from long experience that unresolved disputes about land were only too likely to lead to violence, particularly when an aggressor had stirred up enemies on all sides. The rich priest was not in the least moved by the bishop's words, but hurried off to his own house. Up to this point he had always been favoured by Fortune, but now it turned against him with a sting in its tail. The denouement appears to follow immediately, to demonstrate the fulfilment of Wulfstan's prophecy: most likely several of the priest's victims had listened to the bishop's words, and felt justified in wreaking vengeance at once. The priest's enemies stormed into his house, and his companions fled as best they could, but the priest himself was killed and Wulfstan's prophecy was fulfilled. It was felt in the bishop's circle that the outcome was a warning to others to recognize what is good for them, and in particular, to take care not to transgress the commands of holy men.[13]

Another church dedication outside Wulfstan's own diocese had a happier outcome. Once again a rich Englishman built a church at his own expense, and insisted that only Wulfstan was to perform the consecration and dedication ceremonies. In Wulfstan's *Life*, the episode is set in Wycombe, in Buckinghamshire, and is said to have occurred some years after the incident there when the roof of Wulfstan's lodgings collapsed on his party.[14] In fact, the patron of the new church, Swertlin, together with his brother Herding, held a substantial estate in the little village of Bradenham, adjoining West Wycombe. This land, together with estates which they occupied individually in nearby villages, was held directly of the king in 1086, so that the brothers were probably king's thegns.[15] The new church was almost certainly the present St Botolph's in Bradenham, which has some masonry of the appropriate date.[16]

[13]*Vita Wulfstani*, p. 45.
[14]Ibid., pp. 31–2.
[15]Ibid., p. 32 and note 2. For the estate held jointly by Swertlin, alias Swarting, and Harding, see *Domesday Book 13: Buckinghamshire*, ed. and transl. J. Morris (1978), 57:15. Harding held a further estate of the king in Horsenden: 57:14, while Swertlin (Swarting) held two further estates in chief in Cheddington and Caldecote: 57:16, 17; besides holding a further estate in Cheddington of William Fitz Ansculf: 17:13. Four more French lords each had a tenant named Swarting: 14:30; 21:7; 22:2; 23:27–8.
[16]N. Pevsner, *Buckinghamshire* (1960), p. 70.

Once again, it is emphasized in Wulfstan's *Life* that the patron obtained permission from the diocesan bishop, in this case Rémy of Lincoln (whose seat was moved there from Dorchester-on-Thames in the course of his episcopate, 1067–92).[17] On the pre-arranged day, Wulfstan arrived for the dedication, and as usual preached to the assembled populace and also confirmed those children who were brought to him. When all these duties were completed, he went to dinner at Swertlin's house, where the mother of the family was waiting with a request to make to the bishop. She was afraid to speak to Wulfstan directly, out of modesty, and reverence for him, and so she explained her trouble to Coleman. Her maidservant was suffering cruelly from a monstrous tumour in her head. It caused her tongue to thrust out from her mouth, looking more like that of an ox than of a woman. She could eat nothing. If she did manage to get any food into her mouth, she was unable to chew it, and she could only drink from a spoon. Coleman did all he could for the woman, and at once sent to her some of the water which Wulfstan had blessed that day for use in the consecration ceremony. Next he told Wulfstan about the woman's sufferings. Although the bishop tried to avoid being depicted as a wonder-worker, he was prepared to assist in effecting cures when the healing force was not directly mediated through himself. He possessed a gold coin called a bezant which was regarded as a holy relic, since it was said to have been pierced by the spear which had been thrust into the side of Christ after His crucifixion (John 19:33–4). Wulfstan dipped this bezant in water, to hallow it, and sent the holy water to the maid, since he had effected cures by this means on many previous occasions. It worked again this time, according to the lady of the household and other witnesses, who swore to the truth of this on oath several days later, in evidence to Coleman.[18]

How Wulfstan came to be in possession of this efficacious bezant is quite conjectural. It is generally assumed that throughout most of the Middle Ages the manufacture and sale of reputed relics was widespread, but if these objects were to have any retail value, let alone credibility, the purchasers and subsequent owners must be led to believe that they were genuine, so that the production and initial marketing operations were

---

[17]*Vita Wulfstani*, p. 32. Rémy was nominated to the see of Dorchester *c.*1067, deprived by Pope Alexander II, and then reinstated at the request of Archbishop Lanfranc late in 1070. He transferred his see to Lincoln, with papal approval, probably in 1072. He died in 1092: John Le Neve, *Fasti Ecclesiae Anglicanae 1066–1300 III. Lincoln*, compiled Diana E. Greenway (1977), p. 1. The date of this episode is uncertain, but with hindsight, William of Malmesbury and possibly also Coleman would in any case describe Rémy as bishop of Lincoln, not of Dorchester.

[18]*Vita Wulfstani*, pp. 32–3.

necessarily undocumented. A presumed relic such as Wulfstan possessed wold be a valuable and valued possession, possibly a family heirloom, bearing in mind his affluent clerical connections, or else a gift from one of his much-travelled acquaintances such as Archbishop Ealdred or Harold Godwinson, although the transformation of coin into relic might have occurred in England.[19] Reputed relics of Christ or of His saints were greatly prized because it was believed that they could be employed to mediate bodily and spiritual healing, and also afford physical protection from dangers of many kinds. The demand for relics far exceeded the potential supply, hence the wide, if surreptitious, manufacture of spurious ones. Those who paused to consider how and why a bezant had been pierced by the Holy Lance would be far outnumbered by others anxious for some means of transmitting healing. Really, of course, this was achieved by the faith of the patient. Perceived cures of physical disease could well be effected by such means as that adopted by Wulfstan. Swertlin's household held the bishop in great esteem, and consequently their expectations would already have built up before his arrival. The maidservant's sufferings were cured by her own faith, fortified by that of those around her, including Wulfstan himself. In an age when scientific medicine was available only to the well-off, and not necessarily effective even then, relics were greatly prized as being held to transmit the power of the saint (or in this case, ultimately Our Lord) from whom they emanated.[20] Sceptical readers may doubt the possibility of healing by these means – spiritual renewal and the build-up of the morale inducing physical regeneration – even though their contemporaries place amazing trust in over-rated health foods, unbalanced crash diets and such potentially dangerous activities (for the sedentary) as jogging or playing squash.

The foregoing incidents demonstrate the widespread belief which Wulfstan's contemporaries, and especially his compatriots, placed in his powers as prophet and healer. But the deference which was widely accorded to Wulfstan was not invariably shared by the clerks who accompanied him on his long-distance travels. The discomforts of the journey itself were unavoidable, but the clerks resented the additional

[19]The term bezant took its name from Byzantium (later known as Constantinople, and now called Istanbul). The original *solidus* of the Emperor Constantine weighted 24 carats, and it was possibly such a coin which Wulfstan owned. In the later Middle Ages, west Europeans used the term bezant both for the gold dinar of the Muslim world and also for various units of account which ultimately derived from this: P. Spufford, with the assistance of Wendy Wilkinson and Sarah Tolley, *Handbook of Medieval Exchange* (1986), pp. 286, 294.

[20]On the popularity of relics in this period, see R. C. Finucane, *Miracles and Pilgrims: popular beliefs in Medieval England* (1977), pp. 25–32.

inconvenience caused by Wulfstan's insistence on their sharing his religious observances. Wulfstan always sang the Office of Matins in a church, however far away that might be from his lodgings. Since Matins was sung at dawn – and before dawn in the winter months – his insistence on this point says much for his self-discipline, and also for the discipline he was able to impose on his household staff. He would go to church through snow, rain, storm or gale, struggling over the worst possible roads (and even the best of these would be barely on a par with the worst of modern ones), so that when he reached the church, he could truly say: "I love the house where You live, O Lord" (Psalm 26:8).

Once when he was travelling to the royal court before Christmas, he lodged overnight at Marlow. As usual, he told his servants early in the morning that he was going to the church.[21] This was a considerable distance away, and the road was so deep in mud that it would have impeded a traveller even in daylight. To make matters worse, he was hampered by a raging storm of snow and sleet. His clerks dreaded this foul weather, but Wulfstan was determined, and would not turn back. He insisted that he was going to the church, with only one attendant if necessary – or even alone, if they would show him the road so that he would not wander off course. As Wulfstan was so insistent, the clerks stopped their angry muttering and said nothing more. They hoped that he would tire of his resolve, and take their advice to turn back. Frewin was more daring than the others in his efforts to make Wulfstan change his mind. He grasped the bishop's hand, and led him where the mud was deepest, and the road was most dangerous. Wulfstan was plunged in mud up to his knees, and lost one of his shoes, but he gave no indication that he realized their trickery. By now it was broad daylight, and he returned to the inn half dead with cold. Only then did he speak out about his recent sufferings which had resulted from their scheming. He gently rebuked the impudent clerk Frewin, dismissing his offence with a smile – but sent them off to find his lost shoe. Wulfstan could be long-suffering, and he was said to be so controlled that no disappointment upset him, and no annoyance spurred him into retaliation. This was just as well, because some of his clerks joked about him in secret, or evenly openly spoke against him. But Wulfstan was not deterred by this, or by any other worldly affliction. He was aware of the reactions of his clerks, but never openly expressed anger. On the other hand, Coleman would not

[21] *Vita Wulfstani*, p. 48. The church of St John the Baptist, Little Marlow, contains Romanesque work, whereas those in (Great) Marlow date only from the nineteenth century: Pevsner, *Buckinghamshire*, pp. 191, 198–9.

claim that Wulfstan never felt anger, because this could not be entirely suppressed by even the most intense religious discipline.[22] Coleman, as the bishop's chancellor, would be well aware of the resentment felt by the young clerks at the rigid discipline which Wulfstan imposed on his *familia*. Between the ageing bishop and his clerks there yawned both a generation gap and an ensuing cultural divide. In his last decade, Wulfstan would be sixty years or more older than the junior clerks of his *familia*. He was trained in conservative monastic values while they were products of the new intellectual ferment which was increasingly pervading Western Europe by the last years of the eleventh century. Wulfstan's vocational discipline, his spiritual outlook and his intellectual grounding were all essentially products of the religious revival of the tenth century. Although that movement was influenced by Continental reforms, there is no reason to believe that he assimilated to any great extent the more recent ideas which emanated from across the Channel, despite the growing prevalence of non-native bishops and abbots in post-Conquest England. In marked contrast to his predecessor Ealdred, he himself is not known to have travelled overseas. In one sense there was no reason why he should do so. Unlike Ealdred, Wulfstan was not employed on foreign embassies, and had no obligatory reason to visit the papal court. His commitment to his monastic round, and to his diocese, coupled with the financial constraints on his revenues before 1072,would combine to counter any urge he might have felt to visit distant lands. He was certainly aware of the lure which exotic climes had for others. His former colleague, and near-namesake, Abbot Wilstan of Gloucester, died while on a pilgrimage to Jerusalem.[23] Contingents of dispossessed Englishmen from the Mercian shires entered the service of the Byzantine emperor, allegedly in 1075. In Constantinople their leaders were respectively, if inaccurately, styled earls of Gloucester, Lichfield and Warwick.[24] One of the initial occupants of the hermits' cell of Great

[22]*Vita Wulfstani*, p. 48.
[23]*Historia et Cartularium Monasterii Sancti Petri Gloucestriae*, ed. W. H. Hart, 3 vols (1863, 1865, 1867), I, p. 9. The Gloucester witer is confused about the regnal year, but corroborative evidence supports the date of 1072 given for Wilstan's death: D. Knowles, C. N. L. Brooke and Vera C. M. London, *Heads of Religious Houses* (1972), p. 52. On pilgrimage in the late eleventh century see also A. Grabois, "Anglo–Norman England and the Holy Land," *Anglo-Norman Studies VII*, ed. R. Allen Brown (1985), pp. 132–41.
[24]Krijnie N. Ciggaar, "L'Émigration anglaise à Byzance après 1066: un nouveau texte en Latin sur les Varangues à Constantinople," *Revue des études Byzantines*, 32 (1974), pp. 301–42, esp. pp. 320–1. The activities of these Mercian troops perhaps contributed to the legend of Guy of Warwick: Emma Mason, "Fact and Fiction in the English crusading tradition: the earls of Warwick in the twelfth century," *Journal of Medieval History*, 14 (1988) pp. 81–95, esp. pp. 88–9.

Malvern did set out for Jerusalem, but Wulfstan's dissuasion of Aldwin from following suit reflects the bishop's preference for traditional values over novelties.[25]

Even though Wulfstan did not indulge in foreign travel, he had far-flung correspondents. When his *Life* came to be written, there were still extant at Worcester letters which he received from "the pope of Rome," the archbishop of Bari and the patriarch of Jerusalem. His early biographers made the most of these, claiming that the fame of his holiness had spread to the limits of the known world, since these eminent correspondents requested him to intercede on their behalf in his prayers.[26] There is no reason to doubt that he received letters from these dignitaries, or that their concluding passages included a perfunctory request for the prayers of the recipient, but significantly the main business of these missives is not mentioned. Probably they concerned routine business, or were copies of circulars widely distributed. The papal letter was possibly in the name of Urban II (1088–99), enlisting support in his struggle against the anti-pope,[27] or else from Gregory VII (1073–85), who maintained a flourishing correspondence network with actual and potential supporters of his drastic reform programme.[28] Equally, though, Alexander II (1061–73) perhaps had occasion to write to Wulfstan in the course of the bishop's troubles with Archbishop Thomas of York, and in that event the correspondence was quite likely initiated by Wulfstan himself.

Bari was the capital of a surviving Byzantine enclave in southern Italy until it was captured in 1071 by Norman adventurers who had infiltrated the peninsula. A splendid new basilica was then built in the city, and dedicated to St Nicholas, whose relics it housed. These had formerly been preserved in Myra, in Asia Minor, which was captured by the Turks when they overran the region in 1071. A Norman expedition from Bari then seized the relics and brought them back in triumph. Archbishop Urse (1079/80–1089) ordered his archdeacon John of Bari to write an account of this exploit, and his narrative circulated in Normandy at an early date.[29] It is possible that a copy of this account, together with a

[25]*Vita Wulfstani*, p. 26. In the 1140s, the hermit Wulfric of Haselbury similarly discouraged those who felt the urge to join the Second Crusade: H. Mayr-Harting, "Functions of a Twelfth-Century Recluse," *History*, 60 (1975), pp. 337–52, esp. pp. 345–6.

[26]*Vita Wulfstani*, p. 60.

[27]Ibid., p. 60, note 1.

[28]*The Epistolae Vagantes of Pope Gregory VII*, ed. and transl. H. E. J. Cowdrey (1972), pp. xix–xx.

[29]*Ecclesiastical History of Orderic Vitalis*, IV, pp. 54–68, 353–4.

covering letter from Archbishop Urse, found its way from Normandy into Wulfstan's possession. The other Archbishop of Bari who might have written to Wulfstan is the successor of Urse, Archbishop Elias. He was an Italian, who was successively a monk of La Cava near Naples, and then abbot of St Benedict's abbey in Bari itself, at which time he had charge of the building of the new basilica. Archbishop Urse had supported the anti-pope Clement III, and was in touch with surviving Greeks of the region (who were not only political enemies of the Normans, but also schismatics, following the rupture between the Eastern and Western churches in 1054). Elias, in contrast, staunchly supported the Gregorian papacy. On the death of Urse, Elias was unanimously elected archbishop of Bari, and completed the basilica.[30] Tentative links can be hypothesized between Wulfstan and this exotic world. His acquaintance Bishop Geoffrey de Coutances, who was also a neighbouring landholder in Gloucestershire and Warwickshire,[31] needed funds to complete his own new cathedral in Coutances, in the Cotentin peninsula of Normandy. In or about 1050, he drummed up financial support from the new-rich Normans of southern Italy. Contacts established and maintained over several decades by Bishop Geoffrey may account for Wulfstan's letter from the archbishop of Bari.[32]

The patriarch of Jerusalem who wrote to Wulfstan was certainly a member of the Eastern Orthodox Church, since no Latin patriarch was appointed until 1 August 1099, in the wake of the crusaders' capture of Jerusalem.[33] After the formal split between the Greek and Latin churches in 1054, the Orthodox were officially regarded by the papacy as schismatics. This ruling would have little practical relevance for diocesan clergy outside the Mediterranean lands. When the division occurred, Wulfstan had no reason to take note of the demoted status of the Greeks. In any case, it was the patriarch who took the initiative in writing to him. The nature of his letter can be surmised by analogy with dealings between the patriarch and a major French monastery. In a charter of 8

---

[30]G. A. Loud, *Church and Society in the Norman Principality of Capua, 1058–1197* (1985), p. 83; R. H. C. Davis, *The Normans and their Myth* (1976), p. 93.

[31]*Vita Wulfstani*, p. 46; *Domesday Book 15: Gloucestershire*, ed. and transl. J. S. Moore (1982), 6:1–9; *Domesday Book 23: Warwickshire*, ed. and transl. J. Morris (1976), 5:1.

[32]J. Le Patourel, "Geoffrey of Montbray, bishop of Coutances 1049–1093," *English Historical Review*, 59 (1944), pp. 129–61, esp. pp. 136–7. Tentative links may also be glimpsed between the churches of South Wales and their counterparts in southern Italy: David N. Dumville,"St. Teilo, St. Cadog and St. Buite in Italy," *The Journal of Welsh Ecclesiastical History*, 4 (1987), pp. 1–8.

[33]Y. Katzir, "The Patriarch of Jerusalem, Primate of the Latin Kingdom," in *Crusade and Settlement*, ed. P. W. Edbury (1985), pp. 169–75, esp. p. 169.

May 1088, Sergius, abbot of Jerusalem, described how he had come to France on the instructions of the Patriarch Euthymios. The agreement negotiated beteen this legate and the abbot of Moissac concerned the patriarch's property interests in France. During the eleventh century, and long before the First Crusade, a steady stream of western pilgrims travelled to Jerusalem, and subsequently made donations to the patriarchal see. Information about such gifts depends on the chance survival of related documentation in the west. The full extent of these lands is not now known, due to the virtual dissolution of the Greek church in the Holy Land, and the consequent dispersal of its records. The lands donated in this way could not be managed systematically over so great a distance, and the Moissac evidence shows that the solution was to let them out as tenancies. Patriarchal legates visited the west from time to time, to collect what they could of the revenues due from these properties.[34] Sweyn Godwinson, himself a Mercian landholder, had made this pilgrimage in 1051–2,[35] while in 1072, Abbot Wilstan of Gloucester had set out on the same journey,[36] as did Guy, one of the earliest inhabitants of Great Malvern.[37] Most likely the patriarch's letter to Wulfstan concerned the revenues due from the property donated by one of these men, or from some lesser-known Mercian pilgrim. The writer was perhaps Euthymios, but it is equally likely that the letter came from his successor, Symeon, who died in 1099.[38]

In contrast to many of the bishops appointed to English sees by William I, who were often employed on the king's business in Normandy, Wulfstan is portrayed in his *Life* as an upholder of traditional values, and as a man who seemingly never travelled beyond the boundaries of the English realm. This resulted in the depiction of his mental outlook as being rather circumscribed. Yet while his monastic observance and

---

[34]A. Gieysztor, "The Genesis of the Crusades," *Medievalia et Humanistica*, V (1948), pp. 3–23; VI, pp. 3–34, esp. VI, pp. 24–6.

[35]While the family of Earl Godwin was in exile, Sweyn travelled from Bruges to Jerusalem, but died at Constantinople on his return journey: *The Anglo-Saxon Chronicle*, ed. and transl. Dorothy Whitelock, with D. C. Douglas and Susie I. Tucker (1961), 1052 (C). On Sweyn's lands in Mercia, see *Florentii Wigorniensis monachi Chronicon ex Chronicis*, ed. B. Thorpe, 2 vols (1948–9), I, p. 205; Ann Williams, "The King's nephew: the family and career of Ralph, earl of Hereford," in *Studies in Medieval History presented to R. Allen Brown*, ed. C. Harper-Bill, C. J. Holdsworth and Janet L. Nelson (1989), pp. 327–43, esp. pp. 329–30.

[36]*Historia et Cartularium Monasterii Sancti Petri Gloucestriae*, I, p. 9.

[37]William of Malmesbury, *De Gestis Pontificum Anglorum*, ed. N. E. S. A. Hamilton (1870), p. 286.

[38]Patriarch Symeon II was appointed at some uncertain date in the 1080s, and died in 1099; B. Hamilton, *The Latin Church in the Crusader States: the Secular Church* (1980), pp. 5, 179.

values were conservative, and his geographical horizons apparently limited, he did appreciate some of the new developments in the scholarship of his day. This is certainly the implication of his long and close friendship with Robert of Lotharingia, bishop of Hereford (1079–95). They had been thrown together in the first instance because their sees were contiguous, and on Lanfranc's orders Wulfstan consecrated Robert priest before the archbishop proceeded with the episcopal consecration.[39] Robert's interests were many and varied. He was said to be highly skilled in all the liberal arts, and especially in the use of the abacus, an early accounting device derived from the Muslim world.[40] He was also expert in the study of the phases of the moon, and the movements of the stars. Since the science of astronomy was not yet distinguished from astrology, Robert put his observations to practical use. He was invited by Bishop Rémy to attend the consecration of his new cathedral at Lincoln, but he learned from the stars that Rémy himself would not perform this ceremony, and so declined to attend. Shortly before the date set for the ceremony, Rémy died.[41] Robert built a new church at Hereford in imitation of the basilica of Aix-la-Chapelle, the great church founded by the Emperor Charlemagne. Robert's mathematical studies perhaps enabled him to act as his own architect to some extent, and he certainly modified his original model by the introduction of ideas deriving from the more recent Romanesque architecture of Lotharingia. Robert's designs for his church were probably more influential on those of Abbot Serlo for Gloucester, than were those of Wulfstan's new cathedral at Worcester; acknowledgement of this was perhaps signified in that Robert, and not Wulfstan, the diocesan bishop, laid the first stone of Serlo's new abbey church in June 1089.[42] Robert also sent to the Continent for a text of the Chronicle of Marianus Scotus, and was said to have made so splendid a job of abridging it that his own version was more useful than that of Marianus. From two of the surviving manuscripts of Robert's work, it is clear that his improvements largely comprised an abridgement and simplification of the prefatory chronological material, rather than of the contents of the chronicle itself. Robert's introduction of this chronicle to

[39]*Florentii Wigorniensis monachi Chronicon*, II, p. 13.
[40]William of Malmesbury, *De Gestis Pontificum Anglorum*, p. 300. See also C. H. Haskins, "The Abacus and the King's Curia," *English Historical Review*, 27 (1912), pp. 101–6, esp. pp. 105–6.
[41]William of Malmesbury, *De Gestis Pontificum Anglorum*, pp. 300, 313.
[42]Ibid., p. 300; C. Wilson, "Abbot Serlo's church at Gloucester (1089–1100): its place in Romanesque architecture," in *Medieval Art and Architecture at Gloucester and Tewkesbury*, ed. T. A. Heslop and V. Sekules (1985), pp. 52–83, esp. pp. 55–61.

Wulfstan played an important part in the development of historical writing at Worcester, which was discussed in an earlier chapter.[43] Robert was closer to Wulfstan than he was to any of the other bishops. They were neighbours, and it would be difficult, and probably ill-advised, for either of them to be on terms of complete equality with his own subordinates. Although Robert was often employed on public business far away, when he was at home he enjoyed Wulfstan's company, cherishing his innocence and the purity of his life.[44] Robert needed to cross the diocese of Worcester whenever he travelled away from his own see on public business, so that Worcester, or one or other of Wulfstan's episcopal manor houses, would be a convenient stopover. Robert would find Wulfstan's company a refreshing change after the stress and intrigue of official life, and the more so in that the latter's simplicity derived from his spiritual outlook rather than from any limitations in his mental capacity. Wulfstan had been well educated, and had subsequently been an episcopal clerk, normally a fast route to preferment. Following his monastic conversion, his mental and organizational powers would have been kept fully stretched during his years as an energetic obedientiary, and subsequently prior, of a well-endowed monastic community. Later, the political and social problems which resulted fom the Norman Conquest and settlement would have called for continuing alertness. If Wulfstan had lacked the ability to govern a see in a strategically sensitive region, then some pretext would have been found for his removal. All the same, Robert's scientific interests probably opened new intellectual horizons for Wulfstan. His appreciation of this may be inferred from the appointment of the Lotharingian Walcher to Great Malvern. During Wulfstan's episcopate control of this priory perhaps still rested with the

---

[43]William of Malmesbury, *De Gestis Pontificum Anglorum*, pp. 300–1; Valerie Flint, "World History in the early twelfth century: the *Imago Mundi* of Honorius Augustodunensis," in *The Writing of History in the Middle Ages: essays presented to R. W. Southern*, ed. R. H. C. Davis and J. M. Wallace-Hadrill (1981), pp. 211–38, esp. pp. 214, 226. See also M. Brett, "John of Worcester and his contemporaries," ibid., pp. 101–26, esp. pp. 110–11. Two manuscripts containing work by Robert are Bodl. Auct. F. 5.19, and Bodl. Auct. F. 3.14. These were first mentioned by W. H. Stevenson, "A contemporary description of the Domesday Survey," *English Historical Review*, 22 (1907), pp. 72–84, esp. pp. 72, 78. Bodl. Auct. F. 1.9 is a Worcester manuscript which both includes work by Robert and has writing in the hand of John of Worcester. Other manuscripts containing work by Robert of Hereford are: Cambridge, Trinity College MS 0.7.41; Durham, Dean and Chapter Library MS Hunter 100 (excerpted); Glasgow, Hunterian Museum MS T.4.2; London, British Library MS Cotton Tiberius E.IV, and MS Egerton 3088. On Robert of Hereford's excerpted chronology of Marianus, see also Alfred Cordoliani, "L'activité computistique de Robert, évêque de Hereford," in *Melanges offerts à René Crozet*, ed. P. Galais et Yves-Jean Riou, I (1966),pp. 333–40.

[44]William of Malmesbury, *De Gestis Pontificum Anglorum*, p. 301.

diocesan bishop rather than with Westminster Abbey. There is some uncertainty about Walcher's dates as prior, but he was living in England by 1091. If his appointment can be dated to the early 1090s, the inference is that he was introduced to Wulfstan by Bishop Robert.[45] Walcher, a major scholar in his own right, transmitted the growing corpus of scientific knowledge of his day to the next generation.[46]

Wulfstan is not said in his *Life* to have travelled into Wales. As bishop, he had no cause to do so, but in his young days as an episcopal clerk, it is possible that Worcester's business affairs took him across the Severn. Certainly he had some interest in events there, because the *obit* list in his homiliary (or sermon-collection) includes the following entry for 5 August: *Hic occisus fuit Griffin rex Brutorum* (on this day was slain Gruffyd (ap Llywelyn), king of the British).[47] King Gruffyd's death, at the hands of fellow Welshmen, resulted indirectly from the successful campaigning of Wulfstan's friend Harold Godwinson.[48] The English victory rendered the frontier safe, but Wulfstan perhaps regretted the ignominious end of this national leader. On the other hand, his prayers were perhaps requested by Gruffyd's widow, who later married Harold Godwinson. Contacts between Worcester and the court of King Gruffyd are not easily proved, but there is evidence dating from the early years of the twelfth century to show that in the last years of Wulfstan's episcopate, one of the inmates of his cathedral priory was the priest Urban, who from 1107 to 1134 was bishop of Llandaff, the see which lay to the south-west of the diocese of Worcester, across the Severn estuary.

Urban's early career at Worcester cannot readily be traced. He was aged thirty-two when he became bishop, and therefore he was only a junior inmate of Worcester in the 1090s. Even the name Urban was perhaps adopted only at the time of his episcopal ordination, which

[45]It is not known precisely when Westminster Abbey first asserted its control over Great Malvern: *Vita Wulfstani*, pp. xli–xlii. Bishop Robert was probably instrumental in securing the appointment of his fellow-Lorrainer, Walcher, but it is conjectural whether Wulfstan, or Abbot Gilbert Crispin of Westminster, was the patron concerned. In any case Walcher would be presented to Wulfstan for formal approval and institution.

[46]On Prior Walcher, see Knowles, Brooke and London, *Heads of Religious Houses*, p. 90. A Worcester manuscript, Oxford Bodl. Auct. F. 1.9., which contains writing in the hand of John of Worcester, has Walcher's *Lunar Tables* on folios 86–96, and his *De Dracone* on folios 96–9: see C. Burnett, "Catalogue: The Writings of Adelard of Bath and closely associated works, together with the manuscripts in which they occur," in *Adelard of Bath: an English scientist and Arabist of the early twelfth century*, ed. C. Burnett (1987), pp. 163–96, see p. 185, no. 80.

[47]I. Atkins, "The Church of Worcester from the Eighth to the Twelfth Centuries," Part II, *The Antiquaries Journal*, 20 (1940), pp. 1–38, esp. p. 30.

[48]*Anglo-Saxon Chronicle*, 1063 (C, D). The Worcester Chronicler records this under 1064: *Florentii Wigorniensis monachi Chronicon* I, p. 222.

would blur any chance traces of his activities which there might be in the charters of the church of Worcester. There is a possibility that Urban's family had strong ties with the diocese of Llandaff, perhaps dating from before his consecration.[49] If it was intended by his kinsfolk that Urban should broaden his education and sharpen his administrative skills before progressing to higher things, then Worcester, under the venerable Wulfstan, and subsequently under the competent, if worldly, Samson, was an ideal location for further education, being conveniently within reach of his family in the event of political unrest in the Marches. The skills which Urban acquired at Worcester were later used in the compilation of the *Liber Landavensis* (the *Book of Llandaff*), a compilation of charters which were, or which purported to be, the early title deeds to the property owned by the church of Llandaff. Many of the formulae of these texts strongly resemble some of the charters in the late eleventh century compilation now known as Hemming's Cartulary. The inference is that Urban was at Worcester while this cartulary was being compiled, and that he perceived the value of the formulae commonly used there, including those in some texts of doubtful authenticity, the better to secure the title of the church of Llandaff to its properties. In welding the Llandaff material into a coherent whole, he drew on his own earlier experience at Worcester and, possibly, that of some of the acquaintances whom he had made there.[50]

One of Bishop Urban's major preoccupations was the long struggle he waged to recover properties of the see of Llandaff which had been lost in the time of his predecessor. He tried to organize his bishopric with settled boundaries, like those which existed between English dioceses, rather than the fluctuating demarcations of the Welsh sees. In his struggle against the encroaching lay power, he envisaged St Teilo as the protector of the lands of Llandaff, and a version of the saint's *Life* is accordingly incorporated into the *Liber Landavensis*. But there is another, and apparently earlier, version, which occurs in a collection of Welsh saints' *Lives* apparently made at Worcester.[51] In his concern to document the lands of his see, and in publicizing the cult of the early saint of his church as guarantor of its endowments, Urban followed in the steps of Wulfstan.

[49]Wendy Davies, "Saint Mary's Worcester and the *Liber Landavensis*," *Journal of the Society of Archivists*, 4 (1972), pp. 459–85, esp. pp. 478–9.
[50]Davies, "Saint Mary's Worcester and the *Liber Landavensis*," pp. 474–8, 483–5. For detailed discussion of this material, see Wendy Davies, *The Llandaff Charters* (1979).
[51]Davies, "Saint Mary's Worcester and the *Liber Landavensis*," p. 484, note 216; C. J. Edwards, "St. Teilo at Llandaff," *Journal of the Historical Society of the Church in Wales*, V (1955), pp. 38–44. See also A. Hamilton Thompson, "The Welsh Medieval Dioceses," *Journal of the Historical Society of the Church in Wales*, 1 (1947), pp. 91–111, esp. pp. 95–9.

Links persisted between the church of Worcester and the major religious centres of south and west Wales. Bernard, bishop of St David's (1115–47) witnessed what he took to be the miraculous survival of Wulfstan's tomb during a fire, and unsuccessfully urged Pope Eugenius III (1145–53) to canonize Wulfstan,[52] while in 1212 Worcester established a confraternity agreement (*concordia*) with the important Welsh abbey of Strata Florida.[53] Wulfstan's cult spread throughout Wales and the Marches, drawing Welsh pilgrims to Worcester in considerable numbers. It was probably as a result of this that a text of the mid-thirteenth century *Metrical Life of St Wulfstan*, commissioned by a bishop of Worcester, found its way into Wales.[54]

Welsh and Marchers might have contact both with the living Wulfstan and his diocese, and later with the bishop's cult, not only through routine contacts of trade – in sheep, salt and the like – but also through the administrative and defensive requirements of the lordships of the south March, which were held by men who also possessed lands and exercised authority in Wulfstan's diocese. The pre-Conquest lordships of King Edward's nephew Earl Ralph, and of Harold Godwinson, were forerunners of the earldom held later by William Fitz Osbern and his son Roger.[55] In Worcestershire itself, Earl William shared judicial authority with Wulfstan, and probably exercised comital authority there. He was a major landholder in the shire, where other lords of the March also held estates.[56] Both for administrative reasons and for those emanating from the needs of frontier defence, there would be constant traffic between Worcester and the March, leading to the diffusion of Wulfstan's reputation.

[52]*Vita Wulfstani*, pp. xx, 106.

[53]Annals of Worcester Cathedral Priory, *Annales Monastici*, ed. H. R. Luard, IV (1869), p. 400.

[54]R. Flower, "A Metrical Life of St. Wulfstan of Worcester," *The National Library of Wales Journal*, I (1939–40), pp. 119–30; P. Grosjean, review of the above in *Analecta Bollandiana*, 73 (1955), pp. 259–60. An early bishop of Worcester, St Egwuin, was seemingly venerated at the priory of Monmouth, although the evidence is slight: S. M. Harris, "The Kalendar of the *Vitae Sanctorum Wallensium*," *Journal of the Historical Society of the Church in Wales*, 3 (1953), pp. 3–53, esp. pp. 16, 42–4.

[55]D. Walker, "The Norman Settlement in Wales," *Proceedings of the Battle Conference on Anglo-Norman Studies I. 1978*, ed. R. Allen Brown (1979), pp. 131–43, esp. pp. 132–4; C. Lewis, "The Norman Settlement of Herefordshire under William I," *Anglo-Norman Studies VII*, ed. R. Allen Brown (1985), pp. 195–213. See also Emma Mason, "Change and Continuity in Eleventh-Century Mercia: the experience of St. Wulfstan of Worcester," *Anglo-Norman Studies VIII*, ed. R. Allen Brown (1986), pp. 154–76, esp. pp. 155–7.

[56]W. E. Wightman, "The Palatine Earldom of William Fitz Osbern in Gloucestershire and Worcestershire (1066–1071)," *English Historical Review*, 77 (1962), pp. 6–17.

It is said in Wulfstan's *Life* that the kings of Ireland rendered him many tokens of reverence.[57] Contact would normally be through the seaport of Bristol, at the southern end of Wulfstan's diocese. As we have seen, the crews of Bristol ships contained men from the bishop's see, and he was instrumental in stopping the sale of slaves to Ireland.[58] For this reason, if for none other, he would have been known by reputation in the seaports of its south-east coast. Contacts with religious foundations in Ireland would have existed long before Wulfstan's time, enabling Irish influences to reach the diocese of Worcestershire. This is suggested by the existence of a *Life of St Kyeran* in an eleventh-century booklist thought to be from Wulfstan's diocese.[59]

Influences were exercised in both directions, since Wulfstan's *familia* nourished not only an embryo Welsh bishop, but also an Irish one, Gilla Patraic, alias Patrick bishop of Dublin (1074–84). The evidence for his stay at Worcester is found in a collection of Latin poems which he composed. In their original form, no individual is identified by name, but the lines are glossed to show that he had particularly warm recollections of Bishop Wulfstan, and of Aldwin, the monk who became a hermit at Great Malvern. Whereas Patrick, coming from a land where the eremetical, or solitary, tradition was strong, adopted the communal Benedictine life, Aldwin gravitated from his monastery to the isolated life of a hermit.[60]

Patrick was not merely a short-stay visitor, but was regarded at Worcester as a monk of the house. His name follows immediately after that of Aldwin in the list of Worcester monks contained in the Durham *Liber Vitae*.[61] Some of Patrick's poetry, permeated with the thought of St Augustine, was perhaps composed while he was still at Worcester, but from the internal evidence of his work, it is clear that much of it dates from after his return to Ireland, and perhaps even following his consecration to the episcopate.[62] It is conjectural whether Patrick was the only poet at Worcester in the early 1070s, or whether the cathedral was a

[57] *Vita Wulfstani*, p. 59.
[58] Ibid., p. 43.
[59] M. Lapidge, "Surviving Booklists from Anglo-Saxon England," in *Learning and Literature in Anglo-Saxon England: studies presented to Peter Clemoes on his sixty-fifth birthday*, ed. M. Lapidge and H. Gneuss (1985), pp. 33–89, esp. p. 70. On St Kyeran, see Harris, "The Kalendar of the *Vitae Sanctorum Wallensium*," p. 35.
[60] *The Writings of Bishop Patrick 1074–1084*, ed. and transl. A. Gwynn (1955), esp. pp. 6–7, 9–11, 15–16, 18–19, 42–3, 102–4.
[61] *Durham Liber Vitae*, ed. A. H. Thompson (1923), in facsimile, folio 22 recto.
[62] *The Writings of Bishop Patrick 1074–1084*, pp. 10–11, 16, 19. Evidence for the presence of Augustine's work at Worcester in this period is sparse: Lapidge, "Surviving Booklists from Anglo-Saxon England," p. 73, nos 46–7.

centre of Latin verse writing, like some cathedral schools of France.[63] A substantial poem was composed to commemorate Wulfstan's death and burial,[64] although its author was evidently of a younger generation than Patrick. It was perhaps Patrick who established the Benedictine community which served Dublin cathedral until it was dispersed about 1096. Tangential evidence suggests that monks of Worcester and Winchcombe were among its founder-members.[65] If so, Wulfstan would have played a part in establishing this cathedral priory, since all monks were bound by a vow of stability, and the permission of their superior would be needed before they were able to move to a new cell. Winchcombe's chequered history after the imprisonment of its zealously patriotic Abbot Godric renders it uncertain whether Abbot Ethelwig of Evesham, intermittently acting head of Winchcombe, shares the credit for releasing Mercian monks to help establish the Benedictine life in Dublin.[66] Dublin was formally under the jurisdiction of the archbishop of Canterbury, and Patrick therefore sent his future successor, Donngus alias Donatus (1085–95), to be trained as a monk of Christ Church, Canterbury. The direct link between the Benedictine outpost in Dublin and the Worcester of Wulfstan was ended on 10 October 1084, when Patrick and several of his monks were drowned while crossing the Irish Sea.[67] Yet memory of Wulfstan did not entirely fade, thanks no doubt to the Bristol link. In recent years, excavations on a medieval site in Dublin revealed a pilgrim flask which had been taken back to Ireland from Wulfstan's shrine.[68]

Links with Scotland were much more tenuous, for obvious geographical reasons. In so far as they existed, these comprised a personal connection between Wulfstan and King Malcolm Canmore and his wife Queen Margaret, who commended themselves to his prayers.[69] This request probably occurred towards the end of a letter written on official business. One matter in which they perhaps asked for Wulfstan's good

[63]The Writings of Bishop Patrick, p. 16.

[64]"Latin Verses Lamenting the Death of Saint Wulfstan of Worcester," ed. M. L. Colker, Analecta Bollandiana, 89 (1971), pp. 319–22.

[65]The Writings of Bishop Patrick, p. 7. See also A. Gwynn and R. N. Hadcock, Medieval Religious Houses Ireland (1970), pp. 70–1.

[66]On the governance of Winchcombe during the 1070s, see Chronicon Abbatiae de Evesham ad annum 1418, ed. W. D. Macray (1863), p. 90; Knowles, Brooke and London, Heads of Religious Houses, p. 79.

[67]The Writings of Bishop Patrick, p. 7.

[68]Viking and Medieval Ireland: an Exhibition Catalogue (1973), pp. 19–20, 42, no. 178 and plate 15. A pilgrim from Ireland, named Pippard, was cured of an abscessed tongue at St Wulfstan's tomb in 1212. He built a magnificent church in Ireland in honour of St Wulfstan, and gave it to the church of Worcester with thirty carucates of land: Annals of Worcester, Annales Monastici, IV, p. 401.

[69]Vita Wulfstani, pp. 59–60.

will was that a paternal eye might be kept on their daughter Edith during her residence at the nunnery of Wilton. Margaret probably met Wulfstan in the early 1060s, but it is conjectural whether Malcolm was acquainted with the bishop personally. Some of Malcolm's earlier years were spent as an exile in England. At that period of his life, the most likely occasion when he might have met Wulfstan was at the royal court which met at Gloucester in 1059.[70] The bishop's reputation could also have reached the Scottish court through the rush of eminent English émigrés who found refuge north of the border after the unrest of the late 1060s.[71] As other highly placed Englishmen died, Wulfstan's name would come to the fore on occasions when a sympathetic intermediary was required in the southern kingdom.

The scattered members of the house of Godwin are not known to have kept in touch with Wulfstan. Harold's older sons went to Ireland, and news of them was perhaps brought back to Worcester by traders.[72] Tostig's sons, Scule and Ketel, fought at Stamford Bridge. Evidently they retreated with the survivors of Harold Hardrada's army, because they settled in Norway, where they founded families.[73] Harold Godwinson's mother, Gytha, fled to Flanders and settled at St Omer.[74] A younger Gytha, said to be a daughter of Harold's, was later married to the Russian prince Vladimir of Kiev, conveying English influences to that remote court.[75] News of these exiles is likely to have been sparse, although sea-borne links were frequently maintained over great distances. In Iceland an account circulated concerning the reputed survival of Harold Godwinson. The question which arises here is what part was

[70]On Malcolm's early visits to England, see F. Barlow, *Edward the Confessor* (1970), pp. 19, 164, 202–3. Information reached Worcester about his efforts to secure the throne of Scotland in 1054 and his bitter quarrel with William II at Gloucester in August 1093. *Florentii Wigorniensis monachi Chronicon*, I, p. 212; II, p. 31; see also F. Barlow, *William Rufus* (1983), pp. 309–10. By the latter year, Wulfstan was ailing, and perhaps did not attend this gathering.
[71]*Anglo-Saxon Chronicle*, 1067 (C, D).
[72]*Florentii Wigorniensis monachi Chronicon*, II, pp. 2–3; *Anglo-Saxon Chronicle*, 1068 (D); 1069 (D).
[73]P. Grierson, "The Relations between England and Flanders before the Norman Conquest," reprinted from *Transactions of the Royal Historical Society*, fourth series, 23 (1941), pp. 71–112, in *Essays in Medieval History*, ed. R. W. Southern (1968), pp. 61–92, esp. pp. 90–1.
[74]*Anglo-Saxon Chronicle*, 1067 (D). The correct year is probably 1069. See also *Florentii Wigorniensis monachi Chronicon*, II, p. 2. King Harold Godwinson's sister Gunnhild died at Bruges in 1087; Grierson, "The Relations between England and Flanders before the Norman Conquest," p. 90.
[75]F. Dvornik, "The Kiev State and its Relations with Western Europe," reprinted from *Transactions of the Royal Historical Society*, fourth series, 29 (1947), pp. 27–46, in *Essays in Medieval History*, ed. Southern, pp. 1–23, esp. pp. 17, 23.

played by the Bristol (or Chester) – Dublin-North Atlantic route, and whether there were Mercian antecedents for such a story.[76]

Within England, Wulfstan maintained direct links with religious houses as far away as Chertsey and Ramsey,[77] through his confraternity network, and so long as his health permitted him to attend the royal court and church councils, he could maintain personal contact with clerics and laymen from all corners of the realm. While the bulk of the estates of the church of Worcester lay in his own diocese, there were outlying properties scattered over several others, necessitating dealings with stewards and tenants. There was traffic to and from the mint at Worcester, and the salt-producing town of Droitwich,[78] to the north, besides pilgrims to the shrine of St Oswald, which combined to bring a stream of visitors – not necessarily those whom the bishop would meet personally, but people who would bring news. It is less likely that they carried away information about the bishop and his city, since Wulfstan receives little mention in works which did not draw on Worcester source material. In his own diocese he was greatly valued. His exemplary personal conduct set a standard matched by few clerics in public life, while his concern for the spiritual welfare of all the laity, and the temporal needs of the poorer ones, caused him to be widely appreciated. Mourners of all sorts converged at his funeral: clerics and layman; old and young; rich and poor.[79] He was not a man of the people, but one whose discernment led him to see the true needs of those around him. He would be mourned by those who appreciated his qualities, but especially by his own flock.

---

[76]This account is known only from a thirteenth-century text, and contains no circumstantial details: Margaret Ashdown, "An Icelandic Account of the Survival of Harold Godwinson," in *The Anglo-Saxons*, ed. P. Clemoes (1959), pp. 122–36. Chester, in the ancestral heartland of the estates of the earls of Mercia, was where Harold's wife had taken refuge in the autumn of 1066. Gerald of Wales recorded a legend that Harold survived the battle "of Hastings," and escaped to Chester, where he lived out his days as a hermit: Gerald of Wales, *The Journey through Wales and the description of Wales*, transl. and introd. L. Thorpe (1978), p. 198 and note 407, p. 199.

[77]*The Cartulary of Worcester Cathedral Priory (Register I)*, ed. R. R. Darlington (1968), no. 304; *Diplomatarium Anglicum Aevi Saxonici*, ed. and trans. B. Thorpe (1865), pp. 615–17; *Two Chartularies of the Priory of St. Peter at Bath*, ed. W. Hunt (1893), pp. 3–4.

[78]*Domesday Book 16: Worcestershire*, ed. F. and C. Thorn (1982) (C). 1; 1:a.

[79]"Latin Verses Lamenting the Death of Saint Wulfstan of Worcester," pp. 319–22.

10
Wulfstan the Saint

Wulfstan's stature in his later years as a patriarchal figure among the English, his reputation both for holiness of life and as a mediator of healing, would inspire a party among the monks of Worcester to regard him as a future saint of their church. If the cult of any saint was to be widely recognized, the first requirement was to compose a *Life*, a work of hagiography, which followed a set pattern. This work did not claim to be a comprehensive account of his life and career, but presented his doings and sayings selectively, so as to portray him as a holy man (there were proportionately very few women recognized as saints in the earlier Middle Ages). In a work of this kind, much emphasis was placed upon the pious end of the subject, and his transition from the temporal to the spiritual world. Wulfstan's failing health in the early 1090s would alert those who proposed to promote his cult to note carefully any incident which might contribute to the all-important concluding section of a *Life*. Consequently Wulfstan's last illness, death and burial are recorded in considerable detail, both in the *Life* written c.1100 at Worcester by Coleman and subsequently edited and translated by William of Malmesbury, and also by William alone in his *De Gestis Pontificum Anglorum*, in which the relevant sections on Wulfstan and on his close friend Robert, bishop of Hereford, combine to make a dramatic impact.

Since Wulfstan lived to a ripe old age, and was latterly in a frail state of health, the monks experienced some doubt in knowing when his last days had finally arrived, and two false alarms are recorded. Wulfstan himself sensed that he would live to a great age, and often predicted this. Like many old people, he was inclined to nod off to sleep wherever he happened to be sitting. This occurred one day in chapter when the monks' discussions had gone on for some time. Seeing him slumped in his seat, they became agitated, some of them weeping and crying out that he was about to die and so leave them comfortless. When he woke, and realized why they were so upset, he said, "Believe me, I shall not die as long as my old body can last out, and that will happen only in extreme old age. But after my death, I shall be with you all the more. And if you serve God faithfully, I will prevent all those you fear from harming you."[1] The agitation of the monks at his apparent seizure arose not only from their affection for him, but also from their realization – of which he was well aware – that his death would be followed by drastic changes. The Englishmen among them knew that his successor would be of an alien race, and they all appreciated that it was unlikely that the next bishop would be in monastic orders. Wulfstan's reply was intended to reassure them that if they persevered in upholding the traditional values he had imposed, his spirit would continue to protect them. It may be argued, of course, that the speech was devised by Coleman (or more likely William of Malmesbury) to underline the point that Wulfstan was the champion of traditional Benedictine values, which were undermined by his secular successor.

The second false alarm occurred at Pentecost (28 May) 1094, when Wulfstan experienced the onset of great debilitation throughout his body. He ordered messengers to ride as quickly as possible to his friend Robert, bishop of Hereford, to ask him to come – which Robert did immediately. Wulfstan made his confession, and even "received the discipline," the term which monks used for being beaten with rods upon the bare back by way of penance. It was taken as a remarkable sign of greatness that Wulfstan, although bowed with age and sickness, and at peace in his mind, nevertheless submitted to this scourging in order to be purged of any sin which might still weigh on his spirit. This confession and drastic penance evidently raised Wulfstan's morale, which in turn helped stabilize his physical condition. At times he seemed to be more comfortable, but intermittently took to his bed with a persistent slow fever. His bodily weakness appeared to reinvigorate his mind, as though his raised temperature intensified his spiritual awareness.[2] He felt even more sure of his approaching death when a message reached him that his only sister had died, and said, "The plough's furrow reached me just now, and the brother will follow the sister within a few days."

From the middle of July 1094 he was immobilized with fever, and prepared himself spiritually for his death. He bore his incapacity heroically, and consoled those around him who were weeping because they feared his approaching end, saying to them:

> Stop sighing, and stop crying, because this is not the relinquishing of life, but the changing of its form. I shall never leave you, but will be with you just as much when this frame has crumbled to dust. In

---

[1] *The Vita Wulfstani of William of Malmesbury*, ed. R. R Darlington (1928), p. 61.
[2] Ibid., p. 60.

God, I will be more instantly present, and more speedy in coming to your help. By my intercession, prosperity will come to you, and adversity will recede when I drive it away.

This encouraging speech was perceived to derive from a good conscience, which enabled him to talk in a positive way, helpful to his hearers. While those around him were overwhelmed by sighing and sobbing, he prayed for them. He always spoke with a holy simplicity, one which never doubted the mercy of God.[3] In one sense this scene echoes the deathbed narratives which so frequently concluded works of hagiography, but in another it echoed the personality of Wulfstan as he appeared throughout his *Life*. The monks of Worcester would certainly want to believe that he would support them in the troubles which loomed ahead, and given his paternalistic care for his flock, he himself would want to believe that he would continue to safeguard them. In an age when emotions were freely displayed, those around him probably did weep openly as his end approached – mourning both for the loss of their bishop and for the impending loss of much that he had preserved for them. Few of the monks would even recall a time before he was bishop, and his imminent death would be a destabilizing experience. In contrast to the clerks of the *familia* who accompanied the bishop on his travels, the monks for the most part would live a localized, even an institutionalized existence, so that Wulfstan's death would remove the pivot around which their world turned.

After the feast of the Circumcision (1 January), 1095, Wulfstan received another visit from Robert, bishop of Hereford, together with Abbot Serlo of Gloucester, and Gerald, abbot of Cranborne.[4] He made his confession, and said a last farewell to them. His departure to another existence was now imminent. His illness grew worse each day, but he maintained a constant round of prayer. Often his lips moved as he prayed, but at other times he prayed silently. He sat up, in preference to lying down, listening to the Psalms and gazing at the altar. This was possible because his chair was placed so that he could easily see whatever was taking place in the chapel – presumably a small oratory in his own quarters. Eight days before he died, Prior Thomas administered Holy

[3]William of Malmesbury, *De Gestis Pontificum Anglorum*, ed. N. E. S. A. Hamilton (1870), pp. 287–8.

[4]*Vita Wulfstani*, pp. 60–1. In this source, Gerald is described as abbot of Tewkesbury. He was in fact abbot of Cranborne until 1102, when he and his community moved to their dependent site of Tewkesbury, and Cranborne in its turn became a cell: D. Knowles and R. N. Hadcock, *Medieval Religious Houses England and Wales* (1971), p. 63; D. Knowles, C. N. L. Brooke and Vera C. M. London, *The Heads of Religious Houses England and Wales 940–1216* (1972), p. 87.

Unction, but as Wulfstan lingered on, he received the Eucharist on each succeeding day, to fortify him for his spiritual journey. The end came "a little after midnight, early on Saturday 19 January 1095." In 1095, Friday was the 19th, and therefore the moment of death would have occurred very early on 20th. Born in the reign of Ethelred Unread, he died in the eighth year of the reign of William II. Wulfstan had been bishop for thirty-two years, four months and thirteen days. He was believed to be in, or about, his eighty-seventh year.[5]

When Wulfstan's body was washed for burial, it was seen to shine in an amazing way; it "was bright like a jewel, pure and white as milk." Perhaps it really did look like that, illuminated by candlelight on a dark winter's night – but the simile suggests the work of the hagiographer. Wulfstan's nose, which had been very prominent, now appeared smaller, and grew white after his death, to the amazement of the onlookers. His nose had perhaps seemed disproportionately large in later years because his body became very thin in old age through fasting. For many years before his death the flesh of his fingers was so wasted that the skin scarcely seemed to cover the bones. This had often caused his episcopal ring, which he had received at his consecration, to slip off. The monks became distressed whenever this occurred, taking it as a sign of his approaching death. He used to say pityingly, "There is no need to look so anxious. The ring will be there when you look for it. It came to me without any effort on my part, and I will carry it to the grave." The ring

---

[5]The earliest relevant information on Wulfstan's death occurs in the brief *Life* included by Hemming in his cartulary. He does not give either the date of Wulfstan's death, nor his age, but states that he held the bishropric for "thirty-two winters, four months and three weeks:" *Hemingi Chartularium ecclesiae Wigorniensis*, ed. T. Hearne, 2 vols (1723), II, p. 407. Calculating from the date of his consecration on 8 September 1062 (*Florentii Wigorniensis monachi Chronicon ex Chronicis*, ed. B. Thorpe, 2 vols (1948–9), I, p. 221) and reckoning four weeks to the month, this fixes the date of his death as 19 January 1095. Wulfstan's *Life* concludes with the note that the anniversary of his death is observed on 19 January: *Vita Wulfstani*, p. 67. According to the Worcester chronicler, Wulfstan died "about the middle of the seventh hour" of the night, on Saturday 18 January 1095: *Florentii Wigorniensis monachi Chronicon*, II, p. 36. The only text of William of Malmesbury's *Life* which now survives is not the author's manuscript, and the copyist was confused about the point in question. He gave the date of death as Saturday 19 January, a little after the middle of the night; in 1087; in the tenth regnal year of William II; and when Wulfstan had been bishop for thirty-four years, four months and thirteen days: *Vita Wulfstani*, pp. xliii, 61. The day of the week therefore appears to be agreed, but in 1095, the relevant Saturday fell on 20 January. This date is confirmed by an insertion added in a late eleventh-century hand to the Kalendar contained in Wulfstan's homiliary (or sermon-collection), where Wulfstan's *obit* (the anniversary of his death) is given as the day of Saints Fabian and Sebastian, that is, 20 January: I. Atkins, "The Church of Worcester from the Eighth to the Twelfth Centuries," Part II, *The Antiquaries Journal*, 20 (1940), pp. 1–38 and 203–28, see p. 30.

had frequently slipped off in this way, but was always retrieved. But after his death, some of the monks tried to take the ring from his finger, either to keep it as a relic, or to prove the truth of his saying. Yet however hard they tried, they could not get the ring off, and eventually gave up, thwarted by his knotted joints, and unyielding skin and sinews.[6] When his body was prepared for burial, looking almost lifelike according to his *Life*, it was carried into the church, accompanied by a great crowd of monks and laity – in the first instance the latter would comprise the lay servants of the abbey and their families. The bier was set down before the altar with the clergy sitting around it, maintaining a mournful vigil of prayer. His body lay before the altar, robed in episcopal vestments but with no further covering. It drew great crowds of people who came to venerate the body and make oblations.[7]

Manifestations of Wulfstan were reported immediately after his death, both by the monks of Worcester, and by his friend Robert, bishop of Hereford. The long vigil of prayer at the bier exhausted some of the monks, who crept off into corners to sleep comfortably where no-one would see them. But they continually experienced Wulfstan's presence among them, rousing the sleepers and waking up those who were dozing. "Get up," he said, "And stop snoozing. Recite the psalter right through, and finish up with the commendation of the soul." They did as he ordered, making a virtue out of a necessity. Given Wulfstan's insistence during his lifetime on diligent observance of the round of prayer, it is no wonder that overtired and emotionally strained monks experienced his presence in this way.[8] One of these monks was planning a wicked deed of some unspecified nature, although he had not yet put it into effect. Suddenly Wulfstan appeared to him, very angrily rebuking his wicked intention. He pointed out just how bad it was, and warned him against putting it into effect. The very idea was only too sinful – he must certainly not carry it out. If he hoped to be spared, he must not do as he planned, because otherwise he would be swiftly punished and die that very same year. The monk was terrified both by Wulfstan's threat and by his own guilty conscience. He promised that he would renounce his scheme, and from that time onwards he would remain a faithful servant of the Rule.[9] Lack of sleep, qualms of conscience, and recollection of the

---

[6]*Vita Wulfstani*, p. 62 and notes 1, 4.
[7]Ibid., p. 62; William of Malmesbury, *De Gestis Pontificum Anglorum*, p. 288.
[8]*Vita Wulfstani*, p. 63. For Wulfstan's strict attitude in his lifetime towards monks who were negligent about their prayers, see ibid., pp. 47, 95; William of Malmesbury, *De Gestis Pontificum Anglorum*, p. 282.
[9]*Vita Wulfstani*, p. 63.

moral and disciplinary stance imposed by the late bishop would combine
to generate this manifestation.

Bishop Robert's experiences were of a rather different kind. All were
known at Worcester, but were selectively presented in two related works.
In Wulfstan's *Life* Robert's experiences are related only in so far as they
contribute to the portrayal of Wulfstan after his death, in typical
hagiographical pattern, but in the *Deeds of the English Bishops* the
attention focuses much more on Robert, and the anecdotes build up to a
dramatic climax. The visions began with an incident of a type which is
occasionally experienced by those who have a relation or a friend who is
gravely ill. Robert was at the king's court, engaged in legal matters
relating to the crown, when he suddenly had a vision of Wulfstan, saying
quite distinctly, "If you want to see me alive, come quickly to Worcester
before I die."[10] The version in Wulfstan's *Life* is rather different. At the
very time when Wulfstan died, Robert saw him standing in front of him,
very much changed in appearance from the way he had looked in recent
years. His countenance was fresh and youthful, and shone with light as
though from the stars. He was robed in the vestments of a bishop,
holding his pastoral staff in his hand, and seemed to speak to Robert as
he slept: "Dear brother Robert, come now to Worcester. I want you to
conduct my burial with all proper rites, and commend my soul to God."
Robert dreamed that he replied: "Dear lord and friend, are you telling me
to bury you, when I have not seen you looking so well for the past five
years?" Wulfstan then said, "Be that as it may. It is God's will that you
do this. Go quickly, and do as I say."

Robert believed that his dream was a true vision. He told it to King
William, who gave him permission to leave the court. Robert rode to
Worcester, a journey which passed quickly because of the strength of his
friendship for Wulfstan, whome he had known since the day of his
consecration.[11] So says Wulfstan's *Life*, whereas the other account points
out what a long journey it was, and that Robert took no proper rest by
day or night in his anxiety to see Wulfstan alive. At a staging-post near
Worcester he snatched some sleep, and again saw Wulfstan saying to
him,

> Despite all you have done out of your affection for me, your
> intention has been frustrated, because I have already passed over.
> But you, my dear friend, take thought for your life, and provide for
> your spiritual health, since you will depart this life not long after
> me. And in case you are thinking that this is some fantastic vision,
> here is a token. Tomorrow, after you have buried my body, which

[10]William of Malmesbury, *De Gestis Pontificum Anglorum*, p. 302.
[11]*Vita Wulfstani*, pp. 62–3.

has already been waiting for your arrival for three days, a present will be given to you from me, which you will recognize to be mine.

Robert woke up and continued his journey.[12] He was in time for the burial, because the monks had deliberately delayed the ceremony to wait for his arrival. The Worcester narrative says that Wulfstan was buried on the Sunday. Robert arrived in such a hurry that he scarcely had breath to tell the monks of his vision of the original mandate to conduct Wulfstan's funeral. Requiem Masses were said, and then Wulfstan was buried inside the cathedral. As though no-one had mourned until then, a great weeping and wailing broke out. The whole throng burst into lamentations which echoed and re-echoed around the roof. This display was taken to indicate that Wulfstan's death was seen as the downfall of the monastic life, and a calamity to England. The clergy and people felt their loss equally, some mourning their watchful shepherd; others their master and teacher, young and old alike; some thinking wistfully of his wisdom, and others of his kindness. The rich praised him for not flaunting his wealth; the poor praised his generous charity.[13] This passage from Wulfstan's *Life* is echoed in a poem composed about his funeral, in which it is noted that people of all age groups, and all social classes, mourned his death.[14]

Throughout the long ritual, Bishop Robert kept silent about his more traumatic vision. When all the formalities were over, he said farewell to the monks, and prepared to leave. He mounted his horse, and had already kicked it with his spurs, when the prior approached him, went down on his knees and offered him a present, saying:

My Lord, if it pleases you, accept this cloak which belonged to your dear friend. It is lined inside with lambskins, and he used to wear it when riding. It is a token of your long friendship, and will afford you the protection of our most holy lord.

When the bishop heard this, and recognized the gift, a sudden cold tremor ran through his bones. He immediately postponed his journey and summoned the monks to chapter. With the tears and sighs which were only to be expected on such an occasion, he described his vision, and how it had been fulfilled. He commended his death to them all, and then departed, glad of the admonition (which would give him time to

---

[12]William of Malmesbury, *De Gestis Pontificum Anglorum*, p. 302.

[13]*Vita Wulfstani*, pp. 63–4. It is stated in a derivative account that Wulfstan's funeral took place "on the fourth day" (counting inclusively): *De Gestis Pontificum Anglorum*, p. 288.

[14]"Latin Verses Lamenting the Death of Saint Wulfstan of Worcester," ed. M. L. Colker, *Analecta Bollandiana*, 89 (1971), pp. 319–22.

make spiritual preparation) but continually uneasy with holy fear. He died on 26 June 1095, five months after Wulfstan.[15]

This sad tale concerning Bishop Robert was not included in Wulfstan's *Life*, but it was probably related to William of Malmesbury when he visited Worcester about 1115 to collect material for his *Deeds of the English Bishops*. At the time of this visit, Nicholas was prior.[16] It was perhaps he who donated Wulfstan's riding-cloak to Robert, something which he might take upon himself to do in view of his close relationship to the bishop.[17] On the other hand, it was Prior Thomas who was in charge of the cathedral priory at the time, and acting host to distinguished visitors during the episcopal vacancy. As Robert was told, the gift was intended as a keepsake for practical use, but overtones of the conferring of the mantle of Elijah to his designated successor (1 Kings 19:19; 2 Kings 2:13) might occur to a clerical readership. Had Robert lived to enjoy further promotion, Worcester was not an obvious step upwards, but in terms of spirituality he was seen by the monks there to be closer to Wulfstan than any of their episcopal colleagues.

There is also the question of how far Robert's visions came to him completely spontaneously, and how far they represent a rationalizing of his awareness that Wulfstan's death was imminent. Robert's premonition of his own death was perhaps heightened by a previous awareness that he was driving himself too hard. His hasty visit to Worcester would have its difficulties even if, as a senior royal official, he was entitled to commandeer changes of horses for himself and his retinue. Such facilities might be available to the king's servants on the main routeways, but not if they tried to cut across country. Robert experienced his vision at Cricklade in Wiltshire, when the king and his entourage were apparently heading for Wales.[18] In that event, they would in any case be heading for the Severn, so that Robert was allowed to take a brief leave of absence to make his detour to Worcester, and then rejoin the main party at some pre-arranged spot. But he could not be spared for long. He was a busy administrator, employed not only in important legal business, but also, as his skill in the use of the abacus suggests, in helping to devise and implement the financial policies which would enable the king to hire the

---

[15]William of Malmesbury, *De Gestis Pontificum Anglorum*, pp. 302–3.

[16]*Vita Wulfstani*, pp. ix, 51, 54; John Le Neve, *Fasti Ecclesiae Anglicanae 1066–1300: II. Monastic Cathedrals*, compiled by Diana E. Greenway (1971), p. 102.

[17]Nicholas was described as a "special foster-child (or pupil) of Wulfstan" by William of Malmesbury, *De Gestis Pontificum Anglorum*, p. 287. See also *Vita Wulfstani*, p. 56.

[18]For the king's itinerary in January 1095, see F.Barlow, *William Rufus* (1983), pp. 338, 450. Bishop Robert experienced his vision at Cricklade: *Florentii Wigorniensis monachi Chronicon*, II, p. 36.

mercenaries employed on his frequent campaigns.[19] The grave illness of Robert's closest friend, culminating in the strain of a hurried midwinter journey to a deathbed, perhaps exacerbated a pre-existing stress-related illness.

Wulfstan's tomb was described by William of Malmesbury as lying between two pyramids – small obelisks which were sometimes used to demarcate the graves of dignitaries in this period. A beautiful stone arch was raised over the tomb and overall a wooden framework projected, supporting decorative iron traceries of the kind which contemporaries called spiders' webs.[20] The tombstone was therefore clearly visible, but its protective grill saved it from wear and tear and from possible depredations by pilgrims, who might otherwise chip off pieces of the stone as relics. Wulfstan was widely commemorated in religious houses throughout the country – the terms of his confraternity associations would ensure this – and venerated in many cities, presumably by their English inhabitants at least. At Worcester, and perhaps elsewhere for a time, he was commemorated on every weekday on which there was not already some saint's day. On the annual commemoration of his *obit* (the anniversary of his death) the monks sang psalms and Masses, and the citizens gave alms lavishly.[21] From the care taken, both over his tomb and over his commemoration, it seems that the monks of Worcester encouraged a local cult to develop very quickly after Wulfstan's death. It was said that he freely granted the petitions of those who entreated him, and that everyone who asked in faith received the benefit of his intercession.[22] From accounts of incidents occurring at his tomb through-out the twelfth century, it is clear that from the outset the tombstone was raised above ground level, and that from an early date it was covered by a tapestry. These both indicated recognition of the sanctity of the deceased, as did the burning of candles there, and the provision of a kneeling mat

---

[19]C. H. Haskins, "The Abacus and the King's Curia," *English Historical Review*, 27 (1912), pp. 101–6. On the financing of the royal campaigns, see also J. O. Prestwich, "War and Finance in the Anglo-Norman State," *Transactions of the Royal Historical Society*, fifth series, 4 (1954), pp. 19–43.

[20]William of Malmesbury, *De Gestis Pontificum Anglorum*, p. 288. Analogies might be drawn with the Pyramid of Cestio in Rome, and with the grill which protected the *Confessio* of St Peter, but it is conjectural how these might have come to be used as models by the monks of Worcester. Much nearer home, the cemetery at Glastonbury abbey contained two early Anglo-Saxon free-standing crosses, described as pyramids by William of Malmesbury: *The Early History of Glastonbury*, ed. and transl. by John Scott (1981), pp. 84–5. See also A. Watkin, "The Glastonbury 'Pyramids' and St. Patrick's 'Companions'," *The Downside Review*, 65 (1947), pp. 30–41.

[21]*Vita Wulfstani*, p. 64.

[22]Ibid., p. 64.

for petitioners. Wulfstan's cult was clearly sanctioned to some degree by prior and monks, if not by his immediate episcopal successors.

Very soon two episodes occurred which were seen to denote that even in small matters Wulfstan did not permit those who loved him to suffer distress. Soon after he died, an epistle-book was stolen from the cathedral church, and the blame fell on the sacrist, who had charge of it. He is not named but was perhaps Alfhere, who as sacrist was one of those charged by Wulfstan in 1092 to investigate the dispute over St Helen's church.[23] It was the duty of a sacrist to take care of all the items of church furnishing and equipment. A book such as this would be required for regular use, quite apart from being a valuable object in its own right. All books were, of course, carefully handwritten, and one such as this might also be illuminated. Epistle-books from that period have survived only rarely, and they were perhaps never produced in large numbers. The prior, presumably Thomas, raged at the sacrist for his negligence, and threatened him with a heavy penance if the book was not restored. The sacrist looked for it everywhere but without success. At last he prayed to Wulfstan to intercede for him, hoping that since the bishop was known to be so kindly, his prayers would not be wasted. He lay on his face at Wulfstan's tomb, praying and imploring him to recall his kindness of earlier days; to cause the book to be restored, and silence the threats of the prior. He bargained that in return he would burn a candle for a whole year at the tomb, and say fifteen psalms. That same day "the people" – the lay servants of the cathedral priory – were questioned about the book's whereabouts, and there was an intensive search for it. A "little woman" (*muliercula*) then accused the thief and revealed where the book had been hidden.[24]

A second book was stolen about the same time, seemingly by another thief. A lay servant of the cathedral, who had often been employed by the sacrist, and found to be honest, complained that a book had been stolen from him. He was particularly anxious because it was one he had borrowed, and the owner was pressing him to return it. Every day he prostrated himself at Wulfstan's tomb and prayed to God, asking that through Wulfstan's merits he would bring back the book and punish the greedy thief. Bargaining, like the earlier petitioner, he added that if his prayer was granted, he would from then on continue to render faithful service to the cathedral church. He persevered in his prayers for several days and on the feast of the Ascension prayed longer and more earnestly than ever, and continued until dusk. The thief entered the cathedral, but

---

[23]Ibid., p. 64; *The Cartulary of Worcester Cathedral Priory (Register I)*, ed. R. R. Darlington (1968), no. 52.

[24]*Vita Wulfstani*, pp. 64–5. The prior is not named, but was probably Thomas, since the episode seems to have occurred soon after Wulfstan's death.

was suddenly seized with madness (probably on hearing his crime brought before God in these agitated petitions). He began to scream horribly; pulled out the stolen book, which was hidden in his clothes, held it out and explained when and how he had stolen it. The brother of this thief was a monk of Worcester, an able and astute man, who quickly persuaded the monks to beg Wulfstan in his gentleness to restore the madman to sanity. The monks agreed to do so, and not long afterwards their prayer was answered. It came to be the custom among the monks of Worcester that if they were suffering physical illness, or mental distress, they whispered it to the bishop just as though he were still alive. He generously received their prayers, and granted so many of their petitions that Coleman considered that if any prayer remained unanswered, it was not that Wulfstan could not intercede, but that either the man who asked was unworthy (that is, had not prepared spiritually before making his request), or else the thing requested was unnecessary.[25]

Recourse to Wulfstan as an intercessor seems therefore to have begun spontaneously on the part of individual monks and laity associated with the cathedral priory. There is no hint that this initial stage of the development of his cult was encouraged by Wulfstan's episcopal successor. The monastic chapter would naturally observe the annual *obit* of their bishop, and the frequent commemoration on weekdays perhaps began when the monks and laity in their employ began to experience miracles at Wulfstan's tomb. Fairly soon, however, the cult spread beyond the confines of the cathedral priory. A growing number of people experienced dreams, or else waking visions, in which they saw Wulfstan in sanctified glory. Wulfstan's *Life* records two successive religious experiences of an anchorite. Like others of his profession, he spent much of his existence in isolation and prayer, but his devotions were increasingly disrupted by fantasies which he believed to be the work of the Devil. These continued non-stop, exhausting the hermit, but not breaking him down entirely because he was fortified by Divine help. His spiritual conflict was eventually ended by the mediation of Wulfstan. An under-garment which he had worn when he lay dying was sent from Worcester. As soon as the hermit received it – and in fact as soon as he caught sight of it – his fantasies dispersed and he recovered his peace of mind. From this time onwards he experienced no more temptations or evil suggestions. He appreciated that Wulfstan's merits were far greater than his own, and reverenced this garment as a relic. He folded it carefully, and when he was settling down to sleep, he would lay it carefully over his head to guard himself from any more false temptations.[26]

[25] Ibid., p. 65.
[26] Ibid., pp. 65–6.

The spiritual comfort which the hermit received in this way was followed some time afterwards by a symbolic vision. One day at sunset there was loud knocking on his window. The noise alarmed him – hermits were sometimes attacked by robbers because they were believed to have in their keeping bullion or valuables they were guarding for the local populace. The hermit asked who was knocking and a voice said that his friend Wulfstan, bishop of Worcester, was outside. He wanted to know if the hermit could bring any water so that he (the bishop) might wash his hands. In return, Wulfstan would go into the church and say the Monastic Hours for his friend. Many anchorholds adjoined parish churches, but the anchorite, sealed in his cell, had no means of entry, and could only glimpse the liturgy through a window. The anchorite was told that as a further pledge of friendship, he should give Wulfstan a cloak which he possessed. The man said that he had no such thing, as Wulfstan well knew, but the bishop promised that he would soon have one, if he fixed his mind on God. Wulfstan's body radiated a brilliant light, which illuminated everything round about it. He went into the church; genuflected; said a prayer and crossed himself, and began the Office of the (Monastic) Hours. The responses were said by three maidens, all amazingly beautiful and graceful. When they had finished chanting, the tallest maiden, the middle one of the three, was seen to give a blessing to Wulfstan, who accepted it. The anchorite now thought he saw a bed with rich coverings, and a cloak spread on top of it. He invited Wulfstan to accept what he had asked for, and Wulfstan replied that subsequently he would receive by grace a pledge of greater glory, but the anchorite must now convey his most loving greetings to those at Worcester who had maintained vigils of prayer for so long. Their good work would be accounted to their credit, and whatever they had intended to do for his sake would be to their spiritual advantage. The vision faded, and the next day the anchorite faithfully reported it. The monks at Worcester dutifully did as they had been instructed. They sent letters throughout England with the news of their sad loss, and testifying to their love of Wulfstan. It was requested that if a Divine revelation were to be made to anyone concerning Wulfstan's spiritual status, then the recipient would let them know by a reliable messenger.[27]

This sequence of events incorporated into Wulfstan's *Life* indicates that at Worcester cathedral, once the obligatory Requiems were said, and the customary letter had been circulated to other religious houses, notifying their inmates of the death of the bishop, and requesting prayers for his soul, there was little immediate effort to promote his cult on any formal basis. The early, unnamed petitioners at his tomb seem by

[27]Ibid., p. 66.

inference to have been obscure individuals, looking for release from their anxieties. The anchorite, a prey to neuroses, as lonely people often are, found comfort in the garment which was sent to him from Worcester. Clearly it was regarded as a relic of the bishop, and was sent in the hope that it might fortify the man, but the fact that he was permitted to keep it suggests that it was not initially highly valued. Once the hermit found that it cured his distracting symptoms, this obviously led him to consider Wulfstan as a saintly intercessor, one who had already been admitted to heavenly glory.

Conscious of Wulfstan's spiritual support, he experienced his new perception of the bishop in a vision. Wulfstan's request for water for washing was on one level a preliminary to reciting the Office, but on another plane it indicated that he was now shedding any remaining temporal associations. The request for the cloak, a symbol of protection, might represent a rationalization of the man's aspiration to uphold the merits of his spiritual champion but could also be interpreted as a belief that Wulfstan's tomb should be dignified by a tapestry covering. Next, the deceased bishop was seen praying on his behalf in the company of the Blessed Virgin (to whom the cathedral was dedicated). The blessing of Wulfstan by the Blessed Virgin would symbolize the recognition of his sanctity by the personification of his cathedral church, while the lesser maidens personified the Marian dedications of other religious communities (including Evesham, Perstone and Winchcombe), symbolizing the acclamation of Wulfstan's sanctity by the Benedictine houses) throughout the diocese. This vision helped the anchorite to formulate the conclusion that, since Wulfstan had rescued him from spiritual assault, he in turn could now do something for the bishop. The anchorite was encouraged in his vision to urge those at Worcester who did have Wulfstan's interests at heart to spread the fame of his spiritual merits. The men who had maintained the vigils were most likely those who had sent the garment to the anchorite, but he in turn reinforced their efforts by reporting his vision of Wulfstan in glory. It is implied that the anchorite experienced this vision even before the monks had circulated the customary mortuary-roll, and that by doing so belatedly, they could incorporate the anchorite's revelation of Wulfstan's sanctity, and request news of supporting revelations from other sources.

The anchorite is not identified, but he seems to have lived not far from the cathedral priory. Information on the anchorite population of eleventh-century Worcester is limited, but it is known that in the twelfth century there were six anchorholds in the shire, with one inmate apiece.[28]

[28]Ann K. Warren, *Anchorites and their Patrons in Medieval England* (1985), Appendix I.

Circumstantial evidence suggests a connection between this particular anchorite and the priory of Great Malvern, which began its existence as a hermitage. The tentative link is provided by a relic of Wulfstan. In January 1269, William de Beauchamp III dictated a will in which he bequeathed to his son John the *surcella* of St Wulfstan.[29] The word most readily translates as surplice, or tunic, but this garment may have been reputed to be the relic of Wulfstan which was sent from Worcester to the anchorite. Although Wulfstan gave initial encouragement to the establishment of Great Malvern by his former monk Aldwin, the site was on land donated by King Edward to Westminster Abbey, which asserted control over the priory in the early twelfth century.[30] A century later again, Great Malvern secured the protection of Walter de Beauchamp (II), father of the testator William (III).[31] These men were direct descendants of the eleventh-century sheriff Urse de Abetot, who became a benefactor of Great Malvern shortly after Wulfstan's death.[32] By the early fourteenth century, when the head of the Beauchamp family was earl of Warwick, the priory claimed Urse himself as its founder.[33] Arguably the relic of Wulfstan was given either to Urse or to one of the descendants of his daughter, in return for their protection.

The early impetus for the spread of Wulfstan's cult was reinforced by two obscure people living at an unidentified placed called Brumeton. One was a worthy priest named Dunstan. William of Malmesbury, in his boyhood, heard of this man's reputation for holiness. The other was an unnamed anchoress, who equalled any man in her reputation for holiness. William of Malmesbury could not say which of the two should be esteemed above the other, because they were so evenly matched in their pursuit of holiness, the priest performing the work of instruction and the woman maintaining the discipline of religious obedience. They were both quite outstanding in their devotions, and were rewarded by a

[29] *Register of Bishop Godfrey Giffard, September 23 1268 to August 15 1301*, ed. J. W. Willis Bund, 2 vols (1902), II, p. 8.

[30] *Westminster Abbey Charters, 1066–c.1214*, ed. Emma Mason, assisted by the late Jennifer Bray, continuing the work of the late Desmond J. Murphy (1988), nos 164, 243 and note. See also nos 166, 171.

[31] *The Beauchamp Cartulary: charters 1100–1268*, ed. Emma Mason (1980), no. 61.

[32] T. Habington, *A Survey of Worcestershire*, ed. J. Amphlett, 2 vols (1895–9), II, pp. 178, 263. The attestations of Bishop Samson and Prior Thomas to Urse's charter might suggest that Worcester claimed jurisdiction over Great Malvern at this period, but the witness Hugh the dapifer was perhaps Hugh of Colham, the dapifer and proctor of Westminster Abbey in this period: *Westminster Abbey Charters 1066–c.1214*, nos 47, 488.

[33] *Placitorum in Domo Capitulari Westmonasteriensi Asservatorum Abbreviatio* (1811), p. 331.

vision of Heaven while they were still in this mortal life. They sent a joint message to those at Worcester that they should have no doubt about Wulfstan's merits, because they had seen him among the choirs of the saints, appearing just as glorious as those around him, and in fact more glorious than some of those in the lower ranks. These two visionaries were so constant in their devotions that William considered it would be an offence against religion to doubt their story, which was accepted as though it came direct from Heaven.[34]

In the generations after the Norman Conquest there were many hermits, anchorites and anchoresses of English or Anglo-Danish race scattered throughout the country.[35] People of such origins, upholding simple and traditional values, would be those beyond the cathedral priory who were quickest to appreciate Wulfstan's spiritual merits. These solitaries, devoting their lives to prayer and contemplation, would be more likely to experience Wulfstan's spiritual stature in visionary form than would the better-educated monks of the cathedral priory, or the sophisticated secular clergy of the episcopal *familia*. Before these visions were reported, it is doubtful whether the question of publicly promoting Wulfstan's cult had been seriously debated in the cathedral itself. His mediation of spiritual and physical healing during his lifetime had largely been experienced by laity. A few clerics had appreciated his merits, including the prior of Evesham, and the austere priest Eilmer, besides Bishop Robert, who in any case was largely preoccupied either with the business of his own diocese or with his administrative responsibilities at the royal court; but the inmates of the cathedral were generally less appreciative. As was shown in preceding chapters, Wulfstan's maintenance of traditional values was not popular during his later years, especially among the sharp-tongued young clerks of his *familia*, and towards the end of his episcopate he was possibly experiencing conflict with the monastic chapter over their respective shares of the lands and jurisdiction of the church of Worcester.

But if the monastic community was looking for changes after Wulfstan's death, then they got these with a vengeance. King William quickly addressed a writ to the free tenants of the bishopric, announcing that the honour (or feudal barony) of Worcester had now reverted into his possession. He had discussed with his barons the question of a feudal relief on the estate (the levy which a king customarily made before

[34]*Vita Wulfstani*, p. 67. The place-name cannot readily be identified, but may be a corruption of Bynton, that is, Bevington, in south-west Warwickshire, which was held by Evesham abbey.
[35]H. Mayr-Harting, "Functions of a Twelfth-Century Recluse," *History*, 60 (1975), pp. 337–52, see esp. 337–8.

permitting a new occupant to take possession of a vacant barony) and now proceeded to list the sums he required from thirty named tenants – of these, two were jointly assessed for one payment, and Roger Fitz Durand was acquitted (as a royal servant). The others comprised "French" feudal lords, two of whom were each charged £20; church dignitaries, including Bishop Robert (£10); and the abbot of Evesham (£30); Archdeacon Ailric (£5); Orderic the dapifer (£40) – perhaps a payment on behalf of the episcopal demesne lands; Coleman (£2) – perhaps a payment on behalf of the Westbury lands; Saewulf (£15), and various less prominent figures. No charge was levied on one of Worcester's most substantial tenants, the sheriff Urse de Abetot. On the contrary, he witnessed this writ in company with his associates in the royal administration, Ranulf Flambard, the king's chancellor, and Eudo the king's dapifer. A postcript was added: if anyone resisted making payment, then Urse, together with Bernard (Fitz Ospac, a royal chaplain), would seize his lands and goods for the king.[36]

The bishopric was left vacant for more than a year, until the appointment of Samson, a complete contrast to his predecessor. He was a former canon of Bayeux in Normandy; brother of Archbishop Thomas I of York, and father of Archbishop Thomas II.[37] The old link between diocese and archbishopric was thus renewed again, but only in terms of these personal relationships. Samson was a shrewd and intelligent administrator, not a man to be browbeaten by his archiepiscopal kindred.[38] William of Malmesbury spoke admiringly of his learning, and commented on his gargantuan appetite. He approved of Samson's generosity, both towards the poor, and towards the cathedral church, to which he regularly donated precious objects for its embellishment. On the other hand, Samson wound up the monastery which Wulfstan had re-established at Westbury-on-Trym. William seemed to find a morose satisfaction in noting that it was at that manor that Samson died, on 5 May 1112.[39]

Coleman was most likely inspired to write his English *Life of Wulfstan* as a reaction against the changes made by Bishop Samson, notably his

---

[36]*Regesta Regum Anglo-Normannorum 1066–1154: I. Regesta Willelmi Conquestoris et Willelmi Rufi 1066–1100*, ed. H. W. C. Davis with R. J. Whitwell (1913), no 387; J. H. Round, *Feudal England*, 2nd edn (1964), pp. 241–5. See also Barlow, *William Rufus*, pp. 235–6; C. Dyer, *Lords and Peasants in a Changing Society: The estates of the bishopric of Worcester, 680–1540* (1980), pp. 45–6.

[37]William of Malmesbury, *De Gestis Pontificum Anglorum*, p. 289 and note 3; Le Neve, *Fasti Ecclesiae Anglicanae II*, p. 99.

[38]V. H. Galbraith, "Notes on the career of Samson, bishop of Worcester (1096–1112)," reprinted from *English Historical Review*, 82 (1967), pp. 86–101, in his *Kings and Chroniclers: essays in English medieval history* (1982), pp. IV 86–101.

[39]William of Malmesbury, *De Gestis Pontificum Anglorum*, p. 289 and note 3, p.290.

demotion of Coleman himself by disbanding the priory of Westbury. As episcopal chancellor, Coleman was perfectly capable of writing in Latin. His choice of the English language indicates that it was a work intended for those who believed in the old values which Wulfstan had upheld, and which would be vindicated by his recognition as a saint. When Coleman wrote, around the year 1100, a considerable number of the older monks would still be Englishmen, with a fluent reading knowledge of their native language. As was mentioned in an earlier chapter, manuscripts were produced in English throughout Wulfstan's episcopate. But the circulation of this English *Life* of the bishop was effectively confined to a dwindling group among the monks. New recruits might still be of English or part-English race, but they would be progressively less likely to be able to read this work. There was no longer a standard written form of the language once the production of official documents in English ceased, in the 1070s, and there was a growing discrepancy between the various spoken regional dialects and the written form of Old English. Such further English works as were composed were in one or other of those dialects, readily intelligible only within a limited radius.[40] There was no great incentive for the younger generation to learn to read or write in English, even though it was the first spoken language of all but the court circle.

Coleman's *Life of Wulfstan*, composed within a few years of the bishop's death, was consciously written in hagiographical vein, the model adopted for the biographies of ecclesiastics. He set out to depict Wulfstan in the role of an Old Testament prophetic hero – adding a touch of the Celtic ascetic – and selecting and presenting his material so as to achieve this effect. Consequently there is a discrepancy between the historic figure of Wulfstan and the central character of Coleman's work. Reading between the lines of the *Life*, it is clear that Wulfstan's real strengths were his simplicity and purity of heart; his commitment to the traditional Benedictine life and to the pastoral welfare of those committed to his charge. A pen-portrait of Wulfstan, included in Hemming's cartulary and dating from within a few years of the bishop's death, is the oldest surviving source to single out Wulfstan's simplicity as one of his dominant characteristics.[41] Coleman grasped Wulfstan's real

[40]For discussion of changes in written English in the late eleventh and early twelfth centuries, see *The Peterborough Chronicle*, ed. Cecily Clark, 2nd edn (1970), pp. xxxvii–lxxiv.

[41]*Hemingi Chartularium*, II, pp. 45–6. This section of the cartulary is the work of Hemming himself: N. R. Ker, "Hemming's Cartulary: a description of the two Worcester cartularies in Cotton Tiberius A.XIII," reprinted from *Studies in Medieval History presented to Frederick Maurice Powicke*, ed. R. W. Hunt, W. A. Pantin and R. W. Southern

strengths to a large extent, but apparently believed that the bishop's merits would make a bigger impact if he was depicted as a wonder-worker. Coleman scoured the countryside for stories which could be depicted in this way. His fellow monks criticized these on occasion – as exaggerations, if not downright fabrications – but he was undeterred.[42] The *Life* of any saintly character contains many set-piece "typical" episodes and miracles. While some of these are based on actual events, they combine to present a picture of the subject suitable for instilling into the members of his religious order those virtues which they should admire; consequently it is likely that in many such works their central characters diverge considerably from the historical figures on whom they are based. Writers, particularly if they were outsiders to the communities which commissioned these works, might have little interest in their real-life subjects. Coleman, even though he knew Wulfstan well in the bishop's later years, was inclined on occasion to treat him as a typical hagiographical hero, hence the criticisms of the monks of Worcester, and those which may be inferred from William of Malmesbury's preference for information supplied by Nicholas.

Despite Coleman's efforts, Wulfstan's cult does not seem to have been widely observed in this period. This was due in part to the fact that Wulfstan's real merits were not those most valued in contemporary ecclesiastical circles. The promulgation of the cult of an episcopal saint might be used to justify territorial aggression on the part of an eccle-siastical landholder, but in the late eleventh century, Worcester was on the defensive, notwithstanding Wulfstan's valiant efforts over many years to recover its alienated properties. A cleric would be more readily perceived as a saint if he could defend the estates of his church. Innocence and sanctity were all very well in their way, but a bishop could usually obtain more advantages for his community if he earned the goodwill of the secular ruler for his astute political advice, or his decisive military support. Coleman depicted Wulfstan's support for Harold Godwinson, but not for William I or William II. When Coleman wrote, a bishop's spirituality was more likely to be perceived if he was a worldly success in political terms, and if by reason of his political influence he could gain or recover lands for the use of his monks. In Benedictine houses throughout the country there was an increasing emphasis in this period on the episcopal duty of safeguarding and enlarging the monks' share of the *mensa*; the paternalistic Wulfstan was perhaps not so assertive in this sphere as his monks would have liked, despite his advice to Hemming on

(1948), pp. 49–75, in N. R. Ker, *Books, Collectors and Libraries: Studies in the Medieval Heritage*, ed. A. G. Watson (1985), pp. 31–59, see p. 56.

[42] *Vita Wulfstani*, p. 42.

the need to register the title deeds of the monks' estates. Many contemporaries would perceive sanctity in a prelate precisely because of his success in gaining lands, as though Divine approval was denoted in this way. Wulfstan's devotional practices led him to detach himself to a large extent from worldly concerns, whereas in the later eleventh century Benedictine monks were respected for their successful involvement with the world, not for their withdrawal from it. Ecclesiastical biographers around the turn of the century liked to depict their subjects as conforming to the new ideals of church reform.[43] Wulfstan was certainly free from any taint of the simony alleged against certain other bishops in his day, but his ideals were not the radical ones of the mid– and late eleventh century, but those of the Tenth Century Reform. In a sense, Coleman's work was outside the mainstream of clerical biography in this period. Like his fellow biographers, he was striving to establish a local cult, in his subject's own diocese, but it was less a work for public consumption than a vindication, within the cathedral precincts, of all that Wulfstan represented.

The elaborate tomb accorded to Wulfstan indicates that he was revered by his former monks – but perhaps primarily as a patriarchal figure – and even within the confines of the cathedral the cult of Wulfstan developed slowly. The death of Bishop Samson was followed by a three-year vacancy before the appointment in 1115 of Theulf, like his predecessor a former canon of Bayeux and royal chaplain, and a man very much in the same mould. For self-evident reasons, no attempt was made to foster the cult of either of these men, and they were both buried in the nave of the cathedral church, "before the Crucifix."[44] Down to the death of Theulf in 1123, Wulfstan's cult gained no widespread publicity, although there were two developments which paved the way for things to come. First, Worcester was devastated by a major fire in 1113. The flames spread throughout the town, and the cathedral roof caught alight. The lead liquefied; great rafters the size of trees caught fire and crashed to the ground, and the interior of the church was devastated. Amazingly Wulfstan's tomb survived intact. Not only was it spared from the flames, but it emerged from the ordeal neither stained with soot nor covered with ashes. More sensationally, the reed mat, on which those praying used to kneel, was discovered undamaged before the tomb. Even the wooden structure which extended beyond the stonework was found to be whole,

---

[43]By way of analogy, see Marylou Ruud, "Monks in the World: the case of Gundulf of Rochester," in *Anglo-Norman Studies XI*, ed. R. Allen Brown (1989), pp. 245–60.

[44]William of Malmesbury, *De Gestis Pontificum Anglorum*, p. 290; see note 3 for a comment on Theulf's admission of simony; John Le Neve, *Fasti Ecclesiae Anglicanae II*, p. 99.

although that which was incorporated with the masonry of the tomb had burned to ashes.[45] The kneeling-mat would have been authorized by the chapter, and, together with the elaborate structure of the tomb, its presence shows that Wulfstan's cult was encouraged to some extent in this period. The survival of tomb and mat would considerably enhance Wulfstan's prestige in the locality.

A few years after this event, Worcester was visited by the historian William of Malmesbury, who came to collect material for his major projects, the *De Gestis Regum Anglorum* and *De Gestis Pontificum Anglorum*.[46] He read Coleman's *Life* of Wulfstan and drew on it extensively for his volume on the bishops.[47] It is clear from the extracts he used, and his own emendations, that he recognized Wulfstan's sanctity. Prior Nicholas provided him with several anecdotes on Wulfstan and it was William's opinion that Nicholas would have been the ideal biographer of the bishop.[48]

Following Nicholas's failure to secure a free election of a successor to Theulf,[49] the next bishop to be selected was Simon (1125–50), the chaplain and chancellor of Queen Alice, second wife of Henry I.[50] As a secular clerk, Simon would have no obvious interest in promoting the cult of his monastic predessor, but Wulfstan's cult does appear to have developed over these years. Indirect evidence comes from Henry of Huntingdon, a secular clerk who, in his *Historia Anglorum* (*History of the English*) styled Wulfstan *sanctus* (saint, holy), in references found in a section of his work composed no later than 1131. Henry certainly travelled around the country, but it is not known that he went to Worcester, nor how he picked up the growing consciousness there of Wulfstan's sanctity.[51] William of Malmesbury noted that petitioners to Wulfstan's tomb regularly received a favourable response to their prayers. By traditional standards, therefore, he should be proclaimed a

---

[45]William of Malmesbury, *De Gestis Pontificum Anglorum*, pp. 288–9. *Florentii Wigorniensis monachi Chronicon*, II, p. 66.

[46]R. Thomson, *William of Malmesbury* (1987), p. 73; Antonia Gransden, "Cultural Transition at Worcester in the Anglo-Norman Period," in *Medieval Art and Architecture at Worcester Cathedral*, ed. Glenys Popper (1978), pp. 1–14, esp. p. 9.

[47]*Vita Wulfstani*, p. ix.

[48]Ibid., pp. 51–2, 54, 56–7.

[49]D. L. Bethell, "English Black Monks and Episcopal Elections in the 1120s," *English Historical Review*, 84 (1969), pp. 673–98, esp. pp. 681–4, 689–90, 694–8.

[50]William of Malmesbury, *De Gestis Pontificum Anglorum*, pp. 290–1; Le Neve, *Fasti Ecclesiae Anglicanae II*, p. 99.

[51]Henry of Huntingdon, *Historia Anglorum*, ed. T. Arnold (1879), pp. 211, 214. For the date of composition of the passages in which Wulfstan is named, see Diana Greenway, "Henry of Huntingdon and the Manuscripts of his *Historia Anglorum*," *Anglo-Norman Studies IX*, ed. R. Allen Brown (1987), pp. 103–21, see esp. pp. 107–8.

saint in Heaven, but this was prevented by the scepticism of unnamed contemporaries.[52]

The simple spirituality of Wulfstan would have little appeal to many of the sophisticated secular clerics of Worcester in the mid-twelfth century, and they would be unimpressed by the experiences of plebeian petitioners at his tomb. But if the successive bishops, Samson, Theulf and Simon, were indifferent to Wulfstan's cult, the same was not true of Prior Warin, who succeeded Nicholas in or after 1124, and remained in office until 1140–2.[53] A resident prior might be expected to be able to give more time and energy to promoting a religious cult than a bishop who was frequently absent, either on episcopal business or on the king's service, although as will be seen, some of the later twelfth-century bishops became directly involved in enhancing Wulfstan's reputation. Warin, like his name, was probaly of "French" origin, even though Englishmen were rapidly adopting Norman names in this period. By the latter part of Henry I's reign, and indeed long before that, Continental clerics had come to venerate the native cults.[54] Moreoever, Worcester, like any other self-respecting cathedral or religious house, needed to promote an up-to-date cult. St Oswald retained his stature in the cathedral itself, but he had a limited appeal to the laity of the diocese. People in the immediate vicinity were spreading Wulfstan's reputation by word of mouth, but if his merits were to be advertised more widely, then his *Life* needed to be made available in Latin. Since this language was standardized in its written form, unlike the English of the twelfth century, it was the most suitable medium in which to write a revised *Life*, from which could be made multiple texts to circulate throughout the country. Prior Warin therefore invited William of Malmesbury to translate Coleman's *Life of Wulfstan*, asking him to follow the text closely, without making changes in the narrative or in the order of events.[55] In the course of his translation, William added those anecdotes he had learned from Prior Nicholas[56] together with an occasional amplifying remark of his own,[57] besides making textual amendments which did not affect the flow of the narrative.[58] The most important change which affects the reader's

---

[52]William of Malmesbury, *De Gestis Pontificum Anglorum*, p. 289.

[53]Knowles, Brooke and London, *Heads of Religious Houses*, p. 83; Le Neve, *Fasti Ecclesiae Anglicanae II*, p. 102.

[54]Susan J. Ridyard, "*Condigna Veneratio*: Post-Conquest Attitudes to the Saints of the Anglo-Saxons," in *Anglo-Norman Studies IX*, pp. 179–206.

[55]*Vita Wulfstani*, pp. viii, 1–2.

[56]Ibid., pp. 51–2, 56–7.

[57]The reference to the priest Dunstan is clearly a comment by William himself: ibid., p. 67.

[58]Ibid., pp. 11, 58.

understanding of Wulfstan comes from William's introduction of direct speech. He said the he had freely amended and amplified Wulfstan's sayings, or what he might have said on any given occasion, but always in line with the facts of the narrative.[59] This literary licence had been commonly used since the time of the Classical Greek historians, running the risk that the portrait of the subject would owe more to the biographer than to the original. The only words of Wulfstan of which we can now be sure are his regular opening phrase "Believe me" or "Believe you me."

It is arguable that William's portrayal of Wulfstan diverges from that of Coleman, and equally questionable whether Coleman conveyed a full and rounded portrayal of the bishop. William himself implied that Nicholas came nearer to understanding the essential qualities of Wulfstan than Coleman did.[60] By the time the translation was made, few of the monks who had known Wulfstan would still be active, and of those who were, such as John of Worcester, the majority would have been *oblates* or novices during the bishop's last years. Their recollections, however sharp, would have been fragmentary, and insufficient to challenge the "received portrait" drawn by William.

Prior Warin, as the effective head of the cathedral priory, was the man who would have a natural, even a vested, interest in promoting Wulfstan's cult. The secular clerics who were appointed to the bishopric in the earlier twelfth century would not be greatly interested in Wulfstan's championing of traditional Benedictine values. If any of them read his *Life*, they would find his spirituality, character and conduct old-fashioned by their cosmopolitan standards. A cult which attracted pilgrims, and hence a steady flow of offerings, would be welcome, but the tomb-miracles reported from this period were comparatively rare. Prior Warin's commissioning of the Latin *Life* perhaps followed a renewed spate of tomb-miracles – but it is equally arguable that these would occur after a renewal of official interest in the cult. At all events, one such incident was recorded in 1130 when a woman who had undergone the ordeal of the hot iron experienced the dramatic healing of her badly burned hands.[61] (Accused persons who were condemned to this ordeal were required to carry a red-hot iron for a specified number of paces. The hands were then bandaged for three days, and innocence was proved only if the burns showed clear signs of healing.)

There seems to have followed a lull for some fifteen years or more, until another fire raged through Worcester, devastating the city and

[59]Ibid., p. 2.
[60]Ibid., p. 57.
[61]*The Chronicle of John of Worcester*, ed. J. R. H. Weaver (1908), p. 30. On the ordeal of the hot iron, see Robert Bartlett, *Trial by Fire and Water: The Medieval Judicial Ordeal* (Clarendon Press, Oxford, 1986), pp. 19–23, 25.

spreading to the cathedral. As many of its furnishings as possible were removed, although the tapestry spread over Wulfstan's tomb was left behind. The fire burned up everything in its path, except for this tapestry itself, which remained undamaged. More surprisingly, even the reed mats spread before the tomb were intact. Everything else, all around, was buried in smouldering embers, but the tomb-covering remained untouched by the flames. At first sight, this story looks like a re-working of the comparable episode related by William of Malmesbury, but it has an independent witness. Among the crowds who saw this sight, and appreciated its significance, was Bernard, bishop of St David's (1115–48), who was passing through the city. He came into the church; stared at the tomb-covering and mats; ascertained that everything else was covered in embers, and was astounded.[62] Even if Wulfstan's tomb was located out of the main path of the successive fires, the survival of its furnishings on each occasion would be perceived locally as a miraculous occurrence. Bernard was not a man to be lightly impressed. He was a former royal clerk, and chancellor to the first wife of Henry I; an experienced royal ambassador, chiefly to the papal court, and above all, extremely ambitious for his own see.[63] Yet he was so impressed by the survival of Wulfstan's tomb-covering that he later wrote to Pope Eugenius III (1145–53), describing what he had seen, and petitioning the pope to order Wulfstan to be acknowledged as a saint throughout the universal church.[64] Nothing came of this petition. One such incident would not in itself prompt a mid-twelfth century pope to proclaim a new saint. In December 1139, Pope Innocent II had rejected Westminster's petition for the canonization of King Edward, on the grounds that stronger supporting evidence was needed than had been presented, and that the petition for canonization should be presented by the whole realm of England.[65]

Shortly after this second fire, another miracle was reported at Wulfstan's tomb. There was a woman who had been cruelly crippled from birth. She could propel herself only by means of her hands, "like a serpent," using her knees instead of her feet. Her early years were spent on the Worcester manor of Ripple, and then she was brought to the city, where she spent more than seven years begging in the porch of the cathedral. She was then told in a dream that her disability would be

---

[62]*Vita Wulfstani*, p. 106.

[63]M. Brett, *The English Church under Henry I* (1975), pp. 30, 41, 50, 52, 55, 62, 107, 239–41, 243, 245; F. Barlow, *The English Church 1066–1154*, 2nd edn (1979), pp. 36, 83–4, 96, 111, 312.

[64]*Vita Wulfstani*, p. 106.

[65]*Westminster Abbey Charters*, no. 158.

cured, if only she could enter the church. Slowly she crept in, and made her way laboriously to Wulfstan's tomb. The people who knew her were amazed to see her there, and asked how and why she had come, but she seemed to be in a trance, and did not reply. Then a crowd began to gather, as people had hopes of seeing a miracle. The woman began to writhe and twist, shouting out loud, at times in exultation, and at other times weeping. The crowd joined in, praying that she would be healed by Wulfstan's merits. She writhed from side to side and then gradually her body straightened out, and she was able to stand upright. She had never walked before, but now she could, although slowly and unsteadily. The monks all chanted the *Te Deum Laudamus* (We Praise you, O Lord), and a procession, with the woman at its head, moved towards the high altar. Bishop Simon had been about to set out from the city, and had already mounted his horse when he was told of the miracle. He dismounted and ran into the church, where the woman was standing upright and walking about. By this time everyone was in tears, and giving thanks for the cure of the beggar woman through Wulfstan's mediation. Soon afterwards, she became an anchoress.[66]

There is an absence of recorded tomb-miracles for the period between about 1150 and 1190, although one important step forward was taken in this period to publicize Wulfstan's cult. This development was most likely prompted by the spectacular success of the cult of St Thomas Becket at Canterbury, following the murder of the archbishop in his cathedral in December 1170. Several other religious houses were quick to see the possibility of reviving cults associated with their churches, and commissioned *Lives* of the saints whose relics they housed.[67] The bishop of Worcester between 1163 and 1179 was Roger of Gloucester, a cousin of King Henry II. Unlike his predecessors, Roger was involved to some extent in publicizing Wulfstan's cult. His monk Master Senatus (his title shows that he had studied in the schools), sent the bishop a letter in which he claimed authorship both of a *Life* of St Oswald and of an *Abridged Life of Wulfstan*.[68] This latter work was most likely intended to serve as an introduction to a collection of those miracles which had been reported at Wulfstan's tomb since William of Malmesbury com-

[66]*Vita Wulfstani*, pp. 106–8.
[67]These diverse cults included those of St Frideswide (Oxford) and St Amphibalus, alias the Holy Cloak (St Albans): see Antonia Gransden, *Historical Writing in England c.550 to c.1307* (1974), pp. 358, 434.
[68]Bodl. MS 633 (1966), f. 197v. See also R. W. Hunt, "English Learning in the Late Twelfth Century," reprinted from *Transactions of the Royal Historical Society*, fourth series, 19 (1936), pp. 19–42, in *Essays in Medieval History*, ed. R. W. Southern (1968), pp. 106–28; see p. 116 and note 4.

pleted his Latin translation of the *Life* by Coleman.[69] The *Abridged Life* by Senatus circulated in England to some extent, but does not seem to have been used to press Wulfstan's cause at the papal *Curia*.[70] Senatus was a learned man, appointed by Bishop Roger as his penitentiary, that is, having responsibility for penitents and oversight of their confessions. In his letter to Bishop Roger, he styles himself *famulus* of the church of Worcester, a member of the community, or of the episcopal household. From the mid-1170s he held successively the offices of precentor, chamberlain and prior, resigning from that office some years before his death.[71]

Bishop Roger's four immediate successors, who all had short episcopates, seem to have taken no interest in Wulfstan's cult. During the time of Bishop John of Coutances (1196–8), on the other hand, many people experienced visions of Wulfstan commanding that his body should be translated to a shrine, a step which traditionally denoted formal recognition as a saint. On the night of 6 September 1198, after all the laity were excluded from the cathedral, and only the bishop and monks were present, the tomb was opened. Wulfstan's bones were distentangled, with some difficulty, both from one another and from the hair of his head, on which the corona, or tonsure, was still visible. His chasuble had survived, but of his mitre only the gold embroidery remained, and the shroud had disintegrated. The vestments and ornaments were taken out and deposited in one shrine, and Wulfstan's bones were placed in another. Just over three weeks later, on 28 September, Bishop John died. It was felt that this was a punishment for his irreverent procedure, in that his actions, which had not been approved by the pope, were conducted without due reverence.[72] This severe monastic verdict suggests that the initiative in the promotion of the cult at this date was taken by Bishop John rather than by his chapter.

John's successor was Mauger, a former royal clerk and physician, elected in 1199. Pope Innocent III was forced to quash this election in February 1200, on grounds of illegitimacy, but empowered the chapter of Worcester to postulate Mauger "on his exceptional merits" and he was consecrated in June of that year.[73] On 19 January 1201, the

[69]*Vita Wulfstani*, pp. xix–xxi, 68–108.

[70]For the later derivatives of the *Abridged Life of St Wulfstan*, see ibid., pp. xxi–xxii, 109–14.

[71]Le Neve, *Fasti Ecclesiae Anglicanae II*, p. 103; Mary G. Cheney, *Roger, Bishop of Worcester 1164–1179* (1980), pp. 58–67.

[72]*Vita Wulfstani*, pp. xlvi–xlvii, 181–3.

[73]Le Neve, *Fasti Ecclesiae Anglicanae II*, p. 100. For the detailed reasoning of the pope in this case, see *Selected Letters of Pope Innocent III concerning England (1198–1216)*, ed. C. R. Cheney and W. H. Semple (1953), no. 6.

"official" anniversary of Wulfstan's death, there began a new wave of miracles at Wulfstan's tomb. These continued for well over a year, growing in number until as many as fifteen or sixteen were reported in a single day.[74] On 17 April 1202, Worcester was swept by yet another devastating fire which damaged part of the cathedral precincts, including the domestic ranges.[75] Funds for rebuilding could most readily be acquired by popularizing Wulfstan's cult still further, because growing numbers of pilgrims would inevitably bring increasing oblations. Moreover, following the embarrassing circumstances under which he had come to Worcester, Mauger perhaps felt the need to prove himself a worthy bishop, one who identified with his cathedral church and had its interests at heart. The bishop consulted the chapter on whether to petition for Wulfstan's canonization,[76] and meanwhile he rectified his predecessor's error by replacing Wulfstan's body in its former tomb. A petition was then sent to the pope.

Innocent III appointed a high-powered commission to investigate Wulfstan's sanctity and the nature of his miracles. Its members comprised Hubert Walter, archbishop of Canterbury; Eustace, bishop of Ely; Samson, abbot of Bury St Edmunds; and Peter, abbot of Woburn.[77] Their deliberations were perhaps expedited by the fact that Bishop Mauger had recently hosted at Worcester a large assembly of prelates and magnates, over which the archbishop, the king's justiciar, had presided in the king's absence, to discuss affairs of state and the situation in Wales. These distinguished visitors had then had an opportunity to observe the occurrences at Wulfstan's tomb.[78] The commissioners arrived on 1 September 1202, and conducted their investigation for three days. They concluded that the miracles were genuine.[79] The archbishop's report with supporting letters from all the other English bishops, testifying to the miracles worked through Wulfstan's mediation, was taken to Rome by a team of Worcester monks, led by Walter of Broadwas and Randulf of Evesham. Bishop Mauger also visited the pope at this time. The hazards of his journey included not only dangerous Alpine roads but also robbers, near Bologna, who looted his party's baggage and horses.[80]

---

[74]Annals of Worcester Cathedral Priory, *Annales Monastici*, ed. H. R. Luard, IV (1869), p. 391; *Vita Wulfstani*, pp. 115–16, 183–4.

[75]Annals of Worcester Cathedral Priory, p. 391.

[76]*Vita Wulfstani*, p. 184; Annals of Worcester Cathedral Priory, p. 392, under 1204, inserted into unrelated material.

[77]*Vita Wulfstani*, p. 184; Annals of Worcester Cathedral Priory, p. 391.

[78]*Vita Wulfstani*, pp. 119–20.

[79]Ibid., p. 184; Annals of Worcester Cathedral Priory, p. 391.

[80]*Vita Wulfstani*, pp. xlviii, 116, 150, 184.

On 21 April 1203 Wulfstan was canonized, and on 14 May, Pope
Innocent issued at Ferentino a bull recording the circumstances leading
up to the canonization, setting out the evidence required, the visitation of
his commissioners to Worcester, and the unanimous testimony produced
both by the cathedral chapter and by the citizens of Worcester concerning both Wulfstan's good works in his lifetime and also the many
miracles performed at his tomb, which were taken as a sign that his
merits were acknowledged in Heaven. As further supportive evidence,
the pope had received under Bishop Mauger's seal a certain ancient
manuscript concerning Wulfstan's life, written in English more than a
hundred years earlier. In view of all the foregoing, the pope now declared
that Wulfstan, the blessed bishop and confessor, should be enrolled
among the saints. This spiritually minded and zealous pastor personified
the ideals which Pope Innocent was to promulgate through the decrees of
the Fourth Lateran Council in 1216. Wulfstan's canonization was due to
his own merits, rather than to hidden diplomatic considerations.[81.]

The formalities observed in the case of Wulfstan were in line with
recent papal rulings and practice concerning canonization. Pope Alexander III (1159–81) attempted to reserve all recognition of new saints for
the papacy, although this monopoly was frequently disregarded in
various provinces of the church until well into the thirteenth century.
English clerics, however, were punctilious in observing the formalities.
Consequently Pope Alexander used his prescribed procedures concerning
the taking of evidence before canonizing two Englishmen: King Edward
the Confessor (1163); and Archbishop Thomas Becket (1173). Pope
Innocent III (1198–1216) rigorously vetted not only candidates for
canonization, but also the witnesses who testified on their behalf. He
required evidence of miracles together with good works, and consequently created only four new saints: Homobuono, a merchant of
Cremona (1199); the Empress Cunegunda (1200); and two Englishmen:
the priest Gilbert of Sempringham, founder of the religious order which
bears his name (1202), and Wulfstan, bishop of Worcester (1203). The

[81]Ibid., pp. xlvi–xlviii, 148–50, 184. The papal registers record only an abridged version
of this bull: The Letters of Pope Innocent III (1198–1216) concerning England and Wales:
a calendar with an appendix of texts, ed. C. R. Cheney and Mary G. Cheney (1967), nos
432, 472. Evidently the papal registers served as formularies. The four bulls of canonization
issued by Innocent III between 1199 and 1203 are expressed in partly identical terms, and
the abridged entry of the bull concerning Wulfstan is cross-referenced in the register to that
of 30 January 1202 in favour of Gilbert of Sempringham: Selected Letters of Pope Innocent
III, pp. xxiii–xxiv. While relations between King John and the pope improved considerably
in the earlier part of 1202, there was a renewed coolness by February 1203, and relations
were little warmer by October of that year (ibid., nos 13–14, 17, 20). For a translation of
the decrees of the Fourth Lateran Council, see English Historical Documents III.
1189–1327, ed. H. Rothwell (1975), no. 136, pp. 643–76.

bishop's credentials of sanctity were assured indeed when he passed the rigorous tests inspired by so able a pope.[82]

Wulfstan's translation was delayed for some fifteen years. At the outset, this might in part have been due to repairs necessitated by the fire of 1202, but then public events took a hand. In 1207 King John quarrelled with Pope Innocent III over the appointment of Stephen Langton as archbishop of Canterbury. The pope intervened with his own choice after king and monks put forward rival candidates, but John continued to insist that archbishops and other prelates were chosen by the king alone. In his struggle, he turned to the newly-canonized St Wulfstan for support. The bishop's appeal lay not so much in his spirituality as recorded in his *Vita* or *Life*, but in a legendary story which was incorporated by Osbert de Clare, prior of Westminster, into his *Life of King Edward*, composed for use in the first attempt to secure that king's canonization in 1139. Prior Osbert depicted Edward as posthumously defending Wulfstan when he was about to be deposed by William the Conqueror. According to this story, Wulfstan declined to surrender his pastoral staff, the symbol of his office, and instead rammed it into the stonework of King Edward's tomb, declaring that he would surrender it only to the king who had appointed him. The story was transmitted in later, vernacular *Lives* of King Edward, and it was apparently in this form that it reached King John.[83] About 8 September 1207, he made a visit to Worcester cathedral, where he was received in solemn procession. He prayed for a long time at Wulfstan's tomb, and it was probably then that he committed himself to Wulfstan's protection.[84] The quarrel with the papacy continued, and the pope placed England under Interdict, a ban on public worship. On 9 May 1208 Innocent III ordered Bishop Mauger, together with the bishops of London and Ely, to proclaim this sentence. Mauger did as he was ordered, and then prudently fled into

[82]E. W. Kemp, *Canonization and Authority in the Western Church* (1948), p. 105. The pope insisted that, besides the evidence of a commission, sworn depositions of witnesses should be submitted, and some of the witnesses should be produced in Rome. The deputation of Worcester monks presumably included some who could testify to occurrences at Wulfstan's tomb. For procedure in the case of Gilbert of Sempringham, see *The Book of St. Gilbert*, ed. Raymonde Foreville and Gillian Keir (1987), pp. lxii–lxiii, 168–78.

[83]Emma Mason, "St. Wulfstan's staff: a legend and its uses," *Medium Aevum*, 53 (1984), pp. 157–79, esp. pp. 161–2. For the story of St. Wulfstan's staff, see "La Vie de S. Edouard le Confesseur par Osbert de Clare," ed. M. Bloch, *Analecta Bollandiana*, 41 (1923), pp. 5–131; see pp. 116–20. The story also appears in Wulfstan's *Abridged Life* by Senatus: *Vita Wulfstani*, pp. 77–8.

[84]King John remitted the payment of a hundred marks (£66 13s 4d) due from the monks for privileges he granted them on this occasion, so that they could use this money to rebuild the fire-damaged cloister and domestic buildings: Annals of Worcester Cathedral Priory, p.395.

exile at Pontigny in Burgundy, where he died in 1212.[85] The actions of the current bishop of Worcester did not shake John's adherence to Mauger's saintly predecessor. In 1211, when papal legates came to negotiate on the dispute, John countered with the legend of St Wulfstan's staff as justification of his right to appoint the higher clergy of his realm. The king's reported words were:

> All my predecessors made appointments to archbishoprics, bishoprics and abbeys in their private apartments. As you can read in holy works, the blessed and glorious king, St. Edward, granted the bishopric of Worcester in his day to St. Wulfstan. When William the Bastard, conqueror of England, wanted to deprive him of the bishopric because he did not know French, St. Wulfstan answered, "You did not grant me my pastoral staff, and I will not surrender it to you." Instead, he went to the tomb of St. Edward, and said in his native language, "Edward, you gave me my staff, and now I cannot hold it, because of the king, so I commit it to you. And if you can keep it, then defend it." He rammed the staff into the carving on the tombstone and the staff was miraculously transfixed to St. Edward's tomb, so that nobody present could dislodge it except St. Wulfstan.[86]

The legates were unmoved, but John continued to place his trust in Wulfstan. As he lay dying in October 1216, he dictated a will in which he insisted on being buried beside St. Wulfstan. His followers succeeded in conveying his body across Midland shires which were torn by civil war, and in burying John beside his patron saint.[87] After the country was

[85]*Selected Letters of Pope Innocent III*, no. 34. *Vita Wulfstani*, p. 184; Annals of Worcester Cathedral Priory, p. 396.

[86]The Latin text of King John's speech is printed in the Burton Annals in *Annales Monastici*, ed. H. R. Luard, I (1864), p. 211. There is another account of the dialogue between king and legates in the Waverley Annals, *Annales Monastici*, ed. H. R. Luard, II (1865), pp. 268–71. There are reasons why the Burton account may represent the recollection of eye-witnesses: Mason, "St. Wulfstan's staff," p. 159. Wulfstan was cited even though John also deployed formidable intellectual arguments. At the end of March 1208, he requisitioned from Reading Abbey (of which he was the founder's great-grandson) several scriptural and canonistic works: six volumes of the Bible, including all the Old Testament; Hugh of St Victor on the Sacraments; the *Sentences* of Peter Lombard; St Augustine's *City of God*; St Augustine, *On the third part of the Psalter*; Valerianus, *De Moribus*; Origen, *On the Old Testament*, and Candidus Arianus: *Rotuli Litterarum Clausarum in Turri Londiniensi asservati (1204–27)*, ed. T. Duffus Hardy, 2 vols (1833–44), I, p. 108.

[87]King John's will is printed in *Foedera, Conventiones, Litterae et cuiuscunque generis Acta Publica*, ed. T. Rymer and R. Sanderson (816–69), I, i, 144. At this date the cathedral was dedicated to the Blessed Virgin alone, but John's dying words to the abbot of Croxton were reported as: "I commend my body and my soul to God and St. Wulfstan," Roger of

restored to peace, the solemn translation of Wulfstan could at last take place. In a magnificent ceremony held on 7 June 1218, Wulfstan's body was translated from his tomb to a feretory, or shrine.[88] St Oswald's relics were also translated, and King John was laid to rest between them. It was held that this fulfilled one of the prophecies of Merlin: "And he shall be buried between the saints."[89] The young King Henry III attended, together with many of the magnates of church and state. On this occasion, Bishop Silvester enlarged the dedication of his cathedral church. The high altar was now dedicated in honour both of the Blessed Virgin (the tenth-century dedicatee) and also St Oswald, while the middle altar was dedicated to Saints Peter (the dedicatee of the original cathedral church) and Wulfstan.[90]

It was probably King John's recourse to St Wulfstan which prompted his son Henry III to turn to other English saints – notably Edward, of course, but also Edmund. John is known to have read romanticized English history[91] and although he would not have considered himself an Englishman in the modern sense of the word, he did travel extensively throughout his realm, and governed it energetically, if arbitrarily. By the later twelfth century, even the uppermost tiers of society were taking an active interest in their English predecessors; John's trust in Wulfstan is but one manifestation of a much wider phenomenon. Most likely he became aware of Wulfstan through his reading, although some prompting from Bishop Mauger, the former royal physician, is conjectural.

Wulfstan featured in the popular literature of the thirteenth and early fourteenth centuries as the archetypal "little man" who was derided and bullied by authority figures but was always vindicated in the outcome; these tales reflect little of the historic Wulfstan, and all owe their origins, sometimes at several removes, to the story first composed by Osbert de Clare. The barely literate character of these tales bears slight resemblance to the actual bishop, but what did survive was the legend of his "simplicity."[92] On a more serious and genuinely popular level, he was

Wendover, *Flores Historiarum*, ed. H. G. Hewlett, 3 vols (1886–9), II, p. 196. On the cortege which accompanied the king's body to Worcester, see the Barnwell Annals, in *Memoriale Fratris Walteri de Coventria*, ed. W. Stubbs, 2 vols (1872–3), II, p. 232.

[88] *Vita Wulfstani*, p. 185.

[89] Annals of Worcester Cathedral Priory, pp. 407, 409. The annals survive only in a late text (ibid., xxxv) and the arrangement of the tombs was probably that of 1218. The king's tomb-effigy, dating from about 1232, depicts him flanked by miniature figures of Saints Wulfstan and Oswald, censing him: see P. Draper, "King John and St. Wulfstan," *Journal of Medieval History*, 10 (1984), pp. 41–50, esp. pp.41–2.

[90] Annals of Worcester Cathedral Priory, pp. 409–10.

[91] *Rotuli Litterarum Clausarum in Turri Londiniensi asservati (1204–27)*, I, p. 29. See also Mason, "St. Wulfstan's staff," p. 162 and notes 77–9.

[92] Mason, "St. Wulfstan's staff," pp. 166–9.

revered throughout Mercia, the Welsh Marches and Wales itself as a mediator of physical healing, and as a spiritual champion who could rescue his devotees from shipwreck and other dangers.[93] Clerical leaders from the later twelfth century onwards, notably St Thomas Becket himself, and Stephen Langton, archbishop of Canterbury (1207–28), prized relics of Wulfstan. In 1163 Archbishop Thomas claimed as his fee for participating in the translation of St Edward in Westminster Abbey the tombstone in which St Wulfstan's staff was said to have lodged,[94] and Archbishop Stephen secured the right arm of Wulfstan during his translation in 1218.[95] To them, Wulfstan's defiance of William the Conqueror was the key point. Wulfstan therefore came to be seen in varying lights by those who had never met him, and who did not know of his real spirituality and pastoral achievement.[96] Even at Worcester itself, he perhaps came to be revered chiefly as a wonder-worker, and in the twelfth century, the very portrait on his tomb took on such connotations.[97] The legend of his staff had great appeal. It was included in two cycles of paintings commissioned for the cathedral in the thirteenth century,[98] and also in a window in the cloister, perhaps dating from the earlier fifteenth century.[99]

It can be argued that few people, in any age, truly understand even their close friends and associates. Wulfstan experienced a good deal of browbeating in his earlier years, and as he aged, found that his cherished values were rejected by many of the rising generation among his chapter and *familia*. Yet he was also regarded with warmth by those who appreciated his true worth. The riddle which is an affectionate play on the name of Wulfstan was devised by one of the scribes of Hemming's cartulary.[100] Some of the recorded miracles also show that after Wulfstan's death, many of the poorer laity of his diocese put their faith in his affectionate concern for their well-being.[101] At various times in his life

[93] *Vita Wulfstani*, pp. xlviii–lii, 115–88.
[94] Continuation of the *De Gestis Regum* in *The Historical Works of Gervase of Canterbury*, ed. W. Stubbs, 2 vols (1880), II, p. 285. The writer stated that the story of the staff occurred in Wulfstan's *Life*, which may indicate the existence of a popular version, probably in French verse.
[95] *The Historical Works of Gervase of Canterbury*, II, p. 298.
[96] Mason, "St. Wulfstan's staff," pp. 169–71.
[97] *Vita Wulfstani*, p. 162.
[98] R. Flower, "A Metrical Life of St. Wulfstan of Worcester," *The National Library of Wales Journal*, 1 (1939–40), pp. 119–30, esp. pp. 125–7,
[99] Ibid., pp. 128–9.
[100] *Hemingi Chartularium*, I, p. 217.
[101] *Vita Wulfstani*, p. 162. R. C. Finucane, *Miracles and Pilgrims: popular beliefs in Medieval England* (1977), pp. 131, 169. Analysis of the recorded miracles indicates that Wulfstan's cult was almost equally popular with men and women, mainly from the lowest

the bishop enjoyed the support of a wide range of people; assertive, outgoing men such as King Harold, Abbot Ethelwig and Geoffrey of Coutances, besides others such as Nicholas, Eilmer and Bishop Robert, whose clerical conditioning led them to appreciate his spiritual qualities. Through the eyes of Nicholas, William of Malmesbury in his turn came to appreciate the calibre of Wulfstan's spirituality. William, in his prologue to the Latin *Life*, expressed a hope that those who read it would try to follow in the bishop's footsteps as Wulfstan followed in those of Christ.[102]

Those reading of Wulfstan's life almost nine hundred years after his time can at best have only a fragmentary understanding of the bishop. So much of his true portrait is still missing when all the surviving evidence is pieced together. Our interpretation of events may be very different from that of his contemporaries, or of other generations than ours, who try to understand the man in his environment.[103] There are inevitable difficulties in grasping the constraints of the harsh world in which he lived. The repeated political crises, the discipline of the religious life, and the absence of many amenities of physical comfort which are commonplace today, all combined to mould the man in his environment. At times Wulfstan seems excessively authoritarian, driving himself and others in a way that few now would tolerate. But as a dedicated soldier of Christ, he performed his duty as he understood it. On other occasions, Wulfstan's love of God, and his compassionate response to those around him, come to life even in cold print. Within the constraints of his time and vocation, he strove to follow in the footsteps of his Saviour.

levels of society. Those whose domicile is known chiefly lived within a 40–mile radius of Worcester. Clergy of any rank are not strongly represented among successful petitioners.

[102] *Vita Wulfstani*, p. 3.

[103] For a discussion of the problems facing interpreters of earlier medieval sources, see Eleanor Searle, "Possible History," *Speculum*, 61 (1986), pp. 779–86.

Appendix
Sources for the Life of St Wulfstan

Wulfstan's life is better documented than those of most of his contempo-
ries, even those who attained high office. He was the last surviving
English bishop. His saintly character and his activities, his policies and
priorities represented landmarks in a changing monastic world. Soon
after his death, a full-scale biography was written as a reminder of
Wulfstan's sanctity for those who had known him, and for those who
were subsequently admitted to the community which he had done so
much to build up. Wulfstan himself believed firmly in the value of
documentation, instilling in his monks the need to preserve old records,
and to keep a proper chronicle. Inevitably his name recurs in such works
continued after his death. Throughout his long career as bishop of
Worcester, his activities were also intermittently reflected in royal
administrative documents, both those directed to him, and those which
he witnessed. In the twelfth century and the thirteenth, further biographical works were written to publicize his growing cult more widely, but
their hagiographical content is progressively more predominant. They
have very limited value as sources for Wulfstan's life, although they are a
useful quarry for social and literary historians.

The English Life of St Wulfstan, *by Coleman*

Even in the lifetime of Wulfstan, the monks of Worcester perceived their
bishop as a holy man. It is uderstandable that those who had known him
would want to transmit their perception to posterity. The writing of the
biographies of notable clerics was a feature of the church reform
movement of the later tenth century[1] which in some important respects
continued to imbue life at Worcester a hundred years later. In the late

---

[1]Antonia Gransden, *Historical Writing in England c.550 to c.1307* (1974), pp.79–87.

eleventh century, there was a new wave of ecclesiastical biographies, usually written when a religious community hoped to promote the cult of the deceased.[2] In the case of Saint Wulfstan, it is conjectural whether the impetus to compose a biography came from the monk Coleman himself rather than from a chapter at Worcester now dominated by a Norman bishop as well as by a long-entrenched Norman prior. The initiative is more likely to have been that of Coleman, rather than that of the worldly Bishop Samson, who was, though, astute enough to see the advantage likely to accrue to Worcester if a successful cult developed around his predecessor.

Coleman had been chaplain to Wulfstan during the last fifteen years of the latter's life, and had also served as his chancellor.[3] This combination of close and confidential proximity to the subject of his work would both provide him with the information on which to base a well-informed *Life* and also give him a clear insight into the bishop's character and personal values. The exact date of composition is uncertain. Coleman died in 1113,[4] and administrative commitments are unlikely to have left him with much leisure for literary activity immediately after Wulfstan's death in January 1095.[5] In 1093 Coleman was appointed prior of the revived priory of Westbury-on-Trym, in Gloucestershire, and he continued there until this daughter-house was disbanded by Wulfstan's successor, Samson (1096–1112).[6] On his return to Worcester, Coleman would probably be something of an elder-statesman among the monks, no longer pressurized by formal duties, and with the leisure to write his *Life of Saint Wulfstan*. Rejoining the Worcester community from the outside, as it were, Coleman was perhaps struck by the increasing impact of Normanization under the rule of the new bishop. Even though this was not the prime cause of his decision to write, it probably contributed to the underlying tone of his biography, which emphasized Wulfstan's promulgation of traditional values. In many respects, Bishop Samson was the antithesis of Wulfstan.[7] Recognition of the contrasting personalities and lifestyles of the bishops, combined with resentment at demotion

[2]Ibid., pp. 105–35.
[3]*The Cartulary of Worcester Cathedral Priory (Register I)*, ed. R. R. Darlington (1968), no. 3; *The Vita Wulfstani of William of Malmesbury*, ed. R. R. Darlington (1928), p. 2.
[4]*Florentii Wigorniensis monachi Chronicon ex Chronicis*, ed. B. Thorpe, 2 vols (1848–9), II, p. 66.
[5]*Vita Wulfstani*, pp. xliii, 61.
[6]Ibid., pp. xxxix–xl, 52; *De Gestis Pontificum Anglorum*, ed. N. E. S. A. Hamilton (1870), p. 290. On Wulfstan's revival of Westbury, see *Hemingi Chartularium ecclesiae Wigorniensis*, ed. T. Hearne, 2 vols (1723), pp. 421–4.
[7]V. H. Galbraith, "Notes on the career of Samson, bishop of Worcester," *English Historical Review*, 82 (1967), pp. 86–101, reprinted in V. H. Galbraith, *Kings and Chroniclers: essays in English medieval history* (1982), pp. IV, 86–101, esp. p. 86.

from being a prior, would give added incentive to Coleman to shape his work as he did.

In writing his *Life* of Wulfstan, Coleman was consciously reviving an English tradition, which can be dated back to the eighth century, whereby within a few years of the death of any remarkable bishop, his life was written up by someone who had been in contact with him. The Tenth-Century Reform of English monasticism had been the work of several eminent clerics: Dunstan, Oswald and Ethelwold, whose *Lives* had borne witness to their merits and achievement, but the ensuing generations witnessed the production of little in the way of clerical biography.[8] Wulfstan himself treasured the biographies of Dunstan and Oswald,[9] and Coleman's inspiration was probably this earlier wave of writing, rather than the new wave of works which contemporaries were writing about other eminent clerics around the turn of the century.[10] The influence of this Anglo-Saxon tradition of ecclesiastical biography on Coleman's work is quite marked. He perhaps modelled his work on Elfric's *Life of St Ethelwold*, with a similar division into three sections: (1) the early life and education of his subject, to the time of his consecration; (2) episcopate; (3) character, personal habits and miracles, both those performed in his lifetime and posthumously. Wulfstan is therefore presented in the same mould as the great figures of the Tenth-Century Reform.[11] In Wulfstan's biography, though, there is an additional element, introduced as a result of Wulfstan's struggle to secure the lands and rights of the church of Worcester against the church of York. His eventual triumph was extended by Coleman into a wider emphasis on the independence of Worcester from this archbishopric.[12]

It is remarkable that Coleman chose to write his biography in English, since the *Lives* of earlier distinguished clerics had usually been written in Latin. Annotations, in English, written by Coleman in the margins of several Worcester manuscripts suggest that his preferred literary language was English.[13] At the time he wrote the *Life*, a considerable number of the Worcester monks would probably have been native English, or, in some cases, the sons of mixed marriages between French-speakers and

[8]Gransden, *Historical Writing in England*, pp. 67–91.
[9]*Vita Wulfstani*, pp. 25, 79.
[10]Ibid., p. x. On the new wave of biographies, see Gransden, *Historical Writing in England*, pp. 87–91.
[11]Gransden, *Historical Writing in England*, pp. 87–8.
[12]*Vita Wulfstani*, pp. xxv–xxxi; pp. 19–20, 24–5; Gransden, *Historical Writing in England*, p. 89.
[13]N. R. Ker, *Catalogue of Manuscripts containing Anglo-Saxon* (1957), p. lvi.

Englishwomen, for whom English would be their first language.[14] For Coleman, the English language perhaps seemed the appropriate medium through which to convey a record of an eminent English cleric, and of a traditional lifestyle which was now under threat.[15]

The exact contents of Coleman's biography are now lost, because this work was sent to Pope Innocent III, along with other evidence in support of Wulfstan's canonization.[16] It is not known to have been returned to England, and exhaustive searches in the Vatican Library have failed to produce it there.[17] While Pope Innocent III accepted the authenticity of this English *Life*,[18] it is questionable whether any of his entourage would have been able to read it. The monks of Worcester could the more readily part with Coleman's English-language biography because, long before the canonization proceedings in 1203, they had possessed a Latin version, better suited to publicizing Wulfstan's cult in the world at large.

The Vita Wulfstani *of William of Malmesbury*

William, a monk of Malmesbury in Wiltshire, was a celebrated writer in the early twelfth century. His work was based on detailed research, and, thanks to his family background, he had the added advantage of being able to read documents in English.[19] His extensive travels, which enabled him to unearth old documentary source material, infringed the monastic vow of stability, and it is surmised that they were facilitated by Queen Matilda. As a descendant of the English royal house, she had a vested interest in Malmesbury's first major work, the *De Gestis Regum*, which recounted the deeds of her ancestors.[20] Research for a companion

---

[14]See Cecily Clark, "Women's names in post-Conquest England: observations and speculations," *Speculum*, 53 (1978), pp. 223–51, esp. pp. 224–5. The chronicler Orderic Vitalis, born in Atcham, Shropshire, of one such mixed union, was still unable to understand spoken French at the age of ten: *The Ecclesiastical History of Orderic Vitalis*, ed. and transl. Marjorie Chibnall, 6 vols (1969–80), VI, p. 554.

[15]Elizabeth A. McIntyre, "Early Twelfth-Century Worcester Cathedral Priory, with special reference to the manuscripts there" (Oxford University D.Phil. thesis, 1978), pp. 137–8; Gransden, *Historical Writing in England*, p. 88.

[16]Bull of Pope Innocent III, dated 14 May 1203, printed following the prologue to the second book of miracles of Saint Wulfstan, *Vita Wulfstani*, p. 149; *Patrologiae Latina*, ed. J. P. Migne and others, vol. 215 (1891), no. LXII (137), p. 59.

[17]Correspondence on the search for Coleman's *Life* is in Worcester Cathedral Library, Additional MS 218.

[18]Papal Bull of 14 May 1203, *Vita Wulfstani*, p. 149.

[19]Rodney M. Thomson, "William of Malmesbury as Historian and Man of Letters," *Journal of Ecclesiastical History*, 29 (1978), pp. 387–413, reprinted in R. M. Thomson, *William of Malmesbury* (1987), pp. 11–38, esp. pp. 12–13, 15, 19–20.

[20]Ibid., p. 15.

volume, the *De Gestis Pontificum*, a survey of the achievements of English bishops, brought William to Worcester. Here he made use of Coleman's *Life* of Bishop Wulfstan and became acquainted with Prior Nicholas (c.1113–24), formerly a pupil of the bishop. Later, he was invited by Prior Warin (c.1124–c.1142) and the monks of Worcester to make a Latin translation.[21] After Wulfstan's death, few Worcester manuscripts were written or copied in English.[22] If the monks of Worcester hoped to spread the fame of Wulfstan, in the hope of promoting his cult, they could not do this simply by making copies even of excerpts from Coleman's text. The royal court had used only Latin in official documents from the mid-1070s, and consequently there was now no longer any central authority dictating the form of "received" English. The scribes at each centre which continued to produce manuscripts in English now wrote them in the local spoken dialect, and such texts would usually be difficult to follow outside a narrow radius. Material intended for a wider audience, and particularly anything so dignified as an "official" episcopal biography, could best be disseminated if it was composed in Latin, a language which remained standardized in its written form.[23]

The invitation to William of Malmesbury to make a translation of Coleman's *Life* of Wulfstan came at a time when miracles were persistently being linked with his name, and the publication of his cult on a widespread basis evidently seemed desirable. In a prefatory letter attached to the *Vita Wulfstani*, William of Malmesbury stated that he had agreed to make this translation in order to help keep alive the memory of Wulfstan.[24] It is conjectural whether the religious houses targeted for receipt of this publicity material were those with which Wulfstan had established links of confraternity.[25]

William of Malmesbury's *Vita Wulfstani* now survives in only one manuscript, BL MS Cotton Claudius A.V. This volume is a composite one, containing three separate works brought together later, probably by William Cotton in the early seventeenth century. The first work is a fourteenth-century Peterborough chronicle (folios 2–45), which once

---

[21]Ibid., pp. 15, 19–20. *Vita Wulfstani*, pp. ix–x; Gransden, *Historical Writing in England*, p. 87 and note 156; pp. 167–73.

[22]McIntyre, "Early Twelfth-Century Worcester Cathedral Priory," pp. 92–3.

[23]M. T. Clanchy, *From Memory to Written Record: England 1066–1272* (1979), pp. 165–7, 169–71.

[24]*Vita Wulfstani*, p. 1.

[25]*Diplomatarium Anglicum Aevi Saxonici*, ed. and transl. B. Thorpe (1865), p. 615; William Thomas, *A Survey of the Cathedral Church of Worcester* (1736), appendix, nos 2–3, pp. 3–4; *Cartulary of Worcester Cathedral Priory*, nos 304–5; *Vita Wulfstani*, p. xl.

belonged to the library of Peterborough abbey. The second work is a twelfth-century copy of William of Malmesbury's *De Gestis Pontificum* (folios 46–134a) which belonged to the Benedictine priory of Belvoir (Lincs), a cell of St Albans. The third work (folios 135–99) is a later twelfth- or early thirteenth-century collection of four saints' lives. The pressmark, *liber cciii primus*, indicates that it belonged at one time to the Cistercian abbey of Holme Cultram, Cumberland. This concludes with the *Vita Wulfstani* on folios 160 verso to 198 recto, column 1. There follow a prefatory letter, and a prologue, on folios 198 recto, column 2 to 199 verso, column 2. The *Vita Wulfstani* is well written, in double columns, but has very little ornamentation. The prefatory letter and prologue, which are restored to their proper place in the modern published edition, are the work of the scribe who also began, and concluded, the main text, although the bulk of that is in a second hand.[26]

The author identifies himself as "William" in the prefatory letter, and refers to his *De Gestis Regum* and "our other writings," so that the identification with William of Malmesbury can be safely assumed.[27] It is unlikely that this late twelfth-century copy is substantially different from William's author-manuscript, written perhaps sixty or more years earlier than the text which now survives. Internal consistency suggests that there was no drastic revision. The *Abridged Lives*, discussed below, present few facts which are not in the surviving text of the *Vita*, apart from supplying the contents of one folio which is now missing from the Cotton manuscript. Occasionally, textual readings are also better in these abridgements.[28] Since there are some textual variations between the various *Abridged Lives*, it may be assumed that several copies were made of the *Vita Wulfstani* itself.

In his prefatory letter, William claims that his *Vita* is a close Latin translation of Coleman's *Life*.[29] There are textual indications that William did generally follow Coleman's structure, but he used editorial discretion in several respects: (1) Coleman had translated into English, and incorporated, passages from Gregory the Great, but William now restored these to Latin. (2) William omitted the names of witnesses to miracles. Some of these people would have died since Coleman wrote, and in any case, it would be pointless to cite Worcestershire residents in a

---

[26]N. R. Ker, *Medieval Libraries of Great Britain: a list of surviving books*, second edn (1964), pp. 9, 102, 151, *Vita Wulfstani*, p. vii and note 4.

[27]*Vita Wulfstani*, p. viii and note 1, pp. 19, 56.

[28]*Ibid., pp. xx–xxii;* McIntyre, "Early Twelfth-Century Worcester Cathedral Priory," pp. 141–2.

[29]This statement is accepted by Rodney Thomson, *William of Malmesbury*, pp. 20, 45 and note 45. See, however D. H. Farmer, "Two Biographies by William of Malmesbury," in *Latin Biography*, ed. T. A. Dorey (1967), pp. 157–76, esp. pp. 165–74.

work intended for wider circulation. (3) Coleman had ended his first book with Wulfstan's promotion to the bishopric, in 1062, but William of Malmesbury moved the break to the Norman Conquest – on the consequences of which he had strong feelings. Coleman, writing a traditional work of hagiography, for a local audience, would perceive Wulfstan's election and consecration as a high-spot at which a natural break could best be made. William, with his greater literary experience, and flair for the dramatic, would see the potential effects to be gained by breaking at 1066. The implications of changing this divide would be to shift the emphasis of the later section from Wulfstan's pastoral activities as bishop to Wulfstan facing up to the consequences of the Norman settlement. (4) William exercised a more general editorial discretion, enlivening Coleman's work by suppressing long passages of rhetoric and quotations from saints' lives, besides deleting words and passages where Coleman digressed to describe the episcopal office as such.[30]

These changes might be viewed simply as the exercise of editorial discretion, the up-dating of the work of a previous generation for a wider audience. Yet the revisions incorporated in the *Vita Wulfstani* go some way towards portraying Wulfstan as the wonder-working holy man, almost in the role of an Old Testament prophet, triumphing over the nefarious invaders, and spokesman for native values. It is questionable whether the monks of Worcester would have dictated – or even anticipated – precisely these changes. Probably rather it was a case of their calling in a well-known expert, with whom the chapter had already had dealings, and allowing him discretion. It might even be wondered whether the prefatory letter to Prior Warin and the monks was to some extent a piece of self-justification for an edited translation which, in spirit at least, had parted company with the original on which it was based.

Further alterations to Coleman's material were the result of a friendly relationship which William had established, on an earlier research visit, with the then Prior, Nicholas, who had been a favourite pupil of Wulfstan. Nicholas evidently supplied William with additional anecdotes about the bishop, since he is several times cited as a source.[31] Since these stories were not, apparently, in the English *Life* we might infer that Coleman wrote largely from his own recollections, and according to his own understanding of his subject, perhaps declining to accept for inclusion episodes or viewpoint suggested by the young generation. Having lost his various offices, he perahps preferred to distance himself

[30]*Vita Wulfstani*, p. ix and note 2, pp. 23, 58. For William of Malmesbury's jaundiced views of the impact of the Norman Conquest upon English life, see his *De Gestis Regum Anglorum*, ed. W. Stubbs, 2 vols (1887, 1889), I, p. 278.
[31]*Vita Wulfstani*, p. ix, pp. 51–2, 54, 56–7.

from the new high-flyers, particularly those who claimed personal insights into the views of the former bishop, notably Wulfstan's protégé, Nicholas, who had been seconded to Canterbury to train in the Norman style of monasticism.[32] These tensions may be hypothetical, but in any event, the nature of Nicholas's personal recollections struck a different note from that which Coleman evidently tried to convey. The use of Nicholas's material is clearest in Book III of the *Vita*, the section which deals with the saintly aspects of Wulfstan: his conduct, humility and prayer life. It is interesting that Nicholas, the pupil, rather than Coleman, the chaplain, is the chief source cited for anecdotes illustrating this section.[33]

Several episodes in Wulfstan's life feature the extrovert episcopal clerk Frewin, who later became a monk of Worcester. He is presumably the original source for these incidents, but since they occurred while he was a clerk, and hence subject to the chancellor, it is likely that these stories were included in Coleman's *Life*, rather than told later to William of Malmesbury.

The *Vita Wulfstani* is silent about some aspects of Wulfstan's activities which are known from other sources, probably on the grounds that such topics had no place in a work of hagiography. Litigation receives little mention, and there is no record of Wulfstan's part in the suppression of the rebellions of 1075 and 1088. Moreover, both Coleman and William of Malmesbury would have been reluctant to depict the bishop's support of the new Norman dynasty. On the other hand, Wulfstan's close relationship with the last English king, Harold Godwinson, is emphasized.[34]

William of Malmesbury stated that he completed the *Vita Wulfstani* in six weeks, a creditable achievement for a translation of this length, taking into account the work of editing, incorporating new material, and writing out the whole in formal style.[35] Moreover, a Benedictine monk himself, William was also under obligation to attend the daily Offices.[36]

[32]Ibid., p. 57.
[33]McIntyre, "Early Twelfth-Century Worcester Cathedral Priory," pp. 131, 133.
[34]Ibid., p. 136. On Wulfstan's good relations with Harold Godwinson, see *Vita Wulfstani*, pp. 13, 18, 22–3.
[35]*Vita Wulfstani*, p. 67. On William's small and elegant handwriting, see N. R. Ker, "William of Malmesbury's Handwriting," *English Historical Review*, 59 (1944), pp. 371–6; reprinted in N. R. Ker, *Books, Collectors and Libraries: studies in the medieval heritage*, ed. A. G. Watson (1985), pp. 61–6; and also R. M. Thomson, "William's Scriptorium," *William of Malmesbury*, pp. 76–97.
[36]See however Thomson, *William of Malmesbury*, p. 4, where it is suggested that William "must have been released from a good deal of regular discipline" in order to compose his major works, at least.

The first complete, critical edition of the *Vita Wulfstani* was published in 1928, and has twice been translated.[37] The *Vita Wulfstani* is by far the fullest source for the life of Saint Wulfstan.

Hemming

A second, short, biography was inserted by the Worcester monk Hemming in the cartulary which he began to compile on the instructions of Bishop Wulfstan. This *Life*, written in Old English, is given with a Latin translation.[38] Hemming's monastic career at Worcester perhaps began earlier than those of Coleman. He is cited as an informant of Coleman in the *Vita Wulfstani*, where he is styled sub-prior.[39] Hemming's cartulary was intended to record Worcester's title-deeds, and more especially those which had been assigned for the income of the monks.[40] This biography recounts Wulfstan's successive tenure of the various offices in the priory. It provides useful corroborative evidence on names and chronology,[41] and while it lacks the perception of William's *Vita*, it is a salutary reminder that a monastic community particularly esteemed any head who could safeguard their landed interests. While Hemming began preparing his cartulary in Wulfstan's lifetime, it is likely that much of this manuscript was written during the episcopate of Bishop Samson.[42] In addition to the biographical section, there are other passages relating to

[37]*Vita Wulfstani*. This volume also contains all but one of the Abridged Lives, and the official account of Wulfstan's miracles and translation. For earlier editions of parts of the texts, see ibid., p. vii, and for the excluded *Abridged Life*, p. xxii. The first translation was by J. H. F. Peile, *William of Malmesbury's Life of St. Wulfstan bishop of Worcester, now rendered into English* (1934). The *Life* is also included in *Three Lives of the Last Englishmen*, transl. and introd. by Michael Swanton (1984), pp. 91–148.

[38]*Hemingi Chartularium*, II, pp. 403–5 (Old English *Life*); pp. 405–8 (Latin *Life*). A separate manuscript of the Latin version existed at Worcester down to the early eighteenth century. It was published in *Anglia Sacra*, ed. H. Wharton, 2 vols (1691), I, pp. 541–2, and later by G. Hickes, *Linguarum vett. septentrionalium thesaurus grammaticocriticus et archaeologicus*, 2 vols in 3 (1703–1705), I, pp. 175–6. A modern translation of Hemming's *Life* is printed by I. Atkins, "The Church of Worcester from the Eighth to the Twelfth Centuries," Part II, *The Antiquaries Journal*, 20 (1940), pp. 208–9.

[39]*Vita Wulfstani*, p. 7.

[40]N. R. Ker, "Hemming's Cartulary: a description of the two Worcester cartularies in Cotton Tiberius A.XIII," in *Studies in Medieval History Presented to F. M. Powicke*, ed. R. W. Hunt, W. A. Pantin and R. W. Southern (1948), pp. 49–75, esp. p. 63. (This work is reprinted in Ker, *Books, Collectors and Libraries*, pp. 31–59.) Galbraith, "Notes on the career of Samson," pp. 86–101, esp. p. 98.

[41]*Vita Wulfstani*, p. xix and note 5.

[42]Ker, "Hemming's Cartulary," p. 51; Galbraith, "Notes on the career of Samson," p. 96.

Wulfstan's administration, notably the much-quoted account of his sorting the ancient charters relating to Worcester's lands, and his orders for their preservation.[43] The cartulary compiled by Hemming forms the second part of BL MS Cotton Tiberius A.XIII, folios 119–42,144–52 and 154–200. It is now bound together with another Worcester cartulary, compiled some generations previously.[44] At least three main scribes worked on Hemming's own cartulary, but Hemming, who names himself in the work, appears to be its main author. His own sections include both the *Enucleatio*, the rationale underlying the composition, and also the biography of Wulfstan.[45] The text was first published in 1723.[46]

William of Malmesbury: The De Gestis Regum and De Gestis Pontificum

William of Malmesbury in his two major works, *De Gestis Regum Anglorum* and *De Gestis Pontificum Anglorum*[47] includes some passages relating to Wulfstan. The first edition of the *De Gestis Regum* was written before 1118, and the first edition of the *De Gestis Pontificum* was completed in 1125.[48] The relevant passages in the two major works are evidently based on documents which he saw, and traditions current in Worcester, when he was gathering reseach material there. Most of the relevant passages in these works are closely parallel to material in the *Vita Wulfstani*, which is some years later in date.[49] Since the *De Gestis Regum* was designed to glorify the kings of England, relevant entries on Wulfstan are understandably brief. The *De Gestis Pontificum*, on the other hand, was specifically designed to recall the memorable deeds of former English bishops. It contains an extensive passage on Wulfstan, evidently a comprehensive summary of Coleman's *Life*, with some additional items of information, chiefly hagiographical in tone.[50] Since

[43]*Hemingi Chartularium*, pp. 282–6; Galbraith, "Notes on the career of Samson," p. 98.

[44]Ker, "Hemming's Cartulary," pp. 49–75.

[45]Ibid., pp. 57, 72.

[46]*Hemingi Chartularium*.

[47]William of Malmesbury, *De Gestis Regum Anglorum* and *De Gestis Pontificum Anglorum*.

[48]Thomson, *William of Malmesbury*, p. 4.

[49]*Vita Wulfstani*, pp. viii–ix. Thomson, *William of Malmesbury*, pp. 5, 15.

[50]*Vita Wulfstani*, p. ix; William of Malmesbury, *De Gestis Pontificum Anglorum*, pp. 278–89. The *Vita Wulfstani* dates from between 1124 and 1142 (Thomson, *William of Malmesbury*, p. 5, following Darlington, *Vita Wulfstani*, pp. viii–ix). It is not apparent that William had begun it before completing the first edition of the *De Gestis Pontificum Anglorum*.

this work was not particulary composed for a Worcester readership, William had no qualms about recounting Wulfstan's part in the rebellion of 1088,[51] but he does not relate Wulfstan's defensive role in 1075. The *De Gestis Pontificum* also incorporates passages on clerical contemporaries of Wulfstan, and notably on Archbishop Ealdred and Bishop Robert.[52]

Chronicle of John of Worcester

An exiled Irish monk, Marianus Scotus, compiled a world history, working first at Fulda, and then at Mainz, during the second half of the eleventh century. Shortly after his death, in 1082 or 1083, his chronicle was brought to England by Robert, bishop of Hereford. He made it available to Wulfstan, who ordered the English monk, John, to continue it. At some point in Henry I's reign, Orderic Vitalis visited Worcester, and saw the up-dated chronicle. He noted that John had both incorporated additional older material, and had also continued it with information on the reigns of the Norman kings. The resulting work draws heavily on both Bede and the *Anglo-Saxon Chronicle*, in its earlier sections.[53]

Examination of the episodes common to the *Chronicle of John of Worcester* and the *Vita Wulfstani* demonstrates that neither work is dependent upon the other, but that they are both following Coleman, in much the same order, John summarising and William of Malmesbury translating.[54] The *Chronicle* also contains several passages on Wulfstan which are not found in the *Vita Wulfstani*, and had probably also been excluded by Coleman from his *Life*. This additional material perhaps derived in part from documentary sources; partly, perhaps, from local tradition, and perhaps also from some version of the *Anglo-Saxon Chronicle*, most probably a version similar to the D-text which now survives. Some entries also derive from the *De Gestis Regum* and *De Gestis Pontificum* of William of Malmesbury.[55] A further source is the

[51]William of Malmesbury, *De Gestis Pontificum Anglorum*, p. 285; McIntyre,"Early Twelfth-Century Worcester Cathedral Priory," p. 132.
[52]William of Malmesbury, *De Gestis Pontificum Anglorum*, pp. 251–3.
[53]*Orderic Vitalis*, II, pp. 186–8; the late R. R. Darlington and P. M. McGurk, "The *Chronicon ex Chronicis* of 'Florence' of Worcester and its Use of Sources for English History before 1066," *Anglo-Norman Studies V*, ed. R. Allen Brown (1983), pp. 185–96; M. Brett, "John of Worcester and his contemporaries," *The Writing of History in the Middle Ages: essays presented to R. W. Southern*, ed. R. H. C. Davis and J. M. Wallace-Hadrill (1981), pp. 101–26.
[54]*Vita Wulfstani*, pp. xi–xiv, where the comparable passages are set out in parallel columns.
[55]Ibid., p. xviii and note 2.

Historia Novorum (*History of Recent Events*) by the Canterbury monk, Eadmer, who had also drawn on materials from Worcester.[56] John's circuitous use of material of local origin suggests that he had more confidence in the prose of well-established writers than in his own. His diffidence perhaps arose from long-standing orders to conflate the work of celebrated writers of earlier periods into an authoritative-sounding whole, an exercise which might leave little scope for independent judgement or expression.

The most extended passage in the *Chronicle of John of Worcester* relating to Wulfstan is the compressed biography under the year 1062, when he was elected to the bishopric, although this passage derives from William of Malmesbury's *Vita Wulfstani*.[57] There is also a substantial obituary notice under 1095, and accounts of Wulfstan's part in the suppression of the rebellions of 1075 and 1088. These two incidents are not found in the *Vita Wulfstani*, and were probably excluded by William, or by Coleman before him, either as displaying regrettable support for the Norman kings, or as being unsuitable for inclusion in a work of hagiography.[58]

The *Chronicle of John of Worcester* therefore ranks as only a minor independent source on Wulfstan. Some factual errors probably result from the entries concerning him being written down a generation or more after his death.[59] This lack of originality, and even of accuracy, is the more striking in view of Orderic's statement that John had been a member of the community at Worcester since boyhood, and that he had been commissioned by Wulfstan himself as writer of the official chronicle of the house.[60] Yet it may be that John never knew the bishop well, and was perhaps not in a position to know the full details of matters concerning the bishop as they arose. In Wulfstan's later years, there were about fifty monks at Worcester.[61] Since John was still working in 1140,[62] it is arguable that he was still in his teens at the time of Wulfstan's death, and he was perhaps never closely acquainted with the bishop in the way that the older and more senior monks, such as Coleman, Hemming and Nicholas, were. The original choice of John as continuator of the

---

[56]Ibid., p. xvi and note 2, where the borrowings from Eadmer are set out in detail; *Historical Writing in England*, pp. 129–30, 143; R. W. Southern, *Saint Anselm and his Biographer: a study of monastic life and thought 1059–c.1130* (1966), pp. 283–4.

[57]*Florentii Wigorniensis monachi Chronicon*, I, pp. 218–21. The reliance upon Coleman is demonstrated by Darlington, *Vita Wulfstani*, pp.xi–xiv.

[58] *Florentii Wigorniensis monachi Chronicon*, II, pp. 35–7. For the notices of the rebellions, see II, p. 11, 24–6. See also *Vita Wulfstani*, p. xiv and notes.

[59]*Vita Wulfstani*, p. xviii.

[60]*Orderic Vitalis*, II, p. 186.

[61]*Cartulary of Worcester*, no. 3.

[62]Darlington and McGurk, "The *Chronicon ex Chronicis*," p. 185.

chronicle perhaps resulted from little more than his being a biddable young person, who could be entrusted to copy annals clearly and conscientiously. In the earlier stages of his work, research for John's chronicle was apparently largely undertaken by a senior monk, Florence. An obituary of this man, under the annal for 1118, pays tribute to his industry and knowledge, which formed the basis of John's *Chronicle*.[63]

The chief manuscript of the *Chronicle of John of Worcester* is Corpus Christi, Oxford, MS 157, the ancestor of the other four surviving manuscripts of this work. The *Chronicle* was edited in the nineteenth century, and the section ascribed to John was re-edited in 1908.[64] The *Chronicle* was conflated, soon after its completion, with texts of the *De Gestis Regum* and *De Gestis Pontificum*, into a further chronicle, BL MS Cotton Vitellius C.VIII; but episodes relating to Wulfstan in this work are entirely derivative from its sources.[65]

The Abridged Lives of Saint Wulfstan

In the latter part of the twelfth century, it was desirable that Wulfstan's cult and growing number of miracles should be publicized as widely as possible. There are indications that copies of the Latin *Vita Wulfstani* had circulated to some extent, in slightly varying texts,[66] but a more concise version of it was calculated to be better suited to this new publicity drive, and an *Abridged Life* was accordingly made. The earliest surviving text of this is contained in a thirteenth-century manuscript at Durham: Library of the Dean and Chapter, MS B IV. 39b. The scribe also wrote both the *Life of St Oswald*, which precedes that of Wulfstan in this manuscript, and the ensuing account of the posthumous *Miracles of Saint Wulfstan*. The *Abridged Life* is clearly an abbreviation of William of Malmesbury's translation, but was probably not made from the text which now survives. Its source is likely to have been an earlier manuscript, perhaps even that written by William himself. There are

---

[63]*Florentii Wigorniensis monachi Chronicon*, II, p. 72; *Vita Wulfstani*, p. xvii and note 5; Darlington and McGurk, "The *Chronicon ex Chronicis*," p. 185.

[64]*Florentii Wigorniensis monachi Chronicon*; *The Chronicle of John of Worcester 1118–1140*, ed. J. R. H. Weaver (1908). The whole text is now being re-edited with a parallel translation: R. R. Darlington and P. M. McGurk, *The Chronicle of John of Worcester* (in preparation).

[65]*Vita Wulfstani*, p. xix and note 4.

[66]Ibid., pp. xix–xx; McIntyre, "Early Twelfth-Century Worcester Cathedral Priory," p. 141.

some omissions from the *Vita Wulfstani*, and also some variations, not all of which are erroneous.[67]

It has been suggested, on textual grounds, that the author of this *Abridged Life* was Senatus, who held office as prior of Worcester from 1189 to 1196, and died in 1207.[68] Senatus himself wrote a letter claiming authorship both of this *Abridged Life*, which he evidently composed at an early stage in his career, and of the *Life of St Oswald*.[69] Since the letter of Senatus is addressed to Bishop Roger, who held office between 1164 and 1179,[70] the need for the *Abridged Life* was evidently perceived a generation or more before the flurry of new miracles which preceded Wulfstan's canonization in 1203. This abridgement was probably intended as new official *Life* which would introduce a record of the miracles which had occurred intermittently since Wulfstan's death. The promotion of Worcester's saints during Bishop Roger's episcopate perhaps followed in the wake of Canterbury's great success in promulgating the cult of Thomas Becket.

This *Abridged Life* was copied several times, with increasing degrees of compression. One copy was made into the late thirteenth-century collection of saints' lives which is now BL MS Harley 322. A second copy, made from the Durham manuscript but since lost, was the text from which was copied in turn the version in a fourteenth-century collection of saints' lives from Romsey abbey, now BL MS Lansdowne 436. The ending is a much-summarized version of several concluding chapters in each of the longer abridgements. Another manuscript similar to the Durham one was the text from which was made a very much compressed *Life*, contained in BL MS Cotton Vespasian E.IX. This manuscript also contains the cartulary of Westwood priory, Worcestershire. This *Life*, written in the thirteenth century, probably for the nuns of Westwood, is divided into short lections.[71]

---

[67]*Vita Wulfstani*, pp. xix–xxi; Ker, *Medieval Libraries of Great Britain*, p. 69.

[68]For Senatus, see John Le Neve, *Fasti Ecclesiae Anglicanae 1066–1300: II. Monastic Cathedrals*, compiled by Diana E. Greenway (1971), p. 103; Mary G. Cheney, *Roger, Bishop of Worcester 1164–1179* (1980), pp. 58–69. His authorship of both *Lives* is discussed by Darlington, *Vita Wulfstani*, pp. xx–xxi.

[69]Bodleian MS 633 (1966), f. 197v. This bound manuscript is made up of seven separate parts. The binding is early thirteenth century. One part is a letter book made up of six letters by Senatus, beginning on folios 197, 199v, 202v, 209, 212v, 223. The hand changes at least twice. In the letter in question, the author styles himself *humilis eiusdem ecclesie famulus*. See also R. W. Hunt, "English Learning in the Late Twelfth Century," reprinted from *Transactions of the Royal Historical Society*, fourth series, 19 (1936), pp. 19–42, in *Essays in Medieval History*, ed. R. W. Southern (1968), pp. 106–28; esp. p. 116 and note 4.

[70]Le Neve, *Fasti Ecclesiae Anglicanae II*, p. 99.

[71]*Vita Wulfstani*, pp. xxi–xxii, 68–114.

A composite *Life* was also made, utilizing the section on Wulfstan in the *De Gestis Pontificum*, together with material from the *Chronicle of John of Worcester*, possibly acquired indirectly from the *Chronicle of Roger of Wendover*, and the Durham *Abridged Life and Miracles*.[72]

The Metrical Life of Saint Wulfstan

A codex of Worcester origin, dating from the mid-thirteenth century, contains a *Metrical Life of Saint Wulfstan*, written in 380 Leonine hexameters. It largely comprises episodes derived either from the *Vita Wulfstani* or from the *Abridged Life*. The opening lines state that it was composed at the request of a bishop, who can probably be identified with Walter de Cantelupe (1236–66). Given the likely date of the poem, its style and subject matter, authorship can perhaps be ascribed to Henry of Avranches.[73] This manuscript also contains two shorter poems on Wulfstan, one on his miracles, and the other based on episodes in his career. These shorter poems correspond to two series of verse inscriptions which were composed for scenes, actual and legendary, from the life of Wulfstan which were depicted in murals, or in stained glass, in Worcester cathedral.[74]

While this *Metrical Life* is so derivative as to be only a secondary source for Wulfstan's career, it is a valuable illustration of the ways in which his cult appealed to the popular imagination in the generations following his canonization. The catchy rhymes and racy tone would help imprint his deeds on the memories of those able to read this Latin life – presumably clergy, for the most part – who would then rework the stories for vernacular homilies. In the thirteenth century, Saint Wulfstan was regarded throughout the Welsh Marches and in Wales itself as a powerful healer. This is the probable explanation and perhaps even, in part, a consequence, of the transmission of this manuscript into Wales.[75]

[72]Ibid., p. xxii; *Acta Sanctorum*, ed. J. Bollandus, G. Henschenius et al. (1643–1883), January, II, pp. 246–9, under 19 January; *Nova Legenda Angliae*, ed. C. Horstmann, 2 vols (1901), II, pp. 522–30.

[73]The codex containing the *Metrical Life* of Saint Wulfstan is in the National Library of Wales, Peniarth MS 386 (formerly Hengwrt MS 362). For discussion of the *Life*, see R. Flower, "A Metrical Life of St. Wulfstan of Worcester," *The National Library of Wales Journal*, 1 (1939–40), pp. 119–30, where extracts from the *Life* are published. In a detailed review and commentary on Flower's article, P. Grosjean, *Analecta Bollandiana*, 73 (1955), pp. 259–60, suggests Henry d'Avranches as author of this *Life*.

[74]Flower, "A Metrical Life of St. Wulfstan," pp. 121, 125–7, where these shorter poems are published.

[75]Ibid., p. 119.

The Middle English Life

The continuing popularity of Saint Wulfstan's cult is reflected in the wide circulation of a short English *Life*, first recorded in a fourteenth-century manuscript.[76] Although this too is only a secondary source, its dissemination reflects the continuing appeal of the cult in the later Middle Ages.

The Annals of Worcester Cathedral Priory

These cover the period from the Incarnation of Christ to 1308, with a few later fourteenth-century entries. These annals depend directly upon a set of annals from Waverley abbey, and indirectly upon a lost Winchester set which ran to 1281. In the copy made at Worcester, this derivative material has been supplemented by local information. Almost all of the references directly relating to Wulfstan are derived from the *Chronicle of John of Worcester*. The Worcester annals for the years 1202 to 1266 are apparently independent.[77] These later annals are useful in helping to document the spread of Saint Wulfstan's cult in the thirteenth century.

Other local chronicle sources have little to add. The *History and Cartulary of the Monastery of St Peter's, Gloucester*, provides a few points of supplementary detail.[78] The *Annals of Winchcombe* depend heavily on the *Chronicle of John of Worcester* for the years down to 1181, although they occasionally add brief, independent obituary notices.[79] The *Tewkesbury Annals* have little, if any independent information to add.[80]

[76]This English *Life* is found in five fourteenth-century manuscripts and two fifteenth-century ones. The texts vary in details from one another. Robert of Gloucester has been suggested as the author: *Descriptive Catalogue of Materials relating to the History of Great Britain and Ireland to the end of the reign of Henry VII*, ed. T. D. Hardy, 3 vols (1862, 1865, 1871), II, no. 107, pp. 74–5. For published texts of some of these variants, see *The South English Legendary*, ed. Charlotte d'Evelyn and Anna J. Mill, 3 vols (1956–9), I, pp. 8–15; *The Early South English Legendary*, ed. C. Horstmann (1887), I, pp. 70–7.
[77]The Worcester annals are printed in *Annales Monastici*, ed. H. R. Luard (1869), IV, pp. 355–564. On their sources, see Luard, *Annales Monastici*, ed. IV, pp. xxxv–xlii; N. Denholm-Young, "The Winchester-Hyde Chronicle," *English Historical Review*, 49 (1934), pp. 85–93, reprinted in his *Collected Papers of N. Denholm-Young* (1969), pp. 236–44; Gransden, *Historical Writing in England*, p. 319, and note 7, pp. 333, 449.
[78]*Historia et Cartularium Monasterii Sancti Petri Gloucestriae*, ed. W. H. Hart, 3 vols (1863, 1865, 1867).
[79]Winchcombe Annals 1049–1181, ed. R. R. Darlington, in *A Medieval Miscellany for Doris Mary Stenton*, ed. Patricia M. Barnes and C. F. Slade (1962), pp. 111–37. From 1182 down to 1232, they depend heavily upon the Tewkesbury annals.
[80]The Annals of Tewkesbury, *Annales Monastici*, ed. H. R. Luard, I (1864), pp. 43–180. There are terse references to the death, and to the canonization, of Wulfstan (pp. 44, 47). On these annals, their derivation, and their relationship to those of Worcester, see Denholm-Young, "The Winchester-Hyde Chronicle," pp. 85–93, esp. p. 85; Gransden, *Historical Writing in England*, p. 405 and note 13.

Charters issued by Bishop Wulfstan

One charter issued by Bishop Wulfstan still exists in its original form, and has also been copied into the cartulary of Worcester cathedral priory.[81] This cartulary also contains entries concerning four other documents issued in his name. Two of these are texts of charters,[82] and the other two are detailed memoranda of confraternity agreements which the bishop and monks made with other religious houses.[83] Transcripts in this cartulary of documents dating from the twelfth century occasionally give references to his grants or rulings, although they add little new information.[84] Hemming's cartulary, discussed above, contains the text of one further charter.[85] Other entries provide useful information, both on lands acquired in earlier generations, and on the Worcester estates during the lifetime of Bishop Wulfstan.

In Wulfstan's day, bishops had not yet begun the practice of keeping formal registers of their charters, or of their administrative decisions and rulings. His charters are recorded in Hemming's cartulary, and in the cartulary of Worcester cathedral priory, in so far as they related to the material interests of the monks. Similarly, other recipients of documents issued by Wulfstan would safeguard them, either in their original form or as cartulary copies, only if these documents guaranteed their rights or their properties. Administrative instructions which Wulfstan committed to writing would have a short life expectancy.

Royal charters concerning Bishop Wulfstan

King Edward issued one writ concerning Wulfstan's appointment to the bishopric of Worcester; a second writ concerning the judicial and financial rights of Wulfstan's brother, as dean, or prior, and a third concerning income due to Wulfstan from local tolls.[86]

Charters and writs issued by William I and William II contribute further details about the activities of Wulfstan, chiefly in his roles as a

---

[81]Worcester cathedral library, B. 1680; *Cartulary of Worcester*, no. 3.
[82]*Cartulary of Worcester*, nos 4, 52.
[83]Ibid., nos 304–5.
[84]Ibid., nos 55, 59, 61–2, 79, 300 note.
[85]*Hemingi Chartularium*, II, pp. 421–4.
[86]King Edward's charter appointing Wulfstan bishop is BL Additional Charter 19802, reproduced in *Facsimiles of English Royal Writs to A.D. 1100 presented to Vivian Hunter Galbraith* (1957), plate XXVI, with text printed on the facing page (no foliation). *Anglo-Saxon Writs*, ed. F. E. Harmer (1952), nos 115–17; *Anglo-Saxon Charters: an annotated list and bibliography*, ed. P. H. Sawyer (1968), nos 1156–8. All are authentic.

regional administrator and as a royal counsellor. The texts of half of these are genuine; seven are forgeries; and the remainder are suspect to a greater or lesser degree. There are nine surviving writs addressed to Wulfstan concerning his administrative responsibilities in Worcestershire and Gloucestershire;[87] four writs name him as beneficiary of some royal favour;[88] he is named as witness to a further fifteen writs concerning royal decisions, although the authenticity of eleven of these is suspect, to a greater or lesser extent;[89] one writ refers to him as the adjudicator of an earlier lawsuit, and he is mentioned in two writs of William Rufus issued shortly after the bishop's death.[90]

Latin Poems on the death of Bishop Wulfstan

A Latin verse lament was composed on the death of Wulfstan, describing his funeral in some detail, and reflecting the grief of contemporaries. Internal evidence suggests that the poet was perhaps a member of the chapter of Worcester at the end of the eleventh century. This poem survives as an interpolation in a twelfth-century *chronicula* (little chronicle) by John of Worcester which is based on his *Chronicle*.[91] Another, shorter, poem, *De Wistano Wigornensi Episcopo*, also composed after Wulfstan's death, reflects the feelings of contemporaries; this work, however, is probably by Serlo of Bayeux, a poet of the later eleventh

---

[87]*Regesta Regum Anglo-Normannorum 1066–1154: I. Regesta Willelmi Conquestoris et Willelmi Rufi 1066–1100*, ed. H. W. C. Davis, with R. J. Whitwell (1913), nos 9, 32, 36, 104, 106, 186, 245, 252, 282. Nos 9, 32 and, probably, 252, are genuine. The others are suspect to a greater or lesser degree.

[88]Ibid., I, nos 10, 184, 221, 230. All appear to be authentic.

[89]The writs which seem to be above suspicion are: *Regesta I*, nos 64–5, 315, and, probably, no. 137; *Regesta Regum Anglo-Normannorum 1066–1154: II. Regesta Henrici Primi 1100–1135*, ed. C. Johnson and H. A. Cronne (1956), appendix, no. 328. The following writs are suspect to varying degrees: *Regesta I*, nos 11, 34, 90, 95, 141, 144, 148, 196–7, 262.

[90]*Regesta I*, nos 213, 387–8. All appear to be genuine.

[91]This poem is published in full, and discussed, by M. L. Colker, "Latin Verses Lamenting the Death of Saint Wulfstan of Worcester," *Analecta Bollandiana*, 89 (1971), pp. 319–22. Colker draws attention to parallels between verses 16–20 of this poem and a section in the Short Life contained in BL MS Cotton Vespasian E.IX. The chronicle in which the poem is interpolated is contained in Trinity College, Dublin Codex 503 (E.6.4). This manuscript also contains a continuation at Gloucester of the Worcester *Chronicon ex Chronicis*. Folios 37r–113v line 23 seem to be written in the hand of John of Worcester. The manuscript is entitled a *Chronicula* by John, and is based on the longer chronicle contained in Oxford Corpus Christi College MS 197, although it has much additional matter; Darlington and McGurk, "The Chronicon ex Chronicis," p. 195; Brett, "John of Worcester and his contemporaries," p. 110.

century, who composed a number of verse epitaphs on well-known public figures.[92]

The Chronicon Abbatiae de Evesham

The *Chronicon*[93] supplies interesting information, which counterpoints certain episodes found in Worcester sources. This work, in its present form, dates from the early thirteenth century but incorporated within it is an earlier history of the abbey, probably written in the late eleventh or the early twelfth century. Embedded within this, in turn, is a short *Life* of Wulfstan's contemporary, Abbot Ethelwig. This probably once existed as a separate work, composed soon after the abbot's death in 1077; the author of this *Life* claims that some of his information came from personal observation. The *Life* incorporates some charter material into the narrative.[94] The wider early Evesham history embedded within the *Chronicon* continued into the rule of Ethelwig's successor, Abbot Walter, but, since this abbot's death (in 1104) is not mentioned, this early history presumably ended before that year.[95] A major theme of the thirteenth-century writer of the *Chronicon*, Thomas of Marlborough, is the independence of Evesham abbey from the jursidiction of the bishop of Worcester.[96] It may be inferred that earlier material which he incorpo-

[92]*De Wilstano Wigornensi Episcopo* was published by T. Grey, *Scalachronica*, ed. J. Stevenson (1836), p. 211, from BL MS Cotton Vitellius A.XII, f. 129. This manuscript was copied at Salisbury in the later eleventh century from an unknown exemplar, N. R. Ker, "The Beginnings of Salisbury Cathedral," *Medieval Learning and Literature: Essays presented to Richard William Hunt*, ed. J. Alexander and M. Gibson (1976), pp. 23–49, reprinted in N. R. Ker, *Books, Collectors and Libraries*, pp. 143–73, esp. pp. 143–5, 150, 159, 161. The poem is one of several in this manuscript (ff. 128v–9) attributed to Serlo, a canon of Bayeux. The other late eleventh-century notables on whom he wrote epitaphs include William I, his wife Queen Matilda and their son Richard; Archbishop Lanfranc, and Walcher bishop of Durham: *Scalachronica*, pp. 207, 213–14, 217–19. See also *Descriptive Catalogue of Materials relating to the History of Great Britain and Ireland*, II, nos 96, 106. It is noted in this volume (no. 106) that Godfrey, prior of Winchester, has also been suggested as author of the poem on Wulfstan. For further bibliography on Serlo of Bayeux, see also A. Potthast, *Bibliotheca Historica Medii Aevi*, 2 vols (1896), II, p. 103; *Tusculum-Lexicon*, ed. W. Buchwald, A. Holweg and O. Prinz, third edn (1982), p. 772.
[93]*Chronicon Abbatiae de Evesham*, ed. W. D. Macray (1863).
[94]Ibid., p. xl, note 1; Gransden, *Historical Writing in England*, pp. 89–90; R. R. Darlington, "Aethelwig, abbot of Evesham," *English Historical Review*, 48 (1933), pp. 1–22, 177–98. The eyewitness account of Abbot Ethelwig's rule was probably that of the monk Dominic: J. C. Jennings, "The Writings of Prior Dominic of Evesham," *English Historical Review*, 77 (1962), pp. 298, 302–3.
[95]Gransden, *Historical Writing in England*, pp. 89, 111–12.
[96]*Chronicon Abbatiae de Evesham*, pp. xxiii–xxviii, 142–200; Gransden, *Historical Writing in England*, pp. 112, 519.

rated has perhaps occasionally been edited and even interpolated in order to support his case.

Chronicles written outside the diocese of Worcester

Beyond the diocese of Worcester, Wulfstan generally attracted little notice in chronicles, or in other documentation apart from royal writs and charters.[97] The *Anglo-Saxon Chronicle* mentions him only once, under the year 1088.[98] This passage was later re-worked, from a different angle, by Henry of Huntingdon, who added one further brief reference to the bishop.[99] In the collected letters of Lanfranc, archbishop of Canterbury, Wulfstan is addressed once; attests one document, and, possibly, a letter of Thomas, archbishop of York, apart from being listed among those present at the Council of London in 1075.[100] There is a record of his episcopal profession only in the *Vita Wulfstani*.[101] Eadmer, the biographer of Archbishop Anselm, mentioned Wulfstan only once,[102] as did the York chronicler, Hugh the Chantor.[103] There are three references to Wulfstan in the *Ecclesiastical History of Orderic Vitalis*, which add little new information, except on the inauguration of the Worcester Chronicle.[104] Apart from the references in Lanfranc's letters, most of these references occur in texts written after Wulfstan's death.

Minor References

The *Liber Vitae* of Durham cathedral is a manuscript designed to record the names of members, and of benefactors, of the Northumbrian church.

---

[97]*Vita Wulfstani*, p. xix.

[98]*The Anglo-Saxon Chronicle*, transl. and ed. Dorothy Whitelock with D. C. Douglas and Susie I. Tucker (1961), p. 166.

[99]Henry of Huntingdon, *Historia Anglorum*, ed. Thomas Arnold (1879), p. 214; see also p. 211.

[100]*The Letters of Lanfranc archbishop of Canterbury*, ed. and transl. Helen Clover and Margaret Gibson (1979), Items 4, 11–12; Letter 13.

[101]*Vita Wulfstani*, p. 190. See also *Canterbury Professions*, ed. M. Richter (1973), pp. lxi, 26, no. 31.

[102]Eadmer, *Historia Novorum*, ed. M. Rule (1884), pp. 45–6. There is also a comment that Wulfstan was prevented by infirmity from attending Archbishop Anselm's consecration (p. 42).

[103]Hugh the Chantor: *The History of the Church of York 1066–1127*, transl. and introd. C. Johnson (1961), p. 1.

[104]*Ecclesiastical History of Orderic Vitalis*, II, p. 186; Iv, pp. 124, 170. See also Gransden, *Historical Writing in England*, p. 157.

It was begun at Lindisfarne in the ninth century; subsequently travelled with the body of St Cuthbert, when the monks fled from marauding Vikings, and was continued at Durham cathedral. This manuscript contains, on facing folios, one list of the monks of Evesham, and another of the monks of Worcester. While these lists are headed respectively by the names of Abbot Ethelwig and Bishop Wulfstan, those of their immediate successors in office duly follow. The Worcester list, in addition to the names of Bishop Wulfstan and Bishop Samson, contains a further sixty names written in the same hand. An additional sixteen names, including those of four women, have been added by later hands.[105] Internal evidence strongly suggests that these two lists date from the early months of 1104, and that the Durham scribe has copied information which the abbey and the cathedral priory were requested to supply.[106]

Patrick, bishop of Dublin (1074–84), has left a collection of prose and verse. Allusions within the verse, and in particular, interlinear glosses upon them, identify members of the monastic community at Worcester. From these allusions, it is clear that Patrick trained there, and that he had an affectionate regard for Bishop Wulfstan.[107]

Attestations of Wulfstan, first as monk, and later as prior, occur in several charters of his predecessors in the bishopric, Lyfing and Ealdred, in one charter of King Edward, and in one of Leofric, earl of Mercia.[108]

Obit lists are found with kalendars in two manuscripts closely associated with St Wulfstan. The *obit* was the notice of the death of someone who was to be commemorated annually, hence its inclusion in a kalendar which tabulated the various religious festivals: saints' days and solemn occasions observed throughout the monastic year in a particular monastery. The longer of the two *obit* lists occurs in a kalendar in a manuscript containing homilies by Wulfstan's namesake, the early eleventh-century archbishop of York. Wulfstan is said to have used this collection. While most of the monks and benefactors included in this list were associated with the church of Worcester in the late tenth and early eleventh centuries, others would have been known to Wulfstan at the outset of his monastic career. The original list copied into this manuscript

---

[105]*Durham Liber Vitae*, ed. A. H. Thompson (1923), reproduces this manuscript in facsimile. The Evesham list is on folio 21 verso, and the Worcester list on folio 22 recto.

[106]For detailed analysis of these lists, and for discussion both of their probable date and of the significance of their inclusion in this manuscript, see Atkins, "The Church of Worcester," Part II, pp. 212–20.

[107]*The Writings of Bishop Patrick 1074–1084*, ed. and transl. A Gwynn (1955), pp. 6–7, 10–11, 15.

[108]The attestations of Wulfstan as monk and prior are printed and discussed by Atkins,"The Church of Worcester," Part II, pp. 19–27.

probably belonged to a bishop or prior. Wulfstan's own name, and those of some of his close contemporaries, have been added to the list in later hands.

The shorter obit list occurs in a service book known as *Wulfstan's Collectar*, a work which, on the evidence of its kalendar, dates from St Wulfstan's episcopate. Both lists include the names of laity who had been benefactors of the abbey.[109] These lists provide corroborative information on the identities of the monks of Worcester, and on their dates of death. In some case, family relationships are noted, and in others, the office which the individual held within the monastic community.

In 1122, the abbey of Savigny, in France, notified the English Benedictine houses of the death of Abbot Vitalis, and asked for prayers for his soul. Several monasteries, when replying, asked that the monks of Savigny should in turn pray for certain of their own deceased members, whose names were given. Worcester's list, headed by Bishop Wulfstan, names six senior monks who are mentioned in sources for his life, besides his successor, Bishop Samson. These names, and those given by other monasteries in the diocese of Worcester, were entered on Savigny's Mortuary Roll.[110]

[109]The kalendars contained in both Wulfstan's Homiliary and Wulfstan's Collectar were printed in *The Leofric Collectar*, ed. W. H. Frere and E. S. Dewick, 2 vols (1918–21), II, pp. 589–600. On the kalendar in Wulfstan's Homiliary, see I. Atkins, "An Investigation of two Anglo-Saxon Kalendars (Missal of Robert of Jumièges and St. Wulfstan's Homiliary)," *Archaeologia*, second series, 78 (1928), pp. 219–54. See also H. M. Bannister's Note on the Kalendar in *Early Worcester Manuscripts*, ed. C. H. Turner (1916), pp. lx–lxii; the two *obit* lists have been printed and analysed in detail by Atkins, "The Church of Worcester," Part II, pp. 28–33. These Worcester *obit* lists have subsequently been included in *Die Gedenkuberlieferung der Angelsachsen*, ed. J. Gerchow (1988), items 20–1, but it has not been possible to consult this work.

[110]The abbeys of Gloucester and Pershore also asked for prayers for certain monks. No names were included in the replies of Evesham and Tewkesbury. Rouleau du bienheureux Vital, abbé de Savigny, *Rouleaux des Morts du IXe au XVe siècle*, ed. L. Delisle (1866, reprinted 1966), XXXVIII, nos 83–7, pp. 312–13. See also Atkins, "The Church of Worcester," Part II, p. 266.

Chronological List of Key Events

*A selection of key dates in Wulfstan's life
and events leading to his canonization
together with dates of selected political events*

1008 (?)   Birth of Wulfstan.
           Danish incursions increasingly devastating in this and subse-
           quent years.
1013 (?)   Wulfstan begins school at Evesham abbey.
1016 (?)   Wulfstan begins school at Peterborough abbey.
1016   Death of King Ethelred II; warfare between his son, Edmund
           Ironside and Cnut.
           Accession of King Cnut
1023   Death of Archbishop Wulfstan.
1023 (?)   Wulfstan's schooling at Peterborough ends.
1033   Brihtheah elected bishop of Worcester.
1033 (?)   Wulfstan becomes an episcopal clerk.
1034 (?)   Wulfstan consecrated priest.
1035   Death of King Cnut; accession of his son, Harold I Harefoot,
           as regent for himself and his half-brother Harthacnut.
1037   Harold Harefoot recognized as sole king.
1037 (?)   Wulfstan becomes a monk of Worcester cathedral priory.
1038   Death of Bishop Brihtheah.
1040   Accession of King Harthacnut.
1041   Harrying of Worcester on orders of Harthacnut.
1042   Accession of King Edward "the Confessor."
1046   Ealdred elected bishop of Worcester.
1053   Harold Godwinson becomes earl of Wessex.
1055 (?)   Wulfstan appointed prior of Worcester.
1057   Death of Leofric, earl of Mercia.
           Death of Ralph, earl of Hereford.
1061   Ealdred elected archbishop of York   .
           (Spring) Visit of Archbishop Ealdred and Tostig Godwinson
           to Pope Nicholas II.
1062   (Lent) Visit of Ermenfrid and another papal envoy to Wor-
           cester cathedral priory.

	(Easter) Election of Wulfstan as bishop of Worcester.
	(8 Sept.) Consecration of Wulfstan as bishop of Worcester.
1062 (?)	(Autumn) Death of Alfgar, earl of Mercia.
1065	(Autumn) Northumbrians revolt; expulsion of Tostig Godwinson.
	(Christmas) Bishop Wulfstan attends King Edward's court.
1066	(5 Jan.) Death of King Edward "the Confessor."
	(6 Jan.) Coronation of King Harold II Godwinson.
	(Early months) Wulfstan's mission to pacify the Northumbrians.
	(14 October) Battle "of Hastings;" death of King Harold II. Submission of Archbishop Ealdred, Bishop Wulfstan and other English magnates to Duke William of Normandy.
	(25 Dec.) Coronation of William I "the Conqueror."
1067	William Fitz Osbern created earl of Hereford.
1067–70	Resistance movement of Edric "the Wild" in Herefordshire.
1069 (?)	Urse de Abetot begins the building of Worcester Castle.
1069	Rising in the North.
	(8 Sept.) Invasion of King Sweyn Estrithson of Denmark.
	(11 Sept.) Death of Archbishop Ealdred.
1070	(Jan.–March) Harrying of the North.
	Refugees head for Evesham Abbey.
	(April) Ecclesiastical Council at Winchester. Deposition of Archbishop Stigand.
	Thomas I elected archbishop of York.
	(August) Lanfranc elected archbishop of Canterbury.
1070 (late)–1072 (late)	Wulfstan administers the diocese of Lichfield.
1071	Death of Edwin, earl of Mercia; intensive Norman settlement of the region.
	Mission of Archbishops Lanfranc and Thomas to the papal court.
1072	(April) Ecclesiastical Council at Winchester.
	(Pentecost) Royal council at Windsor; restoration of Wulfstan's manors.
1073	(March) Wulfstan takes part in consecration of Bishop Radulf of Orkney.
1073/4	Monks of Evesham and Winchcombe begin revival of Northumbrian monasticism.
1075	Revolt of the Earls.
	Wulfstan and Ethelwig defend the Severn fords.
1077	Wulfstan institutes his confraternity league.
	Death of Abbot Ethelwig of Evesham.
1077/9	Confraternity agreement between Worcester and Ramsey.

1079/83   Worcester's plea against Evesham.
1084   Death of Bishop Patrick of Dublin.
1085   (Dec.) William I's Christmas court at Gloucester; the Domes-
          day Survey of England is planned.
1086   Domesday Survey of England.
1087   (Sept.) Death of William I.
          Accession of William II "Rufus."
1088   Wulfstan's defence of Worcester against the rebels.
1089   Death of Archbishop Lanfranc.
          Crypt and east end of Romanesque cathedral of Worcester
          completed.
          Wulfstan, conscious of short life expectancy, issues Alveston
          charter for the monks.
1090s   Compilation of Hemming's Cartulary, initiated by Bishop
          Wulfstan.
1091   (Jan.) Wulfstan's last recorded visit to the royal court (at
          Dover).
1092   Wulfstan's diocesan synod; dispute over St Helen's church.
1093   Anselm elected archbishop of Canterbury; Wulfstan's frail
          health prevents him from attending consecration.
1093 (?) Correspondence between Anselm and Wulfstan on prerogat-
          ives of the archbishopric.
1094   Wulfstan's last Maundy ritual and Easter banquet.
          (July) Wulfstan's health gravely declines.
1095   (20 Jan.) Death of Wulfstan.
          King William II levies feudal relief on tenants of the bishopric.
          (26 June) Death of Robert, bishop of Hereford.
          Miracles at Wulfstan's tomb.
          Visions of the anchorite.
1096   Samson elected bishop of Worcester; closes the priory at
          Westbury-on-Trym.
1097/8 (?) Urse de Abetot becomes benefactor of Great Malvern priory.
1100 (?) Coleman writes English *Life* of Bishop Wulfstan.
1100   (August) Death of William II "Rufus."
1113   Wulfstan's tomb survives fire in the cathedral.
1115 (?) William of Malmesbury visits Worcester to undertake histo-
          rical research.
1124   Death of Prior Nicholas.
1124/42   Prior Warin commissions William of Malmesbury to translate
          Coleman's *Life of Wulfstan* into Latin.
1130 (?) Henry of Huntingdon writes of "Saint" Wulfstan.
          Healing of the woman at Wulfstan's tomb after ordeal of hot
          iron.

1145/7	Bishop Bernard of St David's writes to Pope Eugenius III testifying to survival of Wulfstan's tomb, undamaged, after fire.
1148/50	Healing of crippled beggar woman at Wulfstan's tomb.
1170	(Dec.) Murder of Thomas Becket, archbishop of Canterbury; rapid spread of his cult.
1172/4	Senatus writes *Abridged Life of Wulfstan*.
1190s	Visions reported of Wulfstan ordering his translation.
1198	(6 Sept.) Bishop John orders opening of Wulfstan's tomb. (28 Sept.) Death of Bishop John.
1199	Accession of King John. Mauger, royal physician, elected bishop of Worcester; election quashed on grounds of illegitimacy but Pope Innocent III willing to approve if Mauger is supported by monks.
1200	(June) Mauger consecrated bishop of Worcester.
1201	Renewed wave of miracles at Wulfstan's tomb.
1202	(17 April) Fire in cathedral precincts. (Lent) Archbishop Hubert, presiding at council of magnates, witnesses daily miracles at Wulfstan's tomb. Petition to pope for Wulfstan's canonization. (1–3 Sept.) Investigation of Wulfstan by Archbishop Hubert and other papal commissioners.
1202/3	Bishop Mauger and a delegation of Worcester monks visit Pope Innocent III.
1203	(21 April) Pope Innocent canonizes Wulfstan. (14 May) Papal bull issued announcing Wulfstan's canonization.
1207	King John's quarrel with Pope Innocent III over Canterbury election. (*c.*8 Sept.) King John's solemn visit to St Wulfstan's tomb.
1208	(May) Bishop Mauger proclaims Interdict in England and flees into exile.
1211	King John narrates legend of St Wulfstan's staff to papal legates.
1216	(Oct.) Death of King John; his burial beside St Wulfstan.
1218	(7 June) Translation of St Wulfstan.

Map 1 England in the eleventh century
Source: David Hill *An Atlas of Anglo-Saxon England 700–1066*, Basil
Blackwell, 1981.

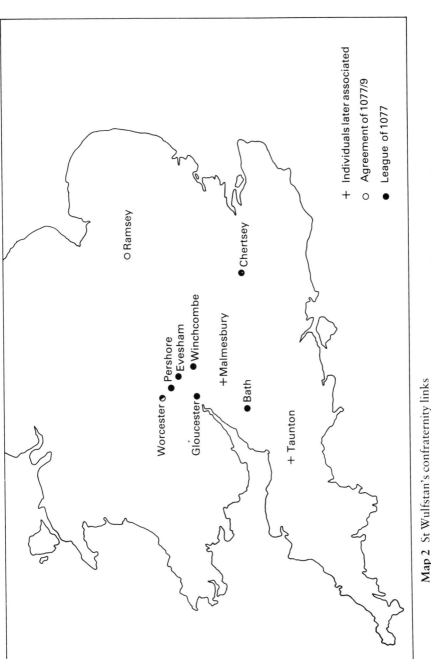

Map 2 St Wulfstan's confraternity links
Source: David Hill An Atlas of Anglo-Saxon England 700–1066, Basil
Blackwell, 1981.

Legend:
+ Individuals later associated
○ Agreement of 1077/9
● League of 1077

Ramsey
Chertsey
Worcester
Pershore
Evesham
Winchcombe
Gloucester
+Malmesbury
Bath
+ Taunton

Bibliography

MANUSCRIPTS

Cambridge, Trinity College: MS 0.7.41
Durham, Dean and Chapter Library: MS Hunter 100
Glasgow, Hunterian Museum: MS T.4.2
London, British Library: MS Cotton Tiberius E.IV
    MS Egerton 3088
Oxford: Bodl. Auct. F. 1.9
    Bodl. Auct. F. 3.14
    Bodl. Auct. F. 5.19
    Bodl. MS 633 (1966)
Worcester Cathedral Library: Additional MS 218

PRINTED SOURCES

Acta Lanfranci, in Two of the Saxon Chronicles Parallel, ed. C. Plummer
   and J. Earle (The Clarendon Press, Oxford, 1892–9).
Acta Sanctorum, Société des Bollandistes, 67 vols (Brussels, 1902–70),
   mainly facsimile reprints of original vols, ed. J. Bollandus, G. Hensche-
   nius and others (Antwerp, Brussels, Tongerloo and Paris, 1643–1883).
Adomnan's Life of Columba, ed. and transl. A. O. Anderson and M. O.
   Anderson (Thomas Nelson and Sons Ltd, Edinburgh and London,
   1961).
Anglia Sacra, ed. H. Wharton, 2 vols (London, 1691).
Anglo-Saxon Charters, ed. and transl. A. J. Robertson (Cambridge
   University Press, Cambridge, 1956).
Anglo-Saxon Charters: an annotated list and bibliography, compiled by
   P. H. Sawyer (Royal Historical Society, London, 1968).

The Anglo-Saxon Chronicle, transl. and ed. Dorothy Whitelock, with D. C. Douglas and Susie I. Tucker (Eyre and Spottiswoode, London, 1961).

Anglo-Saxon Writs, ed. F. E. Harmer (Manchester Univeristy Press, Manchester, 1952).

Annales Monastici, ed. H. R. Luard, 5 vols (Rolls Series, London, 1864–9).

Annals of Barnwell, *Memoriale Fratris Walteri de Coventria*, ed. W. Stubbs, 2 vols (Rolls Series, London, 1872–3), II, pp. 196–279.

Annals of Burton, *Annales Monastici*, ed. H. R. Luard (Rolls Series, London, 1864), I, pp. 181–510.

Annals of Tewkesbury, *Annales Monastici*, ed. H. R. Luard (Rolls Series, London, 1864), I, pp. 43–180.

Annals of Waverley, *Annales Monastici*, ed. H. R. Luard (Rolls Series, London, 1865), II, pp. 127–411.

Annals of Worcester Cathedral Priory, *Annales Monastici*, ed. H. R. Luard, (Rolls Series, London, 1869), IV, pp. 355–562.

Antiphonaire Monastique XIIIe siècle: Codex E 160 de la Bibliothèque de la Cathédrale de Worcester, introd. Laurentia MacLachlan (Paléographie Musicale XII, Société Saint-Jean l'Evangéliste, Desclee & Cie., Tournay, Belgium, 1922).

The Beauchamp Cartulary: charters 1100–1268, ed. Emma Mason (Pipe Roll Society, new series 43, London, 1980).

Bede's Ecclesiastical History of the English People, ed. B. Colgrave and R. A. B. Mynors (The Clarendon Press, Oxford, 1969).

The Book of St. Gilbert, ed. Raymonde Foreville and Gillian Keir (Clarendon Press, Oxford, 1987).

Canterbury Professions, ed. M. Richter (Canterbury and York Society, 67, 1973).

Cartularium Abbathiae de Whiteby, ed. J. C. Atkinson, 2 vols (Surtees Soc., 69, Durham, London and Edinburgh, 1878–9).

The Cartulary of Shrewsbury Abbey, ed. Una Rees, 2 vols (The National Library of Wales, Aberystwyth, 1975).

The Cartulary of Worcester Cathedral Priory (Register I), ed. R. R. Darlington (Pipe Roll Society, new series 38, London, 1968).

The Chronicle of Hugh Candidus, a monk of Peterborough, ed. W. T. Mellows, with *La Geste de Burch*, ed. A. Bell (Oxford University Press, on behalf of the Friends of Peterborough Cathedral, London, 1949).

The Chronicle of John of Worcester 1118–1140, ed. J. R. H. Weaver (Clarendon Press, Oxford, 1908).

Chronicon Abbatiae de Evesham ad annum 1418, ed. W. D. Macray (Rolls Series, London, 1863).

Chronicon Abbatiae Ramesiensis, ed. W. D. Macray (Rolls Series,

London, 1886).

Chronicon Monasterii de Abingdon, ed. J. Stevenson, 2 vols (Rolls Series, London, 1858).

Conciliorum Oecumenicorum Decreta, ed. J. Alberigo et al., third edn (Institutio per le Scienze Religiose, Bologna, 1973).

Councils and Ecclesiastical Documents, ed. A. W. Haddan and W. Stubbs, 3 vols. in 4 (The Clarendon Press, Oxford, 1869–73).

Councils and Synods, with other documents relating to the English Church, I. A.D. 871–1204, ed. D. Whitelock, M. Brett and C. N. L. Brooke, 2 vols (Clarendon Press, Oxford, 1981).

Descriptive Catalogue of Materials relating to the History of Great Britain and Ireland to the end of the reign of Henry VII, ed. T. D. Hardy, 3 vols (Rolls Series, London, 1862, 1865, 1871).

De Wlstano Wigornensi Episcopo, in T. Grey, Scalalchronica, ed. J. Stevenson (The Maitland Club, Edinburgh, 1836), p. 211.

Diplomatarium Anglicum Aevi Saxonici, ed. and transl. B. Thorpe (Macmillan and Co., London, 1865).

Domesday Book, seu liber censualis, ed. A. Farley, 2 vols (Record Commission, London, 1783); vols III and IV ed. H. Ellis (Record Commission, London, 1816).

Domesday Book: Gloucestershire, ed. R. W. H. Erskine and A. Williams (Alecto Historical Editions, London, 1989).

Domesday Book: Worcestershire, ed. R. W. H. Erskine and A. Williams (Alecto Historical Editions, London, 1989).

Domesday Book 13: Buckinghamshire, ed. and transl. J. Morris (Phillimore, Chichester, 1978).

Domesday Book 15: Gloucestershire, ed. and transl. J. S. Moore (Phillimore, Chichester, 1982).

Domesday Book 23: Warwickshire, ed. J. Morris (Phillimore, Chichester, 1976).

Domesday Book 16: Worcestershire, ed. F. and C. Thorn (Phillimore, Chichester, 1982).

Durham Liber Vitae, ed. A. H. Thompson (Surtees Society, 136, Durham and London, 1923), in facsimile.

Eadmer, Historia Novorum in Anglia, ed. M. Rule (Rolls Series, London, 1884).

, The Life of St. Anselm, ed. and transl. R. W. Southern (Clarendon Press, Oxford, 1962).

The Early History of Glastonbury: an edition, translation and study of William of Malmesbury's De Antiquitate Glastonie Ecclesie, by John Scott (The Boydell Press, Woodbridge, 1981).

Early Sources of Scottish History A.D. 500 to 1286, collected and translated A. O. Anderson, 2 vols (Oliver and Boyd, Edinburgh and London, 1922).

The Early South English Legendary, ed. C. Horstmann, I (Early English Text Society, London, 1887).

Early Worcester Manuscripts, ed. C. H. Turner (The Clarendon Press, Oxford, 1916).

The Ecclesiastical History of Orderic Vitalis, ed. and transl. Marjorie Chibnall, 6 vols (Oxford University Press, Oxford, 1969–80).

Encomium Emmae Reginae, ed. A. Campbell (Camden Third Series, LXXII, Royal Historical Society, London, 1949).

English Historical Documents. I: c.500–1042, ed. Dorothy Whitelock, second edn (Eyre Methuen, London; Oxford University Press, New York, 1979).

English Historical Documents. II: 1042–1189, ed. D. C. Douglas and G. W. Greenaway, second edn (Eyre Methuen, London; Oxford University Press, New York, 1981).

English Historical Documents. III: 1189–1327, ed. H. Rothwell (Eyre and Spottiswoode, London, 1975).

English Kalendars before A.D. 1100, ed. Francis Wormald; I: Texts (Henry Bradshaw Society, LXXII, London, 1934).

The Epistolae Vagantes of Pope Gregory VII, ed. and transl. H. E. J. Cowdrey (The Clarendon Press, Oxford, 1972).

Facsimiles of English Royal Writs to A.D. 1100 presented to Vivian Hunter Galbraith, ed. T. A. M. Bishop and P. Chaplais (Clarendon Press, Oxford, 1957).

Florentii Wigorniensis monachi Chronicon ex Chronicis, ed. B. Thorpe, 2 vols (English Historical Society, London, 1848–9).

Foedera, Conventiones, Litterae et cuiuscunque generis Acta Publica, ed. T. Rymer, R. Sanderson and others, 3 vols (Record Commission, London, 1816–30).

Die Gedenküberlieferung der Angelsachsen, mit einem Katalog der libri vitae und Necrologien, ed. Jan Gerchow (Arbeiten zur Frühmittelalterforschung 20, Walter de Gruyter, Berlin and New York, 1988).

Gerald of Wales, *The Journey through Wales and the Description of Wales*, transl. and introd. L. Thorpe (Penguin Books, Harmondsworth, 1978).

Die Gesetze der Angelsachsen, ed. F. Liebermann, 3 vols (Halle-am-Saale, 1903–16).

A Handbook to the Land-Charters, and other Saxonic Documents, ed. J. Earle (The Clarendon Press, Oxford, 1888).

Hemingi Chartularium ecclesiae Wigorniensis, ed. T. Hearne, 2 vols (Sheldonian Theatre, Oxford, 1723).

Henry of Huntingdon, *Historia Anglorum*, ed. Thomas Arnold (Rolls Series, London, 1879; Kraus Reprint, 1965).

Historia et Cartularium Monasterii Sancti Petri Gloucestriae, ed. W. H.

Hart, 3 vols (Rolls Series, London, 1863, 1865, 1867).
The Historians of the Church of York and its archbishops, ed. J. Raine, 3 vols (Rolls Series, London, 1879, 1886, 1894).
The Historical Works of Gervase of Canterbury, ed. W. Stubbs, 2 vols (Rolls Series, London, 1880).
Hugh the Chantor, *The History of the Church of York 1066–1127*, transl. and introd. C. Johnson (Nelson, Edinburgh and London, 1961).
Die "Institutes of Polity, Civil and Ecclesiastical," ein Werk Erzbischof Wulfstans von York, ed. K. Jost (Swiss Studies in English, 47, Bern 1959).
"Latin verses Lamenting the Death of Saint Wulfstan of Worcester," ed. M. L. Colker, *Analecta Bollandiana*, 89 (1971), pp. 319–22.
"La Vie de S. Edouard le Confesseur par Osbert de Clare," introd. and ed. M. Bloch, *Analecta Bollandiana*, 41 (Brussels and Paris, 1923), pp. 5–131.
The Laws of the Earliest English Kings, ed. and transl. F. L. Attenborough (Cambridge University Press, Cambridge, 1922).
The Laws of the Kings of England from Edmund to Henry I, ed. and transl. A. J. Robertson (Cambridge University Press, Cambridge, 1925).
Leges Henrici Primi, ed. and transl. L. J. Downer (The Clarendon Press, Oxford, 1972).
The Leofric Collectar, ed. W. H. Frere and E. S. Dewick, 2 vols (Henry Bradshaw Society, London, 1918–21).
Lestorie des Engles solum la Translacion Maistre Geffrei Gaimar, ed. T. D. Hardy, 2 vols (Rolls Series, London, 1888–9).
The Letters of Lanfranc, archbishop of Canterbury, ed. and transl. Helen Clover and Margaret Gibson (Clarendon Press, Oxford, 1979).
The Letters of Pope Innocent III (1198–1216) concerning England and Wales: a calendar with an appendix of texts, ed. C. R. Cheney and Mary G. Cheney (The Clarendon Press, Oxford, 1967).
Liber Niger Scaccarii, ed. T. Hearne, 2nd edn (Benjamin White, London, 1774).
The Life of Christina of Markyate: a twelfth century recluse, ed. and transl. C. H. Talbot (Clarendon Press, Oxford, 1987).
The Life of King Edward who rests at Westminster, attributed to a monk of St Bertin, ed. and transl. Frank Barlow (Thomas Nelson and Sons Ltd, Edinburgh and London, 1962).
Memorials of Saint Dunstan, archbishop of Canterbury, ed. W. Stubbs (Rolls Series, London, 1874).
The Monastic Constitutions of Lanfranc, transl. and introd. D. Knowles (Thomas Nelson and Sons Ltd, Edinburgh and London, 1951).
Nova Legenda Angliae: collected by John of Tynemouth, John Capgrave

and others, ed. C. Horstmann, 2 vols (Clarendon Press, Oxford, 1901).

Patrologiae (cursus completus, series) Latina, ed. J. -P. Migne and others, LXII (Garnier, Paris, 1891).

The Peterborough Chronicle, ed. Cecily Clark (The Clarendon Press, Oxford, 2nd edn, 1970).

Placita Anglo-Normannica: Law Cases from William I to Richard I preserved in historical records, ed. M. M. Bigelow (Sampson Low, Marston, Searle, and Rivington, London, 1879).

Placitorum in Domo Capitulari Westmonasteriensi Asservatorum Abbreviatio (Record Commissioners, London, 1811).

The Portiforium of Saint Wulfstan (Corpus Christi College, Cambridge, MS 391), ed. Dom Anselm Hughes, 2 vols (The Henry Bradshaw Society, London, vols. 89–90, 1958–60).

Regesta Regum Anglo-Normannorum 1066–1154: I. Regesta Willelmi Conquestoris et Willelmi Rufi 1066–1100, ed. H. W. C. Davis, with R. J. Whitwell (Clarendon Press, Oxford, 1913).

Regesta Regum Anglo-Normannorum 1066–1154: II. Regesta Henrici Primi 1100–1135, ed. Charles Johnson and H. A. Cronne (Clarendon Press, Oxford, 1956).

Reginald of Durham, *Libellus de vita et miraculis Sancti Godrici, heremitae de Finchale*, ed. J. Stevenson (Surtees Society, 20, London and Edinburgh, 1847).

Register of Bishop Godfrey Giffard, September 23 1268 to August 15 1301, ed. J. W. Willis Bund, 2 vols (Worcestershire Historical Society, XV, Oxford, 1902).

Regularis Concordia, transl. and ed. T. Symons (Thomas Nelson and Sons Ltd, Edinburgh and London, 1953).

Relatio de peregrinatione Saewulfi ad Hyerosolymam et Terram Sanctam, ed. T. Wright, M. d'Avenzac and A. Rogers, *Palestine Pilgrims' Text Society*, IV (London, 1896), pp. 31–52.

Roger of Wendover, *Flores Historiarum*, ed. H. G. Hewlett (Rolls Series, London, 1886–9).

Rotuli Litterarum Clausarum in Turri Londiniensi asservati (1204–27), ed. T. Duffus Hardy, 2 vols (Record Commission, London, 1833–44).

Rouleau du bienheureux Vital, abbé de Savigny, Rouleaux des Morts du ixe au xve siècle, ed. L. Delisle (Libraire de la Société de l'Histoire de France, Paris, 1866; reprinted Johnson Reprint Corporation, New York, 1966), XXXVIII.

The Rule of Saint Benedict, ed. and transl. J. McCann (Burns Oates, London, 1951).

Sancti Anselmi Opera Omnia, ed. F. S. Schmitt, 6 vols (I, III–VI, Thomas Nelson and Sons, Edinburgh, 1946–61; II, Sansaini et Soc., Rome,

1940).

Selected Letters of Pope Innocent III concerning England (1198–1216), ed. C. R. Cheney and W. H. Semple (Thomas Nelson and Sons Ltd, Edinburgh and London, 1953).

The South English Legendary, ed. Charlotte d'Evelyn and Anna J. Mill, 3 vols (Early English Text Society, London, 1956–9).

Symeonis Monachi Opera Omnia, ed. T. Arnold, 2 vols (Rolls Series, London, 1882, 1885).

Theophilus, *The Various Arts: De Diversis Artibus,* ed. and transl. C. R. Dodwell (The Clarendon Press, Oxford, 1986).

Three Lives of the Last Englishmen, transl. and introd. Michael Swanton (Garland Library of Medieval Literature, vol. 10, series B; Garland Publishing Inc., New York and London, 1984).

Turgot, *Vita S. Margaretae Scotorum Reginae,* in *Symeonis Dunelmensis Opera et Collectanea,* vol. I, ed. H. Hinde (Surtees Society, 51; Durham, London and Edinburgh, 1868), pp. 234–54.

Two Chartularies of the Priory of St Peter at Bath, ed. W. Hunt (Somerset Record Society, 7, 1893).

Two Lives of Saint Cuthbert, ed. B. Colgrave (Cambridge University Press, Cambridge, 1985).

Two of the Saxon Chronicles Parallel, ed. C. Plummer and J. Earle (The Clarendon Press, Oxford, 1892–9).

The Vita Wulfstani of William of Malmesbury to which are added the extant abridgements of this work and the Miracles and Translation of St. Wulfstan, ed. Reginald R. Darlington (Camden Society Third Series, XL, London, 1928).

Westminster Abbey Charters, 1066–c.1214, ed. Emma Mason, assisted by the late Jennifer Bray, continuing the work of the late Desmond J. Murphy (London Record Society, vol. 25, London, 1988).

William of Malmesbury, *The Early History of Glastonbury,* ed. and transl. J. Scott (The Boydell Press, Woodbridge, 1981).

———, *De Gestis Pontificum Anglorum,* ed. N. E. S. A. Hamilton (Rolls Series, London, 1870).

———, *De Gestis Regum Anglorum,* ed. W. Stubbs, 2 vols (Rolls Series, London, 1887, 1889).

William of Malmesbury's Life of St. Wulfstan bishop of Worcester, now rendered into English, by J. H. F. Peile (Basil Blackwell, Oxford, 1934).

William of Poitiers, *Histoire de Guillaume le Conquerant,* ed. and transl. Raymonde Foreville (Les Classiques de l'Histoire de France au Moyen Age, Paris, 1952).

Winchcombe Annals 1049–1181, ed. R. R. Darlington, in *A Medieval Miscellany for Doris Mary Stenton,* ed. Patricia M. Barnes and C. F.

Slade (Pipe Roll Society, new series 36, 1962), pp. 111–37.
The Writings of Bishop Patrick 1074–1084, ed. and transl. A. Gwynn (Scriptores Latini Hiberniae, I, Dublin, 1955).

Secondary Works

Abels, R., "Bookland and Fyrd Service in late Anglo-Saxon England," *Anglo-Norman Studies VII: Proceedings of the Battle Conference 1984*, ed. R. Allen Brown (The Boydell Press, Woodbridge, 1985), pp. 1–25.
Addleshaw, G. W. O., *The Beginnings of the Parochial System* (St Anthony's Hall Publications, no. 3, York, second edn, 1959).
Anderson, Freda, "St Pancras Priory, Lewes: its Architectural Development to 1200," *Anglo-Norman Studies XI: Proceedings of the Battle Conference 1988*, ed. R. Allen Brown (The Boydell Press, Woodbridge, 1989), pp. 1–35.
Anderson, O. S., *The English Hundred-Names*, 3 vols (Lund University Yearbook, Lund, 1934–9).
Ashdown, Margaret, "An Icelandic Account of the Survival of Harold Godwinson," in *The Anglo-Saxons: studies in some aspects of their history and culture presented to Bruce Dickens*, ed. P. Clemoes (Bowes and Bowes, London, 1959), pp. 122–36.
Atkins, I., "The Church of Worcester from the Eighth to the Twelfth Century," Part I, *The Antiquaries Journal*, 17 (1937), pp. 371–91; Part II, ibid., 20 (1940), pp. 1–38, and 203–28.
———, "An Investigation of two Anglo-Saxon Kalendars (Missal of Robert of Jumièges and St. Wulfstan's Homiliary)," *Archaeologia*, second series, 78 (1928), pp. 219–54.
Backhouse, Janet, Turner, D. H. and Webster, Leslie (eds), *The Golden Age of Anglo-Saxon Art 966–1066* (British Museum Publications Ltd, London, 1984).
Barker, P. A., Cubberley, A. L., Crowfoot, Elisabeth and Ralegh Radford, C. A., "Two Burials under the refectory of Worcester Cathedral," *Medieval Archaeology*, 18 (1974), pp. 146–51.
Barlow, Frank, *Edward the Confessor* (Eyre and Spottiswoode, London, 1970).
———, *The English Church 1000–1066* (Longman, London and New York, second edn, 1979).
———, *The English Church 1066–1154* (2nd edn, Longman, London, 1979).
———, "The King's Evil," reprinted from *English Historical Review*, 95 (1980), pp. 3–27, in F. Barlow, *The Norman Conquest and Beyond*

(The Hambledon Press, London, 1983), pp. 24–47.
——, *William Rufus* (Methuen, London, 1983).
Bartlett, Robert, *Trial by Fire and Water: the Medieval Judicial Ordeal* (Clarendon Press, Oxford,1986).
Bassett, S. R., "A Probable Mercian Royal Mausoleum at Winchcombe, Gloucestershire," *The Antiquaries Journal*, LXV (1985), pp. 82–100.
Bates, D., "The Building of a Great Church: The Abbey of St. Peter's, Gloucester, and its early Norman Benefactors," *Transactions of the Bristol and Gloucestershire Archaeological Society*, 102 (1984), pp. 129–32.
——, "The Land Pleas of William I's Reign: Penenden Heath Revisited," *Bulletin of the Institute of Historical Research*, 51 (1978), pp. 1–19.
Beresford, M. W. and Finberg, H. P. R., *English Medieval Boroughs, a Hand-List* (David and Charles, Newton Abbot, 1973).
Bernstein, D. J. *The Mystery of the Bayeux Tapestry* (Weidenfeld and Nicolson, London, 1986).
Bethell, D. L., "English Black Monks and Episcopal Elections in the 1120s," *English Historical Review*, 84 (1969), pp. 673–98.
Bethurum, Dorothy *The Homilies of Wulfstan* (The Clarendon Press, Oxford, 1957).
Biddle, M., "Seasonal Festivals and Residence: Winchester, Westminster and Gloucester in the tenth to twelfth centuries," in *Anglo-Norman Studies VIII. Proceedings of the Battle Conference 1985*, ed. R. Allen Brown (The Boydell Press, Woodbridge, 1986), pp. 51–72.
Blair, J., "From Minster to Parish Church," in *Minsters and Parish Churches: the Local Church in Transition 950–1200*, ed. John Blair (Oxford University Committee for Archaeology, Monograph no. 17, 1988), pp. 1–19.
——, "Minister Churches in the Landscape," in *Anglo-Saxon Settlements*, ed. Della Hooke (Basil Blackwell, Oxford, 1988), pp. 35–58.
Brett, M., *The English Church under Henry I* (Oxford University Press, Oxford, 1975).
——, "John of Worcester and his contemporaries," in *The Writing of History in the Middle Ages: essays presented to R. W. Southern*, ed. R. H. C. Davis and J. M. Wallace-Hadrill (Clarendon Press, Oxford, 1981), pp. 101–26.
Brown, P. R. L. "The Rise and Function of the Holy Man in Late Antiquity," *Journal of Roman Studies*, 61 (1971), pp. 80–101.
Brown, R. A., *Origins of English Feudalism* (Allen and Unwin, London, 1973).
Brundage, J. A. *Law, Sex and Christian Society in Medieval Europe* (University of Chicago Press, Chicago and London, 1987).
Burnett, C., "Catalogue: The Writings of Adelard of Bath and closely associated works, together with the manuscripts in which they occur,"

in *Adelard of Bath: an English scientist and Arabist of the early twelfth century*, ed. C. Burnett (Warburg Institute Surveys and Texts XIV, London, 1987), pp. 163–96.

Cameron, M. L., "Anglo-Saxon Medicine and Magic," *Anglo-Saxon England*, 17 (1988), pp. 191–215.

Campbell, James (ed.), *The Anglo-Saxons* (Phaidon, Oxford, 1982).

——, "Bede's *Reges* and *Principes*," *Jarrow Lecture, 1979*, reprinted in his *Essays in Anglo-Saxon History* (The Hambledon Press, London and Ronceverte, 1986), pp. 85–98.

——,"The Church in Anglo-Saxon Towns," in *The Church in Town and Countryside*, ed. D. Baker (Studies in Church History, 16; Basil Blackwell, Oxford, 1979), pp. 119–35; reprinted in his *Essays in Anglo-Saxon History*, pp. 139–54.

——, "Some Agents and Agencies of the Late Anglo-Saxon State," in *Domesday Studies: papers read at the Novocentenary Conference of the Royal Historical Society and the Institute of British Geographers*, Winchester, 1986, ed. J. C. Holt (The Boydell Press for the Royal Historical Society, Woodbridge, 1987), pp. 201–18.

Campbell, M. W., "A pre-Conquest Norman occupation of England?" *Speculum*, 46 (1971), pp. 21–31.

Carver, M. O. H. (ed.), *Medieval Worcestershire: An Archaeological Framework* (Transactions of the Worcestershire Archaeological Society, third series, vol 7. 1980).

Cheney, C. R. (ed.), *Handbook of Dates for Students of English History* (The Royal Historical Society, London, 1948).

Cheney, Mary G., *Roger, Bishop of Worcester 1164–1179* (The Clarendon Press, Oxford, 1980).

Ciggaar, Krijnie N., "L'Émigration anglaise à Byzance après 1066: un nouveau texte en Latin sur les Varangues à Constantinople," *Revue des études Byzantines*, 32 (1974), pp. 301–42.

Clanchy, M. T., *From Memory to Written Record: England 1066–1272* (Edward Arnold, London, 1979).

Clark, Cecily, "Women's names in post-Conquest England: observations and speculations," *Speculum*, 53 (1978), pp. 223–51.

Cook, D. R., "The Norman Military Revolution in England," *Proceedings of the Battle Conference on Anglo-Norman Studies I. 1978*, ed. R. Allen Brown (The Boydell Press–Rowman and Littlefield, Ipswich and Totava, 1979), pp. 94–102.

Cordoliani, Alfred, "L'activité computistique de Robert, év êque de Hereford," in *Melanges offerts à René Crozet*, ed. P. Galais and Yves-Jean Riou, I (1966), pp. 333–40.

Cowdrey, H. E. J., "The Anglo-Norman *Laudes Regiae*," reprinted from *Viator*, 12 (1981), in his *Popes, Monks and Crusaders* (The Hambledon Press, London, 1984), VIII pp. 37–78.

, "Bishop Ermenfrid of Sion and the Penitential Ordinance following the Battle of Hastings," *Journal of Ecclesiastical History*, 20 (1969), pp. 225–42.

Cox, D. C., "The Vale Estates of the Church of Evesham *c.*700–1086," *Vale of Evesham Historical Society Papers*, 5 (1975), pp. 25–50.

Dales, D., *Dunstan: Saint and Statesman* (Lutterworth Press, Cambridge, 1988).

Darlington, R. R., "Aethelwig, abbot of Evesham," *English Historical Review*, 48 (1933), pp. 1–22, 177–98.

, "Ecclesiastical Reform in the late Old English period," *English Historical Review*, 51 (1936), pp. 385–428.

Darlington, R. R. and McGurk, P. M., "The *Chronicon ex Chronicis of 'Florence' of Worcester and its Use of Sources for English History before 1066*," *Anglo-Norman Studies V: Proceedings of the Battle Conference 1982*, ed. R. Allen Brown (The Boydell Press, Woodbridge, 1983), pp. 185–96.

Davies, Wendy, *The Llandaff Charters* (The National Library of Wales, Aberystwyth, 1979).

, "Saint Mary's Worcester and the *Liber Landavensis*," *Journal of the Society of Archivists*, 4 (1972), p. 459–85.

Davies, Wendy and Vierck, H., "The Contexts of Tribal Hidage: Social Aggregates and Settlement Patterns," *Frühmittelalterliche Studien*, 8 (Walter de Gruyter, Berlin, New York, 1974), pp. 223–93.

Davis, R. H. C., "Bede after Bede," in *Studies in Medieval History presented to R. Allen Brown*, ed. C. Harper-Bill, C. J. Holdsworth and Janet L. Nelson (The Boydell Press, Woodbridge, 1989), pp. 103–16.

, *The Normans and their Myth* (Thames and Hudson, London, 1976).

Dawtry, Anne F., "The Benedictine Revival in the North: the last bulwark of Anglo-Saxon monasticism?" in *Religion and National Identity*, ed. S. Mews (Studies in Church History, 18; Basil Blackwell, Oxford, 1982), pp. 87–98.

, "The *Modus Medendi* and the Benedictine Order in Anglo-Norman England," in *The Church and Healing*, ed. W. J. Sheils (Studies in Church History, 19; Basil Blackwell, Oxford, 1982), pp. 25–38.

de Jong, Mayke, "Growing up in a Carolingian Monastery: Magister Hildemar and his oblates," *Journal of Medieval History*, 9 (1983), pp. 99–128.

Denholm-Young, N., "The Winchester-Hyde Chronicle," *English Historical Review*, 49 (1934), pp. 85–93, reprinted in *Collected Papers of N. Denholm-Young* (University of Wales Press, Cardiff, 1969), pp. 236–44.

Douglas, D. C., *William the Conqueror* (Eyre Methuen, London, 1964).

Draper, Peter, "King John and St Wulfstan," *Journal of Medieval History*, 10 (1984), pp. 41–50.

Du Boulay, F. R. H., *The Lordship of Canterbury* (Nelson, London, 1966).

Dugdale, W., *Monasticon Anglicanum*, revised edn. by J. Caley, H. Ellis and B. Bandinel, 6 vols in 8 (London, 1817–30, repr. 1846).

Dumville, D. N. "St. Teilo, St. Cadog and St. Buite in Italy," *The Journal of Welsh Ecclesiastical History*, 4 (1987), pp.1–8.

Dvornik, F., "The Kiev State and its Relations with Western Europe," reprinted from *Transactions of the Royal Historical Society*, fourth series, 29 (1947), pp. 27–46, in *Essays in Medieval History*, ed. R. W. Southern (Macmillan, London, 1968), pp. 1–23.

Dyer, C., *Lords and Peasants in a Changing Society: the estates of the bishopric of Worcester, 680–1540* (Cambridge University Press, Cambridge, 1980).

Edwards, C. J., "St. Teilo at Llandaff," *Journal of the Historical Society of the Church in Wales*, V (1955), pp. 38–44.

Ekwall, E., *English River Names* (Clarendon Press, Oxford, 1928).

Farmer, D. H., "Two Biographies by William of Malmesbury," in *Latin Biography*, ed. T. A. Dorey (Routledge and Kegan Paul, London, 1967), pp. 157–76.

Finberg, H. P. R., *The Early Charters of the West Midlands* (Leicester University Press, Leicester, 1981).

Finucane, R. C., *Miracles and Pilgrims: popular beliefs in Medieval England* (J. M. Dent and Sons Ltd, London, 1977).

Fisher, D. J. V., *The Anglo-Saxon Age c.400–1042* (Longman, London, 1973).

Fleming, Robin, "Domesday Book and the Tenurial Revolution," *Anglo-Norman Studies IX: Proceedings of the Battle Conference 1986*, ed. R. Allen Brown (The Boydell Press, Woodbridge, 1987), pp. 87–102.

——, "Domesday Estates of the King and the Godwines: a study in late Saxon politics," *Speculum*, 58 (1983), pp. 987–1007.

Flint, Valerie, "World History in the early twelfth century: the *Imago Mundi* of Honorius Augustodunensis," in *The Writing of History in the Middle Ages: essays presented to R. W. Southern*, ed. R. H. C. Davis and J. M. Wallace-Hadrill (The Clarendon Press, Oxford, 1981), pp. 211–38.

Flower, R., "A Metrical Life of St. Wulfstan of Worcester," *The National Library of Wales Journal*, 1 (1939–40), pp. 119–30.

Fryde, E. B., Greenway, D. E., Porter, S. and Roy, I. (eds), *Handbook of British Chronology*, third edn (Royal Historical Society, London, 1986).

Galbraith, V. H., "An Episcopal Land-Grant of 1085," *English Historical Review*, 44 (1929), pp. 353–72.

——, "Notes on the career of Samson, bishop of Worcester (1096–1112)," reprinted from *English Historical Review*, 82 (1967), pp. 86–101, in his *Kings and Chroniclers: essays in English medieval history* (Hambledon Press, London, 1982), IV, pp. 86–101.

Garnett, G., "Coronation and Propaganda: some implications of the Norman claim to the throne of England in 1066," *Transactions of the Royal Historical Society*, fifth series, 36 (1986), pp. 91–116.

Gatch, M. McC., "The Office in late Anglo-Saxon Monasticism," in *Learning and Literature in Anglo-Saxon England: studies presented to Peter Clemoes on his sixty-fifth birthday*, ed. M. Lapidge and H. Gneuss (Cambridge University Press, Cambridge, 1985), pp. 341–62.

Gem, R., "Bishop Wulfstan II and the Romanesque Cathedral Church of Worcester," in *Medieval Art and Architecture at Worcester Cathedral*, ed. Glenys Popper (The British Archaeological Association Conference Transactions for the Year 1975, London, 1978), pp. 15–37.

——, "England and the Resistance to Romanesque Architecture," in *Studies in Medieval History presented to R. Allen Brown*, ed. C. Harper-Bill, C. J. Holdsworth and Janet L. Nelson (The Boydell Press, Woodbridge, 1989), pp. 129–39.

——, "The Romanesque Rebuilding of Westminster Abbey," *Proceedings of the Battle Conference on Anglo-Norman Studies III. 1980*, ed. R. Allen Brown (The Boydell Press, Woodbridge, 1981), pp. 33–60.

Gibson, Margaret, *Lanfranc of Bec* (Clarendon Press, Oxford, 1978).

Gieysztor, A., "The Genesis of the Crusades," *Medievalia et Humanistica*, V (1948), pp. 3–23; VI, (1950), pp. 3–34.

Gillingham, John, "The Introduction of Knight Service into England," *Proceedings of the Battle Conference on Anglo-Norman Studies IV: 1981*, ed. R. Allen Brown (The Boydell Press, Woodbridge, 1982), pp. 53–64.

Gneuss, H., "Liturgical Books in Anglo-Saxon England and their Old English terminology," in *Learning and Literature in Anglo-Saxon England*, ed. M. Lapidge and H. Gneuss (Cambridge University Press, Cambridge, 1985), pp. 91–141.

Goody, J. and Watt, I., "The Consequences of Literacy," reprinted from *Comparative Studies in Society and History*, 5 (1963), pp. 304–45, in *Literacy in Traditional Societies*, ed. J. Goody (Cambridge University Press, Cambridge, 1968), pp. 27–68.

Gover, J. E. B., Mawer, A. and Stenton, F. M., with Houghton, F. T. S., *The Place-Names of Warwickshire* (English Place-Name Society, XIII, Cambridge University Press, Cambridge, 1936).

Grabois, A., "Anglo-Norman England and the Holy Land," *Anglo-Norman Studies VII: Proceedings of the Battle Conference 1984*, ed. R. Allen Brown (The Boydell Press, Woodbridge, 1985), pp. 132–41.

Gransden, Antonia, "Bede's Reputation as an Historian in Medieval England," *Journal of Ecclesiastical History*, 32 (1981), pp. 397–425.

——, "Cultural Transition at Worcester in the Anglo-Norman Period," in *Medieval Art and Architecture at Worcester Cathedral*, ed. Glenys Popper (The British Archaeological Association Conference Transactions for the year 1975, London, 1978).

——, *Historical Writing in England c.550 to c.1307* (Routledge and Kegan Paul, London, 1974).

——, "Traditionalism and Continuity during the last Century of Anglo-Saxon Monasticism," *Journal of Ecclesiastical History*, 40 (1989), pp. 159–207.

Green, Judith, "The Sheriffs of William the Conqueror," *Anglo-Norman Studies V: Proceedings of the Battle Conference 1982*, ed. R. Allen Brown (The Boydell Press, Woodbridge, 1983), pp. 129–45.

Greenway, Diana, "Henry of Huntingdon and the Manuscripts of his *Historia Anglorum*, *Anglo-Norman Studies IX. Proceedings of the Battle Conference 1986*, ed. R. Allen Brown (The Boydell Press, Woodbridge, 1987), pp. 103–21.

Gretsch, Mechtild, "Ethelwold's translation of the Regula Sancti Benedicti and its Latin exemplar," *Anglo-Saxon England*, 3, ed. P. Clemoes (Cambridge University Press, Cambridge, 1974), pp. 125–51.

Grey, T., *Scalachronica*, ed. J. Stevenson (The Maitland Club, Edinburgh, 1836).

Grierson, P., "The Relations between England and Flanders before the Norman Conquest," reprinted from *Transactions of the Royal Historical Society*, fourth series, 23 (1941), pp. 71–112, in *Essays in Medieval History*, ed. R. W. Southern (Macmillan, London, 1968), pp. 61–92.

Grosjean, P., analysis and commentary on R. Flower, "A Metrical Life of St. Wulfstan of Worcester" (*National Library of Wales Journal*, I (Aberystwyth, 1940), pp. 119–30) in *Analecta Bollandiana*, 73 (1955), pp. 259–60.

Gwynn, A. and Hadcock, R. N., *Medieval Religious Houses Ireland* (Longman, London, 1970).

Habington, T., *A Survey of Worcestershire*, ed. J. Amphlett, 2 vols (Worcestershire Historical Society, V, Oxford, 1895–9).

Hackett, Mary, "Le climat moral de Girart de Roussillon," in *Études de Philologie Romane et d'Histoire Littéraire offerts à Jules Horrent*, ed. J. M. D'Heur and Nicoletta Cherubini (Liège, 1980), pp. 165–74.

328   BIBLIOGRAPHY

Hamilton, B., *The Latin Church in the Crusader States: the Secular Church* (Variorum Publications Ltd, London, 1980).

Hamshere, J. D., "Domesday Book: Estate Structures in the West Midlands," *Domesday Studies: papers read at the Novocentenary Conference of the Royal Historical Society and the Institute of British Geographers*, Winchester, 1986, ed. J. C. Holt (The Boydell Press, Woodbridge, 1987), pp. 155–82.

Harper-Bill, C., "The Piety of the Anglo-Norman Knightly Class," in *Proceedings of the Battle Conference on Anglo-Norman Studies II. 1979*, ed. R. Allen Brown (The Boydell Press, Woodbridge, 1980), pp. 63–77.

Harper-Bill, C., Holdsworth, C. J. and Nelson, Janet L. (eds), *Studies in Medieval History presented to R. Allen Brown* (The Boydell Press, Woodbridge, 1989).

Harris, S. M., "The Kalendar of the *Vitae Sanctorum Wallensium*," *Journal of the Historical Society of the Church in Wales*, 3 (1953), pp. 3–53.

Harvey, Barbara, *Westminster Abbey and its Estates in the Middle Ages* (The Clarendon Press, Oxford, 1977).

Haskins, C. H., "The Abacus and the King's Curia," *English Historical Review*, 27 (1912), pp. 101–6.

——, "King Harold's Books," *English Historical Review*, 37 (1922), pp. 398–400.

Hayward, John, "Hereward the Outlaw," *Journal of Medieval History*, 14 (1988), pp. 293–304.

Heslop, T. A., "Seals," in *English Romanesque Art 1066–1200*, ed. G. Zarnecki, Janet Holt and T. Holland (Arts Council of Great Britain, with Weidenfeld and Nicolson, London, 1984).

Hickes, G., *Linguarum vett. septentrionalium thesaurus grammaticocriticus et archaeologicus*, 2 vols in 3 (Oxford, 1703–1705).

Hiley, D., "Thurstan of Caen and Plainchant at Glastonbury: Musicological Reflections on the Norman Conquest," *Proceedings of the British Academy*, 72 (1986), pp. 57–90.

Hill, D., *An Atlas of Anglo-Saxon England* (Basil Blackwell, second edn, Oxford, 1984).

Holdsworth, C. J., "Christina of Markyate," in *Medieval Women*, ed. D. Baker (Basil Blackwell, Oxford, 1978), pp. 185–204.

——, "Visions and Visionaries in the Middle Ages," *History*, 48 (1963), pp. 141–53.

Hollister, C. Warren, *Anglo-Saxon Military Obligations on the Eve of the Norman Conquest* (The Clarendon Press, Oxford, 1962).

——, *The Military Organization of Norman England* (The Clarendon Press, Oxford, 1965).

Holt, J. C. (ed.), *Domesday Studies: papers read at the Novocentenary Conference of the Royal Historical Society and the Institute of British Geographers,* Winchester, 1986 (The Boydell Press for the Royal Historical Society, Woodbridge, 1987).

, "The Introduction of Knight-Service in England," *Anglo-Norman Studies VI: Proceedings of the Battle Conference 1983,* ed. R. Allen Brown (The Boydell Press, Woodbridge, 1984), pp. 89–106.

Hooke, D., *Anglo-Saxon Landscape of the West Midlands: the Charter Evidence* (British Archaeological Reports, British Series 95, Oxford, 1981).

, *The Anglo-Saxon Landscape: the Kingdom of the Hwicce* (Manchester University Press, Manchester, 1985).

Hooper, N., "Anglo-Saxon Warfare on the eve of the Conquest: a brief survey," *Proceedings of the Battle Conference on Anglo-Norman Studies I. 1978,* ed. R. Allen Brown (The Boydell Press–Rowman and Littlefield, Ipswich and Totava, 1979), pp. 84–93.

Hudson, B., "The Family of Harold Godwinsson and the Irish Sea Province," *Journal of the Royal Society of Antiquaries of Ireland,* 109 (1980 for 1979), pp. 92–100.

Hunt, R. W.,"English Learning in the Late Twelfth Century," reprinted from *Transactions of the Royal Historical Society,* fourth series, 19 (1936), pp. 19–42, in *Essays in Medieval History,* ed. R. W. Southern (Macmillan, London, 1968), pp. 106–28.

Hyams, P., "'No Register of Title:' the Domesday Inquest and Land Adjudication," *Anglo-Norman Studies IX. Proceedings of the Battle Conference 1986,* ed. R. Allen Brown (The Boydell Press, Woodbridge, 1987), pp. 127–41.

Jennings, J. C., "The Writings of Prior Dominic of Evesham" *English Historical Review,* 77 (1962), pp. 298–304.

John, E., "An alleged charter of the reign of Edgar," *Bulletin of the John Rylands Library,* 41 (1958), pp. 54–80.

, *Land Tenure in Early England* (Leicester University Press, Leicester, 1960).

, *Orbis Britanniae and other Studies* (Leicester University Press, Leicester, 1966).

, "the World of Abbot Aelfric," in *Ideal and Reality in Frankish and Anglo-Saxon Society: studies presented to J. M. Wallace-Hadrill,* ed. P. Wormald with D. Bullough and R. Collins (Basil Blackwell, Oxford, 1983), pp. 300–16.

Kapelle, W. E., "Domesday Book: F. W. Maitland and His Successors," *Speculum,* 64 (1989), pp. 620–40.

, *The Norman Conquest of the North: the region and its transformation 1000–1135* (Croom Helm, London, 1979).

Katzir, Y., "The Patriarch of Jerusalem, Primate of the Latin Kingdom," in *Crusade and Settlement: papers read at the First Conference of the Society for the Study of the Crusades and the Latin East and presented to R. C. Smail*, ed. P. W. Edbury (University College Cardiff Press, 1985), pp. 169–75.

Kauffmann, C. M. "Manuscript Illumination at Worcester in the Eleventh and Twelfth Centuries," in *Medieval Art and Architecture at Worcester Cathedral*, ed. Glenys Popper (The British Archaeological Association Conference Transactions for the year 1975, London, 1978), pp. 43–50.

Kemp, E. W.,*Canonization and Authority in the Western Church* (Oxford University Press, Oxford, 1948).

Ker, N. R., "The Beginnings of Salisbury cathedral library," in *Medieval Learning and Literature: Essays presented to Richard William Hunt*, ed. J. J. G. Alexander and M. T. Gibson (Clarendon Press, Oxford, 1976), pp. 23–49; reprinted in N. R. Ker, *Books, Collectors and Libraries: studies in the medieval heritage*, ed. A. G. Watson (The Hambledon Press, London and Ronceverte, 1985), pp. 143–73.

, *Books, Collectors and Libraries: studies in the medieval heritage*, ed. A. G. Watson (The Hambledon Press, London and Ronceverte, 1985).

, *Catalogue of Manuscripts containing Anglo-Saxon* (The Clarendon Press, Oxford, 1957).

, Hemming's Cartulary: A description of the two Worcester cartularies in Cotton Tiberius A.XIII," *Studies in Medieval History presented to Frederick Maurice Powicke*, ed. R. W Hunt, W. A. Pantin and R. W. Southern (Clarendon Press, Oxford, 1948), pp. 49–75; reprinted in N. R. Ker, *Books, Collectors and Libraries: Studies in the medieval heritage*, ed. A. G. Watson (The Hambledon Press, London and Ronceverte, 1985), pp. 31–59.

, *Medieval Libraries of Great Britain: a list of surviving books*, second edn (Royal Historical Society, London, 1964).

, "Old English Notes Signed Coleman," reprinted from *Medium Aevum*, 18 (1949), pp. 29–31, in N. R. Ker, *Books, Collectors and Libraries: studies in the medieval heritage*, ed. A. G. Watson (The Hambledon Press, London and Ronceverte, 1985), pp. 27–30.

, "William of Malmesbury's Handwriting," *English Historical Review*, 59 (1944), pp. 371–6; reprinted in N. R. Ker, *Books, Collectors and Libraries: studies in the medieval heritage*, ed. A. G. Watson (The Hambledon Press, London and Ronceverte, 1985), pp. 61–6.

Keynes, S. D., "The Declining Reputation of King Aethelred the Unready," in *Ethelred the Unready: papers from the Millenary Conference*, ed. D. Hill (British Archaeological Reports, British Series 59, Oxford, 1978), pp. 227–53.

, *The Diplomas of King Aethelred "The Unready", 978–1016* (Cambridge University Press, 1980).

, "A Tale of Two Kings: Alfred the Great and Aethelred the Unready," *Transactions of the Royal Historical Society*, fifth series, 36 (1986), pp. 195–217.

Klukas, A. W., "The Architectural Implications of the *Decreta Lanfranci*," *Anglo-Norman Studies VI. Proceedings of the Battle Conference 1983*, ed. R. Allen Brown (The Boydell Press, Woodbridge, 1984), pp. 136–71.

Knowles, D., Brooke, C. N. L., and London, Vera C. M. (eds), *The Heads of Religious Houses England and Wales 940–1216* (Cambridge University Press, Cambridge,1972).

Knowles, D. and Hadcock, R. N., *Medieval Religious Houses England and Wales* (Longman, London, 1971).

Lapidge, M., "Ethelwold as Scholar and Teacher," in *Bishop Aethelwold: His Career and Influence*, ed. Barbara Yorke (The Boydell Press, Woodbridge, 1988), pp. 89–117.

, "Surviving Booklists from Anglo-Saxon England," in *Learning and Literature in Anglo-Saxon England: studies presented to Peter Clemoes on his sixty-fifth birthday*, ed. M. Lapidge and H. Gneuss (Cambridge University Press, Cambridge, 1985), pp. 33–89.

Lapidge, M. and Gneuss, H. (eds), *Learning and Literature in Anglo-Saxon England: studies presented to Peter Clemoes on his sixty-fifth birthday* (Cambridge University Press, Cambridge, 1985).

Le Neve, John, *Fasti Ecclesiae Anglicanae 1066–1300: II. Monastic Cathedrals*, compiled by Diana E. Greenway (Athlone Press, London, 1971).

, *Fasti Ecclesiae Anglicanae 1066–1300: III. Lincoln*, compiled by Diana E. Greenway (Institute of Historical Research, London, 1977).

Le Patourel, J., "Geoffrey of Montbray, bishop of Coutances 1049–1093," *English Historical Review*, 59 (1944), pp. 129–61.

Lewis, C., "The Norman Settlement of Herefordshire under William I," *Anglo-Norman Studies VII. Proceedings of the Battle Conference 1984*, ed. R. Allen Brown (The Boydell Press, Woodbridge, 1985), 195–213.

Little, L. K., "La morphologie des malédictions monastiques," *Annales*, 34 (1979), pp. 43–66.

Loud, G. A., *Church and Society in the Norman Principality of Capua, 1058–1197* (The Clarendon Press, Oxford, 1985).

Loyn, H. R., "Anglo-Saxon England: Reflections and Insights," *History*, 64 (1979), pp. 171–81.

, "Church and State in England in the Tenth and Eleventh Centuries," in *Tenth-Century Studies: Essays in Commemoration of the Millenium of the Council of Winchester and Regularis Concordia*, ed.

D. Parsons (Phillimore, London and Chichester, 1975), pp. 94–102.

———, *The Governance of Anglo-Saxon England 500–1087* (Edward Arnold, London, 1984).

———, *Harold son of Godwin* (The Historical Association, Hastings and Bexhill Branch, 1966; reprinted The Historical Association, London, 1971).

———, "The King and the Structure of Society in Late Anglo-Saxon England," *History*, 42 (1957), pp. 87–100.

———, "William's bishops: some further thoughts," *Anglo-Norman Studies, X: Proceedings of the Battle Conference 1987*, ed. R. Allen Brown (The Boydell Press, Woodbridge, 1988), pp. 223–35.

McIntyre, Elizabeth A., "Early Twelfth-Century Worcester Cathedral Priory, with special reference to the manuscripts there," Oxford University D. Phil. thesis, 1978.

McLachlan, Laurentia, "St Wulstan's Prayer Book," *The Journal of Theological Studies*, 30 (1929), pp. 174–7.

Mâle, E., *The Gothic Image: Religious Art in France of the Thirteenth Century*, transl. from the third edn by Dora Nussey (The Fontana Library, Collins, London, 1961).

Mason, Emma, "Change and Continuity in Eleventh-Century Mercia: the experience of St Wulfstan of Worcester," *Anglo-Norman Studies VIII: Proceedings of the Battle Conference 1985*, ed. R. Allen Brown (The Boydell Press, Woodbridge, 1986), pp. 154–76.

———, "Fact and Fiction in the English crusading tradition: the earls of Warwick in the twelfth century," *Journal of Medieval History*, 14 (1988), pp. 81–95.

———, "St. Wulfstan's staff: a legend and its uses," *Medium Aevum*, 53 (1984), pp. 157–79.

Mason, J. F. A., "Roger de Montgomery and his sons," *Transactions of the Royal Historical Society*, fifth series, 13 (1963), pp. 1–28.

Maund, K. L., "The Welsh Alliances of Earl Aelfgar of Mercia and his family in the mid-eleventh century," *Anglo-Norman Studies XI: Proceedings of the Battle Conference 1988*, ed. R. Allen Brown (The Boydell Press, Woodbridge, 1989), pp. 181–90).

Mawer, A. and Stenton, F. M., with Houghton, F. T. S., *The Place-Names of Worcestershire* (English Place-Name Society, IV, Cambridge University Press, Cambridge, 1927).

Mayr-Harting, H., "Functions of a Twelfth-Century Recluse," *History*, 60 (1975), pp. 337–52.

Moore, J. S., "Domesday Slavery," *Anglo-Norman Studies XI: Proceedings of the eleventh Battle Conference, 1988*, ed. R. Allen Brown (The Boydell Press, Woodbridge, 1989), pp. 191–220.

Moore, R. I., "Family, Community and Cult on the Eve of the Gregorian Reform," *Transactions of the Royal Historical Society*, fifth series, 30 (1980), pp. 49–69.

Murray, A., *Reason and Society in the Middle Ages* (Clarendon Press, Oxford, 1978).

Nelson, Janet L., "The Rites of the Conqueror," *Proceedings of the Battle Conference on Anglo-Norman Studies IV. 1981*, ed. R. Allen Brown (The Boydell Press, Woodbridge, 1982), pp. 117–32; reprinted in her *Politics and Ritual in Early Medieval Europe* (The Hambledon Press, London and Ronceverte, 1986), pp. 375–401.

Noble, P., "Attitudes to Class as revealed by some of the older chansons de geste," *Romania*, 94 (1973), pp. 359–85.

Pelteret, D., "Slave raiding and slave trading in early England," *Anglo-Saxon England*, 9 (1981), pp. 99–114.

Pevsner, N., *Buckinghamshire* (Penguin Books, Harmondsworth, 1960).

, *Worcestershire* (Penguin Books, Harmondsworth, 1968).

Popper, Glenys (ed.), *Medieval Art and Architecture at Worcester Cathedral: The British Archaeological Association Conference Transactions for the Year 1975*(British Archaeological Association, London, 1978).

Potthast, A., *Bibliotheca Historica Medii Aevi*, 2 vols (Berlin, 1896).

Prestwich, J. O., "War and Finance in the Anglo-Norman State," *Transactions of the Royal Historical Society*, fifth series, 4 (1954), pp. 19–43.

Rahtz, P. A., "The Archaeology of West Mercian towns," in A. Dornier (ed.), *Mercian Studies* (Leicester University Press, Leicester, 1977), pp. 107–30.

Rankin, Susan, "The Liturgical Background of the Old English Advent Lyrics: a reappraisal," in *Learning and Literature in Anglo-Saxon England: studies presented to Peter Clemoes on his sixty-fifth birthday*, ed. M. Lapidge and H. Gneuss (Cambridge University Press, Cambridge, 1985), pp. 317–40.

Reynolds, Susan, "Eadric Silvaticus and the English Resistance," *Bulletin of the Institute of Historical Research*, 54 (1981), pp. 102–5.

, *An Introduction to the History of English Medieval Towns* (The Clarendon Press, Oxford, 1977).

Ridyard, Susan J., "*Condigna Veneratio*: Post-Conquest attitudes to the Saints of the Anglo-Saxons," *Anglo-Norman Studies IX: Proceedings of the Battle Conference 1986*, ed. R. Allen Brown (The Boydell Press, Woodbridge, 1987), pp. 179–206.

,*The Royal Saints of Anglo-Saxon England: a study of West Saxon and East Anglian cults* (Cambridge University Press, Cambridge,

1988).

Rivet, A. L. F. and Smith, C., *The Place-Names of Roman Britain* (B. T. Batsford, Ltd, London, 1979).

Robinson, J. Armitage, "Saint Oswald and the Church of Worcester," *British Academy Supplemental Papers*, V (London, 1919).

——, *The Times of Saint Dunstan* (Clarendon Press, Oxford, 1923).

Rosenthal, J. T., "Bede's use of miracles in the 'Ecclesiastical History'," *Traditio*, XXXI (1975), pp. 328–35.

Rosenwein, Barbara H., "Feudal War and Monastic Peace: Cluniac Liturgy as Ritual Aggression," *Viator*, 2 (1971), pp. 129–57.

Round, J. H., *Feudal England. Historical Studies of the Eleventh and Twelfth Centuries*, second edn (Barnes and Noble Inc., New York, 1964).

Ruud, Marylou, "Monks in the World – the case of Gundulf of Rochester," *Anglo-Norman Studies XI. Proceedings of the Battle Conference 1988*, ed. R. Allen Brown (The Boydell Press, Woodbridge, 1989), pp. 245–60.

Sanders, I. J., *English Baronies: a study of their origin and descent 1086–1327* (Clarendon Press, Oxford, 1960).

Sawyer, P. H., "Charters of the Reform Movement: the Worcester archive," in *Tenth Century Studies: essays in commemoration of the Millennium of the Council of Winchester and Regularis Concordia*, ed. D. Parsons (Phillimore, London and Chichester, 1975), pp. 84–93.

Sayers, Jane, " 'Original,' Cartulary and Chronicle: the Case of the Abbey of Evesham," *Falschungen im Mittelalter, Monumenta Germaniae Historica*, ed. H. Furhmann, 6 vols, Teil IV, *Diplomatische Falschungen* II (Hahnsche Buchhandlung, Hanover, 1988), pp. 371–95.

——, "The Proprietary Church in England: a note on Ex ore sedentis (X 5.33.17)," *Zeitschrift der Savigny-Stiftung für Rechtsgeschichte*, Kanonistische Abteilung LXXIV, ed. Th. Mayer-Maly et al. (Hermann Bohlaus Nachf., Vienna, Cologne, Graz, 1988), pp. 231–45.

Searle, Eleanor, "Possible History," *Speculum*, 61 (1986), pp. 779–86.

——, "Women and the legitimization of succession at the Norman Conquest," *Proceedings of the Battle Conference on Anglo-Norman Studies III. 1980*, ed. R. Allen Brown (The Boydell Press, Woodbridge, 1981), pp. 159–70, 226–9.

Short, I., "On Bilingualism in Anglo-Norman England," *Romance Philology*, 33:4 (1980), pp. 467–79.

Slater, T. R. and Jarvis, P. J. (eds), *Field and Forest: an historical geography of Warwickshire and Worcestershire* (Geo Books, Norwich, 1982).

Smalley, Beryl, *Historians in the Middle Ages* (Thames and Hudson,

London, 1974).

Smyth, A. P., *Scandinavian York and Dublin*, 2 vols (Templekeiran Press, Dublin; Humanities Press, New Jersey, 1975–9).

——, *Warlords and Holy Men: Scotland A.D. 80–1000* (Edward Arnold, London, 1984).

Southern, R. W., "Aspects of the European Tradition of Historical Writing: 4. The Sense of the Past," Presidential Address, *Transactions of the Royal Historical Society*, fifth series, 23 (1973), pp. 243–63.

——, *Saint Anselm and his Biographer: a study of monastic life and thought 1059–c.1130* (Cambridge University Press, Cambridge, 1966).

Spufford, P., with the assistance of Wendy Wilkinson and Sarah Tolley, *Handbook of Medieval Exchange* (Royal Historical Society, London, 1986).

Squire, A., "Aelred and King David," *Collectanea Sacri Ordinis Cisterciensium Reformatorum*, 22 (1960), pp. 356–77.

Stenton, F. M., "Medeshamstede and its Colonies," reprinted from J. G. Edwards, V. H. Galbraith and E. F. Jacob (eds), *Historical Essays in Honour of James Tait* (Printed for the Subscribers, Manchester, 1933), pp. 313–26, in *Preparatory to Anglo-Saxon England: being the collected papers of Frank Merry Stenton*, ed. Doris Mary Stenton (The Clarendon Press, Oxford, 1970), pp. 179–92.

Stevenson, W. H., "A contemporary description of the Domesday Survey," *English Historical Review*, 22 (1907), pp. 72–84.

Stratford, N., "Notes on the Norman Chapterhouse at Worcester," in *Medieval Art and Architecture at Worcester Cathedral*, ed. Glenys Popper (The British Archaeological Association Conference Transactions for the Year 1975, London, 1978), pp. 51–70.

Sumption, J., *Pilgrimage: an image of medieval religion* (Faber, London, 1974).

Thomas, William, *A Survey of the Cathedral Church of Worcester* (London, 1736).

Thompson, A. Hamilton, "The Welsh Medieval Dioceses," *Journal of the Historical Society of the Church in Wales*, I (1947), pp. 91–111.

Thomson, R., *William of Malmesbury* (The Boydell Press, Woodbridge, 1987).

——, "William of Malmesbury as Historian and Man of Letters," *Journal of Ecclesiastical History*, 29 (1978), pp. 387–413; reprinted in Thomson, *William of Malmesbury*, pp. 11–38.

Tierney, B., *The Crisis of Church and State, 1050–1300* (Prentice Hall, Englewood Cliffs, N. J., 1964).

Tudor, Victoria, "Reginald of Durham and Saint Godric of Finchale: learning and religion on a personal level," in *Religion and Humanism*,

336 BIBLIOGRAPHY

ed. K. Robbins (Studies in Church History, 17; Basil Blackwell, Oxford, 1981).

Tusculum-Lexicon, ed. W. Buchwald, A. Holweg and O. Prinz, third edn (Artemis Verlag, Munich and Zurich, 1982).

Viking and Medieval Ireland: an Exhibition Catalogue (National Museum of Ireland, Dublin, 1973).

von Feilitzen, Olof, *The Pre-Conquest Personal Names of Domesday Book* (Arkiv för Germansk Namnforskning utgivet av Jöran Sahlgren. 3, Almqvist & Wiksells, Uppsala, 1937).

Walker, D., '"The Norman Settlement in Wales," *Proceedings of the Battle Conference on Anglo-Norman Studies I. 1978*, ed. R. Allen Brown (The Boydell Press-Rowman and Littlefield, Ipswich and Totowa, 1979), pp. 131–43.

Warren, Ann K., *Anchorites and their Patrons in Medieval England* (University of California Press, Berkeley, Los Angeles, London, 1985).

Watkin, A., "The Glastonbury 'Pyramids' and St Patrick's 'Companions'," *The Downside Review*, 65 (1947), pp. 30–41.

Way, A., "Some Notes on the Tradition of Flaying, inflicted in punishment of sacrilege, the skin of the offender being affixed to the church doors," *The Archaeological Journal*, V (1848), pp. 185–92.

Webster, G., "Prehistoric settlement and land use in the West Midlands and the impact of Rome," in *Field and Forest: an historical geography of Warwickshire and Worcestershire*, ed. T. R. Slater and P. Jarvis (Geo Books, Norwich, 1982), pp. 31–58.

West, F., *The Justiciarship in England 1066–1232* (Cambridge University Press, Cambridge, 1966).

Whitelock, Dorothy, "Archbishop Wulfstan, Homilist and Statesman," *Transactions of the Royal Historical Society*, fourth series, 24 (1942), pp. 25–45.

——, "Wulfstan and the Laws of Cnut," *English Historical Review*, 63 (1948), pp. 433–52.

——, "Wulfstan's authorship of Cnut's laws," *English Historical Review*, 70 (1955), pp. 72–85.

Whybra, J., *A Lost English County: Winchcombeshire in the Tenth and Eleventh Centuries* (The Boydell Press, Studies in Anglo-Saxon History, I, Woodbridge, 1990).

Wightman, W. E., "The Palatine Earldom of William Fitz Osbern in Gloucestershire and Worcestershire (1066–1071)," *English Historical Review*, 77 (1962), pp. 6–17.

Williams, Ann, "'Cockles among the Wheat:' Danes and English in the Western Midlands in the first half of the eleventh century," *Midland History*, 11 (1987), pp. 1–22.

——, "The King's nephew: the family and career of Ralph, earl of

Hereford," in *Studies in Medieval History presented to R. Allen Brown*, ed. C. Harper-Bill, C. J. Holdsworth and Janet L. Nelson (The Boydell Press, Woodbridge, 1989), pp. 327–43.

———, "The Knights of Shaftesbury Abbey," *Anglo-Norman Studies VIII. Proceedings of the Battle Conference 1985*, ed. R. Allen Brown (The Boydell Press, Woodbridge, 1986), pp.214–37.

———, "Land and Power in the eleventh century: the estates of Harold Godwineson," *Proceedings of the Battle Conference on Anglo-Norman Studies III. 1980*, ed. R. Allen Brown (The Boydell Press, Woodbridge, 1981), pp. 171–87.

———, "*Princeps Merciorum gentis*: the family, career and connections of Aelfhere, ealdorman of Mercia, 956–83," *Anglo-Saxon England*, 10 (1982), pp. 143–72.

———, "Some Notes and Considerations on Problems connected with the English Royal Succession, 860–1066," *Proceedings of the Battle Conference on Anglo-Norman Studies I. 1978*, ed. R. Allen Brown (The Boydell Press, Woodbridge, 1979), pp. 144–67.

———, "A Vice-Comital family in Pre-Conquest Warwickshire," *Anglo-Norman Studies XI. Proceedings of the Battle Conference 1988*, ed. R. Allen Brown (The Boydell Press, Woodbridge, and Wolfeboro, New Hampshire, 1989), pp. 279–95.

Wilmart, A., "La légende de Sainte Edith en prose et vers par le moine Goscelin," *Analecta Bollandiana*, lvi (1938), pp. 5–101, 265–307.

Wilson, C., "Abbot Serlo's church at Gloucester (1089–1100): its place in Romanesque architecture," in *Medieval Art and Architecture at Gloucester and Tewkesbury*, ed. T. A. Heslop and V. A. Sekules (The British Archaeological Association Conference Transactions for the year 1981, London, 1985), pp. 52–83.

Wormald, F., "The Survival of Anglo-Saxon Illumination after the Noman Conquest," *Proceedings of the British Academy*, 30 (1944), pp. 127–45.

Wormald, P., "Aethelwold and his Continental Counterparts: contact, comparison, contrast," in *Bishop Aethelwold: His Career and Influence*, ed. Barbara Yorke (The Boydell Press, Woodbridge, 1988), pp. 13–42.

Yorke, Barbara, "Aethelwold and the Politics of the Tenth Century," in *Bishop Aethelwold: His Career and Influence*, ed. Barbara Yorke (The Boydell Press, Woodbridge, 1988), pp. 65–88.

Zarnecki, G., "The Romanesque Capitals in the South Transept of Worcester Cathedral," in *Medieval Art and Architecture at Worcester Cathedral*, ed. Glenys Popper (The British Archaeological Association Conference Transactions for the Year 1975, London, 1978), pp. 38–50.

Index

confraternity associations, 197–201, 249
Constantinople (Istanbul) *alias* Byzantium, 60, 152, 241; emperor of, 152, 241
Cookley (Cullacliffe) (Worcs), 135, 160
Corbie (Lotharingia), 204
Cornwall, 220; bishop of *see* Lyfing
coronation oath, 107
Cotswold hills, 4, 5; Edge, 173
Cotton *see* William
courts: ecclesiastical, 140; *see also* synod; hallmoot, 185; hundred, 148, 185; (Court), royal (including Great Council), 80, 83–4, 90, 95, 96, 99, 106, 111, 115, 120, 131–4, 140, 152, 199, 203, 224, 226, 228, 233, 252, 259, 309–10; village, 185; *see also* lawsuits
Coutances (Normandy), 243; bishop of *see* Geoffrey
Coutances *see* John, bishop of Worcester
Coventry (Warwicks), abbey, 28, 29; bishop, 29
Cranborne (Dorset), abbey, 129; abbot *see* Gerald
Crediton (Devon), bishop of *see* Lyfing
Cremona (Italy) *see* Homobuono
Cricklade (Wilts), 261
crippled beggar woman, healed at Wulfstan's tomb, 276–7, 310
Crispin *see* Gilbert
Croome (Worcs), manor, 148; *see also* Sigref
Cropthorne (Worcs), 138
cross, sign of, 64, 69–70, 219, 225
Crowland (Lincs), abbey, 13
Crowle (Worcs) *see* Sigmund
crown-wearing ceremony, 96, 132, 203
Croxton (Lincs), abbot of, 282 n.
crucifix, 204
crypt, 202
Cullacliffe *see* Cookley

Cunegunda, empress, canonization of, 280
cupbearers, 152
Curthose *see* Robert
Cuthwine, son of King Ceawlin of Wessex, 4
Cutsdean (Worcs), 166; church of, 166
Cynesige, archbishop of York (1051–60), 72

Danelaw, the, 22, 226
Danes, 168; defensive measures taken against, 10; invasions by, 9, 20–1, 23–4, 33, 35, 95, 123–4, 152, 308; personal names, 198; settlement of, 21–2, 132, 147, 154, 209, 213
David, O. T. King, 208
deacons *see* Elfwy; Frewin
Deerhurst (Gloucs), 91; abbey, 19
Deira (region of Northumbria), 2, 3
Denmark, king of *see* Harold Bluetooth; Sweyn Estrithson
Devon, 220
dice, 166
"discipline" (penitential beating), 255
Dispenser *see* Robert
Dobunni, tribe, 2
Dolfin, his son *see* Ulf
Domesday Survey, 28–9, 138, 140–1, 145, 148, 153, 160, 173, 309, 310; commissioners for Worcestershire, 138, 140–1, 154
Dominic, monk of Evesham, 304
Donngus *alias* Donatus, bishop of Dublin (1085–95), 251
Dorchester, diocese of, 110; *see also* Lincoln; bishop *see* Rémy; Wulfwig
Dorchester-on-Thames (Oxon), 238
Dover (Kent), 133–4
drinking, social, 152
drinking-horn, 133
Droitwich (Worcs), 181, 234; salt-production at, 253; resident of *see* Segild
Dublin (Ireland), 253; bishop of *see* Donngus; Patrick; cathedral priory, 251

Hereford; steersman *see* Thorkell;
succession to, 100; tomb of, 113,
281–2, 284; translation of, 284;
wife *see* Edith, daughter of Earl
Godwin
Edward the Exile, son of Edmund
Ironside, 61; his children *see*
Christina; Edgar Etheling;
Margaret
Edward "the Martyr", king of
England (975–8), his genealogy,
219
Edwin, abbot of Westminster
(*c.*1049–68), 129
Edwin, brother of Archdeacon Ailric,
214
Edwin, brother of Earl Leofric, 22
Edwin (son of Earl Alfgar), earl of
Mercia, 28, 99, 105, 148, 309
Edwin, son of Harold Godwinson,
220
Egelmer *see* Eilmer
Egwuin, bishop of Worcester (*c.*
693–717), 6–7, 93; cult, 203;
relics, 7, 136; shrine, 92
Eilaf, earl, 22
Eilmer (Egelmer), priest and monk of
Worcester, 179–80, 214, 268
Elfer *see* Alfhere
Elfgiva, abbess of Wilton (1065–7),
225 n.
Elfric, ecclesiastical biographer, 209;
Homilies, 230; *Life of St
Ethelwold*, 288; *Lives of the
Saints*, 206
Elfric Puttoc, bishop of Worcester
(1040–1), archbishop of York
(1023–51), 57, 58, 216
Elfsige, abbot of Ramsey (1080–7),
201
Elfwin, abbot of Ramsey
(1043–79/80), 201
Elfwy, deacon and monk of
Winchcombe, 125
Elias, archbishop of Bari, 243
Elmham, bishop of *see* Ethelmer
Elmley castle (Worcs), 2

Ely (Cambs), abbey, 13; bishop *see*
Eustace
Emma, queen of England (wife of
Ethelred II and of Cnut), 37, 44, 70
England, 74, 76, 186; defence of, 98
England, kings of, 195, 211, 225,
233; and their anointing, 25, 92,
106, 113, 228; chancellor of *see*
Ranulf Flambard; chancellor to
queen, 276; chaplain *see* Bernard
Fitz Ospac; dapifer *see* Eudo;
demesne (*terrae regis*) of, 104;
dispenser (steward) *see* Robert,
Dispenser; prayers for, 12, 200–1;
queen-consort of *see* Alice; Edith;
Emma; *see also* Alfred; Cnut;
Edgar; Edward "the Confessor";
Edward "the Martyr"; Ethelred (II)
Unraed; Harold II Godwinson;
Harold I Harefoot; Harthacnut;
Henry I; Henry III; John; William
I; William II Rufus
English race, 137, 142, 144, 149,
223; cultural values, survival of,
151, 222; demoted status after
Norman Conquest, 89, 149, 197;
intermarriage with French, 151,
225, 229, 288, 289; language, 97;
spoken, 289; written, 206–8, 270,
288–90; landholders, 152, 187,
228–9, 231, 233; *see also* thegns;
long hair of, 97–8; resistance
movements, 108, 145–7; serving
the Eastern emperor, 241
Eric of Hladir, earl of Northumbria,
21; his son *see* Hakon
Ermenfrid, bishop of Sion, papal
legate, 78, 308
Ermer, mason and plasterer of
Worcester, 173
Ernwig, sheriff (of Nottingham), 234
Ernwin, scribe of Peterborough,
37–8, 44, 70
Ernwy, priest of Edric the Wild, 146
Estrith, her son *see* Sweyn
Ethelbald, king of Mercia (716–57),
214